A History of the Behavioral Therapies:

Founders' Personal Histories

Dedication

This book is dedicated to the loving memory of Janet Bijou, a true friend of behavior therapy, and whose intelligence and kindness reflect the humanitarian spirit guiding us all.

A History of the Behavioral Therapies:

Founders' Personal Histories

Edited by

William T. O'Donohue
Deborah A. Henderson
Steven C. Hayes
Jane E. Fisher
Linda J. Hayes

Context Press
Reno, Nevada

A History of the Behavioral Therapies: Founders' Personal Histories

Paperback 357 pp. Includes bibliographies.

Distributed by New Harbinger Publications, Inc.

Library of Congress Cataloging-in-Publication Data

A history of the behavioral therapies : founders' personal theories / edited by William T. O'Donohue ... [et al.].
p. cm.
"Based on a conference held at the University of Nevada, Reno, in June, 1999"–Pref.
Includes bibliographical references.
ISBN-13: 978-1-878978-40-0
ISBN-10: 1-878978-40-3
1. Behavior therapy–History–Congresses. I. O'Donohue, William T.
RC489.B4 H55 2001
616.89'142'09–dc21

2001047081

933 Gear Street, Reno, NV 89503-2729

Printed in the United States of America

Preface

This book is based on a conference held at the University of Nevada, Reno in June, 1999. The editors organized this conference in order to provide an opportunity for us and others to better understand the development of the behavioral therapies and to capture a part of the historical record before it was lost forever. Most importantly, we wanted to honor the founders of the behavioral therapies and to watch as this group of approximately 20 individuals interacted – most of them as old friends, but also perhaps for the last time, at least in this large of a group.

The chapters the arise from this conference show the unique properties of these unique individuals. While participants had an outline of topics to address, each chapter reflects the topics that the presenters felt best revealed their intellectual history and the context and content of their contribution. The difference between chapters in tone and approach could not realistically be eliminated without muffling the very voices we wanted to hear. In the end, we made the conscious decision to give these leaders of the field the freedom to tell their story in their own way.

We want to thank these individuals for taking time from their busy lives to make this conference a huge success. Although many of these founders are certainly of retirement age – all are clearly "flunking" retirement. Old friends met once again, sometimes after years without contact. Others met for the first time. There was much catching up and many great stories were told. We would also like to thank them for sharing the stories of their lives and their work. These stories were often quite moving, and sometimes very funny. What these individuals showed us is that the story of the development of behavior therapy is not a dry story of purely intellectual commitments and technical developments. Rather it is clearly a story of deeply held values, caring, compassion, conflict, fate, and, at times, personal tragedy. This book is dedicated to these (and other) founders of our discipline.

We also dedicate this book to the spouses and families of these founders. Many individuals brought family members and it was both impressive and touching. It was clear that in many cases there was a real partnership in which spouses not only supported but also clearly substantively contributed to the success of their partners.

We also want to comment on one key aspect of the conference. Many of the founders expressed their deep debt and gratitude to two central figures – Sidney Bijou and Albert Bandura. These two individuals often worked quietly and behind the scenes helping others find jobs, training key students, and in general generously giving help and encouragement to others. The special gratitude and honor extended to these two individuals should be noted.

We also want to thank Professor Leo Reyna for presenting a paper at the conference. Leo is one of the great teachers in our profession; for example, his influence on Joseph Wolpe was critical to the development of behavior therapy. Unfortunately, due to serious health problems he was not able to write up his fascinating paper as a chapter for this volume.

We would also like to thank supporters of this conference. Dean Robert Mead and Vice President Ken Hunter were particularly helpful. Their generous help made this conference possible.

Finally, we also want to thank Tuna Townsend for his generous assistance on many aspects of this project.

William T. O'Donohue
Deborah A. Henderson
Steven C. Hayes
Jane E. Fisher
Linda J. Hayes

Table of Contents

Participants in the Nevada Conference on the History of the Behavior Therapies

Top row (from left to right)
Ogden Lindsley, Gordon Paul, Don Baer, Bill O'Donohue,
Mont Wolf, Paul Mountjoy, Deborah Henderson

Second row (from left to right)
Cyril Franks, Jane Fisher, Todd Risley, Sid Bijou, Walter Mischel,
Stewart Agras, Steve Hayes

Bottom row (from left to right)
Roger Poppen, Jerry Davison, Julie Vargas, Leo Reyna,
Len Krasner, Albert Bandura, Linda Hayes

Introduction

A History of the Behavioral Therapies

William T. O'Donohue, Deborah A. Henderson, Steven C. Hayes, Jane E. Fisher, & Linda J. Hayes
University of Nevada, Reno

A complex set of events occurred around the middle of the 20th century that culminated in the development of the behavioral therapies – i.e., the related approaches to understanding and treating problems in living sometimes known more specifically as applied behavior analysis, behavior therapy, and cognitive behavior therapy. Of course, the story of this development is not simple. There were many actors, behaving over a period of many years, in many locations, all influenced by a complex and diverse set of personal, intellectual, historical and social factors. As we will see, some of these actors interacted with other actors in interesting webs of influence, while others were relatively isolated for significant periods. Many were reacting to similar influences – for example, to contemporary conditioning research, to new research standards, to dissatisfactions with the effectiveness of then current treatments – although each of these individuals also has his or her idiosyncratic sources of influence. Moreover, what was produced – the behavioral therapies – is neither simple nor monolithic. Rather, it is a continually evolving family of therapies partly distinguished by their major historical sources of influence – Skinnerian experimental analysis of behavior; Wolpean reciprocal inhibition; or the cognitive emphases of individuals like Albert Ellis, for example. The history of the behavioral therapies is also not the story of a single event; rather it is the longer story of a series of discoveries, developments, innovations, and events all occurring over a number of years.

What is behavior therapy?

But what history are we trying to capture in this volume? What is behavior therapy, or what was it, at least in its beginnings? It might prove useful at least for a general orientation to provide a few definitions of behavior therapy, particularly those that were offered around the time of its formation:

> "Behavior therapy derives its impetus from experimental psychology and is essentially an attempt to apply the findings and methods of this discipline to disorders of human behavior" (Rachman, 1963, p. 3).

> "The attempt to alter human behavior and emotion in a beneficial manner according to the laws of modern learning theory" (Eysenck, 1964, p. 1).

> "Treatment deducible from the sociopsychological model that aims to alter a person's behavior directly through application of general psychological principles" (Krasner & Ullmann, 1965, p. 244).

> "Behavior therapy, or conditioning therapy, is the use of experimentally established principles of learning for the purpose of changing maladaptive behavior" (Wolpe, 1969, p. VII).

> Bandura (1969) placed the principles of behavior modification within the "conceptual framework of social learning...By requiring clear specification of treatment conditions and objective assessment of outcomes the social learning approach...contains a self-corrective feature that distinguishes it from change enterprises in which interventions remain ill-defined and their psychological effects are seldom objectively evaluated" (p. v).

There seems to be some consensus, at least among these various definitions, that behavior therapy is an orientation to understanding and ameliorating human suffering, through behavior change, that is influenced by principles derived from experimental psychology, particularly learning research. Behavior therapists have traditionally emphasized outcome research (and still do) and more recently some of behavior therapy's subdivisions stress the importance of cognitive variables. We can see that these definitions, although containing some similarities, also suggest controversies. What qualifies as a psychological principle? Exactly what psychological principles are the most important and useful? Which learning theory? What is the proper relationship between a psychological principle and a therapy technique? What evidence should be most persuasive? What are the relative advantages and disadvantages of various research methodologies (e.g., single subject vs. group designs)? What constitutes a legitimate problem for the behavior therapist? What constitutes improvement and how is this best to be measured? How important are cognitive factors, and how are they to be accounted for within a behavioral paradigm?

The various answers to these sorts of questions have led to a great deal of variegation in behavior therapy. In fact, Kazdin (1978) stated that in behavior therapy's second decade,

> "By now behavior modification is so variegated in its conceptualization of behavior, research methods and techniques that no unifying schema or set of assumptions about behavior can incorporate all the extant techniques. Many of the theoretical positions expressed within behavior modification represent opposing views about the nature of human motivation, the mechanisms that influence behavior and the relative influence of such factors, and the most suitable focus of treatment for a given problem" (p. 374).

Is this diversity bad? Does it mean there is now no such coherent entity or activity as "behavior therapy"? We answer both of these in the negative for two main reasons. First, clear and simple definitions expressing essential properties are often difficult to provide, as phenomena are often quite complex, variegated and even "fuzzy." Wittgenstein (1958) famously points this out:

> Consider for example the proceedings that we call "games." I mean board-games, card-games, ball-games. Olympic games, and so on. What is common to them all – Don't say: "There must be something common, or they would not be called "games"" – but *look and see* whether there is anything common to all – For if you look at them you will not see something that is common to *all*, but similarities, relationships, and a whole series of them at that...Are they all "amusing"? Compare chess with naught and crosses. Or is there always winning and losing, or competition between players? Think of patience. In ball games there is winning and losing; but when a child throws his ball at the wall and catches it again, this feature has disappeared. Look at the parts played by skill and luck; and at the difference between skill in chess and skill in tennis. Think now of games like ring-aring-aroses; here is the element of amusement, but how many other characteristic features have disappeared! And we can go through the many, many other groups of games in the same way; can see how similarities crop up and disappear. And the result of this examination is; we see a complicated network of similarities overlapping and criss-crossing; sometimes overall similarities, sometimes similarities of detail (p. 31-32).

We believe the streams and strands of behavior therapy are best captured by Wittgenstein's notion of complicated networks of similarities and dissimilarities. Second, Kuhn (1979) has suggested that as a science develops smaller sets of scientists begin to work on more specialized problems and the particular nature of these problems often call for idiosyncratic solutions. Thus, the more mature science then develops a micro-paradigmatic structure where small groups of scientists share similar problem solving exemplars and assumptions that have complicated networks of similarities but the field as a whole does not share one general paradigm.

Some of this diversity can be seen in the various theories associated with behavior therapy (O'Donohue & Krasner, 1995). From its early reliance on reinforcement, punishment, and reciprocal inhibition we can now see behavior therapists relying on the matching law, implosion theory, learned alarms theory, self-efficacy theory, attribution theory, information processing theories, relapse prevention, etc. Some of these theories were developed, as Kuhn described, in response to more particular problems of concern to particular behavior therapists. However, there clearly was diversity from the very beginning of behavior therapy: a key point of difference was the "Iowa school" more influenced by Hull and Mower's learning accounts; and the "Harvard school" more influenced by Skinner and operant psychology. Behaviorism is also one source of influence on many but not all of the early behavior therapists. Behaviorism is often thought to be monolithic but actually there are a variety of behaviorisms (O'Donohue & Kitchener, 1999). In the formation of behavior therapy these unique behaviorisms had unique influences. Skinner certainly was one of the most influential figures in the development of behavior therapy (he and Wolpe would vie for the title of the most influential). Unfortunately many of the more recent behavior therapists have much less understanding of behaviorism, experimental methodology and learning research than did the first generation behavior therapists. The interested reader is directed to O'Donohue and Ferguson (2001) for a brief introduction to Skinner.

Why Study the History of Behavior Therapy?

Why should a history of the behavioral therapies be attempted? Coleman (1988, p. 3-4) provides an interesting set of reasons for studying history:

A first claim is that *history is therapy*. To be unaware of past influences allows them to have unchecked effect upon our present-day research program.

A second claim sees *history as a cautionary tale*. This is the point made in the aphorism attributed to George Santayana, to the effect that those who are ignorant of the past are doomed to repeat its errors.

A third claim is that *the study of history provides a more perfect understanding of the present*. This claim, advanced by Julian Jaynes, postulates understanding rather than error-avoidance as the primary concern, and holds that the only way to understand the present is to study the past history upon which the present depends.

A fourth claim sees *history as a basis for the unification of psychology*. The history of psychology presumably supplies a "more generalized knowledge" that counterbalances specialization and facilitates appreciation of the unity of historically related specializations.

A fifth proposal regards *history as a form of travel*. Reading in the history of psychology enlarges one's horizon of possibilities, and this may provide a liberating influence from the limitations of one's particular time and place and specialty.

Sixth, *studying history is like getting an immunization shot*. Knowledge of the great pendulum swings that have occurred in psychology and of the fads and orthodoxies that have come and gone can reduce the persuasive power of new fads.

A seventh claim is that *history teaches appreciation*. The study of historical background of psychology makes one aware of the cumulative nature of scientific work in psychology.

An eighth claim regards *history as a treasure-hunt*. A few have claimed that the study of history occasionally results in the recovery of material, that is, a neglected idea or theory, which subsequently proves very useful in the present.

Ninth, *history is a crystal ball*. Erwin Esper, an early behaviorist who recorded a history of psychology in his later life, proposed that a knowledge of historical roots could contribute to efforts to predict future developments.

A tenth claim sees *history as a silver bullet*. Knowledge of how a present-day controversy began and how it gradually came to be formulated may be of great and unexpected assistance in resolving that controversy.

Eleventh, *history is a lesson in sobriety*. According to Crutchfiled and Krech, "knowledge of the history of one's science teaches the scientist humility and tolerance of opposing views"

A twelfth and final claim is that *history is a mark of the educated person*. A knowledge of history provides a familiarity with events, concepts, and cultural landmarks that are common coin in literary and conversational context of the larger world of ideas: even the specialist might wish to become better acquainted with such material.

Beyond these general reasons we think there are several reasons for studying the founding of behavior therapy. The most obvious answer is that this history can be of interest in its own right. Many are interested in family genealogy not because momentous ancestors are found, but because of a more basic curiosity regarding simply knowing what has happened in the past – particularly how this chain has lead to where we are now. A history can also attempt to answer key questions that fundamentally are historical: What is the "founding event"? (interestingly in what follows we will see different accounts of who first coined the label "behavior therapy"). What were the major sources of impetus in the creation of behavior therapy? What changes/developments occurred after the founding; what factors were responsible for these? Finally, all sorts of more specific historical questions can be framed; for example, what interactions did Skinner and Wolpe have and what were these like?

Studying history reminds us of how far we've come – how different things were then. When behavior therapy first came on the scene, psychologists were largely just "testers," permitted to do little therapy. Large state mental hospitals warehoused schizophrenics, who were often out of control, as this predated the discovery of effective anti-psychotics. Therapy was controlled by physicians and particularly by psychoanalysts. Today the scene is so different that new behavior therapists are in danger of having little appreciation of how much things have changed.

Origins often interest us and they often relate to other interesting and sometimes watershed events. In this history of the behavioral therapies we see the influence of the Great Depression; World War II; American ascendancy in the 20th century; the Cold War and its arms race; the rise of technology; the economic prosperity of the latter part of the century at least in the West; as well as the rise and spread of the research university.

Knowing where we came from also allows us to assess whether we have lost something; whether we have drifted away from some of the strengths that allowed us to be where we are today. We are now producing our fourth generation of behavior therapists; and many of the third and fourth generation have had little to no direct contact with the founders of our field. A valuable lesson may be that some of what made behavior therapy successful has been lost across the generations. We will discuss some of these possible "object lessons" below.

We also write this history because we think it is worthy to capture what we take to be a unique event in the history of psychotherapy. The famous historian of science Thomas Kuhn (1963) has stated that a key development of a science is when a scientific revolution occurs that allows a field to emerge from a pre-paradigmatic state to a state of normal, paradigmatic science. At the heart of the paradigm is a successful puzzle solution that serves as an exemplar for other scientists to emulate to solve further problems. We suggest that the learning based interventions that were developed, implemented and most importantly tested by the first generation behavior therapist represented the first time psychotherapy emerged from a pre-paradigmatic state to a state that is closer to what Kuhn calls normal science. Clinical problems such as enuresis, chronic skills deficits of the developmentally disabled, and certain anxiety problems were demonstrated to be remediated, for the first time in history. Before this psychotherapy was based on less sophisticated epistemologies. However, this is not to say that before behavior therapists came on the scene no one was taking a scientific approach. Clearly this was not the case. The Minnesota school was taking sophisticated approaches to test development and validation. The Rogerians, and others, were doing outcome research. And in fact some of the key publications of our discipline were short on experimental rigor. Many were case studies demonstrating the possibilities of efficacy. Some were single subject designs with no replications. Some were simply persuasive manifestos. Although we do not have space here it would be interesting to trace developments in the quality of the evidence during the development of behavior therapy. This project could also attempt to examine if philosophies of science can faithfully capture these developments. Were behavior therapists attempting to falsify their commitments, as Popper would claim constitutes good science? Were they extending problem-solving exemplars, as Kuhn would suggest? Were they opportunistic Dadaists, permissively following Feyerabend's recommendation, "Anything goes"? Were they none of these?

Another reason to study the history of behavior therapy is that at times individuals make *arguments from history*. These arguments are generally of the form:

1. In its origins behavior therapy had properties a, b, c ...
2. Properties a, b, c ... accounted for the success of behavior therapy.
3. Now behavior therapy has lost or reduced properties a, b, c, ...
4. Therefore if behavior therapists want to increase their success, they ought to reorient to properties a, b, c,...

Obviously the soundness of this kind of argument depends upon the accuracies of the historical claims contained in the first premise. Glib histories can be useful to someone wanting to make certain points. Glib, superficial histories are plentiful and the reader ought to be on guard against believing these. Smith (1986) has nicely shown that glib histories of behaviorism falsely associated it with logical positivism instead of characterizing it as associated with indigenous psychological epistemologies.

Thus behavior therapists at times might want to assume a meta-scientific perspective to attempt to understand questions such as: How can behavior therapy make better progress? What are the important features of behavior therapy that account for its growth? What factors are hindering its growth? How has it changed over time? These are important questions. Our point is simply that in order to answer these questions adequately a careful, accurate understanding of the historical record in needed. Otherwise the clever rhetorician can attempt to make historical claims that serve his or her particular interests.

Finally, we also record history to give due recognition to those responsible for events. This, also, is a purpose of the present volume. We believe that the individuals in the chapters that follow deserve to be honored. They worked hard, often as a small minority fighting a powerful and entrenched majority, because they would not accept as satisfactory what they saw. What they saw was much human suffering that was not being effectively treated by the standard interventions of the day. And what they also saw was that the alleged evidential basis for claims surrounding these interventions was problematic. They had a vision that things could be better and they were willing to pay the price to attempt to make things better. Their efforts, we believe, are responsible for bettering the lives of many individuals – most importantly the clients who experience more relief from their pain; but these efforts also paved the way for better opportunities and careers for the second and third generation behavior therapists, as journals were launched; professional associations were formed; and inroads to hiring this strange new breed of therapists and researchers were made. To paraphrase Isaac Newton, we see farther because we stand on their shoulders.

Historiography

Behavior therapists tend to be explicitly concerned with method. Writing a history calls for a historical method. Historiography is the study of the method of writing history. As such it concerns itself with a meta-question: How should history be properly studied? Any history attempts to fairly capture part of the story knowing that the story also legitimately could be told in other ways. Because of the complexity of the tale that the historian is attempting to tell, the would-be historian makes hard choices. A key choice is what method is to be used to capture and explicate a slice of the historical record. The historian is constrained by a lack of knowledge. Much is lost in the mists of the past.

Historical Methods

Externalist histories attempt to specify the larger forces (that is, outside of the phenomena to be explained) that influenced the topic of the historical account, in this case behavior therapy. These forces could be economic, technological, political, social, or ideological. *Historicist accounts* are a variation of externalist accounts. Historicism is the view that history should be told from the point of view of inexorable historical forces. This view would attempt to identify the forces that would have made the rise of behavior therapy an historical inevitability. *Marxist historical accounts* utilize historicism and externalist methods as these attempt to identify the economic and technological forces that give rise to historical events.

Internalist histories, on the other hand, take a more microanalytic view, attempting to explain the historical stream by more immediate influences. In these accounts, personal interactions and other more day-to-day personal events comprise the majority of the account. *A "great person" account*, a type of internalist account, attempts to tell history through the influence of extraordinary individuals. Individual acts of genius are the main constituents of this account.

Whiggish accounts of history are often seen as fundamentally flawed historical accounts. In these accounts the past is seen from the lens of what is now judged to be acceptable or true. Those events that can be seen as contributing to the present are seen as good or important. Those that hindered or are seen as irrelevant to what is presently seen as correct are then depicted as bad or unimportant. Whiggish accounts are sometimes referred to as "presentist" accounts.

Cognitive accounts of history attempt to tell history through its propositional content. A cognitivist account would proceed along the lines of key beliefs and arguments. An example would be: In 1952 Eysneck argued that the eventual basis for the superiority of extant psychotherapies over placebo or spontaneous remission was problematic. This claim leads others to believe that new therapies needed to be developed and that these new therapies needed to be more adequately tested.

In this volume we have attempted to tell a history of the behavioral therapies through the autobiographies of some of the key players (and in the case of a few particularly important individuals who have died – Skinner, Wolpe and Kantor, through canonical biographies). This autobiographical approach generally has some externalist qualities but is mainly an internalist approach. It is inherently a "great person" approach. This autobiographical approach has many advantages, particularly in that it allows the major actors to tell their own stories directly. There is no historian making errors that are inevitable when a third party, who often was not present, attempts to reconstruct events. Importantly, this approach is not only a "read" of the historical record; it actually goes a long way toward helping to create the historical record. With some limitations briefly described below, canonical histories are written by obtaining the statements of the key actors. Finally, the autobiographical account is potentially a very personal and hence potentially more "alive" account. However, there are at least two major limitations to the autobiographical approach that also need to be recognized: 1) the biases introduced by allowing individuals to tell their own stories; and 2) errors introduced by the particular sample of individuals chosen.

To be explicit regarding the second possible source of error, a different, more complete account would have been given if three additional sets of autobiographies were obtained. First, autobiographies of some of the basic researchers whose research set the stage for the behavioral therapies. These would include Pavlov, Schenov, Bechterev, Watson, Thorndike, Guthrie, Tolman, Hull, Spence, and Mowrer, among others. Kazdin's (1978) excellent *History of Behavior Modification: Experimental Foundations of Contemporary Research* nicely documents these influences. The reader is highly recommended to read this text to gain a fuller historical account of this stage of the development of the behavior therapies. Second, autobiographies of individuals who engaged in developing proto-behavior therapies – usually practical but fairly isolated applications of conditioning principles – in the first part of the 20th century. These individuals include people such as John Watson, Rosalie Rayner, Mary Cover Jones, Jules Masserman, O. Hobart Mowrer, Andrew Salter, John Dollard, Neal Miller, among others. These individuals often were innovative and produced an exemplar – perhaps of a treatment technique, perhaps of a conceptual framework in which techniques could be developed – that shed light on a path that was followed in the last half of the 20th century. Finally, due to logistical limitations as well as conflicting schedules the set of autobiographies and biographies of first generation behavior therapists is not exhaustive. The stories of Ayllon, Azrin, Becker, Brady, Eysenck, Ferster, Geer, Gewirtz, Goldiamond, Greenspoon, Kalish, Kanfer, Keller, Lan, London, Lovaas, Malott, Marks, Michael, Patterson, Rachman, Salzinger, Sidman, Staats, Stolz, Ullmann, Yates, among others are not told in this volume, but if these were a fuller account would have been made. Another history of the second generation of behavior therapists would also be key to further understand the history of behavior therapy. It should be notes that we largely tell the story of the rise of behavior therapy in the United States, although it also had important roots in Great Britain and South Africa. Part of the South African story is told here in the biography of Wolpe and the autobiography of Lazarus. However, the British story is admittedly slighted, mainly due to the logistics of travel. Finally, a more complete account of the history of the behavioral therapies would track the influences noted by Krasner and Ullmann (1965):

- The concept of *behaviorism* in experimental psychology (e.g., J. R. Kantor, 1924, 1963).
- The instrumental (operant) conditioning concepts of Thorndike (1931) and Skinner (1938).
- The technique of reciprocal inhibition as developed by Wolpe (1958)
- The studies of the group of investigators at Maudsely Hospital in London under the direction of H. J. Eysneck (1960, 1964).
- The investigations (from the 1920s through the 1940's) applying *conditioning* concepts to human behavior problems in the United States (e.g., Mowrer & Mowrer, 1938; Watson & Rayner, 1920).
- Interpretations of psychoanalysis in learning theory terms (e.g., Dollard & Miller, 1950), enhancing learning theory as a respectable base for clinical work.
- Classical conditioning as the basis for explaining and changing normal and deviant behavior (Pavlov, 1928) interactionism, social psychology and sociology.
- Theoretical concepts and research studies of social role learning and research in developmental and child psychology which emphasized vicarious learning and modeling (Bandura, 1970; Jones, 1924).
- Social influence studies of demand characteristics, experimenter bias, hypnosis, and placebo (Frank, 1961).
- An environmental social learning model as an alternative to a disease model of human behavior (Bandura, 1969; Ullmann & Krasner, 1965).
- Dissatisfaction with psychotherapy and the psychoanalytic model.
- The development of the clinical psychologist as scientist-practitioner.
- A group of psychiatrists emphasizing human interaction (e.g., Adolph Meyer, 1948; Harry Stack Sullivan, 1953).
- A utopian stream emphasizing the planning of social environments to elicit and maintain the best of man's behavior (e.g., Skinner's 1976 *Walden Two*).

We chose first generation behavior therapists as we wanted to tell the story of the beginning of behavior therapy. We defined first generation as individuals we found critical to the development of behavior therapy in the 1950's and early 1960's. We chose these particular individuals as they have been the most influential. Others were excluded either due to their early deaths (e.g., Hans Eysneck, Charles Ferster), space limitations, or to their personal decision not to participate.

The structure of most chapters follows suggestions given to the authors by the editors. We asked the authors to give a brief intellectual and personal biography. We wanted to trace their personal histories so we could see the route each took to become an early player in behavior therapy. We then asked them to present an intellectual case study of one of their key works. We wanted to do this as we thought this focus would provide us with specificity regarding the sources of influence and the consequences of one publication. We wanted this story to have both bandwidth and fidelity. Finally, we asked each of these individuals to take a look at the current status of behavior therapy and provide useful object lessons from their perspectives. What should we pay more attention to? What is going right? What is going wrong? We thought that these originators might have some wisdom that ought to be recorded and noticed by current and future generations.

Object Lessons

What might emerge as important lessons from the past? We think there are at least three deserving comment: 1) what struck us as editors was the scholarship of the originators of behavior therapy. They knew experimental psychology well. They knew learning research and theory well. In fact many of them might be reasonably thought of as learning researchers who were utilizing humans with problems as their subjects. They also were often scholars in general psychology, and read in the original language forerunners like Pavlov. They also were intellectuals and read widely in fields like philosophy, sociology, political science and the like. For example, the scholarship contained in Ullmann and Krasner's (1969) early writings has largely been unmatched. Currently we see a more narrow technological focus in behavior therapy. The larger intellectual perspective is largely lost and the behavioral therapies are not enriched by the broader ideas and developments in psychology and other fields.

The second object lesson, in our view, is that the role of process in behavior therapy has been lost. Today most research in behavior therapy is outcome research; horse race studies examine what condition (placebo, no treatment, active treatment) wins. Active treatment is often a packaged manual. Many current behavior therapists see this as sound and satisfactory. Admittedly it certainly can seem so, particularly when compared to the many completely nonscientific approaches to psychotherapy. However we conjecture that there has been a shift. In the early days of behavior therapy process research and outcome research were more frequently intertwined. These early behavior therapists were testing the effects of psychological processes (such as satiation, extinction, etc.) on clinical problems. Now behavior therapists test the effects of complex eclectic, often atheoretically derived packages (many with no clear relation to a known psychological process or principle).

The third object lesson is that we have lost the iconoclastic value of the first generation: they were questioners; they were radical; they had the courage to fight the power structure. They were rule breakers. It is important to remember that they were breaking the rules and they were not assured that this would lead to success. As the discipline has matured it has come to be more conventional, less revolutionary. Part of the reason for this is that some of our values have been assimilated into the power structure; it is also apparent that we have made compromises. We no longer see radical critiques of the medical model; we often use the DSM system; we design treatment packages and research protocols that will get funded by federal agencies; we eclectically adopt assessment or treatment methods from other schools; our ethical challenges to suboptimal treatment are less frequent and more muted; and our goals have become more modest – we seek no longer to change institutions or society but rather to make a living. The boldness, zeal and courage to question radically and to profess one's convictions even when unpopular have largely given way to a discipline which is more conservative and conventional. Part of a mature discipline is to be derivative – to do normal science; but in this we also have lost some of the creativity of the early years. Where are our revolutionaries that fight against the problematic compromises or who see the radical possibilities within our set of commitments and remind us that we are to go in a vastly different direction? Should we be reminded of the ideals of the founders and look again whether our commitments to evidential standards could be improved; whether our extrapolations from basic psychology could be better; whether we seek to properly intertwine process and outcome research; whether behavior therapy is profiting from corrupt larger intellectual developments?

It is our hope that future generations of behavior therapists keep alive the radical critiques of accepted ways of treating changeworthy behavior as well as the commitment to finding ways to improve human lives through a commitment to scientific methods.

References

Bandura, A. (1969). *Principles of behavior modification*. New York: Holt, Rinehart, & Winston.

Bandura, A. (1970). *Social learning theory*. Morristown, NJ: General Learning Press.

Coleman, S. R. (1988, May 28). What does the history of psychology have on sale today? Paper presented at symposium on history, philosophy and behavior analysis, at the 14th annual convention of the Association for Behavior Analysis. Philadelphia, PA.

Dollard, J., & Miller, N. (1950). *Personality and psychotherapy: an analysis in terms of learning, thinking and culture*. New York: McGraw-Hill.

Eysenck, H. J. (1960). *Behaviour therapy and the neuroses; readings in modern methods of treatment derived from learning theory*. New York: Pergamon Press.

Eysenck, H. J. (Ed.). (1964). *Experiments in behaviour therapy: readings in modern methods of treatment of mental disorders derived from learning theory*. New York: Pergamon Press.

Eysenck, H. J. (1952). The effects of psychotherapy: An evaluation. *Journal of Consulting Psychology, 16*, 319-324.

Frank, J. D. (1961). *Persuasion and healing*. Baltimore, MD: Johns Hopkins University Press.

Jones, M. C. (1924). The elimination of children's fears. *Journal of Experimental Psychology, 7*, 382-390.

Kantor, J. R. (1924). *Principles of psychology*. New York: Knopf.

Kantor, J. R. (1963). *The scientific evolution of psychology*. Chicago: Principia.

Kazdin, A. E. (1978). *History of behavior modification: Experimental foundations of contemporary research*. Baltimore: University Park Press.

Krasner, L., & Ullmann, L. P. (Eds.). (1965). *Case studies in behavior modification*. New York: Holt, Rinehart, & Winston.

Kuhn, T. S. (1963). *The structure of scientific revolutions*. Chicago: University of Chicago Press.

Kuhn, T. S. (1979). *The essential tension*. Chicago: University of Chicago Press.

Meyer, A. (1948). *The concept of wholes*. New York: McGraw-Hill.

Mowrer, O. H., & Mowrer, W. M. (1938). Enuresis: A method for its study and treatment. *American Journal of Orthopsychiatry, 8*, 436-459.

O'Donohue, W., & Ferguson, K. (2001). *The psychology of B.F. Skinner*. Thousand Oaks: Sage.

O'Donohue, W., & Kitchener, R. (1999). *Handbook of behaviorism*. San Diego: Academic Press.

O'Donohue, W., & Krasner, L. (1995). *Theories of behavior therapy: exploring behavior change*. Washington, DC: APA Books.

Pavlov, I. P. (1928). *Lectures on conditioned reflexes* (W. H. Gantt, Trans.). New York: International Publishers.

Rachman, S. (1963). Introduction to behavior therapy. *Behaviour Research and Therapy, 1*, 3-15.

Skinner, B. F. (1938). *The behavior of organisms*. New York: Appleton-Century.

Skinner, B. F. (1976). *Walden two*. New York: Macmillan.

Smith, L. D. (1986). *Behaviorism and logical positivism*. Stanford: Stanford University Press.

Sullivan, H. S. (1953). *The interpersonal theory of psychiatry*. New York: Norton.

Thorndike, E. L. (1931). *The fundamentals of learning*. New York: Bureau of Publications, Teachers College.

Ullmann, L. P., & Krasner, L. (1969). *A psychological approach to abnormal behavior*. Englewood Cliffs, NJ: Prentice-Hall.

Watson, J. B., & Rayner, R. (1920). Conditioned emotional reactions. *Journal of Experimental Psychology, 3*(1), 1-14.

Wittgenstein, L. (1958). *Philosophical investigations*. New York: Macmillan.

Wolpe, J. (1958). *Psychotherapy by reciprocal inhibition*. Stanford, CA: Stanford University Press.

Wolpe, J. (1969). *The practice of behavior therapy*. New York: Pergamon Press.

Chapter 1

The Importance of Case Studies to Methodology of Science

Thomas Nickles[1]
University of Nevada, Reno

1. Introduction: Historical Studies of Recent Science

Until the 1960's or so, history of science was concerned almost entirely with *old* science, for example, the scientific revolution from Copernicus to Newton, the chemical revolution of Lavoisier and Priestley, and the experimental revolution of Wundt and company in psychology. Indeed, the very phrases 'history of present science' and (even) 'history of recent science' sounded oxymoronic. To be sure, philosophers of physics were interested in the early 20th-century revolutions in relativity theory and quantum theory, but historians found it difficult to see the 20th-century work of living scientists as *history*, both because it was not really past and because it did not readily lend itself to good *story*, that is, a semi-literary production accessible to the historians' usual audience – the educated general reader. For the technical details were formidable, and, Einstein and Marie Curie aside, it was increasingly difficult to understand scientific breakthroughs as the achievement of great, Romantic geniuses working in isolation, against scientific, religious, or political orthodoxy.

Since the 1960's, the situation has changed radically. Today the field of "science studies" is flourishing. Science studies, which is also called *Social Studies of Science* (the name of its leading journal), emerged in Britain, in the 1970's, in the form of radical sociology of science, and quickly spread to the Continent and to America. This movement attacked standard philosophy of science as too a priori and dogmatic, and it attacked internalist history of science for remaining too much in the old history of ideas genre, in which ideas were often treated as if they develop in a disembodied manner according to their own internal logic and timeless standards of evaluation. Today the field of science and technology studies encompasses not only the sociology of science but also the anthropology, social history, political science, and economics of science and technology. In its generic sense, it includes old-style history and philosophy of science and even psychology of science, but most science studies scholars still hold philosophy, internalist history, and individual psychology in suspicion. A few years ago two prominent scholars (Bruno Latour & Steve Woolgar, 1986) only half facetiously suggested a ten-year moratorium on psychology of science in order to allow genuinely social accounts of cognition to flourish. Many philosophers, meanwhile, continue to appreciate internalist history and also individual psychological treatments of scientific work, be those treatments cognitivist, behavioral, or (occasionally) Freudian.

But beyond warning that individual biography, including psychobiography of any kind, is considered old fashioned in some quarters, my purpose today is not to belabor these differences among the science studies disciplines. The point of bringing up science studies is that its emphasis is on 20th-century science, especially recent science and technology and science policy as they have been transformed by World War II and postwar developments. The historian of technology Derek Price (1963) marked this difference as a distinction between "little science" and "big science."

Even historians have now moved into the 20th century. At George Washington University, for example, there is a Center for History of Recent Science, headed by Horace Judson. In his spring 1999 newsletter, Judson, who works on the history of recent biology and biotechnology, notes that until recently writing about recent and current science was considered a journalistic activity rather than one of serious scholarship (Judson, 1999).

Yet understanding recent history of science is obviously important, for several reasons. One is that, insofar as the character of 20th-century science has changed, it is dangerous to draw one's methodological lessons from the classical, founding cases alone. And, after all, professional psychology is little more than a century old and developing rapidly. Another sort of reason is that, along with the development of market economies and bourgeois life, the rise of modern science and technology has surely done more than anything else to shape modern culture. These changes have become increasingly rapid and pervasive in the 20th century. A fourth point relates to the scale of scientific activity. Price noted that the amount of scientific investigation had increased exponentially from the time of the scientific revolution until it began leveling off in the 1970's. It is sobering to think that about 80% of the scientists who have ever lived are still alive today. There is therefore some urgency in studying the history of recent science before the participants die.

Now it may seem that recent and contemporary history is easy to do. After all, one still has most of the principals available for direct interrogation (or to do the job themselves). The challenging old intellectual mysteries about what scientist X and Y were really doing – and what led them to their problems and then to their epochal solutions – now seem to vanish, for we can simply ask them!

However, things are not so easy. As Judson says, journalistic accounts, with their anecdotal evidence and apocryphal stories, are not to be confused with serious, professional historical scholarship. Moreover, modern communications technology often makes it more, rather than less, difficult to trace the emergence of new ideas and practices. Today's scientists tend not to leave extensive paper trails, as did the likes of Newton, Faraday, and Darwin – in the form of early drafts of papers, frequent, detailed letters to colleagues, lab notebooks, and diaries of personal reflections. Rather, scientists now communicate by telephone, e-mail, and personal contact at conferences and workshops. Circulated preprints and grant proposals rather than the published record are often where the action is – things that often have an evanescent existence. When scientists retire, they often throw away their personal files.

Furthermore, the idea that we can simply ask living scientists what they meant, and what motivated them, turns out to be naïve, an instance of *the intentional fallacy* and *the whig fallacy*, both of which I shall explain later.

In his book, *The Structure of Scientific Revolutions*, originally published in 1962 and expanded in 1970, Thomas Kuhn called attention to these difficulties and remarked that "History, if viewed as a repository for more than anecdote or chronology, could produce a decisive transformation in the image of science by which we are now possessed." Here was a call to do serious case studies, and of recent science as well as old science.

Some philosophers as well as historians took up the call. Kuhn himself had shown the methodological relevance of historical cases by deftly employing them to discredit Karl Popper's and the logical positivists' accounts of scientific research. The new generation of historically-oriented philosophers promoted the idea that philosophical accounts of science, including scientific method, should be tested against the data of history, with historical cases serving as data points, as it were. To that degree, in other words, philosophy, or at least philosophy of science, became an empirical rather than a purely a priori subject. Today science studies is thoroughly empirical in studying every facet of scientific work. But it was the work of people such as Kuhn, Paul Feyerabend, Stephen Toulmin, and Imre Lakatos in the 1960's and early 1970's that introduced this new kind of philosophy of science based on historical case studies. This, I shall contend, was an important step in weaning philosophy of science from the traditional dogma that good science should be constrained by a foundational epistemological program.

A second reason for taking case-studies seriously derives from a more radical suggestion, one that goes to the heart of learning theory as applied to scientists themselves, that is, to the very idea of scientific method. The basic idea of this *deflationary* conception of method is that method itself is better construed as a set of exemplary cases than as a set of rules. This suggestion is at least implicit in *The Structure of Scientific Revolutions*. In the next two sections, I proceed to contrast two approaches to scientific method in this light.

2. Two Approaches to Scientific Method, Rule-Based and Case-Based

The old philosophy of science associated with logical positivism was, in most versions, a rule-based methodology of science. There were rules for testing hypotheses and, occasionally, even rules for generating empirical hypotheses. Moreover, the positivists required that any abstract, theoretical language be linked to observation language by means of so-called correspondence rules, where the link should be as close to explicit definition as possible – although in fact this was rarely possible. This last sort of rule brings out the *empiricism* as well as the *logic* of logical empiricism. For this methodology of science was a conservative epistemological program. One could do good science only by being a good, conservative-empiricist philosopher.

The positivists, of course, recognized that old-time foundational epistemology of the kind sought by Descartes is impossible: we cannot achieve certainty in empirical science. But they nevertheless insisted that every result, indeed, every legitimate term of art, be empirically well-founded before proceeding to the next step. For them the source of all meaning was the data language, and the source of all justification was the empirical data themselves. The result was a one-dimensional, indeed, one-directional conception of justification, a cumulative account of scientific development, both doctrinal and conceptual, and an empiricist, "building-block" theory of language learning and concept formation, whereby each theoretical term could be learned only in terms of less theoretical language and that language in terms of still less, and so on back to the observation language.

A story from the letters of the composer Arnold Schönberg illustrates this idea. A blind man was discoursing with someone who happened to use the term 'white', which for the blind man was tantamount to a theoretical term.

"White?," he asked.

"You know, the color of a swan," came the reply.

"Swan?"

"Yes, the large bird with the long, curved neck."

"Curved?"

"Here, like the shape of my arm as I am holding it now." The blind man felt his friend's arm.

"Oh!" he exclaimed. "Now I know what white means!"

Compare the now-dated behaviorist joke: Two behaviorists meet on the street. One greets the other: "You feel fine. How do I feel?"

Some strands of behaviorism were broadly compatible with logical empiricism, although the connection has been greatly exaggerated (Smith 1986). To be sure, behavioristic psychologists have, by and large, been conservative empiricists when it comes to concept formation and theory formation; however, they (and especially Skinnerian behavior analysts) have largely ignored or explicitly repudiated the linguistic analyses of the positivists. In general they are closer to the Darwinian, naturalistic epistemologies of the American pragmatists. This is most obvious in Skinner's case, given his emphasis on selection by consequences as an extension of Darwinian methodology; but Edward C. Tolman and Clark Hull owed a debt to Darwin as well (Smith, 1986).

Now as everyone knows, no science has been more concerned with method than psychology has. And method is standardly conceived as a set of rules.

The picture of science that we get from Kuhn is quite different. On Kuhn's view, insofar as you are deeply concerned with method, you are in deep trouble! The emergence of rules signals a science in crisis. Normal scientists working under a paradigm don't need to appeal to methodological rules (he says), because their work is directly modeled on exemplary achievements that define the field of inquiry in the first place. Given his severe criticism of the positivists, Popperians, and the entire rules tradition of concept learning and problem solving in general, we can say that Kuhn, the most famous scientific methodologist of our century, was actually an *anti-*

methodologist. Although his one-time colleague, Feyerabend, was notorious for his book, *Against Method* (Feyerabend, 1975), Kuhn himself was against method in his own way.

And yet Kuhn also has a positive message. We can read him as propounding the view that the sciences operate by means of a very different sort of method than the standard, rule-based one. This is not only an alternative method: it is also an alternative learning theory (including an account of concept formation), indeed, an alternative treatment of what it is to engage in *rational* inquiry. Like Ludwig Wittgenstein before him and the cognitive psychologist Eleanor Rosch (e.g., Rosch, 1973) and her associates after him, Kuhn rejected the view that a concept is defined in all-or-nothing fashion in terms of a set of necessary and sufficient conditions or rules. Rather, concepts are based on a resemblance or similarity relation, and hence graded.

This similarity relation is not entirely natural. It itself is in large-part culturally learned, by paying attention to what that culture takes to be exemplary cases or prototypes. Kuhn termed such cases "exemplars," and *exemplar* became the primary meaning of 'paradigm' in the expanded, 1970 edition of *Structure of Scientific Revolutions.* On Kuhn's view, a certain amount of cultural relativity is unavoidable, since we never have direct, unmediated experience of the Kantian Thing-in-Itself. Different linguistic communities lump different things together as similar. Things that are similar in the folk physics or folk psychology of Aristotle or of the person in the street, may be quite distinct in modern scientific physics or psychology; and vice versa.

What this amounts to, I would claim, is a *rhetorical turn* in our conception of human cognition, of learning and inquiry, a turn away from logic and toward rhetoric. For rhetoric is concerned with simile, metaphor, analogy, and such tropes rather than with sets of logically necessary and sufficient conditions. Insofar as Kuhn is right, logical rules, where they function at all in the process of inquiry, are derivative from exemplars. In my next section I will sketch how this view extends to a case-based as against a rule-based conception of scientific inquiry.

First, however, I want to factor in Kuhn's strong contention that science is a problem-solving activity. Inquiry, he insisted, is erotetic, that is, question-centered or puzzle-centered, rather than theory-centered. In itself this idea was not new. One can find it quite explicitly stated in Ernst Mach, Charles Peirce, Popper, and also in artificial intelligence work by Herbert Simon and his colleagues from the mid-1950's on (e.g., Newell & Simon, 1972). But it was Kuhn who made the most convincing case that scientific work is a problem-solving rather than a directly truth-seeking activity and that scientific knowledge in manifested in practical skill more in than the construction of aesthetically pleasing world-views (see Rouse, 1987, chap. 2; Nickles, 1988). In other words, Kuhn not only promoted what I would call a *pragmatic* account of scientific inquiry, in contrast to the epistemological foundationism still present in modern empiricism, but he also shifted the emphasis from *knowing-that* to *knowing-how*. Previous philosophical accounts of all stripes had tended to reduce knowing how to do something to knowing that a set of propositions is true, or that a set of rules suffices for accomplishing a task, a conception largely retained in Chomskian linguistic theory and in standard artificial intelligence.

A related element of this pragmatic, problem-solving construal of scientific inquiry is that what I call *heuristic appraisal* or *heuristic pursuit* becomes at least as important as epistemic appraisal. When one reads the positivists and other philosophers of science, even Popper, one finds most of the emphasis placed on so-called confirmation theory or corroboration, which attempts to answer the question, To what extent can this scientific theoretical claim be justified, and on what logical and empirical basis? This is part and parcel of the epistemic tradition coming down from Descartes and embracing both traditional rationalism and empiricism. Conservatives in both camps want to avoid at all costs the Type II error of accepting a false hypothesis. An extreme case in the empiricist tradition is W. K. Clifford, the late 19th-century British mathematician and physicist. Clifford once wrote: "It is wrong always, everywhere, and for everyone, to believe anything upon insufficient evidence." This is the empiricist counterpart to Descartes's refusing to take the next step until he had achieved absolute certainty.

The American pragmatists sharply rejected this Cartesian conception of science. This sort of epistemological purity, said Peirce, would block the road to inquiry – and that was his own chief constraint on scientific investigation: "Do not block the road to inquiry." In his celebrated article, "The Will to Believe," the psychologist and pragmatist philosopher William James (1897) also rejected this whole conservative ethos of science. In terms of our more recent terminology, his point was that Clifford was so afraid of committing a Type II error that he was likely to commit Type I errors of rejecting true hypotheses, by refusing even to entertain them seriously because they went far beyond currently available evidence. Nothing ventured, nothing gained. Science is inherently a risky business. In managing risk, whether in everyday life, business life, or science, we need to consider the utilities, the possible payoffs, as well as the epistemic probabilities. Accordingly, James stressed the importance of the fertility of a hypothesis. Don't worry so much about where it came from but look to where it might lead.

This is heuristic appraisal, in contrast to epistemic appraisal. Philosophers have long emphasized that science is a long-term, self-correcting enterprise, not one likely to arrive immediately, if ever, at the absolute truth about the universe. Yet they have paid remarkably little attention to the importance of heuristic appraisal. But surely scientists in the trenches are as much concerned with fertility as with truth. A fertile idea or technique is one that can guide you toward interesting problems, help you write good grant proposals, and so on. Your conviction that a thesis is true does not automatically make it fertile, does not suggest that you can do anything with it. Truth does not equate to fertility. Better to have a fertile hypothesis that you know is false than a sterile one that you believe true! One scientific counterpart to writer's block may be to believe something without seeing how to do anything with it.

Those who emphasize epistemic appraisal tend to have a backward-looking perspective. They ask the question: *How strongly does the data, the track record of this hypothesis, justify it as true?* While this is certainly an important activity, no question about it, at least equally important is the forward-looking perspective of heuristic appraisal: *Whether or not this claim is certifiably true or this practice completely unproblematic, does it open up new avenues of inquiry that it would be fruitful to pursue?*

One way of bringing out my point is to note that many times in the history of science research has shifted away from an entrenched theory or problem or practice not because it was considered mistaken but because it was thought to be exhausted of interesting results. Many of the best and brightest scientists shift problem areas in mid-career when they believe that most of the interesting work has already been done in their former area. The question scientists ask of an approach is not "What have you done for me?" or even "What have you done for me lately?" but "What can you do for me tomorrow?" Highly successful scientists, I believe, are pragmatic opportunists. They do not stick faithfully to an older approach that has served them well when they perceive promising new opportunities for exciting work.

Let me now sum up my two, contrasting conceptions of scientific method. The account that I find attractive

a. is a problem-solving versus a directly truth-seeking enterprise.
b. is pragmatic and opportunistic rather than foundational-epistemological.
c. makes constant use of heuristic appraisal and does not leave theory of justification to epistemic appraisal alone.
d. is forward-looking (prospective, future-directed) rather than backward-looking (retrospective, historical).
e. flourishes on case-based thought and practice over thoroughgoing rule-based inquiry.

In my next section I shall say a little more about case-based vs. rule-based problem solving and how exemplars can have heuristic power.

3. Case-based vs. Rule-based Problem Solving

In my view the most interesting methodological and epistemological feature of Kuhn's *Structure of Scientific Revolutions* is not his doctrine of revolutions but his account of concepts-and-categorization, and his corresponding account of problem recognition and puzzle solving as exemplar-based or case-based rather than explicitly rule-based. Although he sometimes allowed that the physical implementation of his model might involve complete physical determinism, and possibly rules, at the neural level, Kuhn insisted that, at the levels of description to which we humans have cognitive and methodological access (levels of human communication and control), scientific inquiry amounts to learning by example, to case-based pattern-matching of new puzzles to exemplary problems and solutions already available. It does so by means of "acquired similarity relations" rather than rule-based derivations of solutions from first principles. Hence the priority of paradigms to rules (*Structure* §V).

In effect, Kuhn argued that physical scientific inquiry is driven by case-based rather than rule-based reasoning and practice. While the terms 'case-based reasoning' and 'rule-based reasoning' (CBR and RBR) are today most commonly used in artificial intelligence (AI), the basic ideas have a long history dating back to debates between medieval logic, with its concern with universality, and rhetoric, with its concern for *exemplum* – and even back to Socrates's attempt to defend rule-based definition over examples. Although I think that Kuhn exaggerated the incompatibility of the two approaches and underestimated the role that rules of various kinds can play, I shall, for present purposes, continue to draw the distinction sharply.

To be sure, most extant case-based problem-solving systems in AI are implemented in terms of rules, but the mode of problem solving is interestingly different from that of the older generation of rule-based problem solvers. As Kuhn already emphasized, there is a genuine difference between case-based and rule-based practice at consciously accessible levels of methodological description and advice. For Kuhn, learning and computation remain largely implicit or tacit at these levels of description and are the more efficient for being so. In many problem domains, requiring explicit inference rules and definitions of concepts blocks the road to inquiry. Over the past twenty years, work in cognitive science, even in AI, seems to teach the same lesson, although to what degree remains controversial.

A rule-based system solves problems by following strategies expressed in terms of rules, e.g., production rules. The basic idea is to solve a problem by deriving its solution from first principles plus any heuristic rules. A problem solution is thus a kind of heuristic proof, and the problem-solving system a kind of logic supplemented by heuristic rules and empirical assumptions. For some, that is what the adjective 'computational' means and requires. In the heyday of expert systems research, or knowledge-based computation, "knowledge engineers" attempted to elicit knowledge-laden heuristic strategies, in the form of rules, from experts in the particular field of the AI application. A major difficulty of this approach was the so-called "knowledge-elicitation bottleneck" or "Feigenbaum's problem." Many experts claimed not to be using rules at all; and when they did offer rules that fit the current problem, they often violated these supposed rules when given new problems. The rules were not uniformly projectable onto new cases.

Now back in the 1960's, Kuhn had made exactly the same prediction of *philosophers* who tried to reduce scientific practice to rules. In today's terminology these philosophers treated methodology of science *either* as a rule-based "general problem solver" (truncated by the logical positivists to a logic of justification only) *or* as a kind of content-laden, rule-based, expert system; whereas, for Kuhn, scientific methodology (insofar as that enterprise can be defended at all) is a case-based rather than a rule-based system. Thus AI's experience with the knowledge-elicitation bottleneck confirms Kuhn's claim that sharing a common practice does not entail sharing a common, rule-based *theory* of that practice (Hoyningen-Huhne, 1993, p. 137). Interestingly, the "expert systems" philosophers were not only the positivists and Popperians. They prominently included the new, historical philosophers of science, who attempted to extract methodological rules from historical cases. However, the latter were more interested than the positivists were in heuristic rules that possess real, problem-solving power.

Another difficulty with rule-based reasoning (RBR) is that rule-based systems do not scale well. Indeed, they typically become slower and clumsier instead of faster as more knowledge-based rules are added. They do not degrade gracefully. Conflicts among rules are hard to avoid, since no one can see all the implications of present rules or of adding new rules. (The unavoidable failure to recognize all the deductive consequences is one aspect of the Meno problem.) Moreover, in order to be reliable, rule-based systems must be pretty complete; but that makes them relatively static and unable to learn from experience, including learning from their mistakes. These and several other difficulties have dampened the early enthusiasm for simple, rule-based expert systems as a model of human scientific inquiry.

A case-based approach can often avoid such difficulties. Case-based reasoning (CBR) is more contextual or situational than RBR, since rules must abstract over a variety of contexts and situations. A case description tends to be more meaningful and easier to remember than an abstract rule, and it may even lend itself to story. Another advantage of CBR over many forms of RBR is that one can solve sufficiently matching problems with confidence even when one has only a few cases in the case library, as when one imitates or copies someone else's way of handling a task. (This sort of learning-by-being-shown falls somewhere between the Skinnerian distinction of contingency-shaped and rule-governed behavior: see §4 below.) Thus CBR is valuable in ill-structured domains where algorithms and strong heuristic rules are lacking – and the research frontier is, by definition, ill-defined in this way. CBR does not perpetually solve each problem "from scratch" but efficiently matches new cases to old and adapts their solutions. It is therefore one form of *adaptive* problem solving. A case-based approach can, in principle, handle difficult, nonlinear problems in this fashion, because it does not require a Cartesian decomposition of a problem or complex system into its simplest logical components. Hence CBR represents a major departure from the traditional method of *logical* analysis and synthesis. Even when we are dealing with logic problems, write Rumelhart *et al.* (1986, 44), "The basic idea is that we succeed in solving problems not so much through the use of logic, but by making the problems we wish to solve conform to problems we are good at solving."

This sounds very Kuhnian. Kuhn went on to say that a theory or paradigm (in the large sense) *is* basically a set of exemplars sufficient to provide solutions to an entire, significant domain of problems. That is, (1) relatively few exemplars provide the basis for solving a potentially infinite number of concrete problems; and (2) these exemplars constitute a "basis set" that "spans" the problem space (my terminology, not Kuhn's). For according to Kuhn a paradigm guarantees that all puzzles in its domain are solvable by clever modeling upon its various exemplars. In saying that the available exemplars are sufficient to generate the complete space of admissible problem solutions, this guarantee amounts to a strong generatability or discoverability claim (cf. Marshall, 1995; Nickles, 1985).

Exemplars can therefore have great heuristic power. Since an exemplar contains a problem-plus-solution and includes components of skilled practice as well as theory, finding a suitable exemplar or three that seem to fit a new problem area can provide considerable heuristic guidance, since much of the necessary know-how is already built in. The relevant exemplary cases show us how to proceed. In fact, drawing attention to the applicability to new problems of off-the-shelf exemplars is probably the most important facet of heuristic appraisal.

4. Various Difficulties

However, not everything here is sweetness and light. A case-based account of problem solving faces difficulties of its own. What is to count as a case? How do we produce the very first exemplars of a new field? At the other end of this spectrum, which of the zillion possible cases are to be retained in the case library? How can relevant cases be indexed and retrieved? By what mechanism is a new case recognized to be relevantly similar to one case but not to another? In scientific research what and where is this case library, anyway? Is it internal to the individual investigator or does it reside externally in the informational resources of the community, e.g., in real libraries or distributed over communities of investigators? Clearly, retaining in accessible, episodic memory all instructive, problem-solving experiences as distinct cases is an impossibility. It is too piecemeal.

So, while it may ameliorate some aspects of the Meno problem and cognitive economy problems, CBR would seem to exacerbate others. After all, one main attraction of general rules is economy: one rule can subsume an infinity of possible cases, and rules can often be organized into a system. (However, an example can also stand for a potential infinity of cases.)

We must ask similar, skeptical questions about Kuhnian exemplars and the processes by which they are constructed, indexed, retrieved, and activated. His own system of case-based reasoning turns out to be too simple. In fact, a CBR perspective already reveals some shortcomings of Kuhn's account of exemplars. For example, Kuhn's exemplars are all positive achievements, whereas, typically, some of the most exemplary lessons are negative. Janet Kolodner (1995) stresses that we need to include the notable failures also – the "war stories." Kuhn 1974 does note the need to learn dissimilarities among things when acquiring the similarity relations, but his scientific exemplars all seem to be achievements rather than failures (Hoyningen, 1993). In neglecting what we learn from negative exemplars, Kuhn's position is *too* far from Popper's!

Second, surprisingly, Kuhn's account of exemplars is not sufficiently historical. He often presented them as fixed historical achievements, as static anchors for future research, when, in fact, exemplars themselves have a history. Insofar as normal research adapts old solutions to new problem environments in a case-based manner, by replicating them with variations and then selectively retaining those that work better, we should expect the set of exemplars to evolve. Think of the history of Planck's black-body radiation law and of Bohr's atom model, from the original papers through the various editions of Sommerfeld's *Atombau und Spektrallinien* (cf. Kuhn, 1978)! The whiggish misremembering and rereading of the past in terms of the present that worried Kuhn the historian also occurs within the incremental development of normal science itself. As Kuhn the historian did recognize, we need to ask not only how the fund of past experience conditions present perception and practice but also how present problems and commitments shape our recall of past work. The scientist *qua* scientist is necessarily a bad historian (Nickles, 1992). We should expect a mutual adjusting, a mutual fitting, of old exemplars to new problems, not a one-way influence. Hence, Kuhn's account is dynamically inadequate. This point is directly relevant to the concerns of this conference on the history and future of behavioral therapy.

One difficulty faced by a case-study approach is that scientists' treatment of cases is quite different from historians'. Historians aim to understand the past in its own terms, e.g., to understand what Wilhelm Wundt and J. B. Watson were trying to do in their own contexts, and not with an eye to what (the historian knows) came later. Attempting to understand and evaluate past work in terms of present conceptions is anathema to historians and is called *the whig fallacy* (Butterfield, 1931). It is actually a collection of several related ways of being unhistorical, but the basic idea is that whig history judges previous work as good or bad, as insightful or wrongheaded, insofar as it anticipates our most recent work. Kuhn and other historians sometimes say that it would be better if historians did not even know how the story eventually turned out.

By contrast, the perspective of scientists working at the frontier of research is necessarily whiggish. They are interested in exemplary cases, positive and negative, insofar as those cases look similar to present problems and suggest solutions. Much of the creative work of research consists in mutually deforming past exemplars and present problems in order to achieve an adequate match. We might say that scientists are forward-looking, whereas historians are backward-looking (or, rather, forward-looking from the point of view of some time now past). Moreover, with each major success, indeed with each grant proposal, scientists rewrite the previous history of their subfield in order to make their present work look like a logically plausible, if not inevitable, continuation of previous work. Scientists, as such, use history to clarify and advance their current projects. In this respect, good science is bad history, and vice versa (see Nickles, 1992).

We can now see why it is dangerous for historians to take scientists' accounts of their earlier work at face value, for scientists, as such, cannot help but perceive that work through the filter of everything that has happened since then in their specialty area, not to mention the filter of their hopes and expectations for the future. Especially when they do not have the opportunity to study carefully their own early drafts, lab notes, and the like, scientists' recollections are notoriously inaccurate. And even when they are accurate, one can question whether the scientists are absolute authorities on what they were and are doing. For, contrary to the standard conception, scientific texts are rather like literary texts in not possessing a single, definitive, "absolute" meaning. Rather, they are susceptible of variant (yet entirely competent) readings. For example, Einstein and Ehrenfest found much in (or read much into) Planck's work that Planck had not realized that he put there and even repudiated. And just before he died, Niels Bohr vehemently denied as crazy some traces of his earlier ideas that Kuhn and his student, John Heilbron, claimed to find in Bohr's famous 1913 papers on the quantum atomic structure of the elements. Historians and scientists are frequently at odds over what the scientists themselves previously thought and did! As in political history, there can be a struggle for authority over the historical record. Are professional historians or the interested participants themselves the authorities?

To take another famous example, E. G. Boring's *History of Psychology* (1929 and later) is whiggish in just the ways that I have described. He wrote history more as a scientist than as a historian. On his conception, as stated in his prefaces to the various editions, what we should include in the history of psychology changes as the field changes. A main criterion of his selection of older material was how well it related to current work.

The issue of authority over the history and meaning of a piece of work provides the transition to a brief discussion of *the intentional fallacy*. This is the mistake of taking the author of a paper or book as the absolute and exhaustive authority on its content and meaning. On this view, the author's intentions determine the meaning completely. People working in literary theory exposed this mistake long ago. That it is a mistake is almost an axiom of literary and art criticism, for such criticism has little point, at least in the case of living artists and authors, if all one has to do is to ask them what the novel or the painting or the musical score means. Once again the question of authority is central. How privileged, if at all, are the author's own claims about what a work means?

Both fallacies caution us that anyone wanting to understand how science is really done has to be very careful of scientists' own accounts of their past work. When Kuhn said that genuine historical work could transform our image of science, he was extolling the virtues of professional history not only over journalistic, anecdotal history, and skeletal chronologies (i.e., history as a list of established facts and dates), but also over history as the late-career reflections of practicing scientists themselves.

However, the important question I want to raise is this: *Is it equally dangerous for you scientists to write case histories not as genuine history but with methodological intent, for your own practice and that of your students?*

My short response to warnings about the tendency toward whiggism in this context is: *So what?!* After all, *qua* scientists, you are, and must be, whigs at heart. That seems to me no sin as long as you recognize that you are teaching your students to do what you take to be good science rather than to do good history. This use of "history" is an important part of the enculturation into a scientific community that Kuhn himself emphasizes in other passages.

Thus I would urge that we distinguish two rather distinct kinds or uses of historical cases: the whiggish "potted histories" reported by you scientists yourselves, on the one hand, and the cases (sometimes the same cases) as reconstructed by historians and historical sociologists and anthropologists, on the other hand. Still a third use is that made by philosophers in testing their own models of scientific development. Unfortunately, Kuhn tended to conflate all of these things in his notion of exemplar.

Another difficulty of the case-study approach is that we almost cannot resist generalizing from anecdotal cases, an evidentially sloppy practice that attempts to turn cases into rules. A related temptation is to fall into the "just one more case" fallacy, the mistake of forcing new cases into the framework of the few cases already available. This is the mistake, if your only tool is a hammer, of seeing every problem as a nail.

A further problem, one relevant to the business of this conference, is that much scientific knowledge consists of practical skills or know-how rather than knowledge that can be readily articulated. As I noted before, Kuhnian exemplars have a practice dimension. Insofar as this is true, we should all keep in mind that the stories you scientists tell can capture only so much of your scientific work. Are these stories fully effective only to an audience of specialists?

Let me close by raising one last difficulty for a Kuhnian, case-based approach to method. Some of you, our distinguished program participants, have done path-breaking work on rule-governed learning, understanding, and behavior (see, e.g., Hayes, 1989). And, like Skinner himself, you surely believe that your accounts of cognition apply not only to your subjects but also to you yourselves in your scientific behavior. So, in boosting case-based learning over rule-based learning, are Kuhn and I flying in the face of your results?

This issue is a large and difficult one, and my response must be brief. I personally doubt that there is a direct contradiction in most cases. It seems to me that a case-based approach to scientific work does not contradict rule-based learning in the broad senses of that term that many of you employ. For by 'methodological rule' Kuhn meant an abstract generalization of universal applicability, akin to the laws of logic; whereas 'rule-guided' for you normally means behavior guided by verbal instruction (which may involve setting up quite local contingencies of reinforcement on that basis) rather than shaped directly by the contingencies of direct experience. Here I am invoking something like Skinner's distinction between contingency-shaped versus rule-governed learning (Skinner, 1989). In any case, Kuhnian exemplars cannot be fully conveyed by verbal instruction.

Please note that I am not claiming that there are no methodological rules at all, or that rule-based and case-based reasoning are purely incompatible. Clearly, routine procedures do exist, e.g., statistical analysis methods, many of which have been automated in the form of computer programs and have themselves become exemplars. And exemplary cases, as I have described them, often split the difference between contingency-shaped and rule-governed behavior as you psychologists use those terms. Rather, I am claiming that innovative problem-solving research is better considered as case-based rather than as purely rule-based, in the philosophers' sense, which derives from a two-thousand year logical tradition. For innovative research typically matches new problems to old problems-plus-solutions, as nearly as possible, and does not pretend that solutions can be produced by means of general rules.

One consequence of my Kuhnian view is that problem-solving is a more local, domain-relative activity than rule-based methodologists would have us believe. Now if an entire community of investigators has been brought up on the same sets of exemplars, as in Kuhnian normal science, then there will be nearly universal agreement about which problems are genuine and which solutions are successful. But in a field such as psychology, in which one finds distinct schools even within the behavioral approach, we cannot expect such "unanimity of agreement" and "fullness of communication" (Kuhn, 1962). For recognition of problem-solving progress is now more a matter of one's rhetorical tradition than of logic-plus-empirical data. Science turns out to be a highly cultural activity!

References

Boring, E. (1929). *A history of experimental psychology*. New York: Appleton-Century-Crofts.

Butterfield, H. (1931). *The whig interpretation of history*. London: Bell.

Donovan, A., Laudan, L., & Laudan, R. (Eds.). (1988). *Scrutinizing science: Empirical studies of scientific change.* Dordrecht: Kluwer.

Feyerabend, P. (1975). *Against method.* London: NLB.

Fisch, M. (1982). *The writings of Charles S. Peirce: A chronological edition.* Bloomington: Indiana University Press.

Graham, L., Lepenies, W., & Weingart, P. (1983). *Functions and uses of disciplinary histories*. Dordrecht: Reidel.

Hayes, S. C. (Ed.). (1989). *Rule-governed behavior: Cognition, contingencies, and instructional control.* New York: Plenum Press.

Hoyningen-Huene, P. (1993). *Reconstructing science: Thomas Kuhn's philosophy of science.* Chicago: University of Chicago Press.

James, W. (1897). *The will to believe and other essays*. New York: Dover, 1956.

Judson, H. (1999, Spring). Why history of recent science? *Recent Science Newsletter.* Center for History of Recent Science, George Washington University.

Kolodner, J. (1993). *Case-based reasoning.* San Mateo, CA: Morgan Kaufmann.

Kuhn, T. (1962). *The structure of scientific revolutions* (1st ed.). Chicago: University of Chicago Press.

Kuhn, T. (1970). *The structure of scientific revolutions* (2nd ed.). Chicago: University of Chicago Press.

Kuhn, T. (1974). Second thoughts on paradigms. In F. Suppe (Ed.), *The structure of scientific theories* (pp. 459-82). Urbana: University of Illinois Press.

Kuhn, T. (1978). *Black-body theory and the quantum discontinuity, 1894-1912.* Oxford: Oxford University Press.

Lakatos, I. (1970). Falsification and the methodology of scientific research programmes. In I. Lakatos & A. Musgrave (Eds.), *Criticism and the growth of knowledge* (pp. 91-196). Cambridge: Cambridge University Press.

Latour, B., & Woolgar, S. (1986). *Laboratory life* (2nd ed.). Princeton: Princeton University Press.

Laudan, L. (1977). *Progress and its problems.* Berkeley: University of California Press.

Laudan, L. (1981). *Science and hypothesis.* Dordrecht: Reidel.

Marshall, S. (1995). *Schemas in problem solving.* Cambridge: Cambridge University Press.

Nickles, T. (1985). Beyond divorce: Current status of the discovery debate. *Philosophy of Science, 52*, 177-206.

Nickles, T. (1987a). Lakatosian heuristics and epistemic support. *British Journal for the Philosophy of Science, 38*, 181-205.

Nickles, T. (1987b). From natural philosophy to metaphilosophy of science. In R. Kargon & P. Achinstein (Eds.), *Kelvin's* Baltimore lectures *and modern theoretical physics: Historical and philosophical perspectives* (pp. 507-541). Cambridge: MIT Press.

Nickles, T. (1988). Questioning and problems in philosophy of science: Problem-solving versus directly truth-seeking epistemologies. In M. Meyer (Ed.), *Questions and Questioning* (pp. 38-52). Berlin: Walter De Gruyter.

Nickles, T. (1992). Good science as bad history: From order of knowing to order of being. In E. McMullin (Ed.), *The social dimensions of science* (pp. 85-129). Notre Dame: University of Notre Dame Press.

Nickles, T. (1995). History of science and philosophy of science. *Osiris 10*, 139-163.

Nickles, T. (1998a). Kuhn, historical philosophy of science, and case-based reasoning. *Configurations, 6*, 51-85.

Nickles, T. (2000). Kuhnian puzzle solving and schema theory. *Philosophy of Science, 67*, S242-S255.

Polanyi, M. (1958). *Personal knowledge.* Chicago: University of Chicago Press.

Polanyi, M. (1966). *The tacit dimension.* Garden City, NJ: Doubleday.

Price, D. (1963). *Little science, big science* (2nd Ed.). New York: Columbia University Press.

Reese, H. (1989). Rules and rule-governance: Cognitive and behavioristic views. In S. C. Hayes (Ed.), *Rule governed behavior: Cognition, contingencies, and instructional control* (pp. 3-84). New York: Plenum Press.

Rosch, E. (1973). Natural categories. *Cognitive Psychology 4*, 328-350.

Rouse, J. (1987). *Knowledge and power.* Ithaca, NY: Cornell University Press.

Rumelhart, D., Smolensky, P., McClelland, J., & Hinton, G. (1986). Schemata and sequential thought processes in PDP models. In J. McClelland & D. Rumelhart (Eds.), *Parallel distributed processing* (Vol. 2). Cambridge, MA: MIT Press.

Newell, A., & Simon, H. (1972). *Human problem solving.* Englewood Cliffs, NJ: Prentice Hall.

Skinner, B. F. (1981). Selection by consequences. *Science, 213*, 501-4.

Skinner, B. F. (1989). The behavior of the listener. In S. C. Hayes (Ed.), *Rule governed behavior: Cognition, contingencies, and instructional control* (pp. 85-96). New York: Plenum Press.

Smith, L. (1986). *Behaviorism and logical positivism: A reassessment of the alliance.* Stanford: Stanford University Press.

Sommerfeld, A. (1919). *Atombau und Spektrallinien.* Braunschweig: Vieweg.

Whewell, W. (1840). *Philosophy of the inductive sciences founded upon their history.* London.

Young, R. (1966). Scholarship and the history of the behavioral sciences. *History of Science, 5*, 1-51.

Notes

[1] I am indebted to the U. S. National Science Foundation for research support on heuristic appraisal and problem solving, and to the conference participants for helpful discussion. Section 3 and parts of section 4 are borrowed from Nickles (2000).

Chapter 2

Joseph Wolpe: Challenger and Champion for Behavior Therapy

Roger Poppen
Southern Illinois University

When I was younger, I occasionally entered the national Olympic weight-lifting championships. Before a contest, the participants lined up on the stage for introductions and I remember looking at these national and world-class athletes and thinking, "What have I gotten myself into!" I have much the same feeling in the presence of the historic heavyweights who are gathered at this conference.

I have been asked to represent Joseph Wolpe, who was also a competitor, though of a very different and much more effective sort, as I hope to show in describing his contributions to behavior therapy. We were provided with a list of four areas to cover in our presentations and this will serve as an outline: first, a brief intellectual biography; second, important developments in the rise of behavioral therapies; third, a case study of important publications; and fourth, object lessons for the future. A more extensive treatment of these and related topics may be found in Poppen (1995).

Joseph Wolpe's Intellectual Development

Roots

An old proverb states, "As the twig is bent, so grows the tree." The course of Joseph Wolpe's intellectual development can be traced not only to his childhood, but even before that to his family history. His grandparents emigrated from Lithuania at the end of the 19th century, a time of reprisals against its Jewish population, and settled in Johannesburg, South Africa. Lithuanian Jews had a long tradition of scholarship and respect for learning, and this was true in Joseph's own family. His parents, while not religious, maintained traditional values of self-discipline, hard-work, and learning. As the oldest of four children, young Joseph did not disappoint them. He was a precocious and avid reader, fond of sports and sports stories, but was not a gifted athlete himself. Rather, he entered and won numerous scholastic competitions, winning prizes in a wide variety of subjects. Thus, early on a competitive repertoire was shaped, a repertoire that persisted throughout his professional career.

In high school Wolpe developed an interest in chemistry, essentially completing college-level courses while studying on his own. Again, this may be a significant precursor of his later achievements. It reinforced his skills in independent study. And the subject matter itself developed his interest in a systematic, orderly, quantitative, approach to a topic.

Another factor in his early shaping was the politically liberal beliefs of his family. South Africa was a country of sharp class distinctions and institutionalized racism. The ideas of helping the less fortunate, changing an oppressive system, seeking a place of freedom, and standing up for one's beliefs, can be seen throughout Wolpe's life.

Forming the Question

As a compromise between his wishes to be a chemical researcher and his parents' wishes for a respectable career, Joseph chose to study medicine, following the British model of a six-year university curriculum after high school. University provided new intellectual avenues for him to explore. He discovered the joys of discussion and debate of philosophical issues with other young medical students. He was interested in epistemology, finding the empiricist philosophers to be more satisfactory in explaining the origins of knowledge and the operations of the mind.

His interest in epistemology moved him toward psychiatry which, in the 1930's, was dominated by Freudian theory and practice. Wolpe wavered in his acceptance of the notions of unconscious forces that determine behavior, first regarding them as foolish and then giving them credence. Following his usual pattern, once a topic captured his interest he plunged in and read all he could find on it. He even began keeping a dream diary and analyzed his own dreams.

Wolpe completed his studies in the early days of World War II and volunteered as a medical officer in the Cape Corps. He was assigned to a military hospital that saw a considerable number of men with what was then called "war neurosis." He participated eagerly in their treatment, which, according to the psychodynamic model, involved the release of repressed memories through infusion of sodium pentothal, or "narcoanalysis" – the traditional method of psychoanalysis being much too lengthy to carry out in these circumstances. Another characteristic of Wolpe's professional life became apparent at this time – an interest in outcome. However dramatic the processes revealed by narcoanalysis, however strong the emotional "release," the overall results were disappointing. Few young soldiers were returned to adaptive functioning as a result of their treatment. As he did earlier, Wolpe participated in vigorous discussion with his peers. But rather than broad questions of epistemology, these discussions focused on the causes and cures of neurosis.

Wolpe continued to read widely, including anthropology, sociology, and political works. He was interested to find that the Russian allies totally rejected Freudian theory. Karl Marx and Ivan Pavlov suggested that environmental rather than intrapsychic events were important causes of behavior. Pavlov described "experimental neurosis" and proposed neurological mechanisms to explain it. The idea that environmental events resulted in physiologic changes which mediated an individual's behavior appealed to Wolpe.

In 1945, Wolpe met a psychology professor at the University of Cape Town, James G. Taylor, who, upon hearing of his interest in Pavlov, recommended Clark Hull's *Principles of Behavior* (1943). This book had a tremendous impact on Wolpe. Hull's rigorous system described behavior in terms of elemental bits that were combined in quantitative relations, analogous to the way physical matter was comprised of basic particles described by the periodic table of elements. Although Hull did not directly relate these behavioral elements to physiology, Wolpe saw the operation of neural connections. Like Pavlov, Hull's work was based on animal experimentation but described basic principles that could be applied to all species, including humans. Unlike Pavlov, Hull's theory did not address neurosis, but it set Wolpe thinking as to how it could be extended to include such behavior. Wolpe had rejected Pavlov's theory of cortical pathology as responsible for experimental neurosis, as well as Freud's theories of conflicting unconscious forces, and saw in Hull's system an alternative to both. Just how this might take form was unclear, but it provided him a direction for further study.

Upon his discharge from the service in 1946, Wolpe returned to the University of Witwatersrand to pursue the M.D. degree which required a research dissertation. Of course no one on the faculty knew anything about conditioning and learning, so Wolpe again embarked on a course of independent study. Fortuitously, Leo Reyna was appointed to the Psychology Department later that same year. Reyna (1946) had just completed his Ph.D. under Kenneth Spence, Hull's collaborator, and was well-versed in the intricacies of Hull-Spence theory. Wolpe attended Reyna's seminar on learning and joined an informal group of students attracted to this field of study. Reyna's dissertation had dealt with extinction of learned behavior; this seemed particularly relevant to neurosis, which was notoriously persistent. Discovering the principles that enabled the extinction of neurotic behavior, they decided, would be the solution that Freud and Pavlov had sought but failed to find. Reyna continued to provide guidance and feedback as Wolpe carried out his dissertation research.

Finding the Answer

Pavlov's (1927) work on experimental neurosis opened the door for the empirical investigation of its causes and cures. Characteristic of his previous endeavors, Wolpe conducted an exhaustive review of the experimental neurosis literature. There seemed to be a bewildering variety of species and procedural differences, making it difficult to come up with a general paradigm. One feature was fairly consistent, however; once it occurred, experimental neurosis was very difficult to get rid of. This seeming permanence was responsible for Pavlov's suggestion of neurologic damage, a point Wolpe was not willing to concede.

Wolpe found the research conducted by Jules Masserman (1943) very relevant. Masserman had applied noxious stimuli while cats operated a food mechanism, resulting in numerous "neurotic" behaviors, including food refusal, hyperarousal, and excessive timidity or aggressiveness. Masserman, in line with Freudian theory, attributed this result to conflict between motivational states. Wolpe proposed that "conflict" was irrelevant; that the behavior was simply the product of aversive conditioning, as Watson and Rayner (1920) had described many years previously. Accordingly, he replicated Masserman's procedure, shocking cats as they opened a food box, but he included another group of cats that were shocked with no food present, thus eliminating the possibility of "conflicting motivational states." In both groups the effects were the same, supporting his contention that aversive conditioning was responsible for neurotic behavior. The adverse arousal to shock had been conditioned to stimuli associated with it. Wolpe called this conditioned arousal "anxiety." Part of the anxiety response included food refusal; all animals refused to eat even though food had not been paired with shock for some of them. This suggested a means of treatment.

It is instructive to look at Wolpe's reasoning as he adapted Hullian theory to fit his observations of anxiety acquisition, maintenance, and extinction. The main principal he employed was Hull's drive-reduction theory of reinforcement. In brief, anxiety functioned as both a response and a drive. It was evoked during acquisition by the unconditioned stimulus, and during maintenance by the conditioned stimulus. When the stimulus terminated, the anxiety drive was reduced, reinforcing the anxiety response. Thus even though the primary aversive stimulus no longer occurred, anxiety continued to be reinforced through its own reduction, making it remarkably persistent.

Wolpe proposed another feature of anxiety leading to its persistence, namely that as an autonomic response, anxiety generated little "reactive inhibition." According to Hullian theory, each occurrence of a motor response generated a fatigue-like event, reactive inhibition, which could accumulate into a drive state with repeated responding. If a motor response occurred without reinforcement, then the reactive inhibition would build up to the point where its dissipation would reinforce "not-responding," and the response would cease. Thus extinction was seen as resulting from reinforcement of "not-responding" through the reduction of reactive inhibition. Since anxiety generated little reactive inhibition, extinction was greatly delayed.

Faced with such resistance to extinction, it became necessary to find another means to inhibit anxiety. For this, Wolpe invoked a principal used by Sherrington in the description of spinal reflexes, "reciprocal inhibition," in which activation of one muscle group, for example flexors, inhibited the activation of an antagonistic group, for example extensors, and vice versa. Wolpe noted that the autonomic nervous system is comprised of two reciprocally inhibitory branches. Anxiety was largely the response of the sympathetic branch; digestion was largely mediated by the parasympathetic branch. This explained the food refusal in anxious animals and it also suggested a means of overcoming anxiety – by feeding. If feeding could be made to occur in a situation that evoked anxiety, then anxiety would be inhibited in that situation and its bond to that stimulus weakened. This set the stage for the second part of Wolpe's cat experiment, eliminating the experimental neurosis by feeding in the presence of attenuated anxiety-evoking stimuli.

Wolpe's success with this procedure confirmed the utility of the reciprocal inhibition principle and provided the foundation for seeking applications to human neuroses. The first couple of years were difficult ones, as he set about finding responses that could inhibit anxiety and developing ways of presenting anxiety cues in a controllable manner. His solutions are well known – his use of relaxation (adapted from Edmond Jacobson, 1938), assertion (adapted from Andrew Salter, 1949), and sexual arousal (pre-dating Masters and Johnson, 1970) as anxiety inhibitors, and the anxiety hierarchy, both imaginal and in vivo, as a means of controlled exposure.

Wolpe's clinical success further validated the concept of reciprocal inhibition, crystallizing his intellectual development at this point in time. All his medical training and experience, his philosophical discussions and psychological readings, his experimental work and clinical practice, came together – formed a Gestalt (to borrow a term from the cognitive tradition) that organized his past experience and provided the context for all his subsequent work. Wolpe synthesized Hume and Russell, Freud and Hull, Pavlov and Sherrington. From his reading and philosophical discussions of epistemology, Wolpe assumed an empirical, logical, materialistic stance, opposed to mysticism and mentalism. His study of medicine reinforced this position, adding a physiologic reductionist point of view. From Freud he took the idea of anxiety as the core of maladaptive behavior, and also the idea that anxiety was acquired and could be removed – though not in the ways that Freud proposed. From Pavlov came the idea that neurosis could be studied experimentally in the laboratory, its factors teased apart and examined in a quantitative fashion. Pavlov also advanced the idea of a neurologic substrate of behavior, though Wolpe did not accept the mechanisms he suggested. Hull provided the specific stimulus-response-reinforcement framework to organize the study of behavior; Wolpe extrapolated these principles from rats in a runway to people trapped by crippling fears. Finally, Sherrington's principle of reciprocal inhibition suggested how to counteract destructive arousal and replace maladaptive with adaptive behavior.

Developmental Milestones in Behavior Therapy

Before Wolpe, there was no behavior therapy. His work was a major factor in the birth and development of this field. In this section Wolpe's contributions to several major milestones in the growth of behavior therapy are described.

Challenge to Traditional Psychotherapy

Hans Eysenck's 1952 review of treatment outcomes, in which he concluded that psychotherapy was no better than general supportive care, and in some instances was inferior to it, was the first salvo of a revolution in psychotherapy. Wolpe (1952a) published a similar critique, with the added feature of describing the success of his therapy procedures. Eysenck's article seemed to kick open an anthill and traditional therapy proponents swarmed to the counterattack. But the challenge was not simply to prove effectiveness compared to base rates of recovery; the comparison now was with this newfangled therapy based on learning theory.

A few words about Wolpe's relation with Eysenck are in order. In the early 1950's, Eysenck established a group of clinical researchers at Maudsley Hospital,

London, who set about developing and testing therapy interventions based on Hullian learning theory. Eysenck quickly recognized Wolpe as a valuable ally and recruited him into the battle against traditional therapy. Wolpe visited Maudsley in the mid-50's, giving training seminars on his procedures and adopting parts of Eysenck's personality theory. Stanley Rachman, who had studied with Wolpe in South Africa, joined the Maudsley group after completing his Ph.D. and carried out pioneering research on desensitization and related procedures. Wolpe continued to communicate with the Maudsley group during the 60's and participated in the campaign against psychotherapy. The critique of Freud's case of Little Hans, by Wolpe and Rachman (1960), is a classic example of this assault.

Eysenck was probably just the irresistible force needed to go up against the immovable object of traditional psychotherapy. Though not the first to use the term "behavior therapy," he was instrumental in establishing it as the name of the new therapy, for example as the title of a book reviewing the state of the art in 1960, and in the title of the first professional journal (*Behaviour Research and Therapy*) in 1963. Wolpe provided much of the ammunition in these early battles. In addition, his competitive juices were stirred by Eysenck's combativeness, and he carried on as a leader on the American front.

Learning-Theory Foundation of Behavior Therapy

Wolpe was a strong proponent of the need for interconnection between theory, research, and practice. At the most fundamental level, he maintained that basic principles of learning, discovered in animal laboratory research, were applicable to complex human behavior. Theoretical accounts of research findings informed his clinical practice, as for example his use of the reciprocal inhibition principle in developing his therapy procedures. And he sought to include procedures that were developed by others under his theoretical umbrella. He was critical of pure eclecticism, or using techniques that seemed to work with no concern for why they worked or how they were related to other procedures. To the extent that behavior therapy is rooted in a basic science of behavior, it is following the lead of Wolpe.

Of course there had always been widespread disagreement among learning theorists and researchers as to just what the basic principles are. Hullian theory faded from the scene just as Wolpe was extending it to account for neurotic behavior. No one found his drive-reduction theory of anxiety compelling, and he was equivocal about it himself in later years. In the 1960's, Skinnerian theory and research methods were popular, and "behavior modification" (aka "applied behavior analysis") made its appearance in the treatment of people with schizophrenia and autism. Wolpe welcomed these developments but maintained that operant conditioning principles were not relevant for the emotional problems that characterized neurotic behavior. For their part, most behavior analysts did not address the types of clinical problems that Wolpe dealt with and did not consider his physiologic reductionist approach to be consistent with functional analysis.

In the midst of this breech, the "cognitive revolution" gathered momentum in the 1970's. According to this view, operant and respondent learning principles derived from the animal laboratory were at best insufficient, and at worst misleading, in accounting for complex human behavior. Extensive systems of cognitive learning processes were put forth to account for therapeutic change. In Wolpe's view, this was a counter-revolution rather than an advancement, a return to mental mechanisms reminiscent of Freud's psychodynamic forces. He challenged cognitive formulations on philosophical, theoretical, and practical grounds (Wolpe, 1978). Philosophically, he endorsed the approach of Gilbert Ryle (1949), who regarded cognitive theory as a kind of spiritualism, appealing to ghostly mental processes outside the realm of a deterministic physical universe. Theoretically, Wolpe held that so-called cognitive events could be reduced to neurophysiologic processes or could be described as covert behavior, as Skinner (1953) had suggested; no new hypothetical mentalistic processes were necessary. Practically, Wolpe held that cognitive therapy procedures were either ineffective, redundant with behavioral ones, or could be accounted for by learning principles.

In the past decade, behavior analysts have begun to address anxiety disorders and other complex clinical problems – for example, my own work on relaxation training (Poppen, 1998) and, most notably, the work of Steve Hayes and his colleagues on Relational Frame Theory and Acceptance and Commitment Therapy (Hayes & Wilson, 1995). It will be interesting to see if such insurgencies are the beginning of a counter-counterrevolution.

Therapy as Education

Wolpe's view of therapy as a learning process cast the therapist in the role of teacher and the client as student. This stood in marked contrast to other therapy approaches in which, for example, the therapist helped to "uncover conflicts" or "facilitate development," and is the model which today characterizes the broad field of behavior and cognitive therapy.

An educational approach requires a curriculum. Wolpe developed treatment regimens, to be employed for particular types of disorders, in which the behavior of the therapist and the client were clearly specified. Some of the regimens developed by Wolpe are in use today, notably systematic desensitization and assertion training. Relaxation training, which Wolpe introduced as a component of his procedures, has been successfully extended to the treatment of many medical disorders (Poppen, 1998). The many variations, extensions, and new procedures that have been developed by others continue to follow the education model. The behavior therapist today has a variety of curricula at his/her disposal, to be deployed according to client needs, in contrast to one-size-fits-all procedures such as "empathic listening" or "interpreting resistance."

An educational approach also requires assessment. Wolpe proposed to measure the problematic behavior of the client in response to the environment in which it occurred. As with treatment procedures, some of the assessment methods he helped develop are currently useful, such as the Life History Questionnaire and the Fear Survey Schedule. He advocated what he initially called a "stimulus-response analysis" (Wolpe, 1969) and later termed "behavior analysis of case dynamics"

(Wolpe, 1990), that is consistent with what many now term a "functional analysis." The goal is to determine the specific needs of the client which, in turn, determines the therapy procedures to be employed.

The choice of treatment method and the selection of treatment goals hinges on assessment. In addition, assessment throughout the course of intervention allows the teacher/therapist to fine-tune the curriculum and change procedures or goals if necessary. Assessment also allows the effectiveness of therapy to be determined, a necessary requirement for accountability. These all are standard operating procedures for behavior therapists that come to us by way of the educational model that Wolpe was the first to employ and publicize.

Desensitization Research

Wolpe's cat experiment came at the end of an era in which clinical questions were tackled with animal research (Poppen, 1970). However, his clearly specified technique of systematic desensitization triggered an avalanche of research on human subjects with common fears that seemed more relevant to clinical issues. Peter Lang and A. D. Lazovik (1960) were the first to recognize that snake-avoidant college students comprised a huge pool of potential subjects with whom methods of anxiety reduction could be investigated. Jerry Davison's (1968) dissertation, employing this population, was a paragon of experimental rigor that demonstrated the effectiveness of desensitization while controlling for extraneous factors. Gordon Paul's (1966) dissertation, comparing desensitization with insight therapy in college students with public speaking anxiety, was an immediate classic. Hundreds if not thousands of studies followed in the next decade, investigating the variables and parameters that comprised desensitization and, to a lesser extent, assertiveness training, along with alternative methods and explanations. Other procedures, such as flooding and modeling, were investigated in a similar fashion. The net result was an immense bulwark of empirically validated procedures that formed the identifying characteristic of behavior therapy and distinguished it from traditional psychotherapies.

A question about analogue research, either with cats or college students, was its relevance for actual clinical problems. Wolpe himself questioned the utility of studies on "weak fears." The most important conclusion, however, was that therapy could be, indeed must be, empirically studied. If analogue studies omitted too many important factors, than other studies including those factors must be done.

Clinical Trials

The most valid, though most difficult approach, was to study real therapy with real patients. Wolpe first gained widespread attention for his reports of unprecedented therapeutic outcomes. Wolpe's research method, hardly sophisticated but revolutionary in the 1950's, was to rate the outcome of all patients he had seen who had met certain diagnostic and treatment criteria. Wolpe (1952a, 1954, 1958) reported 90% cured or much improved, in contrast with the two-thirds base-rate recovery reported in Eysenck's (1952) review. Traditional psychotherapists were challenged to prove Eysenck wrong, while behavior therapists took up the challenge to prove Wolpe right. Analogue research promoted more sophisticated designs than Wolpe's retrospective case summarization, and controlled prospective studies were soon undertaken with clinical populations as well.

One of the first was Arnold Lazarus' (1961) dissertation, chaired by Wolpe. Lazarus compared matched patients receiving psychodynamic interpretation or systematic desensitization, both administered in a group format, on a variety of self-report and direct observation measures. The outcomes were overwhelmingly in favor of desensitization, but possible experimenter bias was a confounding factor.

A few years later, Wolpe and Lazarus participated in a benchmark study comparing behavior therapy, psychodynamic therapy, and waiting-list controls (Sloane et al., 1975). R. Bruce Sloane recruited Wolpe with this study in mind, and planning began soon after his arrival at Temple in 1967. Not published until 1975, the results presaged a continuing controversy in clinical outcome research. One result, surprising to some but confirming Eysenck (1952), was the degree of improvement in the wait-list controls. A more controversial conclusion was that both behavior therapy and psychodynamic therapy were equally effective. On the one hand, this forced the traditional psychotherapy community to admit behavior therapy into the clubhouse, but Wolpe and others were not content to settle for "equality," they wanted clear superiority. Closer reading of the data indicated a definite edge in favor of behavior therapy (e.g. Giles, 1983; Poppen, 1976), but the "equal effectiveness" conclusion prevailed.

The same controversy was played out a few years later when nearly 500 therapy outcome studies were evaluated with the statistical technique of meta-analysis (Smith, Glass, & Miller, 1980). These authors included the full spectrum of analogue and clinical studies, identifying three major classes of therapy (Behavioral, Verbal, and Developmental), made up of six subclasses, in turn comprised of 18 individual types. The largest contributor to their data pool was desensitization research. Behavioral therapies, at all levels of groupings, showed consistently greater effects than verbal therapies, and both were much superior to developmental counseling. But Smith et al. downplayed the effectiveness of behavior therapy by attributing the differences to measurement bias, recommending that the "benefit of the doubt should be granted to theories that lack technologies readily applicable to outcome evaluation" (p. 31). Traditional psychotherapists felt that meta-analysis research upheld the equal effectiveness notion, while Wolpe and others criticized the meta-analysis procedure, or the studies included in them, or reanalyzed the data to show the superiority of behavior therapy.

Much therapy research, and meta-analyses of that research, has been conducted in the past 20 years, and slowly the superiority of behavioral (and cognitive-behavioral) procedures is being recognized (e.g., Lambert & Bergin, 1992). Although Wolpe did not conduct the research himself, not having mastered the grantsmanship so necessary to carry out such projects, his contributions have been immense. His claims of behavior therapy superiority spurred the showdown studies that led to grudging acceptance of its equality and final recognition as the treatment of choice for many disorders.

Professional Organizations and Journals

A necessary step in any professional movement is for those who form a loose-knit community of persons with similar interests to come together in a more formal organization. Wolpe, through his writing and travels, was certainly responsible for inspiring interest among a large number of people dispersed around the world. He was also instrumental in bringing them together into a professional group.

One of the first steps in this direction was the 1962 conference at the University of Virginia in Charlottesville, that Wolpe chaired and organized with the help of Leo Reyna and Ian Stevenson (Wolpe, Salter, & Reyna, 1964). The conference was called "The Conditioning Therapies: The Challenge to Psychotherapy," reflecting Wolpe's competitive stance toward traditional therapy. The conference reflected the past, present, and future of this new field. The past was represented by Howard Liddell and W. Horsely Gantt on experimental neurosis, and Andrew Salter on "conditioned reflex therapy." Cutting edge research was represented by Peter Lang's presentation of his systematic investigation of systematic desensitization with snake-phobic college students. The future was represented by Stevenson and Reyna, who discussed the need for research on psychotherapy and the issues that would arise in such research. This historic conference provides a valuable reference point for the current one, and the student would be well advised to compare the issues then and now; what has changed and what issues remain?

Another early step was Wolpe's organization of the "June Institute," a one-month summer training program and seminar which drew people from around the world to participate in intensive training and discussion. These began in Virginia in 1965 and continued for about 15 years after Wolpe moved to Temple. The first group included Dorothy Susskind, Alan Goldstein, and Joseph Cautela, all of whom were to make notable contributions in the coming years.

Dorothy Susskind, a clinician in New York, hosted continuing meetings among professionals in the New York area interested in behavior therapy to discuss professional and practice issues. Participants in these meetings included Andrew Salter, Cyril Franks, Joe Cautela, Jerry Davison, Leonard Krasner, Arnold Lazarus and Wolpe. Franks edited the group's newsletter and spearheaded the formalization of the group, holding a convention in 1967 concurrently with the American Psychological Association as the "Association for Advancement of Behavioral Therapies" (later unified as "Behavior Therapy, " or AABT). Franks served as the first president and Wolpe became the second, continuing to be a featured speaker at AABT conventions throughout his life. Wolpe tried to do something similar within the American Psychiatric Association but was rather less successful. In 1970, the AABT Newsletter became the journal, *Behavior Therapy*, and in the same year Wolpe and Reyna cofounded and edited the journal *Behavior Therapy and Experimental Psychiatry*.

Professional Training

An essential feature of a profession is the establishment of teaching and training facilities, typically within university settings. Wolpe's influence as an educator was, first, in providing content through his books and articles, and second, in providing hands-on training through apprenticeship arrangements in workshops and internships at the June Institutes and the Behavior Therapy Unit at Temple. Wolpe was not a daily classroom lecturer but had a marked influence on those of us who are. Wolpe's teaching methods included demonstrations of therapy, live, simulated, or filmed, and participation with students as a co-therapist. One of his chief educational contributions was to open the door of the therapy room. While Carl Rogers had provided audio recordings of therapy sessions, Wolpe showed that much more was involved than "talk" therapy. Indeed, Wolpe put the "behavior" in behavior therapy, and put the behavior of both therapist and patient on display for educational purposes.

To summarize, behavior therapy was born in competition as Wolpe sought to play David to Freud's Goliath. His theories and methods were major protagonists in the psychotherapy wars that have raged in the literature for almost half a century. Although Wolpe was not able to drive psychoanalysis from the field, he was able to wrest grudging recognition that behavior therapy was "equally effective." But Wolpe rejected the offer of equivalency and continued to press for victory. A major point for his side was the increased acceptance of outcome research, as behavior therapists forged ahead on the empirical front. The revolutionary notion that psychotherapy should have measurable outcomes carried the day. Competition continued within the behavior therapy camp, as Wolpe's theories and methods were subjected to rigorous investigation. Variations, additions, and alternatives arose from cognitive and operant learning theories. These challenged the benchmarks established by Wolpe and greatly expanded the scope of behavior therapy. Progress is achieved through competition, and we have all benefited from Wolpe's willingness to take controversial positions.

Significant Publications

Wolpe's publishing career did not begin auspiciously. He at first was determined to be a Hullian learning theorist. However his efforts in this direction were not well received. Only when he published the results of his clinical work did he begin to be noticed. Thus the reaction Wolpe received to his initial publications very much influenced the development of behavior therapy.

Wolpe had dreams of taking Hullian learning theory into the realm of abnormal psychology, and of earning royalties – and perhaps an academic position – based on the hard work he had done on his dissertation. With encouragement from Reyna, Wolpe compiled his research into a book-length manuscript entitled *Conditioning and Neurosis*. This encompassed a complete review and critique of research and theories on experimental neurosis, culminating in his own experiment and his extension of Hullian theory to account for the origins and treatment of neurotic behavior. Ambitiously, he sent this to Clark Hull himself for review and, hopefully, recommendation for publication. Hull, seriously ill and trying to complete his own books, passed the manuscript along to Kenneth Spence, who concluded that there was little market for such a work. Interestingly, the following year saw the publication of *Personality and Psychotherapy* by John Dollard and Neil Miller (1950), and *Learning Theory and Personality Dynamics* by O. H. Mowrer (1950). As two of the most prominent students of Hull, Miller and Mowrer had conducted basic research on anxiety conditioning in the 1940's and in these works extended Hullian theory to account for human neuroses. Both also were influenced greatly by Freudian theory and offered nothing other than psychoanalysis, couched in learning theory terminology, as treatment. It should be remembered that, at this time, Wolpe himself had not developed any new clinical procedures based on his learning principles. Any therapeutic applications were purely speculative and it is perhaps fortunate that his manuscript was not published before he had done the hard work of translating principles into practice.

Somewhat daunted, Wolpe persisted with a series of seven theoretical articles, published over a four-year period (1949 to 1952) in the *Psychological Review*, in which he presented a "neurophysiological view" of various learning phenomena, such as reinforcement via drive-reduction, stimulus generalization, and latent learning. Hull had avoided direct reference to neural structures, preferring to describe hypothetical processes that mediated between environmental stimuli and overt behavior. Nevertheless, it was clear that the operation of the nervous system was to be inferred from these processes, as Skinner (1950) had noted in his critique of the "conceptual nervous system." Wolpe did exactly what Skinner had criticized, filling the gap between stimulus and response with neural sequences having various arrangements of excitatory and inhibitory synaptic connections. These were not based on actual physiological evidence but rather were exercises in logic. The recent surge of interest in "neural network learning theory" (Tryon, 1993) might find it profitable to revisit these neglected papers of Wolpe.

With no prospects as an academician, Wolpe was forced to earn a living as a clinician, a difficult task for a brand new psychiatrist who was shut out of the local referral network and who, besides, was struggling to turn theoretical concepts into procedures that the few patients who came his way would pay for. By 1952 he had developed the main features of systematic desensitization, assertiveness training, and sexual therapy, and began to experience success as a clinician. In that year he published an account of his cat experiment in a British journal (Wolpe, 1952b) and a criticism of psychoanalysis and early report of his alternative methods in a South African journal (Wolpe, 1952a). The latter served only to further alienate him from the local psychiatric professional community. In 1954 he published another outcome survey of a series of patients, reporting 96% cured or much improved (Wolpe, 1954). This publication attracted widespread attention. He received over a hundred reprint requests for this paper, most from the United States. This was in immense contrast to his theoretical papers, telling Wolpe that there was a large potential market for this line of endeavor.

In addition to the attention they generated, these reports were a major factor supporting his application to the Center for Advanced Study in the Behavioral Sciences, in Stanford, California. During his year at the Center, he finished the manuscript for his first book, *Psychotherapy by Reciprocal Inhibition*, published by Stanford University Press the following year (Wolpe, 1958). This book pulled together his work to date, including his neural theory of conditioning (a reprise of his "neuropsychological view" papers), a critical review of the experimental neurosis literature, and a recounting of his cat experiment. He added a theoretical account of the acquisition of various types of human neuroses, including pervasive anxiety, hysteria, and obsessional behavior, providing illustrations from his patients. The last half of the book gave specific details of his therapy procedures. He described the assessment interview and advocated the use of the Willoughby Personality Inventory, both as a means to discover information and as an assessment device to measure therapeutic change. He described his therapeutic procedures in detail, presenting individual cases to illustrate their use. Finally he supplemented his earlier outcome reports with an additional 88 cases, reporting an overall success rate of 90%.

Wolpe's detailed specification of procedures in 1958 had a tremendous impact on clinical researchers and educators. In 1966 he published a book with Arnold Lazarus targeted for clinicians, *Behavior Therapy Techniques*, which, as the name indicates, focused almost entirely on therapeutic procedures. In 1969, the first of four editions of his textbook, *The Practice of Behavior Therapy* appeared (1969, 1973, 1982, 1990). One can look at the proportion of pages in each of these volumes that are devoted to particular topics as reflecting the selective effect of the behavior therapy audience over time. For example, almost half of his 1958 book is devoted to theoretical exposition. This is reduced to about 6% by 1973, but takes a jump to about 13% in 1982 and 1990 as he took on the theoretical issues in cognitive therapy. Wolpe did not mention cognitive issues until the second edition of his textbook in 1973. However, his earlier works included brief descriptions of procedures that he later identified as instances of "cognitive" procedures – if one chose to use that terminology – namely "clarifying misconceptions" and "thought-stopping." These took up about 1% of his first three books. His two final editions included chapters on "cognitive therapeutic techniques" and presented critiques of the "cognitive revolution" in behavior therapy, taking up about 17% of his last book. Finally, Wolpe first recognized operant conditioning in 1969, where he included a brief chapter in an effort to be inclusive of the entire field of behavior therapy. However the topic comprised only 2-3% of this and subsequent editions. In the final analysis, these books reflect the increasing battles Wolpe had with cognitive approaches, his rather cursory recognition of behavior analysis, and his continued faith in the efficacy of his own approach to behavior therapy.

Object Lessons for the Future

Wolpe was a pioneer in proclaiming, both in words and by example, first, that therapy should be measurably effective, second, that procedures should be clearly specified, and third, that learning theory should be a useful guide for research and practice. These are matters of continuing concern that will shape future developments. I will briefly consider these three directives from the perspective of Wolpe's contributions.

Effectiveness of Therapy

Great strides have occurred in assessment of therapy outcomes. What Wolpe began as therapist ratings of improvement based on retrospective review of his own or others' case reports, has evolved into multimethod-multitrait assessment batteries involving direct observation, physiological measurement, self-report, significant-other report, and medical records, in longitudinal, long-term follow-up, blinded clinical trials. The sophistication and expense of outcome research has grown and will continue to do so. However, in his own work and his editorship of *Journal of Behavior Therapy and Experimental Psychiatry*, Wolpe supported the innovative case report and small-n study. This approach continues to provide the seeds for new and more effective procedures, and both large and small-scale studies are necessary for continued development.

A major competitor, or possible ally, in demonstrating effective therapy outcomes is the drug industry (see Hayes & Heiby, 1996). Clinical trials of drugs are driven by companies that earn huge profits from selling pills that soothe dysphoria, relieve migraine, curb appetite, calm hyperactivity, or produce sexual arousal. There is a huge demand for drugs that relieve distress and improve behavior, as the public has come to believe that "better living through chemistry" is an inalienable right. There are no comparable behavioral health companies that profit from promoting behavioral regimens targeting the same ends, though there are some approximations to this approach. As a physician, Wolpe felt that drugs could be useful adjuncts to behavior therapy in individual cases. That is, he did not prescribe drugs as the sole means of treating a condition and he lamented the wholesale shift of psychiatry from the psychoanalyst's couch to the prescription pad. Some clinical trials have examined the combination of drugs and psychotherapy, typically including a drug alone, therapy alone, and combined drug plus therapy groups. Occasionally a drug company recognizes the necessity of concurrent behavioral intervention, such as the combination of behavioral procedures and the nicotine patch for treating smoking. However, these approaches do not address the factors that may make drugs useful in one case and not in another. Nor do they solve the problem of how to make a profit delivering a behavioral program whether or not drugs are involved. "Behavioral health" programs are a definite trend, and their control over treatment is an important issue for the future.

The rise of managed health care, including mental health services, and the focus on cutting costs, has raised many issues of accountability. Not only should treatment be effective, it should be acceptable to the consumer, safe, and efficient (Giles, 1993; Pekarik, 1993). Wolpe observed that many of his patients had undergone years of psychoanalysis with little improvement; and others have reported harmful effects of this approach (e.g., Masson, 1988). Wolpe focused directly on patient complaints, provided a concrete explanation of their problems, and presented a definite plan of action, all of which build patient confidence. He reported number of sessions as an indicator of the efficiency of his approach (although much greater efficiency is required by today's standards). Ironically, traditional approaches have generated "brief psychotherapy" to meet the demands of the payers, the goals and procedures of which appear congruent with behavior therapy: a focus on symptoms and current functioning, directive therapist activity, homework assignments, and use of various procedures to meet client needs (Koss & Butcher, 1986). Convergence of behavior therapy and brief psychotherapy is likely in the future.

Specification of Therapy Procedures

Wolpe opened the door of the consulting room and clearly described desensitization, assertiveness training, sexual therapy, and other procedures. Another important step involved the search for "common factors" across various therapy approaches. Jerome Frank (1961) is known for this line of investigation, but early in his career Wolpe (1958, p. 193) recognized that "the various special points of procedure that the different therapists regarded as so vital to success were not vital at all, and that the effective factor must have been something that all the therapeutic situations generated in common." Wolpe, and many since, have speculated on what those common features are and the mechanism of their action (Arkowitz, 1992). This issue is also likely to continue into the future.

A major tool in analogue desensitization studies was the treatment manual that specified the exact procedures to be followed, the sequence of steps, and even the number and duration of sessions. Manuals were developed to make sure that all persons receiving a particular intervention were treated the same, just as patients in a drug study receive the same course of medication. Manuals allowed patients to be treated with placebos or with particular amounts or combinations of the treatment variables. In short, the treatment manual insured the integrity of the independent variable. Although manuals were developed to test theoretical propositions, the therapist behaviors existed independent of the theory and, as Gordon Paul (1966) showed, could even be carried out by therapists who did not believe in the theory. Treatment manuals were extended to clinical trials with real patients, allowing equivalent treatments to be carried out at multiple sites by many different therapists. Finally, treatments that are empirically shown to be the most effective can be designated as "best practice" to be employed for particular disorders. Managed care companies are interested in best practices and treatment guidelines, and it is likely this trend will markedly increase in the future.

Wolpe (1986) was critical of the use of treatment manuals in the practice of therapy, in which the choice of method is based on the patient's assignment to a DSM diagnostic category. Wolpe felt that an individualized case analysis was necessary to determine the factors important for each patient's behavior, and that these went far beyond DSM classification. He felt that treatment should be selected to meet the unique needs of each person, and that treating a person as a member of a diagnostic group may well result in ineffective therapy. A counter-argument states that it is much better to employ an intervention regimen that is backed by data than by the clinician's seat-of-the-pants intuition as to what is best for a given client. Therapists vary widely in what they might think is appropriate and proceed with their favorite procedure regardless of supporting evidence. Perhaps the treatment manual would not be quite as good as what a highly skilled therapist could come up with, but it would be considerably better than the wild guesses of the not-so-good therapists. This may be seen as another version of the old clinical vs. statistical judgement issue (Meehl, 1954), this time applied to treatment decisions rather than assessment. When it comes to assessment, the evidence favors the statistical "cookbook" approach, and the same may be true here. But it is an empirical question. Can a therapist do better – achieve greater improvement or do it more quickly – by adjusting therapy to what is perceived as the individual needs of the patient as opposed to doing it "by the book?" This would appear to be an important topic for future research. While outcome data on current methods are good, there is still much room for improvement and it would be premature to close the book – or the manual – at this point.

The Role of Theory

Shorn of their theoretical trappings, all effective behavioral and cognitive-behavioral therapies follow the general procedural framework that Wolpe figured out 50 years ago. This framework consists of four steps. First, identify elements of the critical situations – those in which the undesirable or maladaptive behavior is likely to occur – and present them to the patient in a controlled fashion. Second, weaken the undesirable responses. Third, strengthen incompatible adaptive behavior. Fourth, continue steps one through three in a progressive manner until the desirable behavior occurs readily in everyday, uncontrolled environments. This strategy is followed in desensitization for phobic problems and assertiveness training for social anxieties, in exposure and response prevention procedures for obsessive-compulsive disorders, in cognitive therapy for depression and controlled drinking for alcoholics, in toilet training for the incontinent and language training for the autistic, in stress-management for headache sufferers and pain-management for chronic pain. Theories have been useful in suggesting methods to employ at each of these steps. For example, reciprocal inhibition theory has given us relaxation and graded exposure procedures; social learning theory has given us modeling and cognitive theory has given us self-instructions; neurochemical theory has given us anxiolytics and anti-depressives and behavior analysis has given us prompting and reinforcement procedures. Theories will continue to be useful to the extent that they suggest even more effective methods.

No theory has yet provided an overarching account of all methods at all steps that is acceptable to all of us. This conference may be helpful in that regard. It shows us that behavior therapy has progressed along the scientific path that Wolpe was one of the first to point out. Science is a cumulative and corrective process, an evolution born of competitive behavior and professional disputation. Perhaps there is a young Wolpe in the audience who is saying, "I can do better than that," a young person who sees how things fit together in ways that we currently do not, and who can take behavior therapy to yet a higher level of effectiveness or theoretical integration. That would be a fitting legacy to this great champion of behavior therapy.

References

Arkowitz, H. (1992). Integrative theories of therapy. In D. K. Freedman (Ed.), *History of psychotherapy: A century of change* (pp. 261-303). Washington, DC, American Psychological Association.

Davison, G. C. (1968). Systematic desensitization as a counter-conditioning process. *Journal of Abnormal Psychology, 73*, 91-99.

Dollard, J., & Miller, N. E. (1950). *Personality and psychotherapy: An analysis in terms of learning, thinking, and culture.* New York: McGraw-Hill.

Eysenck, H. J. (1952). The effects of psychotherapy: An evaluation. *Journal of Consulting Psychology, 16*, 319-324.

Eysenck, H. J. (Ed.). (1960). *Behaviour therapy and the neuroses.* London: Pergamon Press.

Frank, J. D. (1961). *Persuasion and healing.* New York: Shocken Books.

Giles, T. R. (1983). Probable superiority of behavioral interventions I: Traditional comparative outcome. *Journal of Behavior Therapy and Experimental Psychiatry, 26*, 241-248.

Giles, T. R. (1993). Consumer advocacy and effective psychotherapy: The managed care alternative. In T. R. Giles (Ed.), *Handbook of effective psychotherapy* (pp. 481-488). New York: Plenum.

Hayes, S. C., & Heiby, E. (1996). Psychology's drug problem: Do we need a fix or should we just say no? *American Psychologist, 51*, 198-206.

Hayes, S. C., & Wilson, K. G. (1995). The role of cognition in complex human behavior: A contextualistic perspective. *Journal of Behavior Therapy and Experimental Psychiatry, 14*, 29-32.

Hull, C. (1943). *Principles of behavior.* New York: Appleton-Century-Crofts.

Jacobson, E. (1938). *Progressive relaxation.* Chicago: University of Chicago Press.

Koss, M. P., & Butcher, J. N. (1986). Research on brief psychotherapy. In S. L. Garfield & A. E. Bergin (Eds.), *Handbook of psychotherapy and behavior change* (3rd ed., pp. 627-670). New York: Wiley.

Lambert, M. J., & Bergin, A. E. (1992). Achievements and limitations of psychotherapy research. In D. K. Freedman (Ed.), *History of psychotherapy: A century of change* (pp. 360-390). Washington, DC: American Psychological Association.

Lazarus, A. A. (1961). Group psychotherapy of phobic disorder by systematic desensitization. *Journal of Abnormal and Social Psychology, 63*, 505-510.
Lazovik, A. D., & Lang, P. J. (1960). A laboratory demonstration of systematic desensitization psychotherapy. *Journal of Psychological Studies, 11*, 238-247.
Masserman, J. (1943). *Behavior and neurosis.* Chicago: University of Chicago Press.
Masson, J. (1988). *Against therapy: Emotional tyranny and the myth of psychological healing.* New York: Athenum.
Masters, W. H., & Johnson, V. E. (1970). *Human sexual inadequacy.* Boston: Little, Brown & Co.
Meehl, P. (1954). *Clinical versus statistical prediction.* Minneapolis, MN: University of Minnesota Press.
Mowrer, O. H. (1950). *Learning theory and personality dynamics.* New York: Ronald Press.
Paul, G. (1966). *Insight versus desensitization in psychotherapy.* Stanford, CA: Stanford University Press.
Pavlov, I. P. (1927). *Conditioned reflexes* (G. V. Anrep, Trans.). London: Oxford University Press.
Pekarik, G. (1993). Beyond effectiveness: Uses of consumer-oriented criteria in defining treatment success. In T. R. Giles (Ed.), *Handbook of effective psychotherapy* (pp. 409-436). New York: Plenum.
Poppen, R. (1970). Counterconditioning of conditioned suppression in rats. *Psychological Reports, 27*, 659-671.
Poppen, R. (1976). Review of R. B. Sloane, F. R. Staples, A. H. Cristol, N. J. Yorkston, & K. Whipple, *Psychotherapy versus behavior therapy. Journal of Behavior Therapy and Experimental Psychiatry, 7*, 101.
Poppen, R. (1995). *Joseph Wolpe.* Thousand Oaks, CA: Sage Publications, Inc.
Poppen, R. (1998). *Behavioral relaxation training and assessment* (2nd ed.). Thousand Oaks, CA: Sage Publications, Inc.
Reyna, L. (1946). *Experimental extinction as a function of the interval between extinction trials.* Unpublished doctoral dissertation. University of Iowa.
Ryle, G. (1949). *The concept of mind.* London: Hutchinson.
Salter, A. (1949). *Conditioned reflex therapy.* New York: Creative Age Press.
Skinner, B. F. (1950). Are theories of learning necessary? *Psychological Review, 57*, 193-216.
Skinner, B. F. (1953). *Science and human behavior.* New York: Macmillan.
Sloane, R. B., Staples, F. R., Cristol, A. H., Yorkston, N. J., & Whipple, K. (1975). *Psychotherapy versus behavior therapy.* Cambridge, MA: Harvard University Press.
Smith, M. L., Glass, G. V., & Miller, T. I. (1980) *The benefits of psychotherapy.* Baltimore, MD: Johns Hopkins University Press.
Tryon, W. W. (1993). Neural networks I: Theoretical unification through connectionism. *Clinical Psychology Review, 13*, 341-352.
Watson, J. B., & Rayner, R. (1920). Conditioned emotional reactions. *Journal of Experimental Psychology, 3*, 1-4.

Wolpe, J. (1952a). Objective psychotherapy of the neuroses. *South African Medical Journal, 26*, 825-829.
Wolpe, J. (1952b). Experimental neuroses as learned behavior. *British Journal of Psychology, 43*, 243-268.
Wolpe, J. (1954). Reciprocal inhibition as the main basis for psychotherapeutic effects. *Archives of Neurologic Psychiatry, 72*, 205-226.
Wolpe, J. (1958). *Psychotherapy by reciprocal inhibition.* Stanford, CA: Stanford University Press.
Wolpe, J. (1969). *The practice of behavior therapy.* New York: Pergamon Press.
Wolpe, J. (1973). *The practice of behavior therapy* (2nd ed.). New York: Pergamon Press.
Wolpe, J. (1978). Cognition and causation in human behavior and its therapy. *American Psychologist, 33*, 231-236.
Wolpe, J. (1982). *The practice of behavior therapy* (3rd ed.). New York: Pergamon Press.
Wolpe, J. (1986). Individualization: The categorical imperative of behavior therapy practice. *Journal of Behavior Therapy and Experimental Psychiatry, 17*, 145-153.
Wolpe, J. (1990). *The practice of behavior therapy* (4th ed.). New York: Pergamon Press.
Wolpe, J., & Lazarus, A. A. (1966). *Behavior therapy techniques: A guide to the treatment of the neuroses.* New York: Pergamon Press.
Wolpe, J., & Rachman, S. (1960). Psychoanalytic evidence: A critique based on Freud's case of little Hans. *Journal of Nervous and Mental Disease, 131*, 135-148.
Wolpe, J., Salter, A., & Reyna, L. J. (Eds.). (1964). *The conditioning therapies: The challange in psychotherapy.* New York: Holt, Rinehart, & Winston.

Chapter 3

B. F. Skinner's Contribution to Therapeutic Change: An Agency-less, Contingency Analysis

Julie S. Vargas
West Virginia University

No one in the 20th century has had more impact on methods of changing behavior than B. F. Skinner. Whether attacked or revered, his work continues to affect practices in education, business, cultural design, and behavior therapy. The science he developed is the most comprehensive, the most researched, the most validated analysis of human behavior to date. Yet, in spite of widespread discussion and publicity, Skinner's work is frequently misunderstood.

B. F. Skinner is often erroneously classified as a mechanistic stimulus-response psychologist. True, Skinner began in the behaviorist S-R tradition. But like Darwin, who through detailed observation and recording, found himself unable to support the biblical versions of creation he initially held, Skinner, in working with the behavior of rats, found he could not fit his observations into the classical S-R conception of behavior. Control over the behavior of his rats lay in the consequences of individual actions. Changes in the rate of bar pressing occurred through a process of selection by consequences, not through the pairing of antecedent stimuli. His functional analysis showed how behavior is related to, and thus can be controlled by, factors in an individual's environment, without appealing to psychological processes in the "mind" or physiological processes in the brain. Practices incorporating Skinner's discoveries rippled throughout society, impacting particularly education and behavior therapy. How did a small-town Pennsylvania lad come to make such an impact on the twentieth century?

Intellectual Background

Skinner grew up in a typical family of four in a small railroad town in Pennsylvania. Life was good. His father's law profession was growing and the family could afford the newly appearing fruits of science and industrialization – electricity, the radio, the telephone, silent movies, and when Skinner was six years old, the automobile. Skinner attended the local public school. Early on he began challenging conventional thinking. In his autobiography, Skinner tells of an incident that happened in eighth grade. His English class was studying Shakespeare's *As You Like It*. At home, the young Fred had heard someone question the authorship of the plays and he announced to his class that Shakespeare didn't write the play they were reading. His teacher, Miss Graves, told him he didn't know what he was talking about. As Skinner puts it, "that afternoon I went down to the library and found a copy of Sir Edwin Durning-Lawrence's *Bacon is Shakespeare* which I read in great excitement. The next day, to Miss Graves's dismay I knew only too well what I was talking about." His teacher permitted discussion and Skinner continued to gather evidence for his case, reading "biographies of Bacon, summaries of his philosophical position, and a good deal of the *Advancement of Learning*, the *Essays*, and *Novum Organum*" (Skinner, 1976, p. 129).

Though Skinner says he doubted that he got much out of these readings at the time, it is difficult to imagine a boy continuing to read so much philosophy just to bolster a position in an English class. More likely, Bacon's conception of truth as emanating from the manipulation of objects rather than from the word of authority must have appealed to a youth who loved to tinker. Moreover, Bacon's idealism and belief in bettering the world through scientific inquiry fitted well with Skinner's family's emphasis on leaving the world a better place than one found it. Then, too, Skinner's science courses supported Baconian principles. High school physics revolved around experiments: Showing that a feather falls as fast as a penny in a vacuum, that air has weight, and rolling balls down inclined planes to verify Gallileo's equations. In high school, too, Skinner took botany and chemistry. His intellectual training had begun.

In college, courses in chemistry and biology extended Skinner's scientific training. In biology, Skinner encountered Mach's Occam's razor approach to science. Explanation, Mach asserted, consisted in empirical observation and description. Mach was later to play an important role in Skinner's thinking. But in college, Skinner majored in English and his main activities revolved around literature and the college magazine, of which he was an editor. After college, and an unhappy year and a half living with his parents while trying unsuccessfully to write fiction, Skinner took a job at a bookstore in Greenwich Village in New York, living the bohemian life and subscribing to literary magazines like the *Dial.* It was in the *Dial* that Skinner read a review by Bertrand Russell in which Russell called Watson's *Behaviorism* "massively impressive." Skinner bought Watson's book and also Russell's *Philosophy*. The latter book, Skinner says, "begins with a careful statement of several epistemological issues raised by behaviorism considerably more sophisticated than anything of Watson's" (Skinner, 1979, p. 10). Years later, Skinner told Russell that his book *Philosophy* had converted him to behaviorism. Russell exclaimed, "My God, I thought I demolished that view." But Skinner had stopped reading at chapter eight where Russell talks of that nature of the physical world, and thus missed the last third in which Russell criticizes behaviorism. Towards the end of his Greenwich Village stay, Skinner decided to go back to school to study psychology. Following advice from an old Hamilton professor about where to go, he applied to Harvard. His training was about to begin in earnest.

Graduate Training

Skinner arrived at Harvard in the Fall of 1929 at the age of 24. It was ironic that he chose Harvard for his graduate work. The chair of the Department of Philosophy and Psychology was E. G. Boring, a disciple of Titchener. Following Titchener, Boring defined psychology as the study of the mind or consciousness, exactly the position that Watson had attacked. Boring's students studied topics like how people judged the weights of little pill boxes or how well a person could tell the difference between loudnesses made by swinging a ball on a string from various heights and letting it bang against a block of wood. Boring's presence extended to every psychology classroom in the form of piped compressed air for producing low whistles for students to compare. This was not what Skinner planned to study. But fortunately, when Skinner arrived, Boring was away on Sabbatical finishing his book, the *History of Psychology*. Skinner looked for courses to take and found one in the biology department that looked promising. To his delight, the text discussed Pavlov's work! The course was taught by Hudson Hoagland, a young instructor brought in by William Crozier, chair of a newly created Department of Physiology. Crozier had studied with Jacques Loeb. (It was a small world. Loeb had corresponded with Mach and had taught a course that Watson took at the University of Chicago.) Like Loeb, who was said to "resent the nervous system," Crozier had no use for explanations that appealed to inner processes. Explanation consisted of finding functional relationships between the manipulations of the experimenter and the resulting behavior of the organism – the same platform Watson had espoused. As E. Vargas put it, the match between Crozier and Skinner was " a professional marriage made in heaven: Crozier – caustic, hard-driving and hard-drinking, impatient, contemptuous of what he called organ physiology, an advocate of Loeb in biology and Mach in philosophy; and Skinner – sarcastic, radical and rebellious, impatient, contemptuous of compromisers, and eager to put the investigation of behavior on an independent scientific footing" (Vargas, 1995, p. 108). In his second course in physiology Skinner was assigned research with a more senior student on Crozier's favorite subject, tropisms. This resulted in Skinner first published research article (jointly with T. Cunliffe Barnes). Crozier was an editor of the *Journal of General Psychology*, and the Barnes and Skinner article "The Progressive Increase in the Geotropic Response of the Ant Aphaenogaster," appeared in that journal (Barnes & Skinner, 1930). Predictably, it references Crozier and Loeb.

After his first year of graduate study, Skinner continued to sign up for research credits over in physiology. But Crozier's fascination with tropisms did not appeal to Skinner. It is a tribute to Crozier that he supported Skinner's endeavors and did not insist that the young student conduct tropism research. He encouraged Skinner to pursue his own inclinations. As Skinner describes it,

> In my research courses ... I worked entirely without supervision. No one knew what I was doing until I handed in some kind of flimsy report. Possibly the psychologists thought I was being counseled by Crozier and Hoagland, and they may have thought that someone in psychology was keeping an eye

on me, but the fact was that I was doing exactly as I pleased. (Skinner, 1979, p. 35)

Freed from a dictated program of research, Skinner was shaped by what he experienced. His day to day behavior was controlled by how his rats acted rather than by theories or by hypotheses to prove or disprove. Experimenting with behaving organisms provided perfect contingencies for discovery. Still, it took some time before he broke away from the stimulus-response tradition that dominated not only psychology in general, but also the behaviorism of the time.

Skinner was, of course, familiar with Watson's *Behaviorism*. In that book, Watson proclaimed behavior to be a subject matter in its own right, but he attributed causes to antecedent stimuli even when manipulating consequences. For example, Watson described shaping "da" in an infant as saying "da", and then giving a bottle contingently when the baby uttered "da." He analyzed the process, however, as Pavlovian conditioning to the "da" stimulus *preceding* responding (Watson, 1924 p. 182). Watson's procedure of presenting stimuli in "trials" also made it difficult to see relationships between actions and consequences independently of the role of preceding stimuli.

Skinner started working in this reflex tradition, looking at the responses of rats to prior stimuli. With his tinkering proclivities, however, he kept designing new pieces of equipment for experiment after experiment, and in so doing stumbled onto procedures that did away with trials. The apparatuses that Skinner finally perfected – the operant chamber and the cumulative recorder – enabled him to observe control by consequences when no particular stimulus was present. There were no trials in an operant chamber, and moment to moment changes in rate of bar pressing could thus be related directly to the way in which consequences were arranged. Skinner described the evolution of the apparatus, and the experiments that he conducted in "A Case History in Scientific Method" (Skinner, 1999).

Discovery of the Operant: Selection by Consequences

The "Case History" article Skinner wrote affirms his inductive approach to science. In the early 1950's Skinner was asked to contribute a chapter to a book as part of a "Project A" directed by Sigmund Koch. Contributors were asked to provide "any set of sentences formulated as a tool for ordering empirical knowledge with respect to some specifiable domain of events" (Skinner, 1999, p. 108). To Skinner, this was the reverse of Bacon's dictum that books should follow science, science should not follow books. The "method" of science is what scientists *do*, not a set of rules or procedures. Skinner had already published an article in which he argued against the methodology of statistics and hypothesis testing, offering his own behavior to illustrate how discoveries come about. He submitted a revised version of that article for the book. The only rules provided, such as "When you run onto something interesting, drop everything else and study it," or "Some people are lucky," are serious suggestions, though phrased whimsically as if in contempt for rules of science.

In writing his case history, Skinner spent some time going through old research notes to reconstruct the sequence of his activities as accurately as possible. The sheer number of pieces of apparatus and experiments he built is impressive in itself. Following his tropism experiments with ants in the spring semester of his first year as a graduate student, he was given some rats by a student (Gregory Pincus – the inventor of the birth control pill). Skinner built what he grandly called the "Parthenon" because it had steps descending from a tunnel in a tenuous resemblance to the Greek temple. Skinner was familiar with maze research, but had been bothered by the fact that the position of the rat and the noise of the opening of the door to the maze were not controlled. He developed a "silent release box", watched the rat come down the Parthenon steps, then sounded a click and recorded the rat's behavior. Successive clicks produced less and less of an effect. When some of the rats had babies, Skinner started studying the behavior of the baby rats. He tore up the Parthenon and built a platform on piano wires to measure the motion of baby rats when pulled increasingly by the tail. Extending the work to adult rats and abandoning attachments to the animals, Skinner build an eight-foot runway in a tunnel, again recording the movements of the rats as clicks were sounded. Note that he was still investigating reflexes in a trial format – the responses of the rats to an antecedent click.

To insure that a rat would travel through his tunnel, Skinner gave it a bit of wet mash to eat at the end of the runway. Candidly explaining that he got tired of carrying the rats back and forth, Skinner describes adding a back alley forming a rectangular runway. But the rats would pause after eating the mash. Skinner got interested in those pauses and "dropped everything else". But then the runway did not need to be eight feet long. By January of his second year as a graduate student, Skinner had constructed a shorter rectangular runway with a tilting mechanism permitting the rat to make its own records by moving a needle up and down a moving strip of blackened paper as the rat traveled from one end of the runway to the other. Each trial began when the rat ate the single pellet of food that the tipping of the runway produced. Here, luck entered. Skinner had used scraps to build equipment and had not bothered to cut off a spindle when fashioning the food magazine. One day, his behavior came under control of that spindle, and he saw that by attaching a weighted string that would unwind as the experiment proceeded, he could transform his linear polygraph records into curves. Thus, in early Spring of 1930, the cumulative recorder was born. At about this time, too, Skinner shifted from recording running to recording the rate at which the rat ate pellets of food. One element critical for operant conditioning had fallen into place: Rate as a dependent variable. In a trial format the experimenter produces each stimulus to which the organism is to respond, making rate meaningless. In Skinner's apparatus, the rat could produce a pellet at any time without waiting for any antecedent stimulus. In a letter to his parents he explained that he had demonstrated that "the rate in which a rat eats food, over a period of two hours, is a square function of the time. In other words, what heretofore was supposed to be "free" behavior on the part of the rat is now shown to be just as much subject to natural laws as, for example, the rate of his pulse"

(Skinner, 1979. p. 59). But though freed from the restrictions of "trials", in the publication of his experiments Skinner still talked of "eating reflexes". Time since the beginning of the eating period served as the antecedent stimulus. He had not yet broken free of the stimulus-response tradition. Skinner reported on his work correlating rate of eating as a function of time in two more articles. The first, submitted in July 7, 1931, describes apparatus with a door that the rat *pushes open* to get at pellets. In the article Skinner grapples with the problem of lack of consistency between stimuli and responses that you should get in a reflex: "If it is in fact true that a rat's approach to a bit of food is reflex, why is the response not always evoked by the appropriate stimulus?" (Skinner, 1932a, p. 32). He appeals to a "third variable", conditions such as deprivation of food imposed by the experimenter to take the place of what other psychologists would call "drive", thus avoiding any need to appeal to internal physiology. In the second article, submitted three months later, he describes a "problem box" with a lever – the first mention of an operant chamber in Skinner's published works. In this article, submitted three years after arriving at Harvard, Skinner talks of "eating behavior" as a chain of reflexes, still in an S-R format: "The stimuli for the initial members of this sequence of reflexes emanate from the food or the food tray." (Skinner, 1932b).

The discovery of the control by consequences that shifted Skinner's dependent variable from ingestion to bar pressing began with an accident. One day, the food magazine in the operant box jammed. As Skinner describes it,

> At first I treated this as a defect and hastened to remedy the difficulty. But eventually, of course, I deliberately disconnected the magazine. I can easily recall the excitement of that first complete extinction curve. I had made contact with Pavlov at last: Here was a curve uncorrupted by the physiological process of ingestion. It was an orderly change due to nothing more than a special contingency of reinforcement. It was pure behavior. (Skinner, 1999, p. 117)

The "contact with Pavlov," was, in fact, a complete break with Pavlov's type of conditioning. When Skinner shifted his dependent variable to the rate of bar pressing he began looking at postcedent controls. Here was a "reflex" that did not seem to be explained by conditioning of the antecedent "stimulus substitution" type. He must have written his friend and colleague, Fred Keller about his "discovery" because on October 2, 1931, Keller wrote him back, saying, "The only thing that bothered me about your very welcome and newsy letter was that talk about a brand new theory of learning." (Keller, 1931). By February of the following year Skinner submitted an article making clear the distinction between Type I conditioning (respondent) and Type II conditioning (operant), (Skinner, 1932c). At the age of twenty seven, B. F. Skinner had started onto a line of research that began a whole new science of behavior.

The central relationship Skinner discovered was that of the operant, a class of behaviors defined by a common effect on the environment. The bar press in the operant chamber was defined by the closing of a switch, not by the form of the motions of the rat. Skinner realized that even if the rat falls upon the lever, for example when slipping from climbing up the corner of the box, the depression of the lever is recorded as a bar press. Such data are just as legitimate as a press by a paw, but until bar presses are brought under experimental control of consequences, the actions that close the switch are not considered part of the operant of bar pressing. Unlike respondent conditioning, operant conditioning is controlled not by the stimuli that precede actions, but by those that follow. Operant behavior is a two-term relationship in which no identifiable stimulus need precede a response.

Skinner's dependent variable, probability of behaving, measured as rate of actions, was recorded, in a sense, by the rat itself. Every bar press was captured permitting a fine-grained analysis of functional relationships. Skinner was fortunate to obtain five years of grants that gave him complete freedom to do research. In those five years, he investigated, "deprivation and satiation, reinforcement and non reinforcement, schedules of reinforcement, differential reinforcement with respect to properties or stimuli and responses, aversive consequences, and a few behavioral drugs" (Skinner, 1938). The results were published in 1938, along with a sophisticated analysis of his philosophy of science, in *The Behavior of Organisms* (Skinner, 1938/1991).

In investigating how the probability of responding could be altered by manipulating the way in which food was made contingent upon responding, Skinner opened up a whole new approach to how behavior originates. Reinforcing consequences *select* behavior, making it more likely to occur again under similar circumstances. The process of selection not only increases a particular response, it shifts a whole gradient of properties of responding, gradually producing novel responses, much as new species are created by the selection of individuals. Just as Darwin's analysis provides the mechanism through which the extraordinary variety of species could arise, Skinner's analysis gave a plausible account of the origins of novel or unusual behavior in people including many of the kinds of behaviors with which therapists deal. Interestingly, Skinner didn't draw the selection analogy until very late in his career. It appears in the title of a 1981 article in which Skinner talks of three kinds of selection affecting what people do, natural selection, operant conditioning, and cultural evolution (Skinner, 1981). Of course antecedent stimuli come to gain control over operant behavior, too, but only by being present when action-consequence relationships occur.

Implications for Therapy – Direct Manipulation of Consequences

Had Skinner stopped there, he would have contributed a technology for psychotherapy. By arranging various contingencies of reinforcement, Skinner was able to shape behavior of extreme forms, to produce "negative utility," like pathological gambling, and to demonstrate the harmful effects of punishment. Behavior changes according to contingencies of reinforcement or punishment, providing plausible explanations of how psychoses might have originated, as well as how behaviors could be changed. Direct manipulation of consequences of client behavior was all that was needed. To directly shape behavior, however, the therapist had to interact with patients as behavior occurred. The therapist who sees a client only in office visits is not present to set up consequences following specific problem behaviors of a client. But in institutions, more continuous interactions were possible. Thus it was in institutional settings that operant conditioning as a therapeutic technique first occurred.

As early as 1932, soon after getting his degree, Skinner had talked about setting up some lever-pressing experiments for human subjects at Worcester State Hospital, but nothing came of the talks. His concern with the human condition showed in *Walden Two*, but while in Minnesota and Indiana (1936-1949) he did not address therapy. Even though extensive work with non-human animals demonstrated the variety of behaviors that different contingencies of reinforcement could produce, it wasn't until a student of Skinner's, Ogden Lindsley, took over a project with institutionalized adults, that the first direct applications of operant techniques with human beings was conducted (Lindsley, 1960). Lindsley's human operant chambers consisted of separate rooms, a bit larger than a standard office cubicle. Patients had access to a manipulandum such as a plunger to pull or a panel to press. Behind the row of chambers, equipment controlled the schedules for the dispensing of reinforcers, the latter consisting of everything from candy to cigarettes to visual stimuli. Cumulative records were obtained, showing the same kinds of sensitivities to contingencies found in rats and pigeons. Lindsley had a steady stream of visitors, many of whom set up their own laboratories. Therapeutic applications included work on problems as diverse as stuttering (Flanagan, Goldiamond, & Azrin, 1958, p. 177), multiple tics (Barrett, 1962/66), and wearing or glasses by a child with autism (Wolf, Mees, & Risley, 1964/66). By 1964, Lindsley could report that "more than 100 applications of free-operant methods to human behavioral pathology have been published (Lindsley, 1966, p. 167).

Moving into environments in which patients lived, albeit still in institutions, Ayllon and Michael (1959) trained psychiatric nurses to systematically reinforce or ignore specific behaviors in the patients with whom they interacted every day. (Ayllon & Michael, 1959). For all of the clients served, standard treatments involving counseling or prescription drugs had failed. Only direct manipulation of immediate consequences of client behavior worked as a therapeutic technique. The procedures involved consequences of ongoing behaviors, that is, the continuous flow of a client's actions, rather than behavior as a response to tasks presented in trials. The procedures thus followed directly from Skinner's discovery of the power of consequences over the frequency of behavior. By 1979, operant conditioning was the technique cited most by the members of the Association for Behavior Therapy who responded to a questionnaire about procedures they "frequently used" (Cautela, 1986, p. 5).

When patients are institutionalized, therapists have access to behavior as it occurs, and can alter the consequences of that behavior daily in experimental sessions or on the ward. In the more common therapeutic format of office visits once a week, however, the therapist may not experience the behaviors of concern firsthand, and he or she has little control over the contingencies that occur outside office interactions. The therapist must rely, therefore, not on direct observation and shaping of behavior, but on patient report. Thus verbal behavior enters strongly into the standard therapeutic relationship.

Skinner's Analysis of Verbal Behavior, Covert Behavior, and Feelings

Skinner started working on verbal behavior very early. By the time his first book, *Behavior of Organisms*, came out he was already writing a book on "language." It took him over 20 years to complete what he often called "his most important book." Working on this book, Skinner grappled with topics that had not yet been satisfactorily analyzed, including internal feelings and awareness, as well as the reasons people say, gesture, and write what they do.

The Basic Framework of Verbal Behavior

Verbal behavior is particularly complicated since it has its effect on the world through the mediation other individuals. Where reaching for the salt contacts salt directly, asking for the salt produces salt only through the actions of a second person. In analyzing verbal behavior Skinner asked "Of what variables is a particular response a function?" Extending principles from the laboratory, he sought relationships between what is said and controls in the environment. Consistent with his overall approach, he excluded internal structures or agencies as causes for verbal behavior. That left three basic sources of control: deprivation or aversive stimulation (mand); objects or events in the verbalizer's presence (tact); and verbal stimuli (intraverbal)[1]. Interacting with all three categories, a mediator serves both to reinforce specific verbal responses and to provide a discriminative stimulus for general aspects of verbal behavior, such as starting to speak or the language spoken. Complex relationships such as those involved in "grammatical construction" were also addressed in the book.

Categorizing verbal behavior by its function, rather than by its form, Skinner addressed "meaning". Meaning does not reside in the particular words uttered, but rather in contingencies – the relationship between the particular words emitted, the consequences that have followed similar behavior in the past, and the context in which a statement occurs. "Fire!" means one thing when said by a cold camper in the presence of someone who can make a fire (mand), another when reacting to the presence of flames (tact), and a third when translating the French "feu" (intraverbal). "Milk" said when under the control of "wanting" milk is a different operant (mand) than saying "milk" as a result of "seeing" milk (tact). Tacting is widely misinterpreted as reference, but an example by Skinner illustrates the difference (Skinner, 1986). Saying the word "fishing" instead of, say, "hunting" in the statement, "I'm fishing for a letter I want to show you," is partly a tact if it occurs because of a large swordfish mounted on an office wall. But clearly the speaker is not "referring to the fish."

Conversely, one can refer to Roosevelt without Roosevelt being present. The latter is reference but not a tact, since Roosevelt is not currently present.

Influence of Skinner's Analysis of Verbal Behavior on Therapy

The distinction between mand and tact has led to technological improvements in the field of special education. Traditionally, children with autism were taught first to name objects. When they learned to say "milk" when shown milk, it was assumed that they "knew the word," and could ask for milk if they wanted it, even if milk was not currently visible to them. Mark Sundberg and his colleagues showed that, just as Skinner had predicted in *Verbal Behavior*, the two "milks" were separate operants (Skinner, 1957). Teaching a child to tact did not necessarily enable that child to mand. The same *form* of response (saying "milk") under one set of controls did not always occur under a second set of controls. When different operants are typically learned far apart in time, as with speaking and reading, everyone recognizes the difference in controls: No one would expect a child who can say "milk" to automatically then be able to read that word. Reading has to be taught separately. Similarly mands and tacts may need to be taught separately to children with autism. Since the mand is maintained by getting the specified object or event, while tacts are maintained by generalized reinforcement such as social approval, Sundberg and his associates found that it was easier to teach mands than tacts. Children learn much more quickly to "ask for what they want," than to "name objects". Where it could take literally months to teach a rudimentary tact vocabulary of four to five terms, by reversing the order and teaching mands first, children more rapidly learned a basic vocabulary. (See the journal, *The Analysis of Verbal Behavior*, for additional applications of Skinner's analysis.)

The analysis of verbal behavior also provided insight into some profound dysfunctional social behaviors. Not being able to tell others what you want can be very frustrating. In looking at the function of many of the bizarre behaviors of children, that is, at what usually followed those behaviors, it became clear that many of these behaviors were mands. Throwing oneself on the floor and screaming may not look like verbal behavior, but if it produces a characteristic consequence such as "teacher attention," it is likely to be a mand. By specifically shaping more appropriate ways to bring about the "characteristic" consequence, therapists have been able to eliminate many extreme behaviors without resorting to punishment, which produces its own problems (Bowman, Fisher, Thompson and Piazza (1997). Similar analyses have shown many maladaptive adult behaviors to be mands. Using the "characteristic consequences" as reinforcers to shape more acceptable mands, therapists have been able to eliminate long-standing troublesome behaviors.

Skinner analyzed verbal behavior much as he analyzed the bar press. He looked for factors in the environment responsible for a particular action. Having researched basic principles of reinforcement, shaping, discrimination and generalization, he was sensitive to the nuances of contingencies over behavior. To be sure, the mediated aspect of verbal behavior required a special analysis (470 pages in fact), but the basic principles did not change from one kind of behavior to another. Though the analysis was not different, it became more complex when addressing behaviors going on inside an individual.

Internal Feelings

In *Verbal Behavior* Skinner specifically addresses internal thoughts and feelings. The skin, he maintained, is simply a physical boundary and, as he put it elsewhere, "The skin is not that important as a boundary" (Skinner, 1963, p. 953). Stimuli occurring inside the body can be treated just like those outside, except that they can only be reported by the person observing them. The tooth ache you feel inside is just as much a stimulus as a puncture applied externally. Considering internal events as valid variables in a science (the radical behavioral position) set Skinner apart from methodological behaviorists who follow the logical positivist tradition of intersubjective invariance, or truth by agreement. Where methodological behaviorists insist, for example, on interobserver reliability for reported data, radical behaviorists look for truth in effectiveness at prediction and control. As Skinner pointed out, Robinson Crusoe could develop a science even if his man Friday never turned up.

But the lack of a common contact with internal events poses a problem for teaching tacting. How does a member of a verbal community shape up a reasonably accurate response to an event that only the learner experiences? Skinner described various ways. In "public accompaniment," visible stimuli usually correlated with an internal event help the teacher. A mother, seeing a skinned knee, may say "that must hurt," thus pairing the term "hurt" with whatever the child is feeling. Secondly, through "collateral responses" (a child may wince, for example), the term "hurt" is again mentioned. Metaphor may be used. In asking about a pain, doctors often suggest terms taught in situations where stimuli are external: "Is it a *sharp* pain, or *dull*? Does it *throb*?" People with lower back pain often describe it as feeling "like a red hot poker". Lastly much behavior is learned at the overt level, and then reduces to the covert. We learn to read at first aloud, but gradually the pronunciation of words recedes to the covert level, with, in some readers, a slight movement of the lips revealing the origin of the behavior. (It is also interesting that when the covert level is inadequate, as when reading very difficult directions or in a noisy environment, the behavior is likely to reappear at the overt level.) In a similar way, a person may tact a physical reach for a cigarette in the pocket where she used to keep cigarettes, then only start to reach, and finally reach at such a small magnitude that only the ex-smoker can identify each incident as an "impulse." In researching the origins of dozens of terms describing internal feelings, (such as "anxiety") Skinner found that they originated as terms describing overt behaviors. "Anxiety," for example originated in the word for the overt action "choke." Gradually the word's meaning shifted to describing events inside the skin. Still, a verbal community taught its new members to describe "feeling anxious."

Awareness or Consciousness

Like verbal behavior, awareness or consciousness also requires the mediation of others. We become conscious when those around us arrange contingencies for paying attention to something, whether that something is internal or external. All of us have walked up a set of stairs. But you may not be aware of how many steps you took. If an acquaintance often asked about numbers of steps (particularly if reporting the number accurately resulted in some strong consequence such as winning a $100 bet), it wouldn't be long before you could accurately report the number of steps, and even the numbers of other steps in stairs you encountered. The phrase "conscious of the number of steps" would than be applied to your behavior. The same process occurs when the reinforcement is less conspicuous, such as social approval. Thus the community of people with whom clients interact determines awareness. One part of that community is the therapist. In therapy sessions, the therapist can increase a client's awareness of aspects of his or her life by the kinds of statements to which the therapist attends. The only drawback to working primarily with verbal behavior is that what clients say may not accurately reflect critical components of a their life.

Suppose, for example, instead of a fixed $100 for reporting numbers of steps, you would receive $10 for each step you reported, and the person handing out the money was unable to check on your accuracy. The contingencies in such a case encourage exaggeration, as exemplified by stories of the size of fish caught. The fact that verbal behavior can be shaped independently of actual events confronts anyone who must rely on the description of events he or she has not directly observed. When a client relates feeling better after several therapy sessions, is the client's life better, or has only the client's verbal behavior been shaped? Shaping verbal behavior alone is particularly dangerous with children who are under strong contingencies of pleasing adults, as shown by the graphic descriptions of fictitious sexual abuse. What a therapist reinforces in the interaction during a session thus affects what the client reports during a session as well as what clients notice in their daily lives.

Therapeutic Extensions of Skinner's Analysis of Verbal Behavior

By extending the principles discovered in the laboratory to verbal behavior and to an analysis of how covert behavior comes about, Skinner opened the way for therapists to base therapy on covert behaviors and covert reinforcement. This made it possible to bring a client's problems into the therapist's office, since scenarios, visualized actions, and imagined consequences are not restricted to a particular place. In the 1950's Wolpe used visualization to desensitize patient fears in a respondent conditioning format. If respondent extinction through imaging of antecedent stimuli could help a patient, why couldn't imagery be used in an operant paradigm? In 1966, Joe Cautela began using imagery with operant behaviors. He described his "covert conditioning" procedures as "the modification of a behavior by imagining particular consequences to influence the behavior in the desired directions" (Cautela, 1986, xii). The "particular consequences" were reinforcement, extinction, and punishment, taken directly from Skinner's work. Covert conditioning has been used successfully in treating a wide variety of patient problems, including anxiety, athletic performance, pain, depression, aggression, and sexual disorders (Cautela & Kearny, 1993). Skinner's assertion that verbal and covert behaviors obey the same laws, and that they interact with each other and with overt behaviors has been born out in therapeutic applications.

Lessons for the Future

At the same time that Skinner provided therapists with tools based upon a contingency analysis, Skinner addressed the controls over the therapist. What determines what a therapist does when approached by a client? Certainly training comes into play. Training may guide the initial interview – whether inventories are given or not, and which ones, or what questions are asked. But as interactions continue, other factors enter in. Current cultural practices affect therapeutic practice. Sometime back, therapists would try to change the sexual orientation of a homosexual client. Today that is not necessarily the accepted approach. Standards of ethical conduct also change according to the times. But ultimately, like the experimenter shaping behavior in a rat, chimpanzee, pigeon, or any other convenient platform, and like a teacher shaping behavior of a baby, child, or adult, the therapist, in order to be maximally effective, must come under control of change in behavior of the client. While the precision obtained by cumulative records may not be feasible for tracking daily behavior, direct continuous measurement of the rate of relevant behaviors is the goal to approximate.

Skinner consistently argued against internal agencies. Certainly physiological processes occur as behavioral selection is taking place, but the analysis of brain functioning belongs to another discipline. Furthermore, understanding what is happening in the brain will never provide a parsimonious explanation of why a person sings a particular song at a particular time, or even why a pigeon pecks a particular disk at a particular rate. Behavior must be explained at the behavioral level, and that requires looking at factors in the environment. To change behavior, the therapist must look at the relationships between clinically relevant behaviors and the contingencies over those actions. Appealing to agencies, such as personality traits, short-term and long-term memory processes, or even measurable physiological activities, not only fails to explain behavior of interest but draws attention away from the environment where control actually lies. In his last talk, Skinner warned against "cognitive" approaches, drawing an analogy between them and "creationism." Only by abandoning internal causal agents will therapists turn full attention to the contingency relationships responsible for the behaviors they treat.

Summary

Therapy was not Skinner's field. But, in one sense he was a therapist. For he contributed an analysis of behavior which, combined with the conditioning procedures worked out by Pavlov, encompass all behavior. Skinner discovered the critical role of postcedent events both in selecting actions that become part of an individual's repertoire and in determining how antecedent events, through pairing with selective processes, gain control over behavior. He spent thousands of hours in research, changing every conceivable aspect of contingencies and noting the effects on the probability of behavior, measured as rate of actions. By working out the complexities of how the rate of operant behavior is a function of environmental variables, Skinner showed how maladaptive behaviors could have originated, and how alternative repertoires could be established to take their place.

Psychologists working with institutionalized populations first grasped the significance of the role of postcedent events. By directly altering the kinds of consequences following patient behaviors they were able to solve long-standing behavior problems. Not only were they able to eliminate behavioral excesses, such as tantruming, they also improved the life of patients who had done little but lie about for months or years. They taught these patients to shower, to dress themselves, to make their own beds, get themselves to meals on time, and even to enjoy social events – all by changing contingencies.

Skinner extended his laboratory findings to an analysis of verbal behavior. He categorized verbal operants according to the functional controls over behaviors mediated by the actions of other people. Following Skinner's analysis, therapists have looked at the function rather than the form of behaviors of individuals who do not talk. Many extreme behaviors, such as tantrums and even vomiting, have been found to be verbal. By teaching alternative ways of "asking" for the consequences that followed these extreme behaviors, therapists have, without using punishment, eliminated the maladaptive behaviors.

The analysis of verbal behavior includes covert actions. Behavior inside the skin follows the same laws of reinforcement, extinction, punishment, shaping, and differentiation as behavior occurring overtly. Like overt behaviors, covert behaviors are a function of contingencies. They can be addressed like any other behaviors. Including internal actions in the analysis leads to effective therapies for changing dysfunctional thoughts and feelings.

While Skinner addressed all behavior, internal as well as external, his analysis excluded any kind of internal "agency" as responsible for action. Unlike thoughts and feelings which can be recorded by the behaving person, agencies such as "the mind," or "self" must be inferred from other behaviors, usually the ones to be explained and changed. Including them in an analysis leads to a dead end. At best, attributing behavior to an agency such as "mental illness" or "poor self-concept," raises questions about what caused the mental illness or self concept. At worst, statements that sound like explanations hinder further inquiry. By excluding agency entirely, behavior can be functionally related to environmental events – the same events that an agency analysis must eventually consider. Until Skinner's discovery of the role of consequences in selecting behavior, and the hundreds of experiments investigating the relationship of contingencies to the probability of particular actions, the functional relationship between behavior and environmental events was not well understood. With the science of contingent relationships between behavior and environmental events, the therapist has a comprehensive, well-researched, and effective approach upon which to base practice.

References

Ayllon, T., & Michael, J. (1959). The psychiatric nurse as a behavioral engineer. *Journal of the Experimental Analysis of Behavior, 2*, 323-334.

Barnes, T. C., & Skinner, B. F. (1930). The progressive increase in the geotropic response of the ant *Aphaenogaster. Journal of General Psychology, 4*, 102-112.

Barrett, B. H. (1962/1966). Reduction in rate of multiple tics by free operant conditioning methods. In R. Ulrich, T. Stachnik, & J. Mabry (Eds.), *Control of human behavior* (pp. 143-150). Glenview, IL: Scott, Foresman and Company.

Cautela, J. R., & Kearney, A. J. (1986). *The covert conditioning handbook.* New York: Springer.

Flanagan, B., Goldiamond, I., & Azrin, N. (1958). Operant stuttering: that control of stuttering behavior through response-contingent consequences. *Journal of the Experimental Analysis of Behavior*, 1, 173-177.

Keller, F. S. (1931). *Letter to B. F. Skinner: Skinner-Keller Letters* (Vol 1., pp. 1). Cambridge, MA: B. F. Skinner Foundation Archives.

Lindsley, O. R. (1966). Geriatric behavioral prosthetics. In R. Ulrich, T. Stachnik, & J. Mabry (Eds.), *Control of human behavior* (pp. 156-168). Glenview, IL: Scott, Foresman and Company.

Lindlsey, O. R. (1960). Characterization of the behavior of chronic psychotics as revealed by free operant conditioning methods [Monograph]. *Diseases of the Nervous Systems*, 66-78.

Skinner, B. F. (1932a). Drive and reflex strength. *Journal of General Psychology, 6*, 22-37.

Skinner, B. F. (1932b). Drive and reflex strength II. *Journal of General Psychology, 6*, 38-48.

Skinner, B. F. (1932c). On the rate of formation of a conditioned reflex. *Journal of General Psychology, 6*, 274-286.

Skinner, B. F. (1938/1991). *The behavior of organisms.* New York: Appleton-Century-Crofts. (Reprinted by the B. F. Skinner Foundation, 1991).

Skinner, B. F. (1956/1999). A case history in scientific method. In *Cumulative record: Definitive edition* (pp. 108-131). Acton, MA: Copley Publishing Group.

Skinner, B. F. (1957). *Verbal behavior.* New York: Appleton-Century-Crofts.

Skinner, B. F. (1963). Behaviorism at fifty. *Science, 140*, 951-958

Skinner, B. F. (1976). *Particulars of my life.* New York: Alfred A. Knopf.

Skinner, B. F. (1986). The evolution of verbal behavior. *Journal of the Experimental Analysis of Behavior, 45*, 115-122.

Skinner, B. F. (1979). *The shaping of a behaviorist.* New York: Alfred A. Knopf.

Vargas, E. A. (1995). Prologue, perspectives, and prospects of behaviorology. *Behaviorology, 3*, 107-120.

Watson, J. B. (1924). *Behaviorism.* New York: W. W. Norton & Company.

Wolf, M. M., Ridlsy, T., & Mees, H. (1964/1966). Application of operant conditioning procedures to the behavior problems of an autistic child. In R. Ulrich, T. Stachnik, & J. Mabry (Eds.), *Control of human behavior* (pp. 187-193). Glenview, IL: Scott, Foresman and Company.

Footnotes

[1] Skinner called this category "verbal behavior under control of verbal stimuli" and used "intraverbal" for one special case. E. A. Vargas suggested using "intraverbal" for the whole category and in a private conversation Skinner agreed that such designation would have been better. "But," he said, "it would be too hard to change now." Some of us are still trying.

Chapter 4

Jacob Robert Kantor (1888-1984): Pioneer in the Development of Naturalistic Foundations for Behavior Therapy

Paul T. Mountjoy
Western Michigan University

The name of Kantor has high recognition among psychologists (see O'Donnell, 1985; Popplestone & McPherson, 1994/1999), especially among behaviorally oriented ones, and yet it is commonly stated that he has been relatively non-influential. Perhaps Schoenfeld (1969) indicated an essential point: "It was our wit that was wanting, not his. We demanded too little of ourselves, and expected too much from him." (p. 329)

I add that Kantor suggested a manner of doing scientific work which represented a different approach from the dominant one of the early twentieth-century, and, indeed, which remains in contrast to the most popular approaches of the late twentieth-century as well. This has made mastery of his works difficult. Consequently, the appreciation of his contributions has been limited, and I hope to redress that balance to some extent here.

I accept teaching of (and other efforts at dissemination of) scientific attitudes, as well as innovation in naturalistic and behavioral approaches to psychological events to be of equal importance to that of being an active and/or innovative behavior therapist for purposes of this presentation. We behavioral psychologists are, above all, interested in and devoted to the process of bringing the benefits of a natural science and technology of psychological events to all members of the human species.

Precis of Kantor's Life

Julius, the father of Jacob Robert, emigrated from Vilna, Lithuania to Harrisburg, PA in about 1880, and there became Rabbi of the Orthodox Congregation Chisuk Emuna Bene Russia. Shortly, his wife Mary and their first daughter emigrated to this country. The first child born in this country was Jacob Robert (in 1888), and the family soon included three daughters and four sons. On August 2, 1899 Julius died, which required the eldest son, Jacob Robert, to leave school at the age of 11 years to become an economic asset to the family. About 1900 Mary moved the children to Chicago, Illinois. Jacob Robert never did graduate from high school, but he was able to remediate his academic deficiencies in a year at Valparaiso, so that he was enrolled as a student at the University of Chicago during the summer quarter of 1911. Here, he obtained the Ph.D., *magna cum laude* in 1917, and in 1920 went to Indiana University, where he remained until his retirement in 1959. He then returned to Chicago to live with his daughter (Helene Juliet Kantor – "Bobby"), and in this period created some of his most important works (e.g., Kantor, 1981). (See Kantor, 1976; Mountjoy & Cone, in press; Mountjoy & Hansor, 1986; and Wolf, 1984, for additional details). During his retirement he traveled and lectured frequently, including several visits to Mexico, on the first of which he received a standing ovation and a gold medal (Ribes, 1984). Death came in February of 1984, seemingly in the midst of his creative and active life, since he had published one book and two journal articles in that year, as well as having prepared a book chapter which was published posthumously. A *Festschrift* was presented (Smith, Mountjoy, & Ruben, 1983) only a few months prior to Kantor's death.

Kantor's Approach to Psychological Science

To sum up Kantor in a single sentence I would say something like this: (1) Utmost respect for the complexities of things and events; (2) complete admission of our present ignorance of many of the interrelationships between various things and events; and (3), overwhelming optimism concerning our ability to understand these interrelationships by means of scientific investigation.

Maybe I should be briefer, like this: Even the best living scientists must be judged as fundamentally ignorant of things and events, but given time all will be understood.

Examples of our ignorance are often made obvious by new discoveries. A recent example from physics concerns the speed of light through a medium. As an undergraduate I was taught that although light could be slowed slightly by the medium through which it passed, it was for all practical purposes constant at about 186,300 miles per second in a vacuum. Hau, Harris, Dutton, & Behrooz (1999) announced that with the use of a Bose-Einstein condensate (BEC), they had slowed light to a velocity of 17 meters per second (approximately 38 miles per hour). This was accomplished by shining a "coupling" laser into the opaque BEC, then also firing a second laser beam into the BEC so that the two beams interacted in a process called electromagnetically induced transparency. Only 25% of the luminous energy passed through the formerly opaque BEC, and it was slowed to only 17 meters per second. They expect the technique to further allow them to slow light down to 37 meters per hour. Quite an unusual and unexpected finding.

Another announcement which overthrows a physiological dogma I also learned as an undergraduate actually is confirmed by several replications, so that we even know some of the psychological variables which are involved in this biological event. The report is of actual neurogenesis in the adult human brain (Eriksson, et al, 1998), which I was taught could never occur. The basic research has reported neurogenesis to be a function of running (Van Praag, Kempermann, & Gage, 1999), living in enriched environments (Kempermann, Kuhn & Gage, 1997) and learning (Gould,

Beylin, Tanapat, Reeves, & Shors, 1999). Obviously, these reports also indicate the inevitable interactions between biological and psychological events.

However, we must remember that all scientific constructs (whether utterances, theories, generalizations, or claims) are actually behavior (or if written, a behavior product) by a person who is behaving within a certain space-time framework (setting, or context), and who has a unique interbehavioral (learning, or behavioral) history. This history consists not only of the specialized professional training received in both undergraduate and graduate school, but is also comprised of both the post-training self-learning features of academic-scientific-research activities, and the cultural shaping procedures of pre-professional training. After all, we are usually reasonably law-abiding (follow the rules of our larger cultural group, and the many cultural sub-groups to which we belong), but we all are shaped to be politically conservative or liberal, and some of us are trained to be religious in various degrees, etc. This baggage of our early life does follow us about as we attempt to do the scientific job, and it does to some extent influence our scientific behavior. However when these social preconceptions intrude too much we can have a scientific problem. In other words, science is composed of two complementary and necessary factors: One is empirical investigation, and the second is the logical analysis, by means of which we examine among other things, the influence of cultural factors upon scientific work (Kantor, 1958/1959, 1963-1969). Throughout the history of science we see the constant interplay of these two essential components of our scientific activities (see, e.g., Burtt, 1924/1932; Dampier, 1929/1966).

Here I shall follow Kantor in his use of the term "assumption" in the logical/mathematical sense of a parameter within a scientific system. For example, one of the most important assumptions of interbehavioral psychology is that: Scientific behaviors are continuous with everyday behaviors. That is to say, psychological events may be observed and interpreted by anyone (and they are in everyday life by every lay person!), and it is possible for any person to be trained to apply scientific methodology to the observation and interpretation of those events.

An extremely important role for the scientist to play is that of a critic. This role may be played out in two ways: One is to demythologize our culture, or more precisely, to attempt to abolish the intrusions of cultural myths into our scientific work. This role was embraced heartily by the early behaviorists, who concentrated upon religico-politico myths. Primary interest among these persons was the religico-politico myth of an internal determiner of behavior which transcended space and time. Natural scientists had already partially demolished this myth by demoting Soul to Mind. That is, the Unified Soul, a permanent (immortal) entity with powers of action, such as thinking, remembering, and willing, became an Atomic Mind, in which the atoms were transient mental states. With Soul thus out of science, it became possible actually to turn away from the Mental (Psychic) in an attempt to develop a natural science of behavior. Unfortunately this frequently involved merely substituting a conceptual nervous system (CNS) which was variously endowed with either Soul or Mind properties so that the net gain was very small (e.g., M. Meyer,

1911). Thus, Kantor (1947, 1963-1969) called for the abandonment of the quasi-scientific mythology of the nervous system as a determiner of behavior in all of its guises. Of course, atomic ways of thinking now have merely gone deeper into the unknown and substituted new areas of ignorance for the old ones, and consequently we see the development and triumphant trumpeting of the "new" science of genetic determinism. (See, as an example of a biologist who rejects this doctrine, Rose, 1997. In contrast, Weiner, 1999, lauds the work of Benzer, for demonstrating the genetics of complex human behavior with *drosophila*.)

Actually, the internal inconsistencies of the half-psychic and half-physical universe were evident soon after the development of the construct. For example, shortly after the beginning of the Common Era (CE), Saint Augustine (354-430 CE) lamented that his Soul commanded his body to obey and yet it did not – and asked his god, rhetorically, from whence came this awful thing? (Augustine, ca 399/1912 CE). Augustine, of course, did not allow this empirical observation to interfere with his faith, and thus demonstrated the validity of another of Kantor's generalizations: Philosophical preconceptions determine in large part the manner in which data are interpreted.

It seems to me we could all agree that abnormal behavior, representing as it does a deviation from the norm, might be characterized as "unique" in the sense that it is so unusual as to present problems of classification into categories in spite of the DSM's valiant attempts to do so throughout its various editions (American Psychiatric Association, 1952/1994). Indeed, classification is conventionally regarded as one of the hallmarks of science. However, Kantor swam against the tide because he insisted upon the uniqueness of all (that is, each and every) psychological event. For this reason, among others, his system seems to me to be uniquely suited for an approach to psychopathology. And, remember that Kantor (1963-1969) insisted upon a critico-historical analysis as the foundation for a natural science of behavior, and subsequently (1958/1959, 1987) a system of behavior therapy.

There is a cautionary tale among historians of science which runs something like this. A biologist was investigating diets for cattle at a research station. His superior was a physicalistic reductionist. One day the biologist showed his superior two lists of chemical elements. This sort of thing: Al = x%, C = y%, H = z%, and so forth. The biologist said that these represented the analyses of two diets for cattle, and asked which one was better. The superior stated he could see no difference. The biologist replied that this was strange because while one represented food intake, the other represented the outflow of residual metabolic matter.

This story is one I never discussed with Kantor, but I know he would have approved. I shall follow Kantor's intentions as exemplified by the story, and paraphrase the moral as: In the analysis of psychological events, do not reduce those events to sterile mathematical abstractions (Kantor, 1917). Remember that, in treatment, we always deal with an organism in trouble, and it is embedded in a psychological setting, within which it interacts maladaptively with a stimulus object.

Kantor agreed with other individuals such as Goldstein (1939) and A. Meyer (1934) on this point.

Citation of Goldstein and A. Meyer here is intended to remind you that the topic of abnormal behavior is inextricably entangled with medicine in a historical sense, and that within both psychology and medicine, as well as in science in general, we may discern two major traditions. One is analytic and reductionistic, while the other also analyzes, but does not attempt to reduce unitary psychological events to sterile mathematical abstractions, and thus attempts to do full justice to the event in its entirety. Another way to contrast these two positions is to say that the reductionistic approach treats a temporal mechanistic chain of smaller events as explanatory, while the non-reductionistic attitude treats total events with multiple factors which comprise the complete causal description.

Incidently, one rule that both of these scientific traditions in psychology follow is the emphasis upon the necessity for an outside observer of the psychological event. This was suggested early on by M. Meyer (1922, 1927) with the use of the term "the other one" in the titles of two of his books.

Obviously the reductionistic tradition is dominant today, especially in the popular reports which communicate current science to the lay public. However, it is possible to discriminate the differences between the discrete unit, reductionistic, approach, and the more continuum oriented, non-reductionistic, attitude, as far back as the first stirrings of the philosophy and practice of science among the ancient Greeks, some five centuries Before the Common Era (BCE). Illustrative are the contrasting positions of Democritus (460-370 BCE) (to whom there were irreducible atoms which combined to form everything else), and Heraclitus (540-475 BCE) (who regarded reality as being composed of a dynamic flux of constant change and becoming). Well into the early twentieth century the Heraclitian attitude was still competitive, but the successful application of atomic theory in physics (in spite of strenuous opposition by many physicists, for example, Einstein and Mach) had severe repercussions in all the other sciences.

And, make no mistake about it: All scientific and technologic enterprises are interrelated. For example, biology has been impacted by the successes of atomism in physics so that most biologists are members of the reductionistic school, as described in Wilson's (1998) *Consilience,* which proclaims the desirability, possibility and feasibility of reducing all of sociology (read psychology) as well as all of biology to genetic (i.e., internal) determinants. However, competing traditions do persist, and actually remain healthy and influential. The non-reductionistic approach, which is to be found in Darwin's (1859/1964) *Origin of Species* (along with the opportunity for reductionistic development), also gave rise to the ecological movement (Brewer, 1960). The most easily available scientific and philosophical accounts of the status of non-reductionistic biology are Meyr (1982, 1997) and Rose's (1999) *Lifelines.* Rose, incidently is an active researcher in the molecular mechanisms of memory, while Wilson is also famous for his ecological work. We scientists always strive for consistency, but all too often fail to achieve it.

Examples of the non-reductionistic approach in psychology are not difficult to discover. An excellent example is Lewontin, Rose & Kamin (1984), with their contribution to what has been called "the IQ wars." (See Hunt, 1999, for a discussion of the current impact of political allegiances within contemporary social science.) Marr (1990) has discussed the issue of reductionism in completely behavior analytic terms, and comparison of my statements here with his should be rewarding.

It has been my privilege to not only read the works of three of the authentic geniuses of the twentieth century, but also to have actually been able to interact with all three on a personal level. Alphabetically, Arthur Fisher Bentley (1870-1957), Jacob Robert Kantor (1888-1984), and B. F. Skinner (1904-1990). These men have not only shaped my intellectual life, but enriched my social life as well. In this presentation I shall use some of the technical vocabulary of each, as well as the common language. Please bear with me as I do not do this to confuse, but: (1) Because there is so little agreement regarding technical psychological terminology; and (2), Because all three of these men were constrained by the nature of psychological events to address the same issues, even though they did so with somewhat different terminology and constructs.

Kantor proposed that events be kept separate from their scientific descriptions (that is, constructs regarding events are not the same as the actual events themselves). This rule simply extends and formalizes the ordinary scientific convention of first reporting data, and then secondly, interpreting those data (with the realization that alternative forms of interpretation of those same data are always possible). And the derivation from that rule is that we psychologists should not mistake the constructs of the other sciences for the data of psychology, as Wilson does. Psychology is a relatively independent science among the other relatively independent sciences. We should not use the constructs of the other sciences as our justification for the scientific status of psychology. We do have our own data: The psychological event. This is reflected in Skinner's (1938) construct of the "reflex" and in Kantor's (1924-1926) construct of the "behavior segment."

Here, then, are two complementary, nondualistic or natural science, definitions for the psychological event, and both are derived from empirical observations. Skinner's probably descended more from Sherrington's (1906) biological tradition, and Kantor's probably derived more from the brass instrument aspect of the functionalist school of James (1890). Bentley's (1895) definition may be regarded as one early step toward the elimination of the purported mental explanatory fiction. All three are in agreement that we cannot satisfactorily describe a psychological event in terms of only a portion of that event, i.e., neither solely in terms of the purported mental and/or physiological functioning of the organism, nor in terms of the environment alone. For example, Skinner (1938, p. 35) clearly stated:

> The impossibility of defining a functional stimulus without reference to a functional response, and *vice versa*, has been especially emphasized by Kantor [Italics in original, and citation is to Kantor, 1933b].

These definitions (rules) do not mean that we cannot isolate a portion of the psychological event for study (e.g., the organism and/or the stimulus), but it does mean that we can neither confuse an isolated physiological aspect of the event with the entire event, nor argue that this physiological aspect of the event is the complete explanation and cause of the entire event. Conversely, we cannot argue that the environment is the sole determiner of the behavior of the organism. These rules proscribe not only the reduction of events to one of their actual components, but also the imposition of non-scientific cultural abstractions upon events as the ultimate and final explanation. In psychology the social conventions of Soul and Mind have been especially troublesome, even though severely attacked by most advocates of a natural science of psychology. As we have attempted to approach the status of a natural science some of us have fallen into the error of simply substituting the conceptual nervous system (CNS) for the non-spatio-temporal, and purported, rather than actually isolatable, explanatory device of the Soul or Mind.

At the present time the role of physiological mechanisms in behavior in general, and in abnormal behavior in particular, is controversial, not least among psychologists. I have no doubt that the controversy may be traced, at least in part, to the medical model (Ulmann & Krasner, 1969/1975) and the technology of medicine, as well as to a failure to critically examine basic preconceptions. It has been a problem in American psychology at least since James' *Principles* (1890). Kantor's *Problems of Physiological Psychology* (1947) addressed this problem in his usual iconoclastic manner. Is the science of psychology simply a handmaiden of physiology? Kantor's answer to this question was a resounding "NO!" He regarded psychology as a relatively independent science among the other relatively independent physical and biological sciences, and psychology was of equal validity (Kantor, 1953, 1958/1959). In fact, since scientific research consisted of the interbehavior of an organism (a scientist) with things and events (which essentially was the definition of psychology given by Kantor), psychologists had a special expertise in evaluation of the validity of the actions of all scientists!

Probably this is as good a place as any to insist that Kantor (1947) was correct in all essentials when he argued that physiology was not the ultimate explanation for behavioral events. Although he based his analysis upon the literature prior to that publication year (e.g., Sherrington, 1906, and especially see Leyton & Sherrington, 1917, among others), many recent reports have upheld his statements of some 52 years ago. For example: Vining, et al. (1997) reported on 58 children who had been hemispherectomized in order to control life threatening grand mal episodes. Their behavior was quite normal for such severely injured organisms, and included remarkable voluntary control of the arm and leg contralateral to the missing hemisphere.

Emphasis upon observables was one of Kantor's hallmarks. He regarded the use of physiological factors which had not been observed to be as great a deviation from proper scientific procedures and principals as was the utilization of the, by definition unobservable, Soul or Mind.

Kantor wrote frequently of the necessity for the denial and abandonment of what he called the psychophysical protopostulate, and the substitution of a naturalistic protopostulate in its place. In different words these attitudes are shared by all who attempt to develop a natural science system of psychology. From that point on there may well be competing (or complementary) objective systems of psychology, i.e., the behaviorisms of Watson, M. Meyer, Weiss, Hull, Skinner, and others, as well as the interbehaviorism of Kantor. These somewhat different systems which have been proposed for a natural science of psychology will continue to fight for supremacy in the scientific free market place of ideas in terms of the essential criteria of both empirical support, and logical consistency, and may the best system, or amalgamation of systems, win. [Note well that in the preceding statement I have allowed some covert assumptions to sneak in! Logical analysis indicates that I assume that the optimum form of government for scientific progress is a democracy, and that the optimum form of economic system for scientific progress is capitalism. So, in a definite sense I am, as was Kantor, a true descendant of the eighteenth century enlightenment.]

Remember well that any set of data may be interpreted in myriad manners, as is exemplified in Mazurs (1957/1974) presentation of approximately 700 versions of the periodic table of chemical elements within the last 100 years! These variations were not solely the result of the discovery of new elements, but many definitely depended upon different manners of approaching these data. My son, who was then a teaching assistant in the graduate program in chemistry at the University of Michigan, reacted to Mazurs with the statement that some of the more recent tables had great potential for the teaching of certain aspects of chemistry as over and above the standard table posted on all lecture room walls in chemistry departments.

Perhaps the most productive (heuristic) position to take is that Kantor provided the best philosophical system up to this point in time for an objective and naturalistic science of behavior, while Skinner provided the best investigative system so far for this type of endeavor within science. Note well that, for Kantor, science was applied philosophy (Kantor, 1917), and that philosophy was essentially logical and empirical in nature (Kantor, 1969), and did not deal with specious metaphysical problems such as the nature of god, the existence of evil, etc. (Kantor, 1945-1950, 1981). This attitude or assumption, of course, obviates the usual distinction between the so called "talking cure" which aims to deal with the psychic, and the behavioral therapies which regard language as a type of behavior. Psycholinguistic behaviors comprise both extremely powerful stimuli and very powerful responses (see Kantor, 1936, 1953, 1977, as well as Skinner (1957), and many others too numerous to cite here).

Bentley may be unknown to many, so I simply state that he is the only non-psychologist I know of who as a philosopher of science has consistently and repeatedly denied the psycho-physical protopostulate (1908/1949, 1926/1936, 1932, 1935, 1954). One of Bentley's last works was coauthored with John Dewey (Dewey & Bentley, 1949).

A basic issue is that if the psychophysical protopostulate is denied, abandoned, or rejected, what is to be substituted for it? Some individuals are able to reject only portions of it, and in the false and misguided belief that they have actually completely rejected it, proceed on a reductionistic course of reducing the Soul or Mind to the central nervous system, or as Skinner called it, the conceptual nervous system (CNS). Perhaps concept is a more desirable term than assumption. Kantor's solution (and he did better than most of us have been able to in completely rejecting that mystical concept of a universe which is half physical and half psychic which so permeates our culture and language) was the construct of the coordinate stimulus-response function (1924-1926). Perhaps a quotation from a competent psychologist (long time professor at the University of Michigan) who confesses that he could not comprehend this aspect of Kantor's teaching will make this clear (Walker, nd ca 1993).

> To me his position sounded indistinguishable from Bishop Berkeley's subjective idealism. However, Kantor was vehement in denying that identification. He seemed to be saying there was no real world, therefore no mind-body problem of any stripe. While I 'believed' intensely in what Kantor was teaching us, I was never able to escape the forms of the English language to think, speak and write on the Kantorian theoretical plane (p. 184).

Walker did come close to the point here. To Kantor, there was no problem of a "real world." The so-called problem of whether there is "an external reality" is a pseudo-problem created by that weird, but venerable, politico-religious assumption of a psycho-physical universe. There is no need to assume a dual universe, and to become entangled in problems of "internal" and "external" realities. The simplest solution seems to be to ignore the dual universe assumption, since it leads to scientifically insoluble problems and is itself inherently self-contradictory. In addition, it is not derived directly from scientific investigation, but only indirectly through considerations of social control and cultural cohesiveness. What is needed are other assumptions which will allow the scientist to proceed in a clear, coherent, and productive manner. To the development of these other assumptions, and the explication of their consequences, Kantor was to devote the largest portion of his professional career.

One solution of psychologists to an assumed psychophysical universe is to simply devote themselves to the accumulation of empirical factoids, serene in the misguided and misleading belief that the facts somehow speak for themselves independently of theory. The history of science is filled with such individuals (Dampier, 1929/1966, and others). However, it has long been known that unacknowledged philosophical biases are the fatal flaw in most such persons (Burtt, 1924/1932, Kantor, 1958/1959). Another solution, the one chosen by Kantor, was the mirror image of this, and it was to develop a philosophy suitable for the pursuit of a natural science of psychology, and to this endeavor he remained true throughout his life. For him there were human beings (organisms) who interacted with their surroundings. One adjustment technique was called science, and this was the most satisfactory of all interactions for producing rules which resulted in more and more effective types of interactions with things and events. He elected to: (1) observe what scientists actually did; and (2), develop a set of rules; which (3), if followed, would result in better scientific work. That is, he argued that if one observed scientists at work, and then accurately described the behaviors they performed, and then reacted both critically and constructively, the inevitable result would be better, and more naturalistic science. Up to the point in time at which Kantor began to study there was excess pseudo-scientific verbiage which was not really based upon observation, and which therefore just got in the way of the scientific worker since the job of the scientist, properly conceived, was to observe and describe things and events. The point was discovery. And to discover most effectively the worker must not approach with notions which were not derived from previous observations. Political and religious concepts of a dualistic (half Mental and half Physical) world had been developed to organize and control cultural groups. That may have been a legitimate behavior for people in the distant past, whose aim was to produce a coherent and cohesive society with a high probability of survival in a hostile environment, but it was not scientific work. The scientist does things differently than the priest or politician. And the behavior of priests, politicians, and even scientists, was a proper domain of psychological events which are important objects for observation and study by the psychological natural scientist (see Kantor, 1963-1969 for explication of his natural science approach to the interbehaviors of scientists with their data).

Kantor chose to present his system in the formal manner which is associated with Euclid's *Elements* (ca 300 BCE). Those who have forgotten their high school geometry will find that Artmann (1999) gives a useful review, which should make readers more sympathetic to Kantor's (1958/1959) formal statements of the assumptions and theorems of interbehavioral psychology.

Note well that Kantor was always interested in developing solutions to problems of maladjustment. The first two years after his Ph.D. (1918-1920) were spent as an instructor at the University of Chicago. During this time he taught abnormal psychology two times, experimental psychology once, as well as introductory several times, and published his first independent works. Two of his first four published papers (1918, 1919) were devoted to the topic of abnormal behavior. To be sure, upon reading these it is clear that he was really presenting his first somewhat fumbling attempts to escape psychophysical dualism, and was not yet as successful as he would become in later years. However, a mature presentation was not to be long in appearing. The last chapter of the *Principles* (1924-1926) was a well developed description in terms of both: (1) a lack of necessary reactions; and (2) the acquisition of unsuitable ones (p. 459). Obviously, there are many details which I cannot explicate here.

His last (posthumously published) paper (1987) was an exposition of how interbehavioral psychology qualified as a therapeutic approach. During his long tenure at Indiana University he regularly taught "principles of psychopathology." In addition, he treated abnormal behaviors in both of his introductory textbooks (Kantor, 1933a; Kantor & Smith, 1975). Thus, we can see that his early interest in psychological maladjustment was maintained throughout his scholarly life and career. Other publications which support this generalization include his 1923 paper on personality (which certainly influenced Lundin's treatment of personality (1961, 1969), and which was reiterated, for example, in his introductory texts (1933a, 1975). Actually the first public presentation of Kantor's naturalism was a presentation to "the Psychological Seminar in the University of Minnesota, 1916-17" (Kantor, 1920, p. 260). Here he attacked what was widely thought to be the cutting edge of psychological science at that time: The testing movement (see Mountjoy and Cone, in press) Talk about swimming against the tide! Why, he even defended the concept that women have equal intelligence as compared to men, in this paper.

A Summary of Kantor's System in Brief

There are naturally occurring things and events, and these differ in their duration and inumberable other details. Events are short lived and examples would be my uttering a word, or a sentence. Things are maybe best thought of as slow events, such as a human being. That is, thinking of a normal human life span of say 70 years, as compared to the duration of mere seconds of a verbal utterance. Our time scale in scientific terms has expanded to billions of years for some things. The earth, for example, has existed as an entity for approximately four and one-half billions of years. Now, since we human beings interact with other things (or events), and produce behavior products which may, as in the case of writing, endure for many years, it seems useful to speak of the most effective of these interactions as science.

Scientific interbehaviors simply attempt to discover what is really going on in this concatenation of things and events of which we are an integral part. Yet, everyone has a different history of contacts with things and events, and these inevitably result in different reactions to them. The most deviant reactions serve as the best examples. Some people seek out classes of stimuli which most of us avoid: For example, those we term masochists who obtain sexual orgasm only when tissue injury accompanies other stimulation; or those we term sadists who obtain sexual gratification only by inflicting tissue injury upon others. We attempt to avoid having our scientific work influenced by personal histories which produce behaviors such as these, and among those personal histories we must include exposure to the politico-religico mythologies of our specific cultural group and/or sub-group. For example, bad science is one result of our western European cultural bias toward a single god, which deity some opine, may be influenced by prayer. Anthropologists of western European cultural background (i.e., Christians) have seized upon this notion of intercessionary prayer to separate their "advanced religion" from the "primitive magic" of "uncivilized savages," on the ground that the "primitive" belief is that with magic one can force the gods to bend to one's will. The "advanced" belief is that the deity must be supplicated, and cannot be forced to obey. Why "advanced?" Only because of their membership in a cultural group (Christians) which already so believes. Now, if I could discern the religious origin of this bit of so-called-science as an undergraduate, why is it that Ph.D.'s in anthropology still have problems? Well, in brief, they have not totally rejected the psychophysical protopostulate (I love how that phrase rolls off the tongue).

Serious debate concerning the relationships between scientific work and religious institutions emerged with the advent of the heliocentric hypothesis of our solar system developed by Copernicus (1473-1543). It is well known that Galileo (1564-1642) spent the last years of his life in confinement for advocating the Copernican hypothesis. These battles between science and religion have been described by Draper (1874) and White (1898/1995). An historical analysis of the abandonment of religion during recent times is provided by Turner (1985). A more contemporary viewpoint may be found in a recent issue of a popular magazine (Frazier, 1999).

Kantor's Influences Upon the Behavior Therapies

Name recognition, and Smith's (1990/1993) citation study, both lead to the conclusion that Kantor's influence is a reasonable topic for investigation. Here I present some preliminary data which should be examined in order to determine the extent to which Kantor has been influential, or alternatively, to what extent he should have been influential, but was not. My own examination continues, but replication by independent observers is one of the hallmarks of a natural science. Be reminded that the study of the history of a natural science is itself an example of working as a natural scientist (Kantor, 1963-1969, 1976).

Event Driven (No Direct Contact with Kantor)

Many scientists work in a manner which is compatible with the interbehavioral system, but apparently have had no direct contact with Kantor or his writings. I prefer to call these individuals "event driven" because frequently in our conversations Kantor argued that since he himself was both event oriented, and relatively free of handicapping cultural mythology, all scientists would eventually conform to his position. Examples may be found in Smith (1990/1993) and Smith & Smith (1996), while Rose's (1997) discussion of biological processes serves as a most compelling example.

Formal Students

Kantor rejected the "great man" approach to history, and with equal vigor, the notion that we are all passive victims of our culture. Instead he opted for an interactional approach which included the cultural variables, and each person's individual developmental history, which in combination with biological conditions produced a unique individual. He argued that an interaction between these two variables might combine to produce a scientist who would produce a unique solution to scientific problems (Kantor, 1976; Mountjoy & Cone, in press). In his formal classes he attempted to facilitate a problem solving approach to scientific work rather than a slavish acceptance of his own system. Often he stated that he would be a failure if his students did not progress further than he himself had been able to in the development of a natural science of psychology. However, he did insist upon students' appreciating his own critical approach to the commonly accepted cultural mythology of a psychophysical universe. In my opinion, there was a common core emphasis upon a problem solving approach which was shared by all of the faculty in the psychology department at Indiana University when I was in residence between 1949 and 1954. I assume that Kantor played a role in producing that approach among his colleagues. At any rate, the department did produce a number of individuals who were achievers within psychology.

The students whose dissertations and theses could be ascertained to have involved Kantor as Chair were listed by Hearst and Capshew (1988) (records of faculty directors were not kept carefully in early years), and I present them here in chronological order: 1934: Jerry W. Carter (M.A.); 1936: Paul M. Schroeder (M.A.); 1937: Ignacio T. Briones (M.A.); 1938: Ignacio T. Briones (Ph.D.); 1938: Jerry W. Carter (Ph.D.); 1942: J. W. Bowles (M.A.); 1942: John Bucklew (Ph.D.); 1943: Robert W. Lundin (M.A.); 1944: Annemarie Lehndorff (M.A.); 1944: Nicholas H. Pronko (Ph.D.); 1947: David T. Herman (Ph.D.); 1947: Robert W. Lundin (Ph.D.); 1947: D. Morgan Neu (M.A.); 1948: Harris E. Hill (Ph.D.); 1948: Irvin S. Wolf (Ph.D.); 1951: Marjorie P. Mountjoy (M.A.); 1952: J. W. Bowles (Ph.D.); 1953: Paul T. Mountjoy (M.A.); 1954: Solomon Weinstock (Ph.D.); 1957: Paul T. Mountjoy (Ph.D.). That is a total of 14 individuals, and perhaps more, since the early records (roughly the decade of the 1920's) are so incomplete.

Here, I cite some publications of selected individuals from the above list who have published items which appear to me to be worth consulting: Carter (1937a, 1937b, 1937c, 1938, 1939, 1968), Louttit & Carter (1939); Briones (1937), Bowles & Pronko, (1949), Bucklew (1941, 1943, 1958), Bucklew & Hafner (1951; Lundin (1961, 1965, 1969); Mountjoy (1957, 1976, in press a, in press b), Mountjoy & Cone (1995, 1997, in press); Mountjoy & Ruben (1983); Pronko (1946, 1980,), Pronko & Hill (1949), Pronko & Bowles (1951), Pronko & Herman (1982); Herman et al. (1957); Hill (1944a, 1944b, 1945); and Wolf (1958a, 1958b). The major contributions of Mountjoy are not well represented by the references cited above for him. In fact, his editorial work on *The Record*, and especially his participation in the development of the behavioral graduate program at Western Michigan University, constitute contributions which will impact the scientific culture some years into the future.

Other graduate students at Indiana who were influenced by Kantor (but did not have him as the Chair of their committees, and there are no available public records that I know of as to whether he served on their committees) include (in alphabetical order): Charles Boltuck, John F. Brackman, Sam L. Campbell, Robert S. Daniel, Donald Doehring, Paul Fuller, Frederick P. Gault, Joel Greenspoon, John Grossberg, Adolph Jack Hafner, Lloyd E. Homme, Billy L. Hopkins, Lawson Hughes, Gilbert R. Johns, Arthur Kahn, Fred Kanfer, Neil D. Kent, Parker E. Lichtenstein, David O.

Lyon, Marion W. McPherson, James D. Miller, Edith Neimark, Stanley C. Ratner, Samuel H. Revusky, Julian B. Rotter, Max S. Schoeffler, William A. Shaw, Dewey A. Slough, Edward L. Walker, and Don Zimmerman. In addition, Cromwell (Cromwell & Snyder, 1993), has stated that his undergraduate senior seminar course with Kantor influenced his entire career (see also Wynne, Cromwell & Matthysse, 1978, and Anonymous, 1995). Noel W. Smith also completed the undergraduate senior seminar under Kantor, but was prevented from further academic work with Kantor by his retirement in 1959. My criteria for inclusion of the above list are both personal communications and publications that I have been able to discover.

Here, I cite some publications of selected individuals: Fuller ((1949, 1973, 1987); Greenspoon (1955); Grossberg (1972, 1981), Hafner (1958); Kanfer & Phillips (1970); Lichtenstein (1983, 1984); Mountjoy (1957, 1976, 1980, 1987, in press a, in press b), Ratner (1957), Ratner & Rice (1963), Ratner, Gawronski & Rice (1964); and Rotter (1942, 1954).

Examination of Hearst & Capshew's (1988) listing of MA and Ph.D.'s granted at Indiana reveals that studies of verbal conditioning constitute a noticeable category. While Skinner (1957) certainly played a role here because of his tenure as chair of the department for two years, it is important to note that Kantor treated language interbehaviors naturalistically in a series of papers beginning in 1921 and 1922, and culminating in his book of 1936 (and later in 1977).

Colleagues of Kantor

Many professional psychologists, and other scientists who had already completed their formal training at institutions other than Indiana University, became interested in Kantor as a result of personal contacts/reading, and so on. Herewith, I list some of these in alphabetical order: Don Baer, S. Howard Bartley, Sid Bijou, Joseph V. Brady, Al Cone, Donna Cone, J. J. Gibson, Israel Goldiamond, Emilio Ribes, Nate Schoenfeld, B. F. Skinner, William Stephenson, Paul Swartz, William S. Verplanck, and A. P. Weiss. This list contains 14 names, but many other examples may be found in Smith, Mountjoy and Ruben (1983) and Smith (1990/1993).

Here I shall be extremely selective in citing publications: Bijou (1981), Bijou & Ghezzi (1994), Bijou & Ribes (1996); Brady (1970, 1975); Schoenfeld (1969, 1974, 1993); Swartz (1963); Verplanck (1983); and Weiss (1925/1929).

In some cases, both undergraduates and graduate students at Indiana University were influenced by Kantor, but completed their graduate work at other institutions. These include David Bakan (1952, 1966), Rue Cromwell, Edward Walker, and Donald W. Zimmermann (1979, 1982). Bakan told me in 1997 that he went to Indiana University because he felt that Davis and Kantor were the outstanding psychologists in this country at that time.

Students of Kantor's Students

Also, there are the students of Kantor's students. For convenience and brevity, I list only some of whom I know, however, these have been remarkably productive in terms of publications: Dennis J. Delprato (via Stan Ratner); Linda (nee Parrot) J.

Hayes (via Paul Mountjoy); Ed Morris (via Parker E. Lichtenstein, Irvin S. Wolf, and Sid Bijou); Gerald L. Shook (via Mountjoy); and Douglas Ruben (via Paul Mountjoy).

Selected references include: Delprato, (1995), Delprato and McGlynn (1988), Delprato and Midgley (1992), Ruben and Delprato (1987); Hayes, (Parrot, 1984), Hayes and Ghezzi, (1997); Morris, (1982); Ruben, (1983, 1984a, 1984b, 1985a, 1985b, Barrer & Ruben, 1984, Ruben and Delprato, 1987, Koziol, Stout, & Ruben 1993). Although references could be cited for Shook, it appears most appropriate to indicate that the Society for the Advancement of Behavior Analysis presented a twenty-five year career award for Public Service in Behavior Analysis to him at the 1999 convention of The Association for Behavior Analysis in Chicago, IL. This award was bestowed primarily for his work on developing testing and legislative procedures for National Certification of Behavior Therapists.

The Psychological Record

It may be that the best known of Kantor's actions to further the natural science of psychology was his founding of *The Psychological Record* in 1937 (Mountjoy and Cone, 1997, in press). This was the first psychological journal to actively seek manuscripts which had an authentic natural science orientation. After its rebirth in 1956 by Swartz (Bartlett, 1997), Wolf and Mountjoy accepted the responsibility of editing it, and later passed that duty on to Charles Rice, who is the current Editor. At the time of this writing, *The Record* is in its 49th year of publication, and thus has contributed to the dissemination of psychological research and theory for nearly 50 years. Many papers which may be labeled Experimental Analysis of Behavior and/or Applied Analysis of Behavior types have been published in *The Record*, both prior to and following the establishment of the journals which bear the acronyms of *JEAB* and *JABA*. Additionally, many cognitive behavior therapy papers have appeared in the pages of *The Record.*

Kantor remained deeply involved in the editorial affairs off *The Record* until his death.

Interbehavioral Research

Kantor not only encouraged laboratory work by his students; he also regarded experimentation as essential to scientific work and progress (Kantor, 1978, 1959/1960). In so far as he was concerned, each and every thing and event was subject to experimental manipulation and scrutiny *in principle.* He himself had clinical skills, and actually was the hypnotist in the Davis and Kantor (1935) report on changes in physiological measurement associated with hypnosis. Thus it seems appropriate to cite reports which are either directly related to the interbehavioral framework and/or at least compatible with it. One example which rewards attention is Kantor's analysis of the experimental analysis of behavior (1960).

Other selected examples include these: Wahler was introduced to interbehaviorism by Verplanck. Wahler and his associates have vigorously evaluated the role of setting factors across a spectrum of situations (e.g., Wahler & Dumas,

1989). Hart & Risley (1995, 1999) have diligently recorded the actual (literally millions of them!) linguistic interactions of young children learning to speak. They deserve high praise for these heroic activities. Their two reports clearly indicate the misleading nature of purely physicalistic descriptions of "environments" as influences upon behavior. The data necessary to understand the interbehavioral evolution of language are the sequential interactions of children with their stimulating surroundings. That is, the important sets of data include the smallest details of interactions. If Kantor was alive to peruse these reports I am confident that he would have found them to be praiseworthy.

Plomin (1994) is a geneticist/psychologist who has attempted to transcend the sterility of the conceptual dichotomy between "nature" and "nurture" by actual description of the "interplay" between genetic and experiential factors. This is a stimulating work in spite of what I regard as certain conceptual deficiencies. Diamond (1997) has presented an interesting analysis of the role of geographic factors in cultural evolution. Kantor has spoken of such aspects of events as either hindering or facilitating conditions.

Smith has conducted both empirical (1976a, 1976b) studies and theoretical analyses (1982, 1984), as well as having attempted a generalized description of interbehavioral therapy procedures (1978).

Stephenson (1984) reported a long lasting positive regard for Kantor, and has long associated the Q-Methodology which he has developed with the interbehavioral system. Q-Sorts are one manner of studying those difficult to observe interbehaviors in which the stimulus object is not readily apparent. These events are frequently referred to as "subjective" or "private."

An interesting review of developments within the interbehavioral system of psychology (as reflected in *The Psychological Record* from 1937 to 1983) has been presented by Ruben (1984b). This would serve as useful background and a solid foundation for a review which would include additional published sources.

Summary and Conclusions

Robert Kantor gave us a way of looking at (perceiving) the world which allowed us to bypass the hoary traditions of nearly two millennia of conceiving reality as having two levels of existence: The tangible world of science and its exact linguistic opposite, the purportedly intangible world of spirit, which is the ultimate and absolute cause not only of behavior, but indeed of everything.

We may conceive of his writings as in large part consisting of rules of scientific behavior. Somewhat loosely we may regard them as functioning in the Skinnerian sense of rule governed behavior. Of course, Kantor himself preferred the term "assumption" with a very specific meaning of having been derived from interaction with things and events rather than just some proposition(s) which someone dreamed up arbitrarily out of the blue. (See Artmann, 1999, as well as Kantor, 1945-1950, 1958/1959, for discussions of the roles of assumptions, or axioms, and their origins, in both the deductive sciences and the inductive sciences.)

Assumptions may be ranged on a continuum from the most abstract to the most concrete. For example, from science is the best way to learn about things and events (Kantor, 1958/1959) through many intermediate stages to the discussion of "Applied Subsystems" to which he devoted chapter 17 (Kantor, 1958/1959, p. 170-178).

The psychological event is not an expression of the inner essence of the person, but a complex concatenation, or interaction, among the actual factors involved in, or present in, the event. We can categorize these in a general way as (1) an organism or biological entity, (2) a stimulus object, (3) the surroundings and limits, and (4) the history of interactions of that Organism with that Stimulus Object.

Note that we may substitute other terms as equivalences which are used by other individuals. Surroundings and limits are environment, reinforcement, etc. That is, all scholars have always been interacting with the same things and events that Kantor interacted with. Almost all scholars are limited by concepts that do not truly reflect things and events but instead reflect concepts derived from the general religio-politico conditions of Western European culture to which I have so frequently alluded already, and which Kantor (1963-1969) described so eloquently.

Kantor always sought the most general statement possible. For example, "things and events" are a continuum from relatively stable things such as the earth (four-and one-half billions of years old – though constantly changing) to events such as the relatively fleeting psychological events (such as a linguistic utterance) which may occupy only some portion of a second, or up to a few seconds of time.

Thus, interbehavioral therapy does not deal with the Soul or Mind but with behaviors, with behavioral events, the totality of complete events. No therapist knows prior to interaction with the patient what aspect(s) of the behavioral events may need to be changed or modified to produce the desired (socially acceptable) outcome. And, what assumptions may (must) be made in arriving at the concept of the desired outcome? After all, that concept of a desired outcome is actually a behavior performed by the therapist. Hopefully the construct of a desired outcome is based upon the expectations of the social/cultural group(s) to which the client belongs, not necessarily only those to which the therapist belongs! (See M. Meyer, 1922, 1927 re: "the other one," which is his mnemonic for the necessity of an observer external to the psychological event.)

Choice of words is quintessentially important if we are to communicate with our audience, whether that audience be lay, or patient-client, or professional peers. My interbehavioral history with respect to many words is extremely different from that of other individuals. For example, psychology is the study of the Mind or Soul to the majority of both lay and professional Americans, rather than the study of the interactions of organisms with objects as it was to Kantor, and I devoutly hope it is to me.

Postscript

The evidence discussed above leads me to conclude that Kantor played a reasonably important role in the development of the theoretical foundations for behavior therapy through his efforts at construction of a system for a natural science of psychology. In addition, he devoted a remarkable amount of energy to the dissemination of supportive research activities with his founding and support of *The Psychological Record*, and his teaching activities. Even after retirement, until his hearing impairment made it impossible to react to questions from the audience, he continued to travel and lecture. Indeed, he devoted his life to the pursuit of a natural science of psychology. What better epitaph could there be?

Immediately prior to his fatal seizure, Robert was preparing a never to be completed paper for *The American Psychologist*, and his daughter later found a handwritten note on his desk which may have been intended as a title within the text, or perhaps a general concluding statement for that paper. I quote it in full as it does summarize his life work in one pithy statement (Mountjoy and Hansor, 1986, p. 1297):

> No spirits, wraiths, hobgoblins, spooks, noumena, superstitions, transcendentals, mystics, invisible hands, supreme creator, angels, demons...[ca 1984].

References

With some annotations. Certain of these references may be of antiquarian interest only, but others are quite seminal. This list is, of course, historically incomplete as it centers upon my discovery of items which are by and/or relatable to J. R. Kantor. For a more complete, though, of course now dated by the inevitable passage of relentless time, list of references concerning behavior therapy, see Kazdin (1978). I must admit that my selection criteria might be argued to have been not always consistent. At times a selection was made based upon its early date, and at other times I considered content as more important. For some individuals, I listed more works in order to characterize their career. In my own defence, I state that I used my judgement as to what criteria would serve this audience best, and still produce a reference list of a manageable size. The annotations serve as a substitute for a fuller discussion of the work of many of the individuals cited due to constraints upon space available. Some might object to my inclusion of "popular" works, written for the lay audience, however, I regard the education of mankind into the nature of science to be essential for all citizens. After all, they vote for/against the people who provide the monies to allow us to do our work.

American Psychiatric Association. (1952/1994). *Diagnostic and statistical manual of mental disorders* (4th ed.), 1994. Washington, DC: American Psychiatric Association. (1st ed., 1952.)

Anonymous. (1995). An interbehavioral approach to the study of psychopathology: An interview with Rue Cromwell. *The Interbehaviorist*, *23*, 9-11.

Artmann, B. (1999). *Euclid: The creation of mathematics*. New York: Springer-Verlag. (The first seven chapters (especially) indicate the importance of axioms and definitions in mathematics; a position which Kantor and others have extended to the empirical sciences.)

Augustine, Saint. (ca. 399/1912). *Confessions*. (W. Watts, tr.; Loeb Classical Library). London: Heinemann.

Bakan, D. (1952). The exponential growth function in Herbart and Hull. *American Journal of Psychology, 65*, 307-308.

Bakan, D. (1966). The influence of phrenology on American psychology. *Journal of the History of the Behavioral Sciences, 2*, 200-220.

Barrer, A. E., & Ruben, D. H. (1984). *Readings in brain injury*. Guilford, CT: Special Learning Corp. (Useful for education of lay public, especially family members, because of emphasis upon rehabilitation, social adaptive living, and community reintegration.)

Bartlett, N. R. (1997). The Psychological Record: Rebirth in 1956. *The Psychological Record, 47*. 21-24.

Bentley, A. F. (1895). The units of investigation in the social sciences. *The Annals of the American Academy of Political and Social Sciences*, Philadelphia, *5*(6), 915-941. (Publication version of his Ph.D. dissertation.)

Bentley, A. F. (1908/1949). *The process of government*. Chicago: The University of Chicago Press. (Reissued 1935, Bloomington, IN: The Principia Press; and, 1949, in a new edition, with an introduction by H. T. Davis, Evanston, IL: Principia Press of Illinois.)

Bentley, A. F. (1926/1936). *Relativity in Man and Society*. New York: G. P. Putnam's Sons. (Reissued, 1936, Bloomington, IN: The Principia Press).

Bentley, A. F. (1932). *Linguistic analysis of mathematics*. Bloomington, IN: The Principia Press. (This contains his answer to the Whitehead & Russell *Principia Mathematica* [1910-1912/1926-1927], which argues that all knowledge may be reduced to a few mathematical and logical statements. The converse, that all knowledge may be deduced from a limited number of propositions, is also proposed. Bentley disagrees vehemently.)

Bentley, A. F. (1935). *Behavior, knowledge, fact*. Bloomington, IN: The Principia Press.

Bentley, A. F. (1954). *Inquiry into inquiries*. Boston: Beacon Press. (Contains complete list of his publications.)

Bijou, S. W. (1981, May). Child development and interbehavioral psychology. Presented at the meeting of the Association for Behavior Analysis, Milwaukee, WI.

Bijou, S. W., & Ghezzi, P. M. (1994). *Outline of J. R. Kantor's psychological linguistics*. Reno, NV: Context Press.

Bijou, S. W., & Ribes, E. (1996). *New directions in behavior development*. Reno, NV: Context Press.

Bowles, J. W., & Pronko, N. H. (1949). Reversibility of stimulus function under hypnosis. *The Journal of Psychology, 27* 41-47.

Brady, J. V. (1970). Some conceptual problems and psychophysiological experiments. In M. B. Arnold (Ed.), *Feelings and emotions, the Loyola symposium*. New York: Academic Press.

Brady, J. V. (1975). Toward a behavioral theory of emotion. In L. Levi (Ed.), *Emotions: Their parameters and measurements.* New York: Raven Press.

Brewer, R. (1960). A brief history of ecology: Part I - pre-nineteenth century to 1919. *Occasional Papers of the C. C. Adams Center for Ecological Studies, 1,* 1-18.

Briones, I. T. (1937). An experimental comparison of two forms of linguistic learning, *The Psychological Record, 1,* 205-214. (I must confess that I am deplorably ignorant concerning his later career, although I know that he occupied a special place in Kantor's life. Tears came to the eyes of Bobby when she spoke to me about Briones after her father's death. Briones may have returned to his native land to teach.)

Bucklew, J., Jr. (1941). An experimental set-up for the investigation of language problems. *Journal of Experimental Psychology, 28,* 534-536.

Bucklew, J., Jr. (1943). An exploratory study in the psychology of speech reception. *Journal of Experimental Psychology, 32,* 473-494.

Bucklew, J, Jr. (1958). Evidence from retrograde amnesia for a unit of behavior higher than the stimulus-response. *The Psychological Record, 8,* 13-16.

Bucklew, J., Jr., & Hafner, A. J. (1951). Organismic versus cerebral localization of biological defects in feeblemindedness. *The Journal of Psychology, 32,* 69-78.

Burtt, E. A. (1924/1932). *The metaphysical foundations of modern physical science: A historical and critical essay.* London: Routledge & Kegan Paul Ltd. (Second, revised edition, 1932.) (Argues that it is impossible to understand modern physics without understanding the philosophy of Isaac Newton.)

Carter, J. W., Jr. (1937a). An experimental study of the stimulus function. *The Psychological Record, 1,* 33-48.

Carter, J. W., Jr. (1937b). A case of reactional dissociation (hysterical paralysis). *American Journal of Orthopsychiatry, 7,* 219-224. (Is this the first approximation toward behavior therapy? Perhaps. The date is right, and the content awaits analysis by a competent behavior therapist who is interested in the history of psychology.)

Carter, J. W., Jr. (1937c). A new serial presentation apparatus. *The Journal of General Psychology, 17,* 409-414.

Carter, J. W., Jr. (1938). An experimental study of psychological stimulus-response. *The Psychological Record, 2,* 33-92.

Carter, J. W., Jr. (1939). Manual for the psycho-diagnostic blank: A guide for diagnostic interviewing in psychological clinic work. *The Psychological Record, 3,* 249-290.

Carter, J. W., Jr. (1968). *Research contributions from psychology to community mental health.* New York: Behavioral Publications, Inc.

Cromwell, R. L., & Snyder, C. R. (Eds.). (1993). *Schizophrenia: Origins, processes, treatment, and outcome.* New York: Oxford University Press.

Dampier, W. C. (1929/1966). *A history of science and its relations with philosophy & religion.* London: Cambridge University Press. (Before 1956 there were 15 editions and printings.)

Darwin, C. R. (1859/1964). *On the origin of species*. London: W. Clowes and Sons. (A facsimile of the first edition with an introduction by Ernst Mayr, Cambridge, MA: Harvard University Press, 1964.)

Davis, R. C., & Kantor, J. R. (1935). Skin resistance during hypnotic states. *Journal of General Psychology, 13*, 62-81. (Kantor was the hypnotist in this study.)

Delprato, D., & McGlynn, F. D. (1988). Interactions of response patterns and their implications for behavior therapy. *Journal of Behavior Therapy and Experimental Psychiatry, 19*, 199-205.

Delprato, D. J., & Midgley, B. D. (1992). Some fundamentals of B. F. Skinner's behaviorism. *American Psychologist, 47*, 1507-1520.

Delprato, D. J. (1995). Interbehavioral psychology: Critical, systematic, and integrative approach to clinical services. In W. O'Donohue & L. Krasner (Eds.), *Theories of behavior therapy: Exploring behavior change* (pp. 609-636). Washington, D.C., American Psychological Association.

Dewey, J., & Bentley, A. F. (1949). *Knowing and the known*. Boston: Beacon Press.

Diamond, J. (1997). *Guns, germs, and steel: The fates of human societies*. New York: W. W. Norton & Company.

Draper, J. W. (1874). *History of the conflict between religion and science*. New York: D. Appleton and Company. (About 42 editions and printings up to 1937.)

Eriksson, P. S., Perfilieva, E., Bjork-Eriksson, T., Alborn, A., Nordborg, C., Peterson, D. A., & Gage, F. H. (1998). Neurogenesis in the adult human hippocampus. *Nature Medicine, 4*, No. 11, 1313-1317.

Frazier, K. (Ed.). (1999, July-August). *Skeptical Inquirer, 23*(4), 1-84. This special issue on science and religion is cited here by the name of the editor, and contains papers by many scientists, philosophers, and popular writers.

Fuller, P. R. (1949). Operant conditioning of a vegetative human organism. *American Journal of Psychology, 69*, 587-590.

Fuller, P. R. (1973). Professors Kantor and Skinner: The "Grand Alliance" of the 40's. *The Psychological Record, 23*, 318-324.

Fuller, P. R. (1987). From the classroom to the field and back. In D. H. Ruben & D. J. Delprato (Eds.), *New ideas in therapy*. Westport, CT: Greenwood Press.

Goldstein, K. (1939). *The organism*. New York: American Book Co.

Gould, E., Beylin, A., Tanapat, P., Reeves, A., & Shors, T. J. (1999). Learning enhances adult neurogenesis in the hippocampal formation. *Nature Neuroscience, 2*, No. 3, 260-265.

Greenspoon, J. (1955). The reinforcing effect of two spoken sounds on the frequency of two responses. *The American Journal of Psychology, 68*, 409-416.

Grossberg, J. M. (1972). Brain wave feedback experiments and the concept of mental mechanisms. *Journal of Behavior Therapy and Experimental Psychiatry, 3*, 245-251.

Grossberg, J. M. (1981). Comments about cognitive therapy and behavior therapy. *Journal of Behavior Therapy & Experimental Psychiatry, 7*, 25-33.

Hafner, A. J. (1958). Rorschach test behavior and related variables. *The Psychological Record, 8*, 7-12.

Hart, B., & Risley, T. R. (1995). *Meaningful differences in the everyday experiences of young American children*. Baltimore, MD: Paul H. Brookes Publishing Co.
Hart, B., & Risley, T. R. (1999). *The social world of children learning to talk*. Baltimore, MD: Paul H. Brookes Publishing Co.
Hau, L. V., Harris, S. E., Dutton, A., & Behrooz, C. H. (1999). Letter to *Nature, 397*, 594-598.
Hayes, L. J., & Ghezzi, P. M. (Eds.). (1997). *Investigations in behavioral epistemology*. Reno, NV: Context Press.
Hearst, E., & Capshew, J. H. (1988). *Psychology at Indiana University: A centennial review and compendium*. Bloomington, IN: Indiana University Department of Psychology.
Herman, D. T., Lawless, R. H., & Marshall, R. W. (1957). Variables in the effect of language on the reproduction of visually perceived forms [Monograph]. *Perceptual and Motor Skills, 7*, 171-186.
Hill, H. (1944a). Stuttering: I. A critical review and evaluation of biochemical investigations. *The Journal of Speech Disorders, 9*, 245-261.
Hill, H. (1944b). Stuttering: II. A review and integration of physiological data. *The Journal of Speech Disorders, 9*, 289-324.
Hill, H. (1945). An interbehavioral analysis of several aspects of stuttering. *The Journal of General Psychology, 32*, 289-316.
Honig, W. K. (1959). Perspectives in psychology XII. Behavior as an independent variable. *The Psychological Record, 9*, 121-130.
Hunt, M. (1999). *The new know-nothings: The political foes of the scientific study of human nature*. New Brunswick, NJ: Transaction Publishers.
James, W. (1890). *Principles of psychology* (2 vols.) New York: Holt.
Kanfer, F. H., & Phillips, F. S. (1970). *Learning foundations of behavior therapy*. New York: Wiley. (After Kantor's death a signed presentation copy of this well known book was found in Kantor's personal library: from Frederick Kanfer to J. R. Kantor.)
Kantor, J. R. (1917). *The functional nature of the philosophical categories*. Unpublished Doctoral Dissertation. The University of Chicago.
Kantor, J. R. (1918). Conscious behavior and the abnormal. *Journal of Abnormal Psychology, 13*, 158-167.
Kantor, J. R. (1919). Human personality and its pathology. *Journal of Philosophy, Psychology, Scientific Method, 16*, 236-246.
Kantor, J. R. (1920) Intelligence and mental tests. *Journal of Philosophy, Psychology, Scientific Method. 17*, 260-268.
Kantor, J. R. (1921). An objective interpretation of meanings. *American Journal of Psychology, 32*, 231-248.
Kantor, J. R. (1922). An analysis of psychological language data. *Psychological Review, 29*, 267-309.
Kantor, J. R. (1923). Does psychology need a new conception of personality? [Abstract]. *Psychological Bulletin, 20*, 80-81.

Kantor, J. R. (1924; 1926). *Principles of psychology* (Vols. 1-2). New York: Alfred A. Knopf. (Reissued by Principia Press, 1949. See especially the chapter on Abnormal Reactions and Psychopathic Personalities.)
Kantor, J. R. (1933a). *A survey of the science of psychology*. Bloomington, IN: Principia Press. (His first introductory text.)
Kantor, J. R. (1933b). In defense of stimulus-response psychology. *Psychological Review, 40*, 324-336.
Kantor, J. R. (1936). *An objective psychology of grammar*. Bloomington, IN: Indiana University. Reissued by Principia Press, 1952.
Kantor, J. R. (1945; 1950). *Psychology and logic* (Vols. 1-2). Bloomington, IN: Principia Press.
Kantor, J. R. (1947). *Problems of physiological psychology*. Bloomington, IN: Principia Press. (See especially for his pithy reactions to, and demolitions of, the specious and conventional arguments for the superiority of the human CNS to that of non-human animals, and against the construct of centers in the brain [read powers of the Soul.])
Kantor, J. R. (1953). *The logic of modern science*. Bloomington, IN: Principia Press.
Kantor, J. R. (1959). *Interbehavioral psychology* (2nd ed.). Bloomington, IN: Principia Press. (See especially Chapter 17, Applied Subsystems, the Subsystems of Psychotechnology, Educational Psychology, and Clinical Psychology, pp. 170-178.)
Kantor, J. R. (1963; 1969). *The scientific evolution of psychology* (Vols. 1-2). Chicago and Granville, OH: The Principia Press.
Kantor, J. R. (1969). Scientific psychology and specious philosophy. *The Psychological Record, 19*, 15-27;395-312.
Kantor, J. R. (1970). An analysis of the experimental analysis of behavior (TEAB). *Journal of the Experimental Analysis of Behavior, 13*, 101-108.
Kantor, J. R. (1976). The origin and evolution of interbehavioral psychology. *Mexican Journal of Behavior Analysis, 2*, 120-136.
Kantor, J. R. (1977). *Psychological linguistics*. Chicago, IL: Principia Press.
Kantor, J. R. (1978). Experimentation: The acme of science. *Mexican Journal of Behavior Analysis, 4*, 5-15.
Kantor, J. R. (1981). *Interbehavioral philosophy*. Chicago, IL: Principia Press.
Kantor, J. R. (1987). What qualifies interbehavioral psychology as an approach to treatment? In D. H. Ruben & D. J. Delprato (Eds.), *New Ideas in Therapy: Introduction to an interdisciplinary approach*. Westport, CT: Greenwood Press.
Kantor, J. R., & Smith, N. W. (1975). *The science of psychology: An interbehavioral survey*. Chicago, IL: Principia Press.
Kazden, A. E. (1978). *History of behavior modification*. Baltimore, MD: University Park Press.
Kempermann, G., Kuhn, H. G., & Gage, F. H. (1997). More hippocampal neurons in adult mice living in an enriched environment. *Nature, 386*, 493-495.

Koziol, L. F., Stout, C. E., & Ruben, D. H. (Eds.). (1993) *Handbook of childhood impulse disorders and ADH: Theory and practice.* Springfield, IL: C. C. Thomas.

Leyton, A. S. F., & Sherrington, C. S. (1917). Observations on the excitable cortex of the chimpanzee, orangutan, and gorilla. *Quarterly Journal of Experimental Physiology, 11*, 135-222. (Reports on 22 chimpanzees, three orangutans, and three gorillas, whose motor cortices were mapped by electrical stimulation, portions ablated, and then allowed to recover from the surgery. Upon reexamination, recovery of function was recorded. All experimental subjects were quite young, which is congruent with the report of Vining, et al (1997) concerning recovery of function in young human beings following hemispherectomy.)

Lewontin, R. C., Rose, S., & Kamin, L. (1984). *Not in our genes: Biology, ideology, and human nature.* New York: Pantheon.

Lichtenstein, P. L. (1983). The interbehavioral approach to psychological theory. In N. W. Smith, P. T. Mountjoy, & Rubin, D. H. *Reassessment in psychology.* Washington, DC: University Press of America.

Lichtenstein, P. L. (1984). Interbehaviorism in psychology and in the philosophy of science. *The Psychological Record, 34*, 455-475.

Louttit, C. M., & Carter, J. W., Jr. (1939). The psychodiagnostic blank. *Indiana University Psychological Clinics, 2*(7), 12.

Lundin, R. W. (1961). *Personality, an experimental approach.* Toronto, Ontario: Macmillan.

Lundin, R. W. (1965). *Principles of psychopathology.* Columbus, OH: C. E. Merrill Books.

Lundin, R. W. (1969). *Personality: A behavioral analysis.* Toronto, Ontario: Macmillan.

Marr, M. J. (1990). Behavioral pharmacology: Issues of reductionism and causality. In J. E. Barrett, T. Thompson, & P. B. Dews (Eds.), *Advances in behavioral pharmacology.* Hillsdale, NJ: Lawrence Erlbaum Associates, Publishers.

Mayr, E. (1982). *The growth of biological thought: Diversity, evolution, and inheritance.* Cambridge, MA: Harvard University Press.

Mayr, E. (1997). *This is biology.* Cambridge, MA: Harvard University Press.

Mazurs, E. G. (1957). *Graphic representations of the periodic system during one hundred years.* University, AL: The University of Alabama Press. (Second, revised edition, 1974.)

Meyer, A. (1934). The psychobiological point of view. In M. Bentley & E. V. Cowdry (Eds.), *The problem of mental disorder.* New York, McGraw-Hill.

Meyer, M. (1911). *The fundamental laws of human behavior: lectures on the foundation of any mental or social science.* Boston: Richard G. Badger, The Gorham Press.

Meyer, M. (1922). *Psychology of the other-one: An introductory text-book of psychology.* Columbus, MO: The Missouri Book Company.

Meyer, M. (1927). *Abnormal psychology: When the other-one astonishes us.* Columbia, MO: Lucas Brothers.

Morris, E. K. (1982). Some relationships between interbehavioral psychology and radical behaviorism. *Behaviorism, 10*, 187-216.

Mountjoy, P. T. (1957). Differential behavior in monozygotic twins. *The Psychological Record, 7*, 65-69.

Mountjoy, P. T. (1976). Science in psychology: J. R. Kantor's field theory. *Revista Mexicana de Analisis de la Conducta, 2*, 3-21.

Mountjoy, P. T. (1980). An historical approach to comparative psychology. In. M. R. Denny (Ed.), *Comparative psychology* (pp. 128-152). New York: John Wiley & Sons.

Mountjoy, P. T. (1983). A history of psychological technology. In N. W. Smith, P. T. Mountjoy, & D. H. Ruben, (Eds.), *Reassessment in psychology*, Washington, DC: University Press of America, Inc.

Mountjoy, P. T. (1987). The first systematic account of comparative avian behavior. In E. Toback (Ed.), *Historical perspectives and the international status of comparative psychology* (pp. 5-14). Hillsdale, NJ: Lawrence Erlbaum Associates, Inc.

Mountjoy, P. T. (in press a.) Biographical Entry; Kantor, Jacob Robert. *American National Biography*. New York: Oxford University Press.

Mountjoy, P. T. (in press b). Biographical Entry; Kantor, Jacob Robert. *The encyclopedia of psychology*. Washington, DC: The American Psychological Association.

Mountjoy, P. T., & Hansor, J. D. (1986). Jacob Robert Kantor (1888-1984). *American Psychologist, 41*, 1296-1297.

Mountjoy, P. T., & Ruben, D. H. (1983). *Behavioral genesis: Readings in the science of child psychology*. Lexington, MA: Ginn Custom Publishing. (Used in Psychology 160, Child Psychology, Western Michigan University.

Mountjoy, P. T., & Cone, D. M. (1995). The functional nature of the philosophical categories: Jacob Robert Kantor's doctoral dissertation. *The Interbehaviorist, 23*, 5-8.

Mountjoy, P. T., & Cone, D. M. (1997). Another new journal? *The Psychological Record*: Volumes I-V; 1937-1945. *The Psychological Record, 47*, 3-20.

Mountjoy, P. T., & Cone, D. M. (in press). A biographical sketch of Jacob Robert Kantor. In Morris, E. K. & Midgley, B. D. (Eds.), *Modern perspectives on J. R. Kantor and interbehaviorism*. Westport, CT: Greenwood Press.

O'Donnell, J. M. (1985). *The Origins of Behaviorism: American Psychology, 1870-1920.* New York: New York University Press.

Parrot, L. J. (1983). *Complex behavior: A systematic reformation of radical behavioral analysis*. Unpublished Doctoral Dissertation. Western Michigan University. (As was the case with Kantor's (1917) dissertation, she presents a program for making psychology into a natural science by analyzing the fundamental problem of the linguistic behaviors of scientists and philosophers.)

Parrot, L. J. (1984). J. R. Kantor's contributions to psychology and philosophy: A guide to further study. *The Behavior Analyst, 7*, 169-81.

Popplestone, J. A., & McPherson, M. W. (1994/1999). *An illustrated history of American psychology*. Madison, WI: Brown & Benchmark, Publishers. (Second Edition, 1999, Akron, OH: The University of Akron Press.)

Plomin, R. (1994). *Genetics and experience: The interplay between nature and nurture*. Thousand Oaks, CA: Sage Publications.

Pronko, N. H. (1946). Language and psycholinguistics: A review. *Psychological Bulletin, 43*, 189-239.

Pronko, N. H. (1980). *Psychology from the standpoint of an interbehaviorist*. Monterey, CA: Brooks/Cole Publishing Co.

Pronko, N. H., & Hill, H. (1949). A study of differential stimulus function in hypnosis. *The Journal of Psychology, 27*, 49-53.

Pronko, N. H., & Bowles, J. W. (1951). *Empirical foundations of psychology*. New York: Rinehart & Company, Inc. (With the collaboration of D. T. Herman, H. Hill, & J. Bucklew, Jr.)

Pronko, N. H., & Herman, D. T. (1982). From Dewey's reflex arc concept to transactionalism and beyond. *Behaviorism, 10*, 229-54.

Ratner, S. C. (1957). Toward a description of language behavior: I. The speaking action. *The Psychological Record*, 7, 61-64.

Ratner, S. C., & Rice, F. E. (1963). The effect of the listener on the speaking interaction. *The Psychological Record, 13*, 265-268.

Ratner, S. C., Gawronski, J. J., & Rice, F. E. (1964). The variable of concurrent action in the language of children: Effects of delayed speech feedback. *The Psychological Record, 14*, 47-56.

Ribes, E. (1984). Obituario: J. R. Kantor (1888-1984). *Revista Mexicana de Analisis de la Conducta, 10*, 15-36.

Rose, S. (1997). *Lifelines: Biology beyond determinism*. New York: Oxford University Press.

Rotter, J. B. (1942). A working hypothesis as to the nature and treatment of stuttering. *Journal of Speech Disorders*, 7, 263-288.

Rotter, J. B. (1954). *Social learning and clinical psychology*. Englewood Cliffs, NJ: Prentice-Hall.

Ruben, D. H. (1983) *The validation of a behavioral programmed text for increasing self-control attitudes*. Unpublished MA Thesis, Western Michigan University.

Ruben, D. H. (1984a). *Drug abuse and the elderly: An annotated bibliography*. Metuchen, NJ: Scarecrow Press.

Ruben, D. H. (1984b) Major trends in interbehavioral psychology from articles published in *The Psychological Record* 1937-1983). *The Psychological Record, 34*, 589-617.

Ruben, D. H. (1985a). *Philosophy journals and serials: An analytic guide*. Westport, CT: Greenwood Press.

Ruben, D. H. (1985b). *Progress in assertiveness, 1973-1983: An annotated bibliography*. Metuchen. NJ: Scarecrow Press.

Ruben, D. H., & Delprato, D. J. (Eds.). (1987). *New ideas in therapy: Introduction to an interdisciplinary approach*. Westport, CT: Greenwood Press.

Schoenfeld, W. N. (1969). J. R. Kantor's *Objective psychology of grammar* and *psychology and logic:* A retrospective appreciation. *Journal of the Experimental Analysis of Behavior, 12*, 329-47.

Schoenfeld, W. N. (1974). Notes on a bit of psychological nonsense: "Race differences in intelligence." *The Psychological Record, 24*, 17-32. (His Presidential Address to the Eastern Psychological Association, 1937. Compatibility with Kantor is obvious, even though he is not cited in the references.)

Schoenfeld, W. N. (1993). *Religion and human behavior.* Boston: Authors Cooperative, Inc. (Written in about four months in the Spring of 1971, it was distributed in manuscript form as a "test edition" in 1982, see prefaces, pp vi-xxvi. The volume may be interpreted on many levels as it is largely written in the vernacular.)

Sherrington, C. S. (1906). *The integrative action of the nervous system.* New Haven: Yale University Press.

Skinner, B. F. (1938). *The behavior of organisms.* New York: Appleton-Century-Crofts.

Skinner, B. F. (1957). *Verbal behavior.* New York: Appleton-Century-Crofts.

Smith, N. W. (1976a). Twin studies and heritability. *Human Development, 19*, 65-68.

Smith, N. W. (1976b). Longitudinal personality comparison in one pair of identical twins. JSAS *Catalog of Selected Documents in Psychology*, *6*(4), 106.

Smith, N. W. (1982). Brain, behavior, and evolution. *The Psychological Record, 32*, 483-490.

Smith, N. W. (1984). Fundamentals of interbehavioral psychology. *The Psychological Record, 34*, 479-494.

Smith, N. W. (1990/1993). *Greek and interbehavioral psychology: selected and revised papers of Noel W. Smith* (2nd rev. ed. 1993). Lanham, MD: University Press of America. (Contains a complete list of Kantor's publications, as well as a citation study of references to his works.)

Smith, N. W., & Shaw, N. E. (1979). An analysis of commonplace behaviors: Volitional acts. *The Psychological Record, 29*, 179-186. (Describes an interbehavioral approach to behavior therapy.)

Smith, N. W., Mountjoy, P. T., & Ruben, D. H. (Eds.). (1983). *Reassessment in psychology: The interbehavioral alternative.* Washington, DC: University Press of America. (This is a *Festschrift* for Kantor, and includes contributions both by his students and also by individuals who were not students in the formal sense, but were influenced by his works, and sometimes engaged in correspondence and other personal interactions with him. Although marred by numerous typographical errors due to hasty production, for which Mountjoy takes full responsibility, it was delivered into Kantor's hands by Mountjoy and Ruben late in 1983, shortly before Kantor's death in early 1984.)

Smith, N. W., & Smith, L. L. (1996). Field theory in science: Its role as a necessary and sufficient condition in psychology. *The Psychological Record, 46*, 3-19.

Stephenson, W. (1984). Methodology for statements of problems: Kantor and Spearman conjoined. *The Psychological Record, 34*, 575-588.

Swartz, P. (1963). *Psychology: The study of behavior.* Princeton, NJ: D. Van Nostrand Company, Inc. (An interbehavioral introductory text which has many interesting features.)

Turner, J. (1985). *Without God, without creed: The origins of unbelief in America.* Baltimore, MD: The Johns Hopkins University Press.

Ullmann, L. P., & Krasner, L. (1969/1975). *A psychological approach to abnormal behavior*, Englewood Cliffs, NJ: Prentice-Hall.

Van Praag, H., Kempermann, G., & Gage, F. H. (1999). Running increases cell proliferation and neurogenesis in the adult mouse dentate gyrus. *Nature Neuroscience, 2*, 266-270.

Verplanck, W. S. (1983). Preface. In N. W. Smith, P. T. Mountjoy, & D. H. Ruben (Eds.), *Reassessment in psychology*. Washington, DC: University Press of America.

Vining, E. P. G., Freeman, J. M., Pillas, D. J., Uematsu, S., Carson, B. S., Brandt, J., Boatman, D., Pulsifer, M. B., & Zuckerberg, A. (1997). Why would you remove half a brain? The outcome of 58 children after hemispherectomy–the Johns Hopkins experience: 1968 to 1996. *Pediatrics, 100*, 163-171.

Wahler, R. G., & Dumas, J. E. (1989). Attentional problems in dysfunctional mother-child interactions: An interbehavioral model. *Psychological Bulletin, 105*, 116-130. (Reviews about 100 empirical and theoretical papers. Concludes that environmental stressors, classifiable as interbehavioral setting factors, are important variables.)

Walker, E. L. (nd., ca. 1993). *CHAFF.* Mill Creek, WA: Hedgehog Press. (Walker's birth & death dates are 1914-1997. He was long time Professor at the University of Michigan, and a member of the board of editors of *The Psychological Record.* These reminiscences were privately printed and distributed).

Weiner, J. (1999). *Time, love, memory: A great biologist and his quest for the origins of behavior.* New York: Alfred A. Knopf. (A Pulitzer Prize winning author of popular scientific works describes Seymour Benzer's reduction of complex behavior to genetic components.)

Weiss, A. P. (1925/1929). *A theoretical basis of human behavior.* Columbus, OH: Adams. (Ranks Hunter, Kantor, and Lashly as the three eminent behaviorists of that time.)

White, A. D. (1896/1955). *A history of the warfare of science with theology in Christendom.* London: Macmillan and Company, and New York: D. Appleton & Company. (About 25 editions and printings up to 1955. The most convenient edition is the reissue of 1955, New York: Braziller. Because of its exhaustive treatment of the historical record it remains the definitive source for this topic. White was soon to be the first president of Cornell University, the first American university founded upon sectarian rather than secular principles.)

Whitehead, A. N., & Russell, B. (1910-1912/1925-1927). *Principia mathematica* (Vols. 1-3). Cambridge: Cambridge University Press. (Second Ed., 1925-1927.)

Wilson, E. O. (1998). *Consilience: The unity of knowledge.* New York: Alfred A. Knopff.

Wolf, I. S. (1958a). Stimulus variables in aphasia: I. Setting conditions. *Journal of the Scientific Laboratories, Denison University*, *44*, 203-217.

Wolf, I. S. (1958b). Stimulus variables in aphasia: II. Stimulus objects. *Journal of the Scientific Laboratories, Denison University*, *44*, 218-228. (These two papers of Wolf indicate the important roles of environmental conditions upon the behaviors of brain injured, aphasic, patients.)

Wolf, I. S. (1984). J. R. Kantor, 1888-1984. *The Psychological Record*, *34*, 451-453. (This obituary is in the fall issue, pp 448-634, which is a special issue devoted to the commemoration of Kantor's scholarly contributions to the natural science of psychology; includes his founding of *The Psychological Record* in 1937, and his continuing association with its editorial policies until his death.)

Wynne, L. C., Cromwell, R. L., & Matthysse, S. (Eds.). (1978). *The nature of schizophrenia; New approaches to research and treatment.* New York: John Wiley & Sons.

Zimmerman, D. W. (1979). Quantum theory and interbehavioral psychology. *The Psychological Record*, *29*, 473-485.

Zimmerman, D. W. (1982). The universe – an unscientific concept. *The Psychological Record*, *32*, 337-347.

Acknowledgments

My long term friends and colleagues Dr. Donna M. Cone, Dr. Dennis Delprato, and Dr. Noel W. Smith have read an early draft of this paper and their comments have contributed greatly to its current status. All errors remain, of course, my own responsibility. Dr. Howard E. Farris, Chair, Department of Psychology, Western Michigan University, and Dr. R. R. Hutchinson, President of The Foundation for Behavioral Resources, have provided logistical support in terms of office space, computer access, photocopying and mailing privileges.

Chapter 5

Child Behavior Therapy: Early History

Sidney W. Bijou
University of Nevada, Reno

Introduction

In keeping with the purpose of this conference, I will focus my remarks on the early history of child behavior therapy considered in its broadest sense. To this end I will present them in terms of the four topics suggested by William O'Donohue: (1) my intellectual biography, (2) my perception of the important developments in the rise of child behavior therapy, (3) detailed case studies of selected publications, and finally, (4) possible object lessons learned for the future.

Intellectual Biography

In reviewing my rather long history, I find that my intellectual biography with respect to the early history of child behavior therapy easily falls into two phases. The first pertains to my training and experience as a clinical psychologist, the second, to my training and experiences as a child psychologist focusing on the psychopathologies.

Phase One

The first phase began when I enrolled as a graduate student in psychology at Columbia University in 1935. At that time the department was proudly theoretically eclectic with a faculty consisting, among others, of Henry E . Garrett, Elizabeth Hurlock, Otto Klineberg, A. T. Poffenberger, A. J. Warden, and Robert S. Woodworth. Two events outside of my courses moved me in the direction of child clinical psychology: One, a self-selected internship in mental retardation, the other my thesis research.

The internship consisted of a summer at Letchworth Village, a large residential institution for severely retarded persons, which served families and social agencies mostly in the New York City area. Sponsored and supported by the New York State Department of Mental Health, the purpose was to attract more professionals to the field of mental retardation. Consequently, students in medicine, dentistry, nursing, education, social work, and psychology were recruited.

That summer provided a heady experience for me in that I had many contacts with the members of the staff and particularly the head psychologist, Elaine F. Kinder. It also afforded me an opportunity to learn more about the problems encountered in treating low-functioning persons in a large institution as well as a chance to interact with students in allied professions. But it was disappointing to see how limited the contributions of the clinical psychologists were, their only function being to administer psychological tests (mainly intelligence tests) to help the medical staff diagnose and classify the residents. Their training in areas other than test administration was completely wasted.

Incidentally, Uri Bronfenbrenner, known particularly for his ecological child development (e.g., Bronfenbrenner, 1992), grew up in the environment of Letchworth Village where his father was a well-respected research pathologist.

The second event that nudged me further in the direction of clinical psychology – my thesis research – was in fact a compromise. After reading two books by John B. Watson (1919, 1930), I became intrigued with his views and decided that I would like to do a behavioral experimental study with children. In my enthusiasm and naivete, I wrote to Watson, then vice president of the J. Walter Thompson Advertising Company, telling him of my interest in the behavioral approach to child development and asking him if he would be willing to suggest a topic for my master's degree research. He replied promptly with the suggestion that I study how young children learn "muscle sense." How, for example, does little Jimmy know that his arms are stretched out at shoulder height when his eyes are closed? He mentioned also that for subjects I might contact Patty Hill-Smith, director of the model kindergarten at the nearby Horace Mann School at Columbia's Teachers College. Although this kind of problem appealed to me, I could not find a member of the psychology department who was sufficiently interested to serve as my advisor. I was sorely disappointed but to progress in my graduate studies I undertook to complete a project begun by a faculty member, Louise E. Poole, with whom I had been taking a course. This project involved the measurement of nonverbal intelligence in young retarded children (Bijou, 1938), thus giving me an opportunity to test many retarded children and to learn more about the measurement literature.

After receiving my degree in 1937, I took a position as clinical psychologist at the Delaware State Mental Hygiene Clinic on the campus of the Delaware State Hospital, near Wilmington. The Clinic provided diagnostic services to adult patients in the hospital and to children and adults with mental health problems throughout the small state of Delaware. My job was to administer psychological tests and prepare reports for the psychiatrists to help them make diagnoses and recommendations.

The upside of the appointment was that for the first time I was exposed to patients of all ages and covering the entire range of mental health problems, since the Clinic served all the social and educational agencies in the state. I administered 33 different types of psychological tests to over 2000 patients. The downside was similar to that of the clinical psychologists at Letchworth Village: my duties were largely limited to testing and report writing.

It was at the Delaware Mental Hygiene Clinic that I worked with Joseph Jastak, the chief psychologist, to develop a clinical test of school achievement, the Wide Range Achievement Test (Jastak & Bijou, 1938). The need for such a test arose from Jastak's conviction that all "mental" diagnoses should be based, not on a single score, but on a profile of scores including basic school achievement (Jastak, 1934). Because a brief achievement test of reading, writing, and arithmetic was nonexistent, we constructed one that could be administered and scored in about fifteen minutes.

In addition to its use by many clinical psychologists, and later by psychometricians, the Wide Range Achievement Test was found to be a valuable screening measure for young children nationwide when the Head Start program was launched.

I left Delaware in 1939 to complete my graduate training. Because of Columbia's lack of theoretical focus, I decided to go to a different university. Before leaving Columbia, I confided my disappointment to one of my professors, George W. Hartmann, who suggested I consider studying with Kurt Lewin (1935, 1936), a brilliant neo-Gestaltist who had recently immigrated from Germany and was now at the University of Iowa. Acting on Hartmann's advice, I applied to and was accepted by the department of psychology and to my surprise was offered an assistantship. On my arrival in Iowa City, I learned to my chagrin that Lewin could not serve as my advisor because he was not a member of the psychology department; his appointment was in the Child Welfare Research Station (later the Institute of Child Development). The chairperson, John McGeoch, informed me that if I wanted to study psychology and keep the assistantship, I would have to select an area of concentration in psychology. I decided on learning since it was closest to my interest in child clinical psychology. Kenneth Spence was assigned as my adviser.

I did, though, take a course from Lewin titled, "Theory of Psychology and Personality Development." While Lewin was indeed a stimulating although somewhat disorganized lecturer, the content of his course was appealing inasmuch as it dealt with the behavior of children. But what bothered me was that Lewin's analysis of a child's behavior was in terms of correlated relationships. All the conditions of an interaction – situation, response, and motivation – were entered into a "field" on the basis of an individual's perceptions, hence the relationships among the variables were correlational rather than functional. My interest was on functional relationships. Besides, I was losing interest in Lewin's theory. I was beginning to believe, through the intensive learning course with Spence, that the learning theories of Hull, Tolman, and Guthrie held more promise than Lewin's for the future of psychology as a natural science.

The Iowa department at that time (1939-1941) was an exciting place for graduate students. Spence, armed with Hullian learning theory, was warring against Lewin and his field theory: Spence and his students (among them Isador Farber, Robert Grice, Arthur Irion, Howard and Tracy Kendler, and Benjamin Underwood) were doing research on learning and motivation using animals in mazes while Lewin and his students (among them Leon Festinger, Ronald Lippit, and Ralph White) were researching the similar topics with children in socially structured situations.

Among the highlights of my training at Iowa were Spence's two-semester course in animal learning and conditioning and his informal seminar , The Monday Night Group, which was devoted entirely to an intensive chapter-by-chapter review of Hull's manuscript for his *Principles of Behavior* (Hull, 1943); Gustav Bergmann's course in philosophy of science (mostly logical positivism); E. F. Lindquist's course in advanced statistics (mostly small sample research designs); and John McGeoch's courses, one in systematic psychology and the other in human learning (mostly rote memory studies).

For my stipend, I worked in the Department's clinic as an assistant to Charles Strother, administering psychological tests. The only feature of this experience that was new to me was working with many children and adults with speech problems.

Because of my interest in abnormal behavior, Spence permitted me to do my thesis on experimental neurosis in rats, modeled after Pavlov's studies with dogs . I constructed an apparatus that held the animal in a stationary position but allowed it to raise its head to lift a bar in response to a visual stimulus (Bijou, 1942, 1943). The experimental procedure followed the instrumental rather than the classical conditioning model. In this situation, the animals showed strong emotional behavior when required to make fine visual discriminations (Bijou, 1951).

By the time I received my degree, I was convinced with Hull that the objective of the science of psychology was to develop a general theory of behavior that would account for events between the stimulus input and the response output of an organism and that research should be on testing hypotheses to tease out the properties of the internal variables and their relationships. Although the theory dealt with the behavior of individuals, the research typically involved small-sample, group designs. The fact that, thus far, Hull's approach was based on the behavior of nonverbal organisms was not a matter of concern for him for he believed that the complex human behavior of verbal organisms would eventually be incorporated into the system. In this respect, the task ahead was to redefine Freud's concepts and principles in scientifically acceptable ways. Some of Hull's students had already begun to do that. Sears and his colleagues, for example, had been using Freudian concepts in their studies of children (Sears, Whiting, Nowlis, & Sears, 1953).

There was an interlude of about five years – from 1941 to 1946 – between receiving my degree and my first academic appointment. During that time, I spent two years as a research psychologist at the Wayne County Training School in Northville, Michigan, a residential school for high-grade retarded children, and three years in the military service, first administering intelligence tests at Induction Centers, then Air Force aptitude tests for selecting pilots, bombardiers, and navigators and finally, supervising psychological services at Convalescent Centers in resorts throughout the country.

Phase Two

The second phase of my experience and training began in 1946 with an academic appointment at Indiana University. I was recruited by B. F. Skinner, then chairman of the psychology department, to serve as assistant professor and director of the newly formed clinical program. The Department and Skinner wanted a clinical program with an experimental-learning orientation. My clinical experience in Delaware and in the military service plus my training in learning with Spence qualified me for this position.

I took on the first group of graduate students in clinical psychology with a course in experimental psychopathology which was saturated with references by Hull's students, among them Carl Hovland, Hobart Mowrer, Neal Miller, and Robert Sears. I also set up an animal laboratory to continue my thesis research on conflict. Once when I complained to Skinner that I could not get the differences in approach and avoidance gradients postulated by Miller (1944), he smiled and simply said, "The animal is always right."

Indiana was as intellectually exciting as Iowa, although in a different way. Here, frequent heated discussions took place among faculty and students over the merits and limitations of the Skinnerian, Hullian, and Kantorian views. There was a Skinner-Kantor, standing-room-only, joint seminar plus informal competing seminars by the students of Skinner and Hull. At the same time, ground-breaking research was being done by students, such as Bill Estes, Norman Gutman, Paul Fuller, and Joel Greenspoon.

During this time, I audited several lectures of J. R. Kantor's undergraduate class on psychopathology and had discussions with him about theory construction. I quickly learned that he took issue with Hull's view that psychology should study, almost exclusively, the presumed variables and events between stimulus input and response output of an organism. He argued, furthermore, that Hull's system was physically reductionistic and questioned his emphasis on the hypothetico-deductive method for theory construction and research, averring that both deductive and inductive methods are proper tools for psychology as a natural science.

In 1948, when Skinner left to take a permanent appointment at Harvard, I left to go to the University of Washington where I was appointed associate professor and Director of the Institute of Child Development. I was pleased to join the faculty at Washington for among other attractions (e. g., the ocean and mountains), I would get to know Edwin Guthrie, learn more about his learning theory and his research with George Horton on cats in a puzzle box. Unfortunately, Guthrie was no longer teaching; he was now vice-president of the University. But occasionally "just to keep his hands in" he would give a seminar. I audited one of these rare occasions which consisted of his telling stories, some related to learning, some not. When students raised questions critical of his theory, he would laugh and counter with one even more devastating. The students obviously enjoyed his stories. Incidentally, the undergraduates good-naturedly referred to the psychology department as offering only two courses: An introductory course on the behavior of cats in a puzzle box and a developmental course on the behavior of kittens in a puzzle box.

The Institute, which was established in 1910 to provide state-wide services to children, actually consisted of a two-room clinic, part of the Psychology Department in Denny Hall. The responsibility of the small staff was to provide psychological test services under the supervision of Stevenson Smith, a student of Guthrie. My conception of a child institute was rather different. I visualized it as a research organization consisting of a clinic, a preschool, and a child study unit. With the support of the Institute's Board of Directors, I arranged to move the Institute into the building which then housed only the University Nursery School. By 1950 the "new" Institute consisted of a Child Development Clinic, a two-unit Nursery School and a Research Laboratory.

With this expansion I launched what I hoped would be a research program on children based on Hullian principles, one similar to what Sears and his colleagues were doing at Iowa and Stanford. This group was engaged in two types of research: Correlational group studies of the relationship between parents and their young children (e.g., Sears, Whiting, Nowlis, & Sears, 1953) and laboratory studies of individual children using doll play techniques (e.g., Sears, 1947). I was primarily interested in their studies with individual children. On the basis of a review of the literature, I decided to carry out a study which had implications for the frustration-aggression hypothesis (Bach, 1945). The study would be concerned with the relationship between aggression in a social situation and fantasy aggression as manifested in a doll-play situation (fantasy aggression). In planning the experiment I realized that I would have to obtain teachers' ratings of children's aggressiveness, prepare a doll house simulation of a preschool, find or make a teacher doll and three children dolls, one being of the opposite sex of the subject, train two observers to record data from behind a one-way glass, then analyze their protocols in terms of frequency, direction and latency of aggression, and train a student to perform the task of an "experimenter," the person who interacts with the subject in the course of an experiment. All these requirements made me realize that laboratory research with children in the Hullian tradition was quite different from animal research which was relatively simple and included good control over the antecedent and consequent conditions of an objectively recordable response. The study was never done. Instead I turned to the only other procedure I knew – Skinner's operant conditioning model.

I built a toy-like apparatus, shown in Figure 1, consisting of three parts: a response mechanism, a trinket dispenser, and a recording pad. To make a response

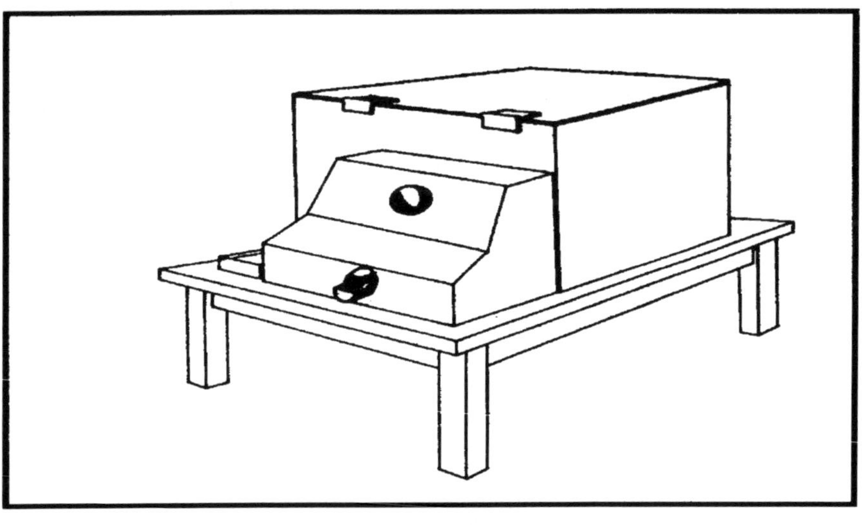

Figure 1. The ball dropping apparatus.

the child would simply take a ball from the receptacle and drop it into the hole above. The ball, a Spaulding handball, would activate the dispenser to deliver a trinket and then return to the receptacle for the next response, thus creating a free operant situation with objective, countable responses, a clearly discernible and manipulable consequence, and a potentially objective antecedent condition (Bijou, 1955).

With this crude device, I carried out two experiments (Bijou, 1957a) each showing that intermittent reinforcement was more resistive to extinction than continuous reinforcement in four-year-boys). However, I was disappointed with the results because the research design, which involved comparison of small groups, produced a relatively small number of responses (the means ranged in the order of 15.3 to 26.2 responses) compared to the large numbers of responses generally seen in operant infra-human studies. It was apparent that the design was more appropriate for theory testing than for demonstrating functional relationships.

For the next study (Bijou, 1957b), I built another apparatus (Fig. 2) which would allow me to follow operant conditioning principles scrupulously. Because the ball dropping response on occasion created recording problems (e. g., a child would miss the hole and go scrambling to retrieve it), I substituted a lever (an O-Cedar sponge mop handle) for a response. In addition, two sophisticated commercial instruments (Gerbrands) replaced my home-made devices: One for recording responses and stimulus events, the other for delivering trinkets as well as other small objects.

With this set-up, I studied the effect of several fixed-internal and fixed ratio-schedules of reinforcement on four-year-old boys and obtained hundred of responses in orderly relationships to the schedules. Samples of the data obtained are shown in Figure 3.

Figure 2. The lever-pressing aparatus.

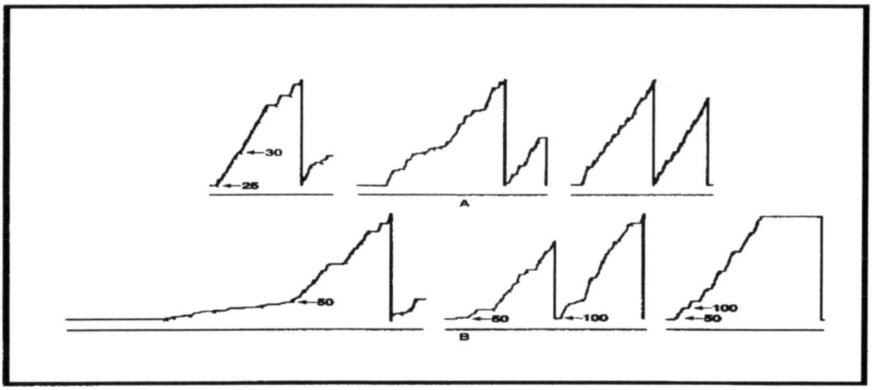

Figure 3. Cumulated responses of the first, third, and fifth sessions of two four-year old boys. Sequence A is on a fixed-interval schedule of reinforcement. Sequence B is on a fixed-ratio schedule of reinforcement.

On my next trip to the East Coast, I stopped to see Skinner in Cambridge and showed him some of these and other data. He was both surprised and pleased. Incidentally, in one of his last papers, Sears recognized that the externalization of the reinforcement mechanism (drive) in Skinner's system helped the behavioral approach move ahead.

I was now convinced that laboratory studies with children should be conducted in controlled settings like infra-human animal studies. To augment the Institute facilities, I built a mobile laboratory, a converted house trailer, shown in Figure 4, that could be easily towed to any nursery school in the Seattle area where additional studies could be carried out (Bijou, 1958a).

I also set up a research laboratory, similar to the one at the Institute, at the nearby Rainier State School for operant studies with retarded children (Orlando, Bijou, Tyler, & Marshall, 1960).

During the 1950's and 60's I recruited several new faculty members for the Institute staff, all of whom had training and experience in experimental studies with animals and/or children. Included were Donald Baer, who did his thesis research with kittens as subjects at the University of Chicago under Howard Hunt; Montrose Wolf who studied remedial reading with Arthur Staats at Arizona State University; Jay Birnbrauer who carried out learning studies at Indiana University, and Robert Orlando who did discrimination learning studies on children with retardation under David Zeaman at the University of Connecticut.

During this period the Institute attracted a group of highly talented graduate students, among them, Douglas Kenny, Ivar Lovaas, Robert Peterson, Donald Pumroy, Shirely Ann Spence Pumroy, Stephanie Stolz, Todd Risley, James Sherman, Robert Wahler, and Ralph Wetzel. A note regarding the training of graduate students at Washington: I had the unique experience of sponsoring the Ph. D. thesis of the daughter of the professor who sponsored my Ph. D. thesis. Shirley Ann Spence

Figure 4. Mobile child study laboratory.

Pumroy, the daughter of Kenneth Spence, carried out an operant study on the effects of reinforcement on resistance to extinction and emotional behavior with preschool children (Pumroy, 1954). As far as I know her father did not object.

Innovative research now flourished in all divisions of the Institute. From the laboratories came studies by Baer on escape and avoidance on two schedules of reinforcement (1960), on the effect of positive reinforcement on extinguishing responses (1961), on laboratory control of thumb sucking by withdrawal and re-presentation of reinforcement (1962a), and behavior avoiding reinforcement withdrawal (1962b); by Baer, Peterson, and Sherman on the development of imitation by reinforcing behavior to a model (1967; by Baer and Sherman on the control of generalized imitation (1964); by Bijou on patterns of reinforcement and resistance to extinction in young children (1957a), on operant extinction after fixed-interval schedules (1958b), on discrimination as a baseline for individual analysis of young children (1961); by Bijou, Lovaas, and Baer on experimental procedures for analyzing the interaction of symbolic social stimuli and children's behavior (1965); by Bijou and Oblinger on responses of normal and retarded children as a function of the experimental situation (1960); by Bijou and Orlando on single and multiple schedules of reinforcement with retarded children (1960, 1961); and by Bijou and Sturges on positive reinforcers for experimental studies with children – consumables and manipulables (1959).

From the nursery school came research after the teachers witnessed the results of a study which showed the power of the application of behavior principles. The director of the nursery school had confided in Montrose Wolf that her teachers had been unsuccessful in eliminating regressive crawling of a three-and-a-half -year-old girl even though they were giving her attention and support when she was crawling or sitting on the floor or ground on the assumption that the behavior was a symptom of stress. Wolf suggested that they do a little study of the problem in which they would give the child attention and support when she was standing and walking and would planfully ignore her when she was crawling or sitting on the floor or ground. Reluctantly, she and the teachers followed his suggestion and in a short time the crawling and floor sitting were eliminated. A brief reversal of conditions convinced them that the intervention was indeed effective (Harris, Johnston, Kelley, & Wolf, 1964). Working with members of the research staff, the nursery school staff then used the same method and procedure to eliminate operant crying and whining, isolate play, excessive passivity and excessive aggression and the development of motor skills (Hart, Allen, Buell, Harris & Wolf, 1964; Harris, Wolf, & Baer, 1964: Hart, Reynolds, Baer, Browley, & Harris, 1968); Johnston, Kelley, Harris, & Wolf, 1966; Sloane, Johnston, & Bijou, 1967).

From the Clinic came studies by Wahler on child-child interactions in free field settings (1967), infant-mother interactions (1969a), and oppositional children (1969b), and by Wahler, Winkel, Peterson, and Morrison on procedures for training mothers to serve as therapists for their own children (1965). A spin-off of this series was one in which a mother was trained in her home to be a therapist for her four-year-old boy with serious aggressive behavior (Hawkins, Peterson, Schweid, & Bijou, 1966). And finally, came the now classic clinical study by Wolf, Risley and Mees (1964) on a three-and- a -half -year-old, hospitalized, "schizophrenic" boy who needed training to wear his glasses to compensate for the surgical removal of cataracts.

These studies and their applications provoked discussions about the role of norm-reference and personality tests in child behavior therapy. It was noted that the investigators and practitioners did not use intelligence or projective tests, did not take into account psychiatric diagnoses, and did not make predictions about the outcome of treatment . All true. These previously almost mandatory practices were unnecessary because treatment was not linked with psychiatric diagnostic categories. Needed were only reliable assessment techniques for evaluating initial behavior repertoires, treatment progress, and follow-up. (Bijou & Peterson, 1971; Marholin & Bijou, 1978) It should be noted, nevertheless, that criterion-reference tests, such as checklists, were useful in many instances for planning treatment and academic programs.

In 1961 I spent a sabbatical year at Harvard with Skinner on a Senior National Institute of Mental Health Fellowship. I set up a laboratory at the Fernald State School near Cambridge to study complex discriminative behavior in retarded children. Using a match-to-sample apparatus developed by James Holland, I explored the programming of antecedent stimuli to facilitate the learning of right-left visual discrimination (Bijou, 1968). I also audited Skinner's large undergraduate lecture course which was the basis of his *Science and Human Behavior* (Skinner, 1953) and his weekly meetings of the "Pigeon Staff", an informal seminar for psychologists in and around Harvard for displaying and discussing data from their research with pigeons. Each session ended on a high note with a round of beer. And I spent considerable time in Skinner's Teaching Machine Project (Skinner, 1968), learning principles and techniques of programmed instruction.

While at Harvard I visited several special classes and programs for young retarded children in the Northeast. All seemed uninspired and relatively ineffectual. That impression together with my exposure to programmed instruction led me, on my return to Seattle, to construct an experimental classroom to individualize instruction for retarded children in residence at the Rainier State School. I recruited two behaviorally trained teachers – Cecilia Tague and John Kidder – and arranged for Montrose Wolf and Jay Birnbrauer to serve as consultants. Together they developed both a motivational system based on a token economy and a programmed curriculum for teaching reading, writing, arithmetic, and related subjects. The children attending the classes were considered serious behavior problems with IQ's in the low 60's. All not only made good progress, but their classroom problem behaviors were eliminated, and they actually enjoyed coming to class (Bijou, Birnbrauer, Kidder, & Tague, (1966). After the project was terminated, the reading program, now known as the Edmark Reading Program, was adapted for use with a computer touch- screen and is distributed by IBM (International Business Machine Company).

As the research of the Institute became nationally known (e.g., Kazdin, 1978), faculty members began to receive attractive offers from other universities. Since the majority of the members of the Psychology Department did not appreciate their accomplishment (many even disparaged their work as "unscientific"), they were unwilling to match their offers. As a result Baer, Wolf, Birnbrauer, and Orlando soon departed. Without the wholehearted support of the Department, it was difficult to recruit replacements. However, I was able, fortunately, to entice Howard Sloane to leave the Johns Hopkins School of Hygiene and Public Health and join the staff. The continued negative attitude of the Department led Howard and me to accept offers from the University of Illinois in 1965.

At Illinois I established the new Child Behavior Laboratory which consisted of six research rooms and two experimental classrooms for teaching and treating young handicapped children. Robert Peterson and Thomas Sajway were added to the staff in 1966 and research continued in the Laboratory (Peterson, 1968; Peterson, Cox, & Bijou, 1971; Sajway, Twardosz, & Burke, 1972; Sloane & MacAulay, 1968) and in the home (Peterson & Peterson, 1968; Zeilberger, Sampen, & Sloane, 1968). Among the talented graduate and post-doctoral students were Richard Amato, Tadashi Azuma, Leroy Ford, Arthur Miller, Edward Morris, Susan O'Leary, Joseph Parsons, Ely Rayek, Emilio Ribes, Howard Rosen, Grover Whitehurst, Barbara Wilcox, and Koaru Yamaguchi.

In the late 1960's I began to disseminate our knowledge in other countries. Most of my effort in this endeavor was devoted to psychologists and educators in Mexico and Japan. My venture into Mexico began with an invitation to give talks and workshops at the University of Veracruz at Xalapa and at the National

Autonomous University of Mexico in Mexico City in 1967. In order to spread "the word" to larger audiences, Emilio Ribes, Professor of Psychology at the University of Veracruz at Xalapa, persuaded his department to appoint him and me as co-presidents of a new organization, The International Symposium on Behavior Modification, to sponsor conferences throughout Mexico and South America. At each meeting we arranged to have six to eight psychologists present their research and describe service programs on a topic selected to be of central interest by the local psychologists. In the ten years, between 1971 and 1981, 13 well-attended conferences were held in Xalapa, Mexico City, Caracas, Panama City, Bogota, Lima, and Brasilia, covering such topics as standards for paraprofessional training, early education, delinquency and aggression, self-control, and various clinical issues.

My dissemination activities in Japan began after I had participated in the 1972 meeting of the International Congress of Psychology held in Tokyo. Kaoru Yamaguichi, Professor of Special Education, Tokyo Gakugei University, invited me to give an address in Tokyo and Tadashi Azuma, Professor of Psychology at the University of Soporo to give one in Hokaido. During the following years, I gave lectures in Nagasaki, Kumonto, Papu, Osaka, and other cities. Then in 1980, Yamaguchi arranged for me to attend a meeting of the Personnel Committee of the Asian Conference on Mental Retardation which was concerned with plans for the future treatment of mentally retarded children. With Yamaguchi's support, I advised the Committee to invest their countries' limited resources to training teachers in the Portage Project, a behaviorally based teaching method, so that they would be able to train parents to treat their young retarded children in their homes or in community centers rather than dissipate their funds on building large institutions. Yamaguichi himself took action by forming the Japan Portage Association, translating and the Portage Program into Japanese, and adapting it for his culture. The Association now has 34 chapters throughout the country. Among them, 28 chapters provide individualized teaching of mothers for about 300 retarded infants and young children; the other six chapters carry out parent training in small groups called Day Care Centers. In Tokyo, about 70 handicapped infants and young children and their parents come to the headquarters facility once or twice a week for individualized instruction and Portage teachers home-visit about 40 families and teach parents of about 60 special children in Day Care Centers.

Our recommendation to the Personnel Committee with respect to Asian countries was largely implemented by the establishment of the Portage International Portage Association in 1980 by Yamaguichi and Portage leaders from England and the United States. This organization, which meets biannually, has been instrumental in having the Portage Model translated into 34 languages and used in about 90 countries, many of which have a national Portage association.

Important Developments in the Rise of Child Behavior Therapy

Looking back over my experiences, I believe there were several indications of the rise of child behavior therapy. The first was a study by a graduate student at Indiana University (Fuller, 1949) showing that the behavior of a profoundly low-functioning institutionalized patient, who, according to the hospital staff, was unable to learn, could in fact learn to increase his arm movements when they were followed by a mixture of warm milk and sugar and to decrease them when the contingency was withheld. This simple demonstration impressed not only the hospital staff but also many psychologists because never before had operant principles been shown to be effective with a human being.

Another indicator was a study by Greenspoon (1955) in which he created an experimental situation parallel to the operant conditioning animal model and demonstrated that the verbal behavior (saying words) of college students could be manipulated by the experimenter's delivery of contingent verbal behavior – "uh-hum" – and visual and auditory stimuli. This finding had a general impact similar to the Rheingold, Gewirtz, and Ross study (1959) which showed that human vocalization and mild physical touching can function as reinforcers for normally developing infants. It also had a specific impact on the then ongoing controversy between Rogers and Skinner (1956) as to whether the therapist is influential in guiding a client's conversation.

Still another harbinger were the studies by Ferster and DeMyer (1961,1962) showing that young autistic children could learn simple responses to vending-type machines in a laboratory setting. The fourth indicator was the previously mentioned clinical study by Wolf, Risley, and Mees (1964) in which operant principles were applied to the treatment of a hospitalized three-and-a-half-year-old "schizophrenic" boy with a serious visual handicap. This was indeed a remarkable study in that the team had not only to create the treatment programs but also had to train the attendants, nurses, and parents to carry out the programs and to record data in a form amenable to a quantitative presentation. This study pointed out the route to the future that child behavior therapy would take.

Case Studies of Publications

Of all the publications that flowed from the work at Washington and Illinois, two appear to have had the greatest impact on psychologists and students: One was the methodology for field studies (Bijou, Peterson, & Ault, 1968; Bijou, Peterson, Harris, Allen, & Johnston, 1969); the other a behavior analysis of child development (Bijou & Baer, 1961).

Methodology for Field Studies

The methodology for studying children's behavior in natural settings was an expansion and adaptation of the laboratory operant conditioning method. It developed with the previously mentioned study in which the regressive crawling of a preschool girl was quickly eliminated (Harris, Wolf, & Baer, 1964). The method used was refined and expanded with the many subsequent studies in the nursery school and clinic.

In addition to the development of a field methodology, these studies had two powerful side effects. One was that the staff's over-arching view of child development and child management was changed from the Freudian-Rogerian position to the behavioral approach (Allen & Goetz, 1982; Goetz & Allen, 1983). The other was that these studies served to redefine the activities of the staff: They were not only teachers; they were now researchers as well. One of the nursery school teachers, Betty Hart, was so inspired by the research that after taking a Ph. D. degree at the University of Kansas, she carried out a series of studies on the role of verbal behavior in the development of children and finally embarked on a multi-year, pioneering study with Todd Risley on how children learn to talk in their home settings (Hart & Risley, 1995, 1999).

Books on Child Development

The other publication that had the most telling effect on psychologists – the small paper-back book by Baer and me – was intended for our large undergraduate courses in child development which both of us were teaching at the time. Dissatisfied with the textbook (Mussen, Conger, & Kagan, 1956) we had been using, we wanted one that would present child development from a behavioral point of view and would also serve as a background for the research being carried out at the Institute.

Our plan was to write a series, the first being a summary of the basic principles, the others, descriptions of their application to the successive stages of development. Hence, the second volume (Bijou & Baer, 1965) presents and describes the application of principles to the prenatal, neonatal, and infancy stages, and the third to the early childhood stage (Bijou, 1976). To our regret, we learned through a review of the literature that we could not extend the series to middle childhood and beyond because of the paucity of studies amenable to a functional analysis at those levels. We therefore supplemented the series with a book of readings to show the application of principles in others areas related to child development (Bijou & Baer, 1967).

Volume One was revised twice. The first revision (Bijou & Baer, 1978) emphasized that the relationship between behavior and stimulating conditions was mutual and reciprocal, and extended the analysis to complex behavior, such as self-management and problem-solving. The second revision (Bijou, 1993) included an analysis of verbal behavior and elaborated on the meaning of setting factors.

I learned from personal contacts that these books were used not only in courses on child development, but also in clinical and introductory courses. The series enjoyed a much wider circulation than we had anticipated.

Lessons Learned for the Future of Child Behavior Therapy

One lesson learned was that insufficient attention was being devoted to the joint treatment of parents and child. This lack of attention refers not to parent training *per se* or to training parents to deal with their child's problem behavior (Dangle & Polster, 1984) but to the treatment of parents and child in relation to each other. Considering that the earliest child therapies evolved from the psychoanalytic-medical model, the oversight is understandable. Believing that the parents were either the cause of the problem or part of it, early-day therapists tended to exclude parents from treatment on the assumption that they would either delay or retard the child's treatment program.

Assuming that parents are the most important social influence in a child's early life, child behavioral therapists should insist on parents' involvement, the extent to which would depend on the severity of the problem. With severe disturbances, autism for example, treatment should be planned and carried out with the child and parents as a *social unit.*

Another lesson learned is that although it was recognized early on that there is a need for training and experience standards for those who practice child behavior therapy, nothing was done about it. As early as 1971 there was an expression of such a need. It was at the first meeting of the International Symposium on Behavior Modification held in Xalapa, Mexico. The entire panel of Mexican and American psychologists was concerned with standards for the training of behavioral paraprofessionals. It is encouraging that six states in the United States now have such requirements and a strong movement exists in the Association for Behavior Analysis to support this movement at the national level.

Summary

The early advances in child behavior therapy have been nothing short of spectacular. A review of therapeutic techniques for children (Bijou, 1954) described five approaches, three of which were offshoots of psychoanalysis: Child analysis (A. Freud, 1946; Kline, 1949), the briefer analytic child therapies (Newell, 1941), and the expressive therapies (Levy, 1939). Of the other two, one was based on the Rankian psychology (Taft, 1933; Allen, 1942), the other on Rogers' client-centered approach (Axline, 1947). There was no mention of learning or behavior therapies. An update of that review, 12 years later (Bijou & Sloane, 1966), included both classical and operant conditioning child therapies. The classical conditioning therapies emphasized the systematic desensitization of children with phobias (e.g., Bentler, 1962; Lazarus, 1959), whereas the operant conditioning therapies stressed a range of problems from autism (Wolf, Risley, & Mees, 1964) to everyday "normal" problems (Harris, et al., 1964) to the rehabilitation of simple motor skills (Johnston, Kelley, Harris, & Wolf, 1966). So rapidly had the field expanded during the next ten years that the editor of the 1975 edition of *American handbook of psychiatry* saw fit to include a separate chapter on the child behavior therapies (Bijou & Redd, 1975).

All the described research and applications served to set the foundation for intensive studies on specific techniques for specific problems which we are now witnessing.

References

Allen, F. H. (1942). *Psychotherapy with children.* New York: W. W. Norton.

Allen, K. E., & Goetz, E. M. (Eds.). (1982). *Early childhood education: Special problems, special solutions.* Rockville, MD: Aspen Systems.

Axline, V. M. (1947). *Play therapy.* New York: Houghton Mifflin.

Bach, G. R. (1945). Young children's play fantasies. *Psychological Monographs, 59*(2), 1-69.

Baer, D. M. (1960). Escape and avoidance response of preschool children to two schedules of reinforcement withdrawal. *Journal of the Experimental Analysis of Behavior, 3*, 155-160.

Baer, D. M. (1961). Effect of withdrawal of positive reinforcement on an extinguishing response in young children. *Child Development, 32,* 67-74.

Baer, D. M. (1962a). Laboratory control of thumb sucking by withdrawal and re-representation of reinforcement. *Journal of the Experimental Analysis of Behavior, 5,* 525-528.

Baer, D. M. (1962b). A technique of social reinforcement for the study of child behavior: Behavior avoiding reinforcement withdrawal. *Child Development 33,* 847-858.

Baer, D. M., Peterson, R. F., & Sherman, J. A. (1967). The development of imitation by reinforcing behavioral similarity to a model. *Journal of the Experimental Analysis of Behavior, 10,* 405-416.

Baer, D. M. & Sherman, J. A. (1964). Reinforcement control of generalized imitation in young children. *Journal of the Experimental Analysis of Behavior, 1,* 37-49.

Bentler, P. M. (1962). An infant's phobia treated with reciprocal inhibition therapy. *Journal of Child Psychology and Psychiatry, 3,* 185-189.

Bijou, S. W. (1938). The performance of normal children on the Randall's Island Performance Series. *Applied Psychology, 22,* 186-191.

Bijou, S. W. (1942). The development of a conditioning methodology for studying experimental neurosis in a rat. *Journal of Comparative Psychology, 44,* 91-106.

Bijou, S. W. (1943). A study of experimental neurosis in the rat by the conditioned response technique. *Journal of Comparative and Physiological Psychology, 36,* 1-20.

Bijou, S. W. (1951). A conditioned response technique to investigate experimental neurosis in the rat. *Journal of Comparative and Physiological Psychology, 44,* 84-87.

Bijou, S. W. (1954). Therapeutic techniques with children. In L. A. Pennington & I. A. Berg (Eds.), *An introduction to clinical psychology* (2nd ed.). New York: Ronald Press.

Bijou, S. W. (1955). A systematic approach to an experimental analysis of young children. *Child Development, 26,* 161-168.

Bijou, S. W. (1957a). Patterns of reinforcement and resistance to extinction in young children. *Child Development, 28,* 47-54.

Bijou, S. W. (1957b). Methodology for an experimental analysis of child behavior. *Psychological Reports, 3,* 243-250.

Bijou, S.W. (1958a). A child study laboratory on wheels. *Child Development, 29,* 425-427.

Bijou, S. W. (1958b). Operant extinction after fixed-interval schedules with young children. *Journal of the Experimental Analysis of Behavior, 1,* 25-29.

Bijou, S. W. (1961). Discrimination performance as a baseline for individual analysis of young children. *Child Development, 32,* 163-170.

Bijou, S. W. (1968). Experimental analysis of left-right concepts in young children. *International Review of Research in Mental Retardation* (Vol. 3, pp. 65-96). New York: Academic Press.

Bijou, S. W. (1976). *Child development: The basic stage of early childhood.* Englewood Cliffs, NJ: Prentice-Hall.

Bijou, S. W. (1993). *Behavior analysis of child development* (2nd rev.). Reno, NV: Context Press.

Bijou, S. W., & Baer, D. M. (1961). *Child development: A systematic and empirical theory* (Vol. 1). Englewood Cliffs, NJ: Prentice-Hall.

Bijou, S. W., & Baer, D. M. (1965). *Child development: II. Universal stage of infancy*. New York: Appleton-Century-Crofts.

Bijou, S. W., & Baer, D. M. (Eds.). (1967). *Child development: Readings in experimental analysis*. Englewood Cliffs, NJ: Prentice-Hall.

Bijou, S. W., & Baer, D. M. (1978). *Behavior analysis of child development*. Englewood Cliffs, NJ: Prentice-Hall.

Bijou, S. W., Birnbrauer, J. S., Kidder, J. D., & Tague, C. E. (1966). Programmed instruction as an approach to the teaching of reading, writing, and arithmetic to retarded children. *Psychological Record, 16*, 505-522.

Bijou, S. W., Lovaas, O. I., & Baer, D. M. (1965). Experimental procedures for analyzing the interaction of symbolic social stimuli and children's behavior. *Child Development, 36*, 237-248.

Bijou, S. W., & Oblinger, B. (1960). Responses of normal and retarded children as a function of the experimental situation. *Psychological Reports, 6*, 447-454.

Bijou, S. W., & Orlando, R. (1960). Single and multiple schedules of reinforcement in developmentally retarded children. *Journal of the Experimental Analysis of Behavior, 4*, 339-348.

Bijou, S.W., & Orlando, R. (1961). Rapid development of multiple schedule performances of retarded children. *Journal of the Experimental Analysis of Behavior, 4*, 7-16.

Bijou, S. W., & Peterson, R. F. (1971). The psychological assessment of children: A functional analysis. In P. McReynolds (Ed.), *Advances in psychological assessment.* (Vol. 2, pp. 63-78). Palo Alto, CA: Science & Behavior Books.

Bijou, S. W., Peterson, R. F., & Ault, M. H. (1968). A method to integrate descriptive and experimental field studies at the level of data and empirical concepts. *Journal of Applied Behavior Analysis, 1*, 175-191.

Bijou, S. W., Peterson, R. F., Harris, F. R., Allen, A. K., & Johnston, M. S. (1969). Methodology for experimental studies of young children in natural settings. *Psychological Record, 19*, 177-210.

Bijou, S. W., & Redd, W. H. (1975). Child behavior therapy. In S. Arieti (Ed.), *American Handbook of Psychiatry*, (Vol. 5 , 2nd Ed., pp. 579-585). New York: Basic Books.

Bijou, S. W., & Sloane, H. N., Jr. (1966). Therapeutic techniques with children. In L. A. Pennington & I. A. Berg (Eds.), *An introduction to clinical psychology* (3rd Rev.). New York: Ronald Press.

Bijou, S. W., & Sturges, P. T. (1959). Positive reinforcers for child experimental studies with children – consumables and manipulables. *Child Development, 30*, 151-170.

Bronfenbrenner, U. (1992). Ecological systems theory. In R. Vasta (Ed.), *Six theories of child development* (pp. 187-249). London: Jessica Kingsley Publishers.

Dangle, R. F., & Polster, R. A. (Eds.). (1984). *Parent training: Foundations of research and practice.* New York: The Guilford Press.

Ferster, C. B., & DeMyer, M. K. (1961). The development of performances in autistic children in an automatically controlled environment. *Journal of Chronic Diseases, 13,* 312-345.

Ferster, C. B., & DeMyer, M. K. (1962). A method for the experimental analysis of the autistic child. *American Journal of Orthopsychiatry, 32,* 89-98.

Freud, A. (1946). *Psychoanalytic treatment of children.* London: Imago Press.

Fuller, P. R. (1949). Operant conditioning of a vegetative human organism. *American Journal of Psychology, 62,* 587-590.

Goetz, E. M., & Allen, K. E. (Eds.). (1983). *Early childhood education: Special environmental, policy, and legal considerations.* Rockville, MD: An Aspen Publication.

Greenspoon, J. (1955). The reinforcing effect of two spoken sounds on the frequency of two responses. *American Journal of Psychology, 68,* 409-416.

Harris, F. R., Johnston, M. K., Kelley, C. S., & Wolf, M. M. (1964). Effects of positive social reinforcement on regressed crawling of a nursery school child. *Journal of Educational Psychology, 55,* 35-41.

Harris, F. R., Wolf, M. M., & Baer, D. M. (1964). Effects of adult social reinforcement on child behavior. *Young Children, 20,* 8-17.

Hart, B. M., Allen, K. E., Buell, J. S., Harris, F. R., & Wolf, M. M. (1964). Effects of social reinforcement on operant crying. *Journal of Experimental Child Psychology, 1,* 145-153.

Hart, B. M., Reynolds, N. J., Baer, D. M., Brawley, E. R., & Harris, F. R. (1968). Effect on contingent and non-contingent social reinforcement of the cooperative play of a preschool child. *Journal of Applied Behavior Analysis, 1,* 73-76.

Hart, B. M., & Risley, T. R. (1995). *Meaningful differences in the everyday experiences of young children.* Baltimore: Paul H. Brooks Publishing Co.

Hart, B. M., & Risley, T. R. (1999). *The social world of children: Learning to talk.* Baltimore: Paul H. Brooks Publishing Co.

Hawkins, R. P., Peterson, R. F., Schweid, E., & Bijou, S. W. (1966). Behavior therapy in the home: Amelioration of problem parent-child relations with the parent in a therapeutic role. *Journal of Experimental Child Psychology, 4,* 99-107.

Hull, C. H. (1943). *Principles of behavior.* New York: Appleton-Century Co.

Jastak, J. F. (1934). *Variability of psychometric performances in mental diagnosis.* New York City.

Jastak, J. F., & Bijou, S. W. (1938). Wide Range Achievement Test. Wilmington, DE: Guidance Associates.

Johnston, M. S., Kelley, C., Harris, F. R., & Wolf, M. M. (1966). An application of reinforcement principles to the development of motor skills of a young child. *Child Development, 37,* 379-387.

Kazdin, A. E. (1978). *History of behavior modification: Experimental foundations of contemporary research.* Baltimore: University Press.

Klein, M. (1949). *The psychoanalysis of children*. London: Hogarth Press.

Lazarus, A. A. (1959). The elimination of children's phobias by deconditioning. *Medical Proceedings of South Africa*, 261-265.

Levy, D. M. (1939). Release therapy. *American Journal of Orthopsychiatry*, *9*, 913-936.

Lewin, K. (1935). *A dynamic theory of personality*. New York: McGraw-Hill.

Lewin, K. (1936). *Principles of topological psychology*. New York: McGraw-Hill.

Marholin II, D., & Bijou, S. W. (1978). Behavioral Assessment: Listen when the data speak. In D. Marholin II (Ed.), *Child behavior therapy* (pp. 13-36). New York: Gardner Press.

Miller, N. E. (1944). Experimental studies of conflict. In J. McV. Hunt (Ed.), *Personality and the behavior disorders* (Vol. 1 pp. 431-465). New York: Ronald Press.

Mussen, P. H., Conger, J. J., & Kagan, J. (1956). *Child development and personality* (1st ed.). New York: Harper & Row.

Newell, H. W. (1941). Play therapy in child psychiatry. *American Journal of Orthopsychiatry*, *11*, 245-251.

Orlando, R., Bijou, S. W., Tyler, R. M., & Marshall, D. A. (1960). A laboratory for the experimental analysis of developmentally retarded children. *Psychological Reports*, *7*, 261-267.

Peterson, R. F. (1968). Imitation: A basic behavioral mechanism. In H. N. Sloane, Jr. & B. D. MacAulay (Eds.), *Operant procedures in remedial speech and language training* (pp. 61-76). Boston: Houghton Mifflin.

Peterson, R. F., Cox, M. A., & Bijou, S. W. (1971). Training children to work productively in classroom groups. *Exceptional Children*, *37*, 419-500.

Peterson, R. F., & Peterson, L. W. (1968). The use of positive reinforcement in the control of self-destructive behavior in a retarded boy. *Journal of Experimental Child Psychology*. *6*, 351-360.

Pumroy, S. A. S. (1954). The effects of amount of reinforcement on resistance to extinction and emotional behavior with preschool children. Unpublished doctoral dissertation, University of Washington.

Rheingold, H. L., Gewirtz, J. L., & Ross, H. W. (1959). Social conditioning of vocalizations in the infant. *Journal of Comparative and Physiological Psychology*, *52*, 68-73.

Rogers, C. R., & Skinner, B. F. (1956). Some issues concerning the control of human behavior. *Science*, *124*, No. 3231, 1057-1066.

Sajway, T. E., Twardosz, S., & Burke, M. (1972). Side effects of extinction procedures in a remedial preschool. *Journal of Applied Behavior Analysis*, *5*, 163-175.

Sears, R. R. (1947). Influence of methodological factors on doll play performance. *Child Development*, *18*, 190-197.

Sears, R. R. (1975). Your ancients revisited: A history of child development. In E. M. Hetherington (Ed.), *Review of Child Development Research* (Vol. 5, pp. 1-73). Chicago: University of Chicago Press.

Sears, R. R., Whiting, J. W. M., Nowlis, V., & Sears, P. S. (1953). Some child rearing antecedents of aggression and dependency in young children. *Genetic Psychology Monographs*, *47*, 135-234.

Skinner, B. F. (1953). *Science and human behavior.* New York: The Macmillan Co.

Skinner, B. F. (1968). *The technology of teaching.* New York: Appleton-Century-Crofts.

Sloane, H. N., Jr., Johnston, M. K., & Bijou, S. W. (1967). Successive modification of aggressive behavior and aggressive fantasy play by management of contingencies. *Journal of Child Psychology and Psychiatry*, *8*, 217-226.

Sloane, H. N. ,Jr. & MacAulay, B. D. (Eds.). (1968). *Operant procedures in remedial speech and language training.* Boston: Houghton Mifflin.

Taft, J. (1933). *The dynamics of therapy in a controlled relationship.* New York: The Macmillan Co.

Wahler, R. G. (1967). Child-child interaction in free field settings: Some experimental analysis. *Journal of Experimental Child Psychology*, *5*, 278-293.

Wahler, R. G. (1969a). Infant social development: Some experimental analyses of an infant-mother interaction during the first year of life. *Journal of Experimental Child Psychology*, *7*, 101-113.

Wahler, R. G. (1969b). Oppositional children: A quest for parental reinforcement control. *Journal of Applied Behavior Analysis*, *2*, 159-170.

Wahler, R. G., Winkel, G. H., Peterson, R. F., & Morrison, D. C. (1965). Mothers as behavior therapists for their own children. *Behaviour Research and Therapy*, *3*, 113-124.

Watson, J. B. (1919). *Psychology from the standpoint of a behaviorist.* Philadelphia: Lippincott.

Watson, J. B. (1930). *Behaviorism.* (Rev. ed.) Chicago: The University Press.

Wolf, M. M., Risley, T. R., & Mees, H. (1964). Application of operant conditioning procedures to the behavior problems of an autistic child. *Behaviour Research and Therapy*, *1*, 305-312.

Zeilberger, J., Sampen, S. E., & Sloane, H. N., Jr. (1968). Modification of a child's problem behaviors in the home with the mother as therapist. *Journal of Applied Behavior Analysis*, *1*. 47-53.

Footnote

[1] Many thanks to my wife, Janet, for her careful and thorough editing of the manuscript and my son, Bob, for preparing the figures.

Chapter 6

Studies in Behavior Therapy and Behavior Research Laboratory: June 1953-1965

Ogden R. Lindsley
University of Kansas and Behavior Research Company

The Beginning

I was born on August 11th, 1922 in Jane Brown Hospital, Providence, Rhode Island. My father was a young Harvard Law School graduate practicing corporate law in Edwards and Angel, Providence's most prestigious law firm. My mother had dropped out of Wheaton College at the end of her junior year to marry my father upon his graduation from law school. We wintered at 282 Wayland Avenue on the upper income East Side of Providence. We summered on the west shore of Narragansett Bay in Quidnessett, Quonset Point, Rhode Island, on our 365-acre farmstead with a house built in 1804 and its own Allen's harbor.

One of my earliest ambitions was to be like my great-grandfather, Isaac Lindsley, who invented hair cloth looms to weave the manes and tails of horses into a stain-proof fabric to cover Victorian furniture. Stories about his genius were family legends. He sailed to London, England, to design looms to weave hair cloth royal coat of arms fabric to cover chair backs and seats in Buckingham Palace. He spent endless hours inventing in a shop behind his house. He invented a very fast early bicycle, and a machine to roll cigars. There was a wonderful oil painting of him in long mustache and beard over the large mahogany Stella music box in grandmother Lindsey's home. The music box stood 37 inches from the floor and 24 inches from the wall. When I was so small that I had to reach up to the edge of the music box, I would pull with both hands standing tippy-toe to peer over the top at Isaac Lindsley's face. I had been given his brass microscope with glass slides in a handsome wooden box with an engraved brass nameplate which read, "Isaac Lindsley, Inventor." I wanted to grow up to be like him!

We had two rooms and a bath on our third floor attic. One was Helen, our maid's bedroom, and my mother, Mildred Flagg Monroe Lindsley, made the other into a little school room with three desks, a chalkboard, a table, and book cases containing first and second grade public school books. I still have some of those books: the McCall Speller-Intermediate, Mother Westwind's Children, the Hiawatha Primer, The Elson Readers Book Three, Stories of American Discovers for Little Americans. Every afternoon my mother taught me school up there. Often one or two of my playmates came over to be taught by my mother. It was wonderful, she was so kind and had such a great sense of humor. Most of the time we were learning and laughing. I learned so much that when it came time for school, the principal at Moses Brown Lower School had me skip first grade so I went into second grade at six years of age. We wore little navy blue short pant suits with white Eaton collars, and little navy blue caps with MBLS, for Moses Brown Lower School, embroidered in white. We had to walk home through some streets where tough poor kids from Fox Point walked home from Nathan Bishop Junior High School. The tough teens chased and terrorized us, throwing rocks and horse chestnuts at us and yelling "Momma's Baby Lemon Sucker," referring to the MBLS on our caps. For a while we had police escorts until the Fox Pointers gave up.

My father, Ogden Richardson Lindsley, taught me to discover. He never directly answered my questions. He always answered by saying, "How could we find out?" When I asked him to teach me how to tie my shoelaces, he said "See if you can figure it out by yourself." When I tiptoed into his room in the morning as he was dressing to see how he tied his shoes, he noticed me and said, "No spying, figure shoe tying out by yourself!" I did, and I now tie my shoes by a very unique method, different from most people's way.

On May 20th, 1935 my father was killed in a head-on automobile accident in a car driven by my mother. He had taken a job as a vice president and sales manager for Everett and Baron, a shoe polish company for which he had done superb legal work. His salary was about three times his old law firm salary. He was late for a keynote speech against Roosevelt's National Recovery Administration at a shoe retailers convention in Boston, about 60 miles on a two-lane, blacktop Route One from Providence. My mother was driving about 70 miles per hour in a brand new Chrysler Airflow Imperial Sedan. She went to pass an eighteen wheeler truck on a curve and ran head-on into a large LaSalle limousine coming the other way. My father writing his speech in the passenger seat took the full force of the collision dying instantly, his body totally crushed. My mother had multiple fractures; her hips were fractured in five places and she was in the hospital almost a year-long enough for the guppy fish pair that my brother and I gave her to have multiplied, filling a bowl in almost every room in the hospital!

Nannie, my grandmother Lindsley, blamed and never forgave my mother for killing her only child. I blamed neither my mother nor my father. I blamed business for driving him so fanatically that he was urging my mother to speed ever faster while he wrote his speech notes in the passenger seat. Had he accepted the Harvard Law Review and stayed in academia, I doubted that he would have been killed strolling across Harvard Yard. This early interpretation of the cause of my father's death laid the groundwork for my avoidance of business as a career.

A few weeks before my father's death I asked him if he believed in life after death. He answered in his typical fashion, "How could we find out?" I had just become a Boy Scout in Troop 8, Providence, and learned Morse code and American Indian smoke signaling. I had had trouble separating L (.-..) from F (..-.), and my father suggested the memory aid, "L is our Lindsley family, mother a dot, father a dash, Ogden a dot, and Brad a dot. And you know that gentlemen always have ladies go first." I remember this to this day. I told my father that if one of us dies the survivor will go by the body on a nice quiet evening with no wind and make a fire with wet leaves so the smoke will go straight up. The dead one may be able to interrupt the column of smoke with short and long interruptions – the dots and dashes of Morse code – and send a message to the survivor that way.

My grandmother and mother could not agree where to bury my father, so for a while he was in a tomb in Swan Point Cemetery, the ritziest one in Providence. I sneaked over to his tomb on a still fall night and built a nice wet fire with lots of smoke beside the tomb and waited for signals from my dead father. Suddenly I felt a hand on my shoulder! A male voice boomed out, "What are you doing here, Lad!" I shook with fright, turned around and saw a large, scowling, uniformed Providence cop. I blurted out, "I'm keeping warm. My dead father is in there!" The cop beamed and said in an Irish brogue, "Sure and the fine young lad is holding a wake for his dear departed father!" He took me to McDonald's drugstore, bought me ice cream, and then to the East Side police station on Sessions Street. At the station he told all the cops what a brave little man I was sitting awake by his father's tomb. I did not have the heart to break his myth and tell him that I was trying to communicate with the dead!

We lost all of our money. The shoe polish company did not pay my father's salary from January to May 1935, when it was customary for executives to get the full year's salary for the year in which they died. A partner in rental housing did not honor the partnership and we received no money from that source. It was the depth of the depression. My father did not believe in insurance, saying he was smarter than insurance people and could better invest his money. My mother had a giant policy drawn up on my father that was to have sent me to Switzerland for prep school if he died. But he had been too busy cornering the shoe polish market to take the physical examination, so this life insurance policy was not in force. We moved to our summer home, the farm in Quidnesset, full-time and became country boys. I put my arm around my little brother's shoulders and said "Don't cry, Brad. I will take care of you!" I never teased Brad or hit him again. I never cried after my father's death, and I assumed his role. I dropped the "junior" from my name and stopped people from calling me "Sonny." I became "Ogden," or "Oggie."

From East Side little rich kids, my brother and I became South County poor country boys. We moved to our former summer home. We grew our own vegetables. We tended our own ponies. We sold city kids pony rides on the beach. I trapped skunks and sold their pelts for money to buy long pants for Brad and me to wear to North Kingstown High and Wickford Grammar schools. We walked half a mile up our road to the mailbox to catch the school bus each day. Whenever we were cut we went to our beach and soaked our wounds in the clear salt water until the bleeding stopped. I raised turkeys from day old chicks and sold them in town for Thanksgiving and Christmas dinners. We raised vegetables and sold them in town. We became country kids.

Mr. Brown, track coach and cross-country coach, taught me to run through pain. I won Class C medals in the mile and cross-country. I could not go out for team sports because there was no late school bus that went north to our farm. I lettered in track and expected to get a nice, leather armed, brown and white, NKHS letter jacket on Class Day. I almost cried and then got super angry when I was handed a little plastic envelope with small felt NKHS letters inside. Track was a minor sport and did not earn the big chenille NKHS that the team sport lettermen got! I became high school paper cartoonist, lead singer in the minstrel show, and held several class offices.

In 1937 my horse, Prince, got a thorn in his head and developed a severe throat infection. It was before penicillin, so he was rapidly dying. I had to walk him about a quarter mile down to our sandpit, where it was easy digging, and dig his grave. Then I injected Prince with the strychnine that the vet had given me to kill him. It was one of the hardest things I had to do up to that point in my life. Having my father killed was hard, but having to kill Prince was even harder!

I continued Boys Scouts in a small town, Troop 3 East Greenwich, and became a patrol leader by recruiting and starting a new patrol for the troop. I earned Eagle Scout and many merit badges beyond. I became a leader at summer scout camp, Yawgoog, and went on 500 mile canoe trips. I won State Jamboree competition with fire by flint and steel by using flint from the family heirloom flintlock rifle and charred linen from my grandmother's linen wedding slip. I learned how to raise and train wasps and hornets to attack other kids who entered my shop without permission. I loved the behavior of farm and wild animals. I spent hundreds of hours stalking them, imitating their calls, and learning their habits. I trapped eels, crabs, skunks, muskrats, mink, woodchuck, rabbits, guinea hens, quail, and pheasants. I dug clams, quohaugs, mussels, and oysters. I caught saltwater fish and lobsters. We were taught not to eat freshwater fish, even though my grandfather had stocked the ice house pond with pickerel. Mother would not let us swim in fresh water. It could be polluted and dangerous. Salt water healed and was always safe. We were north Atlantic kids.

In the great hurricane of 1938, I was out running cross-country practice and the wind blew us down. It was raining salt water! I thought it was the end of the world. We had to walk about 12 miles home through blown over trees across the highway. Refuse from broken Oceanside homes and boats littered our front lawn and pasture. My brother and I found three dead bodies washed up on our side of the harbor. We called the National Guard who had declared an emergency and sealed off our area to prevent looting.

In June 1939 I graduated from North Kingstown High School with a class of about 35 students. I was 16 years of age and went to Providence to work as a mechanic in a gasoline station for a year, to make money and mature a bit before attending Brown University the following year. Atlantic Refining Company checkers came around to the stations in unmarked cars, and if you approached them with the correct Tom's River Lubrication Service spiel they gave you a silver dollar. "Good morning, Sir! Shall I fill it with Atlantic White Flash Plus? Or do you prefer the Ethyl?" "Thank you, Sir! I'll also make sure your oil and water are safe!"

In September 1940 I entered Brown University as a freshman to attain a degree in electrical engineering. The family plan was to train as an engineer but at a liberal arts college. Join a fraternity. Meet all the right people. Build social skills and become a highly paid sales engineer. Richard Fink, my stepfather, was a top salesman for Cook, Dunbar, and Smith manufacturers of rolled gold plate. He often took me on his sales visits when I was in high school.

At Brown I was in the class of '44 and undisciplined. I drank too much, pledged Zeta Psi fraternity and with my piano playing buddy, Phil Simpson, sang duets all night at fraternity parties. I fell asleep in 8:00 A.M. classes, having slept not at all the night before. I got either the highest grade in the class (Analytical Geometry) or the lowest (Advanced Calculus). If I loved it, I exceeded. If I hated it, I flunked. There was no middle ground! The war escalated in Europe. High school friends joined the merchant marine on the Murmansk run. Others joined our U.S. Marines. One was a Navy flier. I thought about joining the war effort every day. I envied uniforms and combat ribbons and *wings*! My heart was in flying a spitfire as an American volunteer for the Royal Air Force over England and chasing Messerschmitts back to Germany. I would rather die in air combat, a hero, than sit here in Providence in a lecture seat.

In January 1942 the U.S. Army Air Force dropped its age requirement for cadets from 21 to 18 years. I immediately joined and was in Class 42J Aviation Cadets at Maxwell Field, Montgomery, Alabama. I went through preflight at the top of my class, but washed out in June on a flight physical eye exam with prism divergence to exceed six diapers. The medics giving the physicals urged us to erase the check marks on the examination forms we carried from exam post to exam post. Some of the cadets did erase physical problem checks. I chose not to erase my prism divergence check. I was so young, naive, and moral that I thought the physicians knew more than I did. I did not want to take nine men on my crew to their death because I wanted silver wings. So I left the check mark on my form, and was washed out. The ophthalmologist said my eyes were not good enough to be a navigator or bombardier. My eyes were not even good enough for glider pilot school! I was discharged from Cadets. I was ashamed to go home as a civilian, so I enlisted in the Army Air Corps as a private at Maxwell field. In July the Air Corps found there were not enough perfect eyes in the country to fight the war, so they dropped mission requirements for flying. Prism divergence dropped from six diopters to 12! Mine was eight diopters! I was so young and inexperienced that I did nothing about it. I let them assign me to the military police and be a guard at the main Maxwell field gate. Because I had been top in my cadet preflight class I really could polish brass, buttons and buckles, stand rather ramrod straight, and salute smartly.

I got promoted to corporal, and drove a jeep on night patrol around the air base perimeter. I still love the throb of that little flat head four engine. I got caught by the officer of the day while lying on the hood of that MP jeep with a beautiful young nurse and counting the stars while on duty! They sent Juanita to combat in Africa and busted me to private and put me on the back of a GI truck cab with a sawed-off shotgun guarding prisoners while they picked up paper along the Birmingham highway fence. I was now a prison chaser! I started drinking too much beer, spending every night in town with an MP pass. One day I fell asleep on the truck cab under my umbrella. When I looked up I saw only three of my four prisoners. The fourth was running toward the airfield fence. I yelled halt three times, pumped a shell into the shotgun, aimed in the direction of the prisoner now running faster, and pulled the trigger. A buck shot hit him in the leg. We put him in the back of the truck and drove him to the base hospital while the other three prisoners swore at me and pledged they would get me some day for this.

On the advice of older, peace time GIs, I had been going about once a week to both Provost Marshal and Base Chaplain complaining that I had army general classification test scores above 150 and should be better used than as a prison chaser. The combination of these appeals, my test scores, my year-and-a-half college engineering experience, and the shooting got me sent to airplane mechanics school at Keesler Field, Biloxi, Mississippi. I studied hard and became a student instructor who went to class an hour before the other students, and then taught a squad of about 15 students the topic of the day. I graduated first in a class of about 800 and was awarded my certificate and engineers badge by the major general in front of the entire school student body massed at attention. As a reward for being top in the class, I was being sent to Helicopter Engineering Officer School at Twenty Nine Palms while all the other graduates were off to gunnery school at Tyndall Field, Florida, to become combat flight engineers. The first sergeant came running out of the orderly room yelling, "Lindsley, we've got to cut you a new set of orders! We have to re-stencil your barracks bags! You can't go to Twenty Nine Palms! You're on detached service from the 831st Military Police Company and have to go back to Maxwell!"

Back at Maxwell I wasn't even in the Air Force anymore. The 831st Guard Squadron had been transferred out of the Army Air Corps into the Army Military Police Branch and made the 831st Military Police Company. We no longer wore a propeller and wings on our uniforms, but wore crossed pistols! And I was an airplane mechanic! I had blue triangles with a gold rotary engine insignia sewn on my right sleeve! I got teased by the former cops and the company. They would bend over, point to their butt and say, "Hey! Engineer! Come over here and check my oil!"

I went back to my provost marshal and chaplain monthly, bitching, and soon got transferred back into the Air Force 82nd training squadron on Maxwell Field as a flight engineer on B24 bombers. I worked up to be crew chief for Major Buttman on Army 00, The Flying Goose, the squadron commander's ship. Soon our squadron was transferred to pilot transition training at Smyrna Field, Tennessee. An instructor pilot and an engineer took up two rookie pilots just out of twin-engine flight school, shot a few landings by each student pilot, then the instructor got out. The flight engineer stayed while the student pilots learned to fly the heavy four engined B24 bomber. We would shoot 30 to 60 landings a day! Landing and takeoff accidents were common. I was flying every day, but not in a spitfire over England chasing Messerschmitts back to Germany.

Tech Sergeant Perez, a former peace time ground machine gunner at Schofield Barracks, Hawaii, had volunteered to switch over to the Air Corps and lay on his belly in the back of an early B-17 and fire a flexible 50 caliber machine gun out of its sawed off tail, becoming one of the B-17's first tail gunners. Perez had flown a tour of duty in the Pacific, told great war stories, and wore an air medal with oak leaf clusters and a yellow and red Asia-Pacific combat ribbon with several battle stars. I admired Perez. He really knew the Air Corps enlisted flight crew life. We were good drinking and woman chasing buddies. One day just as I landed with two rookie pilots, the B-24 in front of us went off the end of the runway and nosed down, twin tail sticking up in the air at a 45-degree angle. A little smoke rose out of one of the starboard engines. We taxied over to operations while civilian fire trucks raced to the nosed up B-24. The waist windows were closed and jammed shut by the fuselage twisting from the crash. You could hear the men inside yelling and pounding the sides of the aircraft. Flames were now coming from the starboard engine. The civilian crash crews had forgotten their asbestos suits and a truck raced back to the hangars to get them. Just then there was a terrible *swoosh* and a wave of hot air as the plane went up in flames from the spilled 120 octane gas.

Back at operations, my student pilots asked, "Who were the student pilots in that plane?" I asked, "Who was the engineer?" The operations officer replied, "Tech Sergeant Perez." I shouted, "S–t! Not Perez! Combat in the Pacific, and now ashes at the end of a runway in Smyrna, Tennessee!" I went into Nashville to our favorite bar, got drunk, and refused to fly. The flight surgeon made me come to his office every day and sign a yellow sheet under the words, "I am yellow. I refuse to fly for my country." I did, but each day added "with rookie pilots in Smyrna. I want to fly in combat!" above my signature. After about two weeks of this, I got sent to gunnery school at Tyndall Field, Florida.

I went through gunnery school at Tyndall, air crew make up and assignment at Savannah, Georgia, and staging for high altitude bombardment at Langley Field, Virginia. We flew our factory new silver B24-J from Langley to Newark, New Jersey; to Bedford, Massachusetts; to Bangor, Maine; to Gander, Newfoundland; the Azores; Marrakech, Morocco; El Aouina, Tunisia; to the U.S. air base in Lecce, Italy. We were a replacement crew to the 415th squadron, 98th Bomb Group, 15th Air Force when Major Habegar, our new squadron commander, took our shiny new plane for his own crew, leaving us to fly as replacements in battle scarred, patched, veteran ships from the African campaign. I was shot down with a crew that I had never seen before on my first real combat mission to the Asta Romani oilfields in Ploesti, Rumania on July 22, 1944.

After parachuting out over the North Albanian Alps we were traded by partisans to the Croatians for guns and then handed over to the Germans in Dubrovnick, Yugoslavia. We were interrogated by the Hungarian Gestapo in Pestvideki Prison in Budapest and imprisoned in Gross Tychow, Pomerania, between Danzig and Berlin.

In January of 1945 our guards marched us from Luft IV to Hamburg across northern Germany to keep us away from the advancing Russian armies. We had only two bowls of hot soup in 63 days. I went from 175 to 114 pounds. I sneaked through the wires into the French prisoners' compound as my fellow Air Force POW's were marched back into Germany. A few days later, dressed as a French POW, I escaped from a wood picking-up detail in the forest with two French POWs. We went through the German front lines to the Queen's Regiment, British 2nd Army. I escaped rather than be marched back into Germany with the rest from Stalag Luft IV. I was afraid that when Germany was only a few hundred kilometers wide, there would be no room for hated prisoners of war, and we might all be machine gunned as we marched.

Mary Elizabeth Moore and I were married in early November 1945 while I was still in the Air Force. I had dated her a few times before the war, and we dated while I was recovering from malnutrition and Pleurisy at Cushing General Hospital in Framingham, Massachusetts. I got discharged in November 1945 and went back to Brown University on the GI Bill. Mary got a job as a secretary in a lawyer's office. We had a small basement apartment on George Street in Providence. Having difficulty back in Advanced Calculus, I chose taking courses that I enjoyed with content that I liked. Most of these courses were in experimental psychology and biology, so that meant dropping out of engineering. I had a double undergraduate major in experimental psychology and histochemistry. I had been influenced by Flanders Dunbar's book, "Psychosomatic Medicine." I planned to personally solve the mind-body problem by becoming expert in both. I became president of Zeta Psi fraternity and help fill the house with returned combat veterans. Notable among them was Dick Check, former chief quartermaster on the aircraft carrier Bunker Hill. I was also proud of getting the first Jewish man into our chapter by blackballing the whole delegation until his box passed with all white balls. With Ben Latt, whose dad was a union organizer, I started the Lincoln Society with its motto of "Fellowship without Fences." I became interested in liberal causes and folk music, and learned to sing and play a six-string guitar. I graduated with Highest Honors in Psychology in June 1948. I did not make Phi Beta Kappa or Cum Laude because Brown averaged in my grades and incompletes (which had become E's) from before the war!

My main mentor at Brown during graduate training was Carl Pfaffman, an electro physiologist who had studied with Lord Adrian while on a Rhodes Scholarship and had earned a Ph.D. from Cambridge University. Carl taught me the details and personal discipline of laboratory science. His fame came from isolating and recording the nerve fibers for taste in the chorda tympani nerve that ran from the anterior two thirds of the tongue. My undergraduate Honors Thesis on handedness in rats showed that you could determine which paw they preferred to use by biasing their first one handed reaches in an angled chute. I received highest honors, because I had the honesty to write in my thesis that I was forced to discard one of the 20 odd rats who was slowest to learn, because in a fit of rage at his slowness I pulled him by his tail from the apparatus and threw him across the room. That was the last time that I angered at slow learners.

I admired Lord Adrian for his creativity from a story that Carl had told me about Adrian's first recording of the electrical discharge from an eel's eye. It was in the days before reliable electronic amplifier tubes. Adrian physically amplified the electrical signal by using a light and a movable mirror. He went into the basement of the longest cathedral he could find and set up his equipment. In the dark a small mirror moved a miniscule distance when the eel eye was stimulated with light. At the other end of the hundred foot long dark cathedral photographic paper was pasted on the wall which recorded the amplified signal. This classy, simple, physical solution fascinated me. I wanted to create similar simple solutions to my own psychological research problems.

I designed and built the psychology department's histochemistry lab for staining nerve fibers. My master's thesis reported the diameters and the conduction velocities of the C fibers used for taste in the chorda tympani nerve of the rat. Carl had taught me the tease method of single nerve fiber recording. You anesthetized a rat, put him under a microscope in a moist chamber and shielded room, and using iridectomy tools surgically exposed the nerve running across its eardrum. While stimulating its tongue from dripping salt or sugar solutions, you watched a cathode ray oscilloscope recording from silver-silver chloride electrodes touching the nerve. You very gradually tweezed off pieces of the nerve until you got down to seeing only a few fiber's spikes showing on the oscilloscope tube from each stimulation. Then you watched with fingers crossed hoping the nerve fibers would die one at a time leaving a single fiber firing. At that moment you stimulated and took as many pictures as you could before it also died. This took 3 to 4 hours, most of a Saturday, and a lot of patience. About 1 in 5 or 1 in 10 operations got a single nerve fiber dose response curve! Here I learned scientific discipline and patience.

About this time Floyd Ratliff, a former artillery officer, and fellow graduate student studying with Lorrin Riggs, conducted a simple creative solution similar to Adrian's eel eye signal amplification in the cathedral basement. Floyd proved that the vibration of the eye is necessary for sight by gluing a small mirror to a contact lens and aiming the visual signal at the mirror on the eye so the eye's motion moved the signal also. The mirror sent the signal to a screen and the signal disappeared. An elegantly simple solution to an age old vision question that even Helmoltz could have solved but did not! It looked like all that you had to do was design one brilliant experiment and your place in textbooks was assured and your professorship was granted and tenured. Such was my plan.

In my courses I learned Behaviorism from Walter Hunter. From him I also learned that it is impossible to improve the name of a discipline once it is accepted by society. Hunter's attempt to change the name of Psychology to Anthroponomy was a dismal failure. His claims to fame were building the top experimental behavioral program at Brown from scratch, and his research design of the double alternation maze. I fought young professor Greg Kimble, fresh from an Iowa Ph.D., who taught us Hull-Spence learning theory when he said you did not need to know what went on in the nervous system to understand and predict behavior. Just before the end of his course, I finally agreed that he was right. He gave me my only B grade at Brown. To this day Greg does not believe he taught me anything, but I know how much he changed me.

I set to work on my doctoral dissertation apparatus. I planned to do with smell what Carl had done with taste. I had learned to surgically expose a rat's olfactory epithelium and nerves under anesthesia. I was designing glass tubing and fans to blow odors over the epithelium at constant flow, temperature, and moisture. I had taken all the courses for the doctorate in experimental at Brown – over 60 credit hours. Everything went smoothly. Then disaster struck! The dean of the Graduate School dropped dead with a coronary. The acting dean was Barnaby C. Keeney, a history professor with all three degrees from different universities. He was convinced that made him a superior scholar, and he put into action "no more three degrees at Brown." Hunter, a strong man, was on sabbatical. Harold Schlosberg, famous for coauthoring a textbook and a weaker, more compromising person than Hunter, was acting department chair. Schlosberg let me and my office mate and friend, William Kessen, be ordered to find another university for our doctorates. Kessen, whose advisor was Kimble, went off to Yale along with Kimble. I had to find a place to conduct my electro-physiological research. There were three options. Johns Hopkins to study with Eliot Stellar who had just written a textbook on Physiological Psychology; McGill to study with Donald Hebb, a wonderful student-supporting professor who let his students conduct any creative research they chose; Harvard with Robert Galambos who had just perfected his micro-electrode method of single nerve fiber recording. I applied to all three. My wife Mary preferred Harvard because she grew up in Weston, a Boston Suburb. I preferred McGill because I loved Canada and knew that all Hebb's students loved him. I was offered a fellowship with preference to Mayflower descendants at Harvard, and Galambos accepted me as a student. Our family – by now Mary Elizabeth and Deborah Melinda had been born – moved to a housing project in Watertown, Massachusetts in June 1950. I wanted an early start at Harvard to learn the ropes and to learn micro-electrode recording from Galambos before classes started in September.

Galambos put me to work sitting at a table measuring nerve discharges on film along with Kathy Safford, another graduate student who knew nothing about electro physiology. The crew in the pit doing the operations on auditory nerve preparations in cats was a closed shop. They were all experienced researchers – Galambos, Walter Rosenblith, and Jerzy Rose. They did not even have lunch with us. They did not invite me to watch their operations and recording. I was their recording slave, and they kept pushing us to read and measure more film records faster and faster. They seemed desperate. So went my summer.

In September I was put in Psychology 101 with Law School drop outs who had never had a psychology course, and started graduate school all over again with absolutely no credit for any course (over 60 graduate credit hours) taken at Brown.

I soon saw why. There was almost no overlap in content with courses with the same title from Brown. Harvard was more past oriented, covering a rich history of European and especially German experimental psychology from E. G. Boring's influence. Harvard was also psychophysics oriented from S. S. Stevens' influence. I essentially embarked on a second Ph.D. program. In June I went to Galambos and asked, "Now will you teach me your micro electrode recording method this summer?" Galambos smiled and said, "Lindsley, you've blown it! I'm going to Walter Reed in 2 weeks." I said, "Wow! And you're taking me with you?" Galambos said, "Nope! You are a graduate student and your fellowship is for here!" I said, "But my fellowship is to study micro electrode recording with you!" He said, "Yes, but I have not asked Walter Reed to support you." Such was the life of a graduate student at Harvard. So different from Brown.

Meanwhile, B. F. Skinner had asked me to assist him teaching sections of his undergraduate course, "Natural Science 114." The dittoed text for this course later became Skinner's book "Science and Human Behavior." The class had a weekly lecture by Skinner with a demonstration of pigeons or rats illustrating the topic of the week. The other two meetings of the class each week were in smaller sections run by graduate students that covered the weekly topic in more detail. Skinner asked me to lead one section. I said, "I haven't even read the text!" He said, "I know, but at least you're a behaviorist having been taught by Hunter at Brown. I am being undermined by graduate student section leaders who tell the Harvard undergraduates "I don't believe it either, but that is what Skinner wants you to say on the final exam." So that spring semester I taught a section of Natural Science 114. Fred assigned me my first job to shape up a high jumping rat for a class demonstration of the astonishing results of shaping. Armed with the Halloween clicker Skinner gave me, I promptly got four naive male rats from the animal colony, two ring stands and a meter stick from the biology labs, and a pellet dispenser from Skinner's pigeon-rat apparatus room. I soon had all four rats magazine trained; when they heard the pellet drop they ran to the pan and ate it.

After several sessions of pairing the clicks with the pellet dispenser the rats were clicker trained, running back to the place where they were last clicked. The four rats were soon stepping over the meter stick lying on edge. When I raised the meter stick up on the ring stands, one rat kept pulling down on one end. I immediately put him back in his home cage and built him a different apparatus, pivoting and putting an adjustable sliding weight on the meter stick. I was going to teach this rat to lift weight. I put a ring handle on the end of the meter stick, because his paws kept slipping off. Within a week of daily training, Samson Rat was pulling down a weight equal to his own body weight. He jumped up, hung on the handle with both fore paws, and tried to bounce down the weight. One time his back feet swung forward and his toe nails stuck into the plywood wall and with this leverage he was able to pull down a weight heavier than his own weight. I put him in his home cage, ran to the Harvard Coop across Harvard Square, getting there just before closing at 5:00 pm. I bought a rubber stair tread to use as an exercise mat on the wall of Samson's weight lifting apparatus, so his back feet would not slip. I was in a hurry to see if Samson's exercise mat would help him lift more weight. Now, what to use for fast drying glue? I remembered the very, very expensive Ambroid, non conductive electrode cement, in the psycho acoustic electro physiological operating room. It cost about $40 a quart but dried in an instant. I smeared the back of the stair tread with Ambroid, ran to the pigeon and rat labs in the other end of Memorial Hall basement, and stuck the tread on Samson's wall. I rushed Samson from his home cage back to his lifting apparatus with its new non-slip mat. Samson leaped up, swung on his ring, planted both hind feet on his rubber mat, arched his back, and pulled the weight all the way down. HOORAY! Samson had taught me what he needed! Within another week he was pulling down weight over two and a half times his own body weight!

Skinner has often said that he did not make free operant conditioners, the rats did! Samson had just made me a free operant conditioner. It was the speed of learning, and the precise control of Samson's behavior that bowled me over. I was a laboratory scientist. I had to admit that I had more control over a whole, free roaming, rat than I ever did over a single rat nerve in a temperature controlled moist chamber. I never again did a physiological experiment. I still kept all my expensive custom designed iridectomy forceps and knives.

For several years I rationalized that I would combine Skinner's methods to improve my physiological research. I dreamt up many such experiments and wrote them down in my notebooks. One such experiment was to teach rats to hold their breath to a sound signal to clean up their motor cortex for study. The giant Betz motor cells in the brain make more electrical discharge than the other cells. As the rat breathes, these motor cells discharge and swamp out the delicate small sensory neural discharges that you are trying to record.

I often discussed these possibilities with Jim Olds, a fellow graduate student. Jim went on to discover the reinforcement center in the brain as a result of combining free operant with neurophysiological research.

When it came time for my doctoral dissertation research, Fred said he had two things I might work on. One, put together a pigeon box and take it over to the medical school where Otto Krayer in the pharmacology department is interested in measuring the effects of drugs on free operant behavior. This was what Peter Dews later did. The other was with Walter Jetter who was a state pathologist and professor of legal medicine at Boston University medical school and who had a grant from the atomic energy commission to study the effects of irradiation on beagle dog's physiology, exercise and behavior. Fred said, "I have been receiving a few hundred dollars a month from him in consultation, which has helped keep Julie in Putney School. All I have done is design a hamburger magazine that Ralph Gerbrands has about half built." I chose to work with the dogs rather than the pigeons because they seemed more social and closer to my goal of researching human behavior. I also knew that dog blood is closer to human blood than that of other animals, and preferred by many pharmacologists for research.

At Boston University I designed and built the first dog operant conditioning apparatus. I studied the dogs in a one-hour behavior sample that included a baseline of pressing a panel on a one minute variable interval schedule for raw hamburger reinforcement. They learned to stop pressing when a light flashed (visual discrimination). They also learned to pause when a buzzer signaled a loud, aversive horn blast (conditioned suppression), going back to work immediately after the horn stopped. This was the first use of loud noise as an aversive stimulus. I ran 63 two year old male beagle dogs for 50 or more one hour long daily sessions to stabilize their behavior samples.

I injected the dogs with alcohol, Nembutal, methamphetamine, and saline placebos to calibrate the effects of well known drugs on this behavior sample. I did this so that we could say enough alcohol to make them stagger had this effect, and enough irradiation to kill them had that effect. The well known drug effects provided a comparison. Then the dogs were taken over to Massachusetts Institute of Technology (MIT) in small body tight cages where they were given 300 Roentgen units of total body irradiation (150 units on each side) from a Van der Graph Generator. That amount of radiation will kill half of the dogs (Lethal Dose of 50% – LD50) from Leukopenia (loss of white cells) about 15 days after irradiation. The survivors gradually recover, taking another 15 days to regain strength and health. Hunter, named for Walter Hunter and the quickest to learn of the 63 dogs, survived and became Fred Skinner's family dog. Hunter lived to a ripe old age, although Eve Skinner was convinced that Hunter's embarrassing flatulence had been caused by his irradiation.

Our free operant behavior sample picked up an immediate effect of the irradiation an hour afterwards by the dogs anticipating and extending their conditioned suppression (experimental anxiety) period when the buzzer signaling the noise blast sounded. Of course, when the dogs became physically ill, their responding dropped off, but their visual discrimination and conditioned anxiety suppression were not changed by their physical deterioration. The same dogs were run every day on an overhead maze by Albert Dimascio, and Nathan Azrin, two BU psychology graduate students. There were no discernible immediate effects of irradiation on their maze times or errors. Azrin was so impressed with the sensitivity of the free operant that after my urging he applied to Harvard's Psychology Department and was accepted to study for his doctorate with Skinner.

This research became my doctoral dissertation, accepted in June 1957. From Walter Jetter I learned the advantage of keeping experimental animals in top physical shape. Our dogs were examined and treated by a veterinary physician every day. They had their temperatures and blood sampled every day. They were washed and combed every day, Their home cages were hosed down and sterilized every day. They exercised on a treadmill at 20 miles per hour at 20 percent grade for 20 minutes every day!

From our free operant research I was strongly rewarded for apparatus design and procedure innovation. I had introduced a new species to the free operant! From the sensitive effects of extended anxiety one hour after irradiation, but not three hours after irradiation, I learned the incredible power and sensitivity of the free operant method. This strengthened my resolve to use the free operant with people.

Whenever Fred and I met to discuss my doctoral dissertation on the effects of total body irradiation and drugs on beagle dog discrimination and fear (Lindsley, 1957a), we always strayed from the topic.

Figure 1. Hunter, the fastest learner of 67 beagle dogs, pressing a panel to get a bit of hamburger delivered up through the magazine hole to his right. Hunter survived his dose of 50% lethal total body radiation and became the household pet of Julie and Debby, B. F. Skinner's daughters.

We wondered whether the catatonic schizophrenic standing in a corner all day was the result of total extinction. We wondered whether the hebephrenic was reinforced for giggling on a variable ratio schedule. If so, all we had to do was find a reinforcer and shape them back to their normal performance.

Fascinated, I promised Fred that if he could get funds, I would give human free operant research with psychotics five years of my life. If it didn't pan out, my parachute plan was to go to Ringling Brothers Circus and shape Gargantua the gorilla to play a piano and simple card games. I ended up spending eleven and a half years studying psychotics from the back wards of Metropolitan State Hospital.

Skinner got support from the Milton Fund of Harvard and the U. S. Office of Naval Research. Harry Solomon, chair of Psychiatry at Harvard and Commissioner of Mental Health for Massachusetts agreed to serve as a co-investigator. I started in June 1953 with $7,500 for the year in "A" Basement (an abandoned hydro therapy unit) of Metropolitan State Hospital, Waltham, Massachusetts. We studied both acute and chronic male and female psychotic patients, autistic children, and even the

Figure 2. Chronic psychotic patient, diagnosed catatonic schizophrenic, standing in his usual position in a corridor of Harvard's Behavior Research Laboratory waiting for his daily session in one of the experimental rooms behind the doors to the left.

most violent patients from the locked wards (it was before routine drug therapy). We studied attendants, adult volunteers, and school children as normal controls.

Figure 3 shows ten minutes of the one hour cumulative record of session 91 for patient number 46 at the right pf the photo. The record shows he pulled the plunger 220 times for 13 reinforcements (diagonal hatch marks) on a fixed ratio 20 schedule. He paused 11 times (flat places on record), but not immediately after reinforcement as do normal animals and normal human adults and children. The patient showed two aspects of normal fixed ratio behavior, high speed and pauses. However the third aspect of fixed ratio behavior, pausing immediately after reinforcement was deficient.

Project Name Selection

Skinner named our project "Experimental Analysis of the Behavior of Psychotic Patients" (Skinner, Solomon, & Lindsley, 1954; Lindsley & Skinner, 1954). Hospital staff, patients, and parents reacted negatively to the words "Experimental Analysis." I made a list of over 12 possible names and chose "Studies in Behavior Therapy." Market tests of the name with staff, patients, and family were positive. I liked the words because they meant we treated behavior problems with behavior. Skinner and Solomon approved this name for our project (Lindsley, Skinner, & Solomon 1953, 1954a, 1954b). This was the first use of the name "Behavior Therapy."

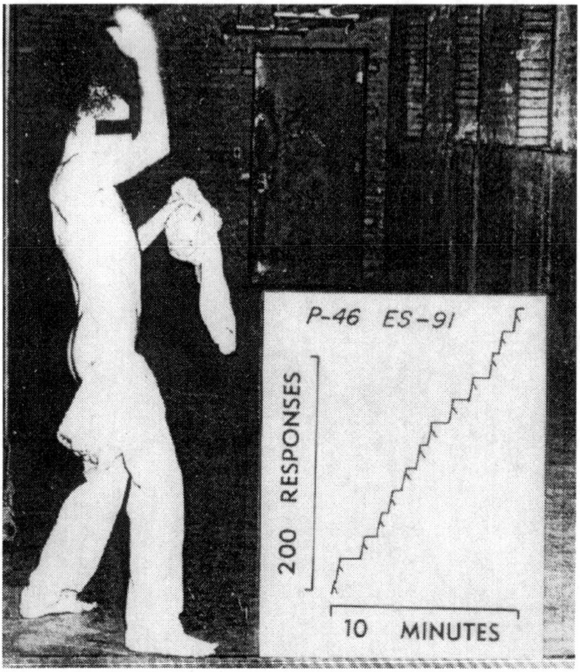

Figure 3. Head banging psychotic on his way from male violent ward to Behavior Research Laboratory for his 91st experimental session. The chart at the right shows ten minutes of his experimental session, which is described in the text.

After two years we were accepted as part of the hospital staff by patients and families. Our stationary and business cards were used up. We felt secure enough to change our name to "Harvard Medical School Behavior Research Laboratory" (Lindsley, Skinner, & Solomon 1955). Strangers would read it in the telephone book and call up and ask, "Do you do laboratory research on behavior?" Mary Hall, our secretary, would laugh and answer, "Of course!" This was the first use of the name "Behavior Research."

Operandum Design

Many chronic psychotic patients occasionally become highly destructive with no advance warning. They throw objects, smash chairs, and break windows. This is the behavior that keeps them in the hospital, and this is the behavior we must study and understand. In order to record the behavior of such patients while in their destructive episodes, we needed indestructible rooms, signals (stimuli), operating switches (operanda), and reward delivery magazines. The operanda had to be able to be moved easily at frequencies above 300 per minute so there would be no ceiling on response frequency. No commercially available switches met these demands, so we designed and Ralph Gerbrands built, our "Lindsley Operandum." Other laboratories later purchased this operandum from Gerbrands, Inc.

Figure 4 shows the condition of the experimental room after a violent patient had a destructive episode during the experimental session. Note the chair is destroyed, but the plexiglass windows to left and right used to yoke rooms or display picture stimuli and rewards are intact. The work panel with a signal light above each of two plunger operanda and the magazine delivery chute on the right is intact. The patient broke his chair against the work panel, but did not harm our indestructible panel.

Symptom Recorders

To record psychotic symptoms we used electrical mats on the floor to record pacing, and voice operated relays hidden in the ceiling to record vocal hallucinating (talking and yelling to no one). These frequencies were recorded minute to minute on cumulative recorders with electrical counters for the hourly and daily totals. Three recorders ran through each session, a manual work recorder, a pacing recorder, and a vocal hallucinating recorder (Lindsley, 1959, 1963a).

Figure 5 diagrams the room and apparatus for directly and continuously recording the vocal and pacing symptoms and the manual plunger pulling for reinforcements. You can see the cumulative recorders at the bottom of the relay racks at the right apparatus alley in figure 6.

Reinforcer Search

I designed and Gerbrands built universal magazines that would carry anything from a penny, an M&M candy, a cigarette, or a slice of apple, to a package of

Figure 4. Interior of experimental room at end of one hour experimental session during which a violent patient had a destructive episode.

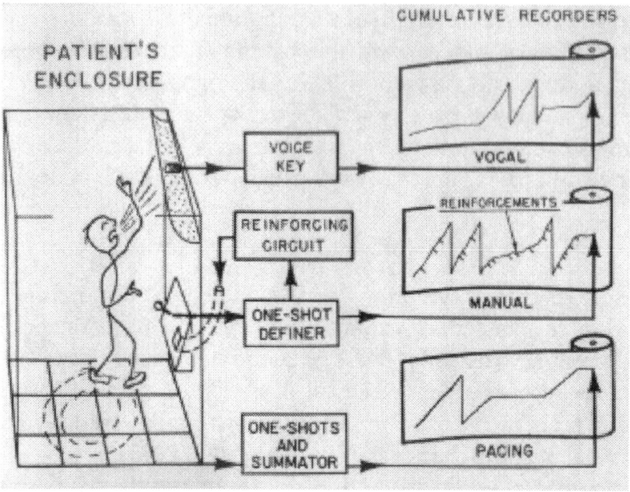

Figure 5. Diagram of experimental room and apparatus for recording vocal symptoms, manual plunger pulling for reinforcements, and pacing symptoms.

Figure 6. Apparatus Alley, a long corridor behind the six experimental rooms contained the controlling and recording apparatus. Details described in the text.

cigarettes, and deliver them rapidly down a chute into the experimental room. You can see four universal feeders mounted up the outside back of the experimental rooms at the left of figure 6. We never found adequate rewards for several of the patients (Lindsley 1956a). In vain we tried projected 2 x 2 slides of various subjects, including nude women for the men. We tried various music selections and movies, but the silent periods in the image and sound when the frequency of responding dropped disturbed the viewers.

Figure 6 shows apparatus alley. You can see the universal magazines mounted vertically along the left back wall of the experimental rooms. The near magazine contains assorted candies on the trays about to be delivered. At the second room down William Nichols stands with his head under a periscope observation hood secretly watching the patient working inside the room. At the right you see vertical wheeled relay racks with the controlling apparatus, counters, timers and recorders. See four reset able counters at the top of the near rack. At the top of the next rack hang two timing tapes. Note the cumulative recorders on shelves with baskets to o catch their records as they roll out. I am the young bearded man wearing hospital keys on a chain and standing while recording some counts on a standard data card resting on top of the fourth recorder down.

Conjugate Reinforcers

We designed and built the first conjugate reinforcer to continuously present narrative movies and music without the brief pauses that destroy narration and mood. The reward is to bring the image or sound louder, closer, or more in focus. The rate of response is directly linked to the intensity of the video or audio channel. The faster the patient presses one switch the louder the audio; the faster they press the other switch the brighter the projected image.

Figure 7 diagrams the two rooms linked by conjugately controlled closed circuit televised psychotherapy sessions. The patient pressed one switch to listen to her therapist and the other switch to look at her therapist (Lindsley 1963b, 1969). We found looking and listening were independent, sometimes occurring together and at other times singly. The looking and listening were related to therapeutic content. Conjugately reinforced loud noises went deeply into sleep (Lindsley 1957b), anesthesia (Lindsley, Hobika, & Etsten, 1961), coma (Lindsley & Conran, 1962), and infancy (Lipsitt, Pederson, & Delucia, 1966), but still did not generate behavior from our most withdrawn chronic psychotics. Conjugately reinforced television commercials were easily calibrated (Lindsley 1962c), and the conjugate schedule is sensitive enough to record preference for stereo over mono phonic music (Morgan & Lindsley, 1966). Over a hundred studies using the conjugate schedule have since been reviewed (Rovee-Collieer & Gekoski, 1979).

Reinforcer Behavior Therapy

We eliminated and reduced symptom frequencies in some patients with differential reward methods (Barrrett, 1962; Lindsley, 1959). However, there were some patients for whom we never found a useful reinforcer.

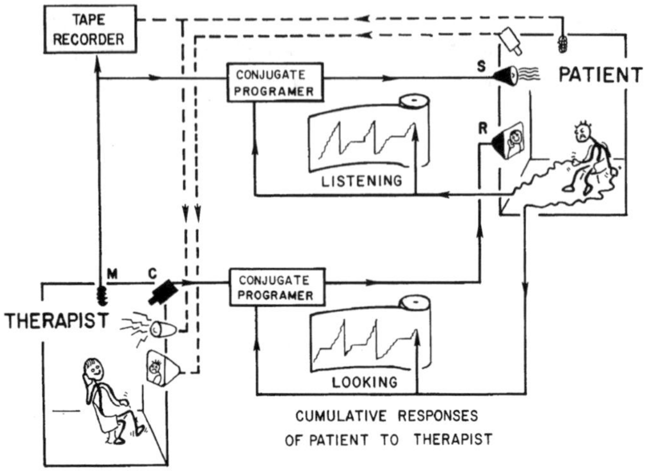

Figure 7. Diagram of experimental rooms and apparatus for recording a patient's listening and looking at her psychotherapist throughout their daily session.

Social Reinforcers

In attempts to see if patients were too guilty to work to reward themselves, we tried giving them the opportunity to feed a hungry kitten as a reward (Lindsley, 1956b). We yoked two experiment al rooms to see whether patients would work to reward a friend, attractive member of the opposite sex, or a stranger (Cohen, 1962; Cohen & Lindsley, 1964). We generated cooperation between children without giving instructions by using reward contingencies alone (Azrin & Lindsley, 1956). None of these attempts were effective with our most depressed inactive patients.

Simultaneous Discrimination and Differentiation SIDAD

One of our most powerful diagnostic methods used a panel with two signal lights. Each was lit for one minute as they switched back and forth. A plunger under each light could be pulled singly or both at once. This work panel is shown in figure 4. Pulling the left plunger with the left light on was reinforced on a fixed ratio 10 schedule (every tenth response rewarded) with a coin or candy. Pulling the left plunger with the right light on, or the right plunger with the left light on, or the right plunger with the right light on was never reinforced. We recorded each of these four reflexes separately on counters and cumulative recorders. A fifth recorder continuously recorded simultaneous plunger pulls (within 125 milliseconds of each other) which were never reinforced (Barret & Lindsley, 1962).

Simultaneous learning to discriminate (tell the lights apart) and differentiate (tell the plungers apart) could be seen developing on the five recorders. Learning deficits in nonverbal and violent patients were easily diagnosed and compared with the learning of normal children and adults (Lindsley, 1962a).

Free Operant Equation, COLAB and IS – DID

It was difficult to determine what part of free operant behavior was deficient in the patients who could not perform. The components of a single operant reflex are, in order: (1) stimulus; (2) response; (3) reinforcing contingency; and (4) consequence or reinforcement. In diagramming the analysis we used capital letters as the symbols for each component and separated them by dashes:

DID	S	-	R	-	K	-	C
	stimulus		response		contingency		consequence

In analyzing a deficient operant to determine which component may be causing the deficiency, each component must be independently tested for operant function on each individual. We gave another set of names to events whose operant function is still unproven, to clearly separate them from components with proven function. These terms are: (1) programmed event; (2) movement; (3) arrangement; and (4) arranged event. They are diagrammed as follows:

IS	PE	-	M	-	A	-	AE
	programmed event		movement		arrangement		arranged event

An example shows how this notation system helped us determine which component of a deficient operant was not functioning. If a child pulled a plunger on the wall when the light was on, every tenth pull produced a piece of candy. The child pulled the plunger and got some candy, but she pulled when the light was off as much as when it was on. What can we say, except that the child could not learn to pull only when the light was on? The operant equation now reads:

IS	PE	-	M	-	A	-	AE
	light on		plunger pull		FR 10		candy

Any one of these four components could be deficient. An operant equation with four unknowns cannot be solved for one unknown.

A prosthetically oriented educator would not assume the child has a visual problem. Nor would he try other rewards. Nor would he change the contingency arrangement. Instead he alters the movement component, because he had notice the plunger pulling seemed "rhythmic" or "mechanical." So, our educator substitutes jumping-on-a-pedal for pulling-the-plunger as the movement component:

IS	PE	-	M	-	A	-	AE
	light on		pedal jump		FR 10		candy

Our child only jumps for candy when the light is on! Our educator has now discovered four operant components and can assign operant functions to the components in the child's equation:

DID	S	-	R	-	K	-	C
	light on		pedal jump		FR 10		candy

The child has visual discrimination Ability, jumping as an operant response, will work on fixed-ratio 10, and is reinforced by candy. She has a response function deficit using her hands, but does not have restricted manual movement.

Our educator analyst can now use the three components with proven function to test to see whether the child will work for tokens:

IS	S	-	R	-	K	-	AE
	light on		pedal jump		FR 10		token

This operant equation, containing three components with known function, can be solved for the unknown consequence (token) being tested. We must have only one unknown in the behavior equation we are trying to solve. These analytic procedures were further detailed in Lindsley, 1964. They later were named a Common Language for Analyzing Behavior (COLAB), and still later named IS-DOES (a set of terms for what it IS, and a set for what it DOES). Still later, I named them IS-DID in an attempt to make people not use the DOES terms until they had actually proven them with that child.

Ten Year Data Histories

Our core group of 50 male chronic psychotic patients participated in our rooms each weekday for as long as 10 years. Several patients had 25 to 29 day rhythms in their performance which we tried to relate to phases of the moon, sun spots, temperature and humidity fluctuations, but none of these held up. Patients whose 10 year histories were without rhythms were good for measuring drug effects because we could rule out mood swings, hospital events, and family visits.

Seven Hour Drug Sessions

Since most psychotic episodes of hyper active shouting to no one or stereotyped pacing in circles lasted from 15 to 45 minutes, we needed sessions as long as two hours to capture an episode from beginning to end. To record the onset and duration of an oral or intra muscular injection of a drug our nurse entered the room after 15 minutes and injected the drug or a placebo. Usually the drug had its onset effects within 15 to 30 minutes after injection. After about 5 hours the effects wore off. Therefore we needed 7 hour sessions to record the full effect of a drug on a patient's work, pacing, and vocal symptoms (Lindsley, 1962b).

Figure 8 shows that fifteen minutes into session 746 our nurse injected 20 mg. of Benactyzine intramuscularly and the effects appear in the top panel. Fifteen minutes into session 747 our nurse injected a lactose placebo whose effects are shown in the bottom panel. Notice that the Benactyzine injection produced sustained vocal hallucinating for a about four hours. During this time the manual work was depressed. Also notice that the vocal cumulative record is less steep for the first 2 hours representing a rate of about 12 per minute. During this time his plunger pulling work fell off from his normal rate of 160 per minute to 6 per minute. During the second 2 hours after injection the vocalizing almost doubled to 21 per minute while his plunger pulling work gradually returned to normal. Benactyzine produced a psychotic type episode lasting almost 4 hours. In the placebo session 747 a short 25 minute and a longer 40 minute psychotic episode occurred. This patient number 7 displayed 15 to 45 minute psychotic episodes of this type every few hours on his ward.

The immediate effects of injected drugs on seven hour sessions produced the same effects as did routine clinical oral administration which usually took weeks to develop. These immediate effects permitted us to screen new drugs with suggested psycho active potential 5 or 6 times faster than the usual oral administration and ward behavior observation.

Coextensive Reflex Emission

These seven hour sessions permitted us to view and quantify the interactions between episodes of psychotic vocalizing and pacing with manual working. With 16

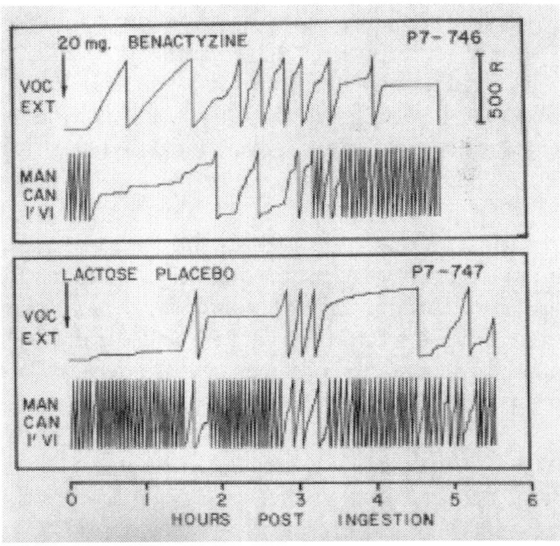

Figure 8. Six hour cumulative response records of never rewarded hallucinatory vocalizing (VOC EXT) and manual plunger pulling reinforced with candy on a 1 minute variable interval schedule (MAN CAN 1'VI) of Benactyzine session 746 and lactose placebo session 747 for Patient number 7.

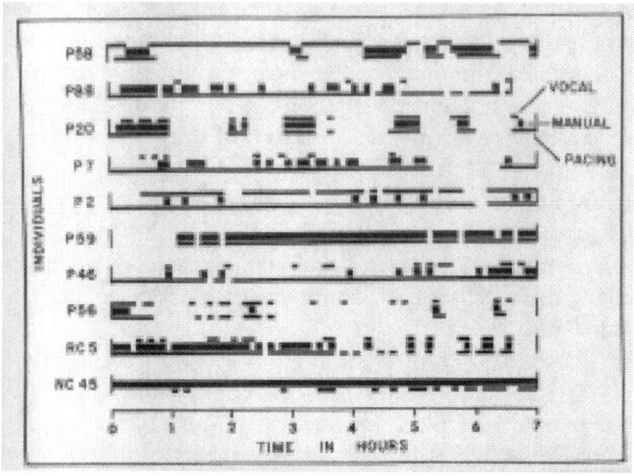

Figure 9. Bar diagrams of 7 hour sessions comparing emission of never rewarded vocalizing (thin top bar), manual working for rewards (thick middle bar), and never rewarded pacing (thin bottom bar) for 8 psychotics, 1 retarded child (RG), and 1 normal child (NC).

patients these episodes were independent as with normal adults and children. In 6 patients, all diagnosed schizophrenic, these episodes coextended of the same time interval. They appeared linked together (See the records of P20, P59, P56 in figure 9), or alternated (See P58 in figure 9). All normal controls manually worked throughout the seven hours with no vocalizing and only a very few brief pacings (See NC 45 in figure 7). The normals did not stop working during their brief pacing episodes.

Figure 9 displays bar diagrams for the never rewarded vocalizing (thin top bar), manual plunger pulling for rewards (thick middle bar)., and never rewarded pacing (thin bottom bar) over continuous 7 hour sessions. The performance of eight adult male psychotic patients, a retarded child (RC), and a normal child (NCV). The retarded child also had emotional problems and had recently been thought of as emotionally disturbed. Note the linked coextension during the last 2 hours of his session.

Except for the vocal hallucinating and pacing symptoms, this reflex coextension was the first emergent diagnostic item that we found. All other diagnostic items that we found were deficiencies, a decrease or absence of some aspect of normal performance.

Folly of Drug Screening

Our seven hour intra muscular injection drug sessions predicted the response of patients to long term (3 months) oral clinical administration of the same drug. This meant we could screen new drugs at the rate of one a week on ten psychotic patients. This screening efficiency appealed to drug companies and to the National Institute of Mental Health. We had a screening device. We could screen one new drug a week on the normal work, pacing and hallucinating of chronic and acute psychotic patients.

We wondered what was the past success of scientists with screening devices in searching for effective active compounds? How many drugs must we try before we would find one that would reduce psychotic symptoms and at the same time restore normal work performance? Edison said he screened 3,000 materials before he found the carbon filament for his electric bulb (Josephson, 1959). Marie Curie tried hundreds of salts, oxides, and ores before she found the radio active pitchblende and chacolite (Pflaum, 1993). Salvarsan™ (arsphenamine), an early treatment for syphilis, was the 606th compound the company tried. The range seemed to be 3,000 to 300 barren attempts before screening success.

If we tried a new compound a week and were lucky we might expect to find a psychotic treatment drug in 300 trials, or 6 years, at the rate of one trial a week. The hooker was that the drug companies were only producing 5 to 10 per year that were of human toxicity. That would take 30 years if we were as lucky as Curie and 300 years if we had Edison's luck!

The kiss of death to our drug screening came in 1957 to 1962 when Thalidomide taken in even a single dose caused pregnant women to miscarry or give birth to horribly deformed babies. Only 17 Thalidomide babies were born in the United States to women who got the drug illegally, since it had not been approved for use in the US. However, the Thalidomide scare caused a shut down in new drugs approved by the United States Health Service for human trial. New drugs available for trial with psychotics went from 5 to 10 per year to 1 in 5 years. With these restrictions, if we had Curie's luck, we would find an effective drug in 5 x 300 or 1500 years! So ended our drug screening plans.

Lab Visitors

Our laboratory guest book shows that in the twelve years from 1953 through 1964 ninety eight university classes from ten universities with a total of 1857 students spent day long field trips in our laboratory. Nine Hundred thirty seven professionals visited our laboratory from the United States and over seventeen other countries. Visiting psychiatrists and psychologists included Carl Rogers, Harry Harlow, Roy Menninger, Piere Pichot, Paolo Nuzzi, Koji Sato, Hudson Hoagland, Otto Kernberg, Andey Snejnenski, Carl Pfaffman, Frank Beach, Donald Lindsley, Carl Pribram, Joe Zubin, and Timothy Leary. Visiting behavior analysts included Don Baer, Harold Weiner, William Morse, Ted Allyon, Dale Brethower, Matthew Israel, Charlie Catania, Thom Verhave, Joe Brady, and Charles Ferster. Sidney Bijou visited in April 1957, November 1961, and April 1962. Bijou built a similar laboratory for children at the University of Washington, as did Ferster at the University of Indiana Medical School, Azrin at Anna State Hospital in Southern Illinois, and Barrett at Fernald State School, Waltham, Massachusetts.

Research Trainees

Larry Fane and Donald Cohen conducted undergraduate honors theses . Julie Rich and Barbara Morgan conducted their Master's theses. Post Doctoral trainees were Nathan Azrin, Beatrice Barrett, Peter Nathan, Martha Mednick, and Paul Blachly. Tom Gilbert conducted research in our laboratory while on a University of Georgia sabbatical.

Awards

In 1962 the American Psychiatric Association awarded one of our research papers its annual Hofheimer Research Prize (Lindsley, 1960). In 1964 the American Academy of Achievement awarded us its Golden Plate Achievement Award. These twelve pioneering years were cited in two recent awards, the 1998 Thomas F. Gilbert Distinguished Professional Achievement Award from the International Society for Performance Improvement and the 1999 Award for Distinguished Service to Behavior Analysis from the Society for the Advancement of Behavior Analysis.

Appliers Abandon Frequency

Most of the behavior analysts who visited our laboratory and then set up studies in clinics, hospitals, and schools did not record their learner's rate of response; they recorded percent. To me this was a crisis because we had proven that frequency was as much as 10 times more sensitive than percent. I considered rate of response and the cumulative self-recorder to be Skinner's greatest contributions, and both were discarded by the appliers. Azrin went so far as to say "suit the metric," which meant use a different measure for every behavior you work with. It may have been easier to do and much easier to sell, but such a loss of measurement standards rules out real science which requires standard measures

Application research grew like wildfire compared to the behavioral laboratory research that had originally triggered it. The laboratories were expensive, hard to fund, and ignored by both clinicians and small animal laboratory researchers. Behavior modification, behavior therapy, and applied behavior analysis were clearly going to dominate the field. Unfortunately they left behind behavior frequency and self charting on standard charts, Skinner's most powerful discoveries.

The crisis was clear. If something was not done soon, frequency and standard self charting would die with Skinner! A few began to apply operant methods to regular and special education. They too did not use frequency or standard self charting. They said teachers preferred percent correct, and percent time on task. They said teachers were dead set against student self charting. Clearly education was a larger industry with far greater market potential than mental health.

Since I could not convince others to do it, I realized that I would have to put frequency and standard self charting into school classrooms. The combination of too few new drugs to try, increased university overhead charges, increased competition for smaller and smaller government research grants, lack of interest in our results, and the crisis of losing frequency and standard self charting to multiplying applications, made continuing our laboratory research a poor choice.

In January 1965, I closed our laboratory and parachuted further into teacher education at the University of Kansas Medical Center than the percent correct appliers had yet gone. My mission was to get teachers using frequency and students charting their own performance. There we developed Precision Teaching and the Standard Celeration Chart used by students to self chart their learning and make their own improvement decisions (Lindsley 1972, 1996, 1997). But that's another story.

References

Azrin, N. H., & Lindsley, O. R. (1956). The reinforcement of cooperation between children. *Journal of Abnormal and Social Psychology, 52,* 100-102.

Barrett, B. H. (1962). Reduction in rate of multiple tics by free operant conditioning methods. *Journal of Nervous and Mental Disease, 135,* 187-195.

Barrett, B. H., & Lindsley, O. R. (1962). Deficits in acquisition of operant discrimination and differentiation shown by institutionalized retarded children. *American Journal of Mental Deficiency, 67,* 424-436.

Cohen, D. J. (1962). Justin and his peers: An experimental analysis of a child's social world. *Child Development, 33,* 697-0717.

Cohen, D. J., & Lindsley, O. R. (1964). Catalysis of controlled leadership in cooperation by human stimulation. *Journal of Child Psychology and Psychiatry, 5,* 119-137.

Jetter, W. W., Lindsley, O. R., & Wohlwill, F. J. (1953). *The effects of irradiation on physical exercise and behavior in the dog: Related hematological and pathological control studies* (AEC Contract AT No. 30-1, pp. 1201). Boston University Medical School.

Josephson, M. (1959). *Edison: A biography.* New York: McGraw-Hill. pp. 207.

Lindsley, O. R. (1950). Neural components of the chorda tympani of the rat. Unpublished masters thesis, Brown University, Providence, RI.

Lindsley, O. R. (1956a). Operant conditioning methods applied to research in chronic schizophrenia. *Psychiatric Research Reports, 5,* 118-139.

Lindsley, O. R. (1956b). Feeding a kitten – a social reinforcer. In annual technical report #3, November, Contract N5-Ori-07662, Office of Naval Research. Waltham MA: Harvard Medical School, Behavior Research laboratory.

Lindsley, O. R. (1957a). *Conditioned suppression of behavior in the dog and some sodium pentobarbital effects.* Unpublished doctoral dissertation, Harvard University.

Lindsley, O. R. (1957b). Operant behavior during sleep: A measure of depth of sleep. *Science, 126,* 1290-1292.

Lindsley, O. R. (1959). Reduction in rate of vocal psychotic symptoms by differential positive reinforcement. *Journal of the Experimental Analysis of Behavior, 2,* 269.

Lindsley, O. R. (1960). Characteristics of the behavior of chronic psychotics as revealed by free-operant conditioning methods [Monograph]. *Diseases of the Nervous System, 21*, 66-78.
Lindsley, O. R. (1962a). Operant conditioning methods in diagnosis. In J. H. Nodine & J. H. Moyer (Eds.), *Psychosomatic medicine: The first Hahnemann symposium* (pp. 41-54). Philadelphia: Lea & Febiger.
Lindsley, O. R. (1962b). Operant conditioning techniques in the measurement of psychopharmacologic response. In J. H. Nodine & J. H. Moyer (Eds.), *Psychosomatic medicine: The first Hahnemann symposium* (pp. 373-383). Philadelphia: Lea & Febiger.
Lindsley, O. R. (1962c). A behavioral measure of television viewing. *Journal of Advertising Research, 2*, 2-12.
Lindsley, O. R. (1963a). Direct measurement and functional definition of vocal hallucinatory symptoms. *Journal of Nervous and Mental Disease, 136*(3), 293-297.
Lindsley, O. R. (1963b). Free-operant conditioning and psychotherapy In J. H. Masserman (Ed.), *Current psychiatric therapies* (Vol. 3) (pp. 47-56). New York: Grune and Stratton.
Lindsley, O. R. (1964). Direct measurement and prosthesis of retarded behavior. *Journal of Education, 147*, 62-81.
Lindsley, O. R. (1969). Direct behavioral analysis of psychotherapy sessions by conjugately programmed closed-circuit television. *Psychotherapy: Theory, Research, and Practice, 6*, 71-81.
Lindsley, O. R. (1972). From Skinner to Precision Teaching: The child knows best. In J. B. Jordan & L. S. Robbins (Eds.), *Let's try doing something else kind of thing: Behavioral principles and the exceptional child* (pp. 1-11). Arlington, VA: Council for Exceptional Children.
Lindsley, O. R. (1996). Is fluency free-operant response-response chaining? *The Behavior Analyst, 19*(2), 211-224.
Lindsley, O. R. (1997). Precise instructional design.: Guidelines from Precision Teaching. In C. R. Dills & A J. Romiszowski (Eds.), *Instructional development paradigms* (pp. 537-554). Englewood Cliffs, NJ: Educational Technology Publications.
Lindsley, O. R., & Conran, P. (1962). Operant behavior during EST: A measure of depth of coma. *Diseases of the Nervous System, 23*, 407-409.
Lindsley, O. R., Hobika, J. H., & Etsten, B. E. (1961). Operant behavior during anesthesia recovery: A continuous and objective method. *Anesthesiology, 22*, 937-946.
Lindsley, O. R., & Jetter, W. W. (1953). The temporary elimination of discrimination and fear by sodium pentobarbital injections (dog). *American Psychologist, 8*, 390.
Lindsley, O. R., & Skinner, B. F. (1954). A method for the experimental analysis of the behavior of psychotic patients. *American Psychologist, 9*, 419-420.
Lindsley, O. R., Skinner, B. F., & Solomon, H. C. (1953). Study of psychotic behavior, Studies in Behavior Therapy, Harvard Medical School, Department

of Psychiatry, Metropolitan State Hospital, Waltham, MA, Office of Naval Research Contract N5-ori-07662, Status Report I, 1 June 1953 - 31 December 1953.

Lindsley, O. R., Skinner, B. F., & Solomon, H. C. (1954a). Study of psychotic behavior, Studies in Behavior Therapy, Harvard Medical School, Department of Psychiatry, Metropolitan State Hospital, Waltham, MA, Office of Naval Research Contract N5-ori-07662, Status Report II, 1 January 1954 - 31 May 1954.

Lindsley, O. R., Skinner, B. F., & Solomon, H. C. (1954b). Study of psychotic behavior, Studies in Behavior Therapy, Harvard Medical School, Department of Psychiatry, Metropolitan State Hospital, Waltham, MA, Office of Naval Research Contract N5-ori-07662, Status Report III, 1 June 1954 - 31 December 1954.

Lindsley, O. R., Skinner, B. F., & Solomon, H. C. (1955). Study of psychotic behavior, Behavior Research Laboratory, Harvard Medical School, Department of Psychiatry, Metropolitan State Hospital, Waltham, MA, Office of Naval Research Contract N5-ori-07662, Status Report IV, 1 January 1955 - 31 August 1955.

Lipsitt, L., Pederson, L. J., & Delucia, C. A. (1966). Conjugate reinforcement of operant responding in infants. *Psychonomic Science, 4,* 67-68.

Morgan, B., & Lindsley, O. R. (1966). Operant preference for stereophonic over monophonic music. *Journal of Music Therapy, 3,* 135-143.

Pflaum, R. (1993). *Marie Curie and Her Daughter Irene.* Minneapolis: Lerner Publications

Rovee-Collier, C. K., & Gekoski, M. J. (1979). The economics of infancy: A review of conjugate reinforcement. *Advances in Child Development, 13,* 195-255.

Skinner, B. F., Solomon, H. C., & Lindsley, O. R. (1954). A new method for the experimental analysis of the behavior of psychotic patients. *Journal of Nervoius and Mental Disease, 120*(5), 403-406.

Chapter 7

A Brief Personal Account of CT (Conditioning Therapy), BT (Behavior Therapy) and CBT (Cognitive-Behavior Therapy): Spanning Three Continents

Arnold A. Lazarus
Rutgers University and the Center for Multimodal Psychological Services

Conditioning Therapy

In South Africa, the forerunners of what came to be known as "Behavior Therapy," were Joseph Wolpe (a general medical practitioner), James Taylor (a university-based psychologist), Abe Adelstein (an epidemiologist and methodologist), Cynthia Adelstein (a psychologist), and Leo Reyna, an American psychologist who served as a senior lecturer at the University of the Witwatersrand in Johannesburg from 1946 to 1950. The foregoing individuals guided and inspired Wolpe and were the driving forces behind the well-known experiments that he conducted on cats. Wolpe first submitted the dissertation that resulted from his animal experiments to the Department of Psychiatry at the University of the Witwatersrand. Given that he had never received any formal training in psychiatry, they turned it down. Similarly, the Department of Psychology rejected it because Wolpe had never enrolled in any psychology courses. Finally, given that he had graduated from the medical school with an M. B., B. Ch. (Bachelor of Medicine and Bachelor of Surgery), the Department of Medicine awarded him an M.D. degree in 1948.

In 1956 when I was a graduate student in psychology at the University of the Witwatersrand one of the senior lecturers arranged for Wolpe to give talks and demonstrations of his CT (conditioning therapy). Wolpe was in full-time private practice, but was not allowed to charge specialist fees because he was not a licensed psychiatrist. This factor coupled with the untenable political climate in South Africa led him to seek for greener pastures. Thus, when he received an appointment in 1960 at the University of Virginia School of Medicine, he emigrated from South Africa. This did not occur before he had gathered together a coterie of clinicians and theoreticians who were interested in learning what the establishment thinkers called "ideas from the lunatic fringe." I became a member of this august group, although it took some time to shed the psychoanalytic precepts that had been drilled into me. S. Rachman, also a graduate student, was an important member of this cabal. He proclaimed Wolpe "The King," and we vied for the position of Crown Prince. Rachman went to London to study with Eysenck, whereas I continued working with Wolpe who chaired my doctoral dissertation. In 1960, when Wolpe left for America, I, a newly minted Ph.D., (but a registered clinical psychologist) inherited his private practice. I also became the leader of the training group seminar in Johannesburg that Wolpe had launched. Later, Rachman was awarded a Ph.D., from the University of London, soon became Eysenck's right hand man, and went on to a distinguished career as a writer, editor and clinical experimenter.

Whereas the mainstream theorists and clinicians in South Africa focused essentially on putative dynamic insights and psychoanalytic concepts, the CT meetings were devoted to learning theory and the use of exciting new techniques – all old hat today – imaginal and in vivo desensitization, relaxation procedures, assertiveness training, thought stopping, aversion relief conditioning, and the like. Animal analogues played a major role at this juncture. Methods or ideas that could not be tested in the animal laboratory were deemed unacceptable.

In 1957, at one of the Wolpe group meetings I proposed that we drop the term "Conditioning Therapy" because too many people tended to attach pejorative connotations to it of bells, whistles and salivating dogs. Instead, why not call ourselves "Behavior Therapists" and describe our area of interest as "Behavior Therapy?" After all, I stated, our main focus is on behavior and the remediation of maladaptive behaviors. This suggestion was not well received. The main objections, as I recall, were that we should not pander to ignorance. Why permit the prejudices of unenlightened people to sway us? Moreover, the New York-based practitioner Andrew Salter (another worthy contender for the title of the father of behavior therapy) reported no down side from calling his book *Conditioned Reflex Therapy* (1949). Wolpe's commitment to CT is exemplified in the proceedings of an important conference held at the University of Virginia that was published under the title *The Conditioning Therapies* (Wolpe, Salter & Reyna, 1964). The conditioning label remained quite popular. Thus, Franks (1964) edited a book he called "Conditioning Techniques in Clinical Practice and Research." Nevertheless, I had published an article (Lazarus, 1958) in which I put forward the terms "behavior therapy" and "behavior therapist." Later, Eysenck (1959) independently used these terms in print, but I lay claim to having been the first person to use them in a scientific journal. (Wolpe, 1968, discovered that in 1953, Skinner, Lindsley and their associates, working at the Metropolitan State Hospital, Waltham, Massachusetts had some mimeographed status reports on operant conditioning with psychotic inmates that they referred to as "Studies in Behavior Therapy.")

Behavior Therapy

After Eysenck (1960, 1964) edited two books on behavior therapy, the term became more widely disseminated and won out over Conditioning Therapy and other designations that had been proposed – e.g., "Behavioristic Psychotherapy,"

"Objective Psychotherapy," and "Reciprocal Inhibition Therapy." Subsequently, Cyril Franks founded the Association for Advancement of the Behavioral Therapies in 1966 (soon afterward called the Association for Advancement of Behavior Therapy) and he later edited a highly significant book on behavior therapy (Franks, 1969). In the 1960's and 1970's, despite denouncements from critics, skeptics and detractors, there was a high degree of interest in behavioral methods among researchers, theoreticians and clinicians. In 1963 when Albert Bandura invited me to spend a year at Stanford University training graduate students in behavioral theories and methods, enthusiasm for this novel and promising approach was high. (My favorite student was a very bright, personable and energetic fellow named G. C. Davison who, as you well know, has played a major role in the field.)

Interestingly, the emphasis in behavioral methods in South Africa and England was primarily Pavlovian and Hullian (see Eysenck, 1956) and focused on *respondent conditioning*, whereas in the United States, the work of Skinner on *operant conditioning* served as the mainstay. Well-known names in this arena include Ayllon, Goldiamond, Ferster, Wolf, Risley, Patterson, Baer, Azrin, Lindsley, Bijou, and many others. The term "behavior modification" was preferred to "behavior therapy." An influential book edited by Ullmann and Krasner (1965) blended the two concepts. Bandura's (1969) seminal studies on social learning theory and modeling served to broaden the base of behavioral interventions. Perry London's (1964) book *The Modes and Morals of Psychotherapy* was widely read and served to pave the way for technical eclecticism and a more elegant behavioral tradition.

From 1960 onward, data driven research on behavioral theories and methods was conducted at many centers. The annual conventions of the Association for Advancement of Behavior Therapy (AABT) traversed such topics as the use of reinforcement schedules, modification of smoking behavior, aversion relief treatment of obsessive neurosis, the use of positive and aversive imagery, the specific effects of modeling and role playing, community-based operant learning environments, and other innovative procedures (see Rubin, Fensterheim, Lazarus, & Franks, 1971). Populations to which these new behavioral methods were applied included such areas as schizophrenia, alcoholism, mental retardation, geriatrics, school settings, and juvenile delinquency. Indeed, the proliferation of books, articles, and popular publications on behavior therapy led Franks and Wilson (1973) to bemoan the fact that "quantity is accelerating at a far greater rate than quality" (p. vii). Thus, they launched their *Annual Review of Behavior Therapy* to provide an integrated distillation of the vast literature. They also offered trenchant commentaries that placed the many developments in perspective. These erudite 800-page tomes were extraordinarily illuminating, and it always astonished me that Franks and Wilson managed to address and fulfill all their other academic and clinical demands and still produce these volumes. Each year from 1973 to 1979 the monumental volumes appeared on time. Gradually, it became evident that the commentaries by Franks and Wilson were becoming equal in length to the reprinted articles. It also became clear that most readers were much more interested in the commentaries than in the reprinted material. Consequently, for Volume 8, Kendall and Brownell were recruited to add their specific areas of expertise to the enterprise. With the advent of Volume 12 written (not edited) by Franks, Wilson, Kendall and Foreyt (1990), the question was posed as to whether there was still a need for these publications. The cost-benefit ratio seemed disproportionate and the series ended with Volume 12. At this stage, formal behavior therapy had been in existence for over 30 years.

Cognitive-Behavior Therapy

Some of the personages associated with Cognitive-behavior therapy (CBT) include Ellis, Beck, Meichenbaum, Goldfried, Mischel, Davison and Mahoney. My book *Behavior Therapy and Beyond* (1971/1996) is arguably one of the first books on cognitive-behavior therapy. It soon became a Citation Classic. In the 1977 *Annual Review of Behavior Therapy*, the transition from BT to CBT was discussed, and Cyril Franks used the term "cognitive-behavior therapy" for the first time in his overview. One of my first forays into cognitive zones occurred when I pointed out to Wolpe that during imaginal desensitization, a finger signal or a head nod, or whatever other nonverbal sign of distress had been agreed upon, merely indicated that discomfort, or displeasure was being experienced. It did not speak to the content of the uneasiness or anxiety. When a client signaled distress during a desensitization procedure, the standard response was to say, "Stop picturing that scene, take in a few deep breaths and go back to the pure relaxation." But I pointed out that by examining the meaning behind the finger signal, this often shed light on hitherto unknown components and associations. Wolpe claimed that to conduct discussions in the middle of the desensitization procedure would dilute the process and interrupt the relaxation. This procedural difference was perhaps the first indication that within a few years, an extensive parting of the ways between us would take place.

The aforementioned procedural shift was the harbinger of a significant modification in my thinking. My understanding of the process of change had gone from "insights into putative unconscious complexes," to "reciprocal inhibition, counter-conditioning, and extinction." At this juncture, I started to view *cognitive restructuring* as one of the primary psychotherapeutic change agents. I was influenced by Ellis's (1962) *Reason and Emotion in Psychotherapy*, and London's (1964) *The Modes and Morals of Psychotherapy*, and began to embrace the notion that the power of a person's beliefs can often override his or her operant or respondent conditioning. When I stated that in addition to focusing on behavior, elegant therapy called for attention to cognitive processes – beliefs, attitudes, values, and opinions – my behavioral peers were unimpressed. They saw it as an atavistic regression to mentalism, and I was wrongly accused of being a closet psychoanalyst.

I wrote a series of articles on what I termed "broad-spectrum behavior therapy," that culminated in my 1971 book *Behavior Therapy and Beyond.* This book places emphasis on the notion that "effective psychotherapy must teach people to think, feel, and act differently" (p. 166). This was the beginning of an even broader application of treatment dimensions that I termed "multimodal therapy" (see

Lazarus, 1997) which Cyril Franks (1997) dubbed "behavior therapy in one of its most advanced forms" (p. xii). The multimodal orientation goes beyond the scope of this paper.

A Pivotal Case

A clinical event that played a crucial role in my outlook occurred in 1966. I was treating a severely agoraphobic and fearful 35-year-old woman. She was a cooperative and highly motivated client who responded well to a standard range of behavioral techniques consisting primarily of deep muscle relaxation, imaginal and in vivo desensitization, behavior rehearsal, and assertiveness training. After 5 months of therapy she was able to enjoy taking long walks alone, shopping, visiting and traveling without distress. Important changes had accrued above and beyond the client's capacity to venture out of her home – she was no longer socially submissive and enjoyed a wider range of social outlets; she found that relaxation and positive imagery were capable of quelling any residual fears or anxieties; and her marriage relationship and sexual experiences were more gratifying. Nevertheless, although the client was delighted by her newfound ability to remain anxiety-free while traveling and engaging in the niceties of social interaction, she continued to view herself as a worthless person. She referred to herself as being like a 12-year-old who was now able to cross the street alone, but was contributing nothing to society. At this juncture, what is now called 'cognitive therapy" was clearly indicated, and we launched into an assessment of her more fundamental attitudes and beliefs. This led her to conclude: "If you want to *feel* useful, you have to *be* useful." Consequently, she founded an organization that distributed basic essentials such as food and clothing to impoverished people. This *behavior*, based upon her *attitudes* and *self-concept* led her to view herself as "eminently worthwhile." In a follow-up interview she stated: "Thanks to the fact that I exist and care, thousands of people now derive benefit," and she proclaimed herself "eminently worthwhile." This case is described in greater detail in *Behavior Therapy and Beyond* (Lazarus, 1971/1996).

It was this woman who first led me to realize that "behavior therapy" alone might be insufficient (to use a football analogy) to take people into the end zone. It became quite apparent to me that it was often necessary to venture beyond the customary parameters of behavioral interventions into such territory as values, attitudes and beliefs. Although the early books on behavior therapy discussed the need to "correct misconceptions" (Wolpe, 1958; Wolpe & Lazarus, 1966), the focus was solely on erroneous ideas and did not address the realm of the client's self-talk, his or her basic values, or other cognitive processes. When I emphasized the need to explore and modify such concerns, and when I drew a distinction between what I termed "narrow band behavior therapy," and "broad-spectrum behavior therapy," the reactions from Wolpe and many of my fellow behavior therapists were less than positive. Eysenck (1970), who was after all a theorist who had never treated a patient in his life, wrote a strident criticism and said that my ideas would lead to "nothing but a mishmash of theories, a huggermugger of procedures, a gallimaufry of therapies, and a charivaria of activities having no proper rationale, and incapable of being tested and evaluated" (p. 145). It took about ten years before the need to add cognitive interventions to standard behavioral methods became widely recognized. Goldfried and Davison (1994) in their updated edition of *Clinical Behavior Therapy* (first published in 1976) state: "One no longer needs to argue for the admissibility of cognitive variables into the clinical practice of behavior therapy. Indeed, more than two-thirds of the membership of the Association for Advancement of Behavior Therapy now view themselves as "cognitive-behavior therapists'" (p. 282). As an aside, I took Eysenck thoroughly to task in a chapter I called "On Sterile Paradigms and the Realities of Clinical Practice," (Lazarus, 1986).

As we move into the 21st Century, the emphasis on empirically supported methods and the use of carefully crafted treatment manuals have already begun to clarify the issue of treatments of choice for specific disorders. They supply much needed information about the active ingredients of therapeutic techniques (see Wilson 1995, 1998). Add various breakthroughs that have occurred in the biological arena to the greater precision that is now taking place in the field of cognitive-behavior therapy, and it becomes evident that quantum leaps are in the immediate offing.

So what about the training for future generations? In my own view, in addition to a thorough grounding in psychology and biology, students must fully comprehend science, methodology, and gain a meticulous understanding of the difference between "data" and "anecdotes" (as well as a fundamental schooling in treatments of choice for specific disorders). Moreover, students need to be taught how to implement *relationships of choice* (Lazarus, 1993). Much has been written about "techniques of choice," whereas "relationships of choice" have more or less been taken for granted. Trainees need to acquire a flexible repertoire of relationship styles to enhance treatment outcomes. Decisions regarding different relationship stances include when and how to be directive, supportive, reflective, cold, warm, tepid, formal, informal and so forth. Talking in generalities about rapport, good working alliances, empathy, compatibility and the like will not suffice.

One other important consideration is worth underscoring. Good therapists, in my estimation, have few (if any) "buttons" – hypersensitivities that can trigger untoward affective reactions. For example, recently, two of my students took offense at ethnic slurs uttered by clients during a therapy session. In one case, the client had made an anti-Semitic remark. The Jewish trainee took exception to it and handled the matter emotionally, not clinically. In the other instance, a Hispanic student refused to continue working with a client who made an ethnic remark about Puerto Ricans. My recommendation was that, at the very least, these students should be urged to undergo a course of systematic desensitization.

The foregoing considerations are idealistic. The vast majority of practitioners are drawn from the ranks of counselors, social workers, and psychotherapists who have scanty scientific backgrounds, a distant awareness of psychological principles, and very little understanding of basic behavioral facts and factors. The marketplace is flooded with extremely poorly trained personnel. Nevertheless, it is my contention that if we can move beyond empirically supported methods and develop explicit and well-established treatments of choice, it will become mandatory for anyone who practices psychotherapy to know how, when and where to administer what needs to be employed. Having lived to see behavior therapy evolve (in the span of about 40 years) from a laughable, lunatic fringe, naïve and mechanistic joke, to an orientation that almost occupies center stage, I can but hope that our findings will be consolidated and extended throughout the 21st Century to the benefit of all.

References

Bandura, A. (1969). *Principles of behavior modification*. New York: Holt, Rinehart, & Winston.

Ellis, A. (1962). *Reason and emotion in psychotherapy*. New York: Lyle Stuart.

Eysenck, H. J. (1956). Modern learning theory. *Proceedings of the Royal Society of Social Medicine, 49*, 1024-1026.

Eysenck, H. J. (1959). Learning theory and behaviour therapy. *Journal of Mental Science, 105*, 61-75.

Eysenck, H. J. (Ed.). (1960). *Behaviour therapy and the neuroses*. Oxford: Pergamon Press.

Eysenck, H. J. (Ed.). (1964). *Experiments in behaviour therapy*. Oxford: Pergamon Press.

Eysenck, H. J. (1970). A mish-mash of theories. *International Journal of Psychiatry, 9*, 140-146.

Franks, C. M. (Ed.). (1964). *Conditioning techniques in clinical practice and research*. New York: Springer.

Franks, C. M. (Ed.). (1969). *Behavior therapy: Appraisal and status*. New York: McGraw-Hill.

Franks, C. M. (1997). Foreword. In A. A. Lazarus, *Brief but comprehensive psychotherapy: The multimodal way* (pp. ix-xii). New York: Springer

Franks, C. M., & Wilson, G. T. (Eds.). (1973). *Annual review of behavior therapy*. New York: Brunner/Mazel.

Franks, C. M., Wilson, G. T., Kendall, P. C., & Foreyt, J. P. (1990). *Review of Behavior Therapy*. New York: Guilford.

Goldfried, M. R., & Davison, G. C. (1994). *Clinical behavior therapy*. New York, NY: Wiley.

Lazarus, A. A. (1958). New methods in psychotherapy: A case study. *South African Medical Journal, 32*, 660-664.

Lazarus, A. A. (1971). *Behavior therapy and beyond*. New York: McGraw-Hill.

Lazarus, A. A. (1986). On sterile paradigms and the realities of clinical practice: Critical comments on Eysenck's contribution to behaviour therapy. In S. Modgil and C. Modgil (Eds.), *Hans Eysenck: Consensus and controversy*. London: The Falmer Press.

Lazarus, A. A. (1993). Tailoring the therapeutic relationship, or being an authentic chameleon. *Psychotherapy, 30*, 404-407.

Lazarus, A. A. (1996). *Behavior therapy and beyond.* Northvale, NJ: Jason Aronson.

Lazarus, A. A. (1997). *Brief but comprehensive psychotherapy: The multimodal way.* New York: Springer.

London, P. (1964). *The modes and morals of psychotherapy.* New York: Holt, Rinehart & Winston.

Rubin, R. D., Fensterheim, H., Lazarus, A. A., & Franks, C. M. (Eds.). (1971). *Advances in behavior therapy.* New York: Academic Press.

Salter, A. (1949). *Conditioned reflex therapy.* New York: Creative Age Press.

Ullmann, L. P., & Krasner, L. (Eds.). (1965). *Case studies in behavior modification.* New York: Holt, Rinehart, & Winston.

Wilson, G. T. (1995). Empirically validated treatments as a basis for clinical practice: Problems and prospects. In S. C. Hayes, V. M. Follette, T. Risley, R. D. Dawes, & K. Grady (Eds.), *Scientific standards of psychological practice: Issues and recommendations.* Reno, Nevada: Context Press.

Wilson, G. T. (1998). Manual-based treatment and clinical practice. *Clinical Psychology: Science and Practice, 5,* 363-375.

Wolpe, J. (1958). *Psychotherapy by reciprocal inhibition.* Stanford, CA: Stanford University Press.

Wolpe, J. (1968). From the president. *Newsletter of the Association for Advancement of Behavior Therapy, 3,* 1-2.

Wolpe, J., Salter, A., & Reyna, L. J. (Eds.). (1964). *The conditioning therapies.* New York: Holt, Rinehart, & Winston.

Wolpe, J., & Lazarus, A. A. (1966). *Behavior therapy techniques.* Oxford: Pergamon Press.

Chapter 8

Swimming Against the Mainstream: The Early Years in Chilly Waters

Albert Bandura
Stanford University

Behaviorally-oriented approaches evolved in an inhospitable historical climate. In the early 50's, the field of personal change was dominated by the psychodynamic drive model of human behavior. There were several variants to this model, but they shared three characteristics.

They all emphasized psychic determinism as their guiding causal model. In this approach, behavior was regulated by the interplay of inner impulses and complexes. Most of this inner life operated subterraneously below the level of consciousness, disguised by defensive mental operations. To circumvent the defensiveness, surreptitious projective methods were devised to reveal them. People were asked to respond to inkblots, ambiguous pictures, sentence stems, or simply to free associate. Although the theory postulated a thoroughgoing psychic determinism, the unconscious inner life was only loosely linked to behavior. The same inner dynamics could produce any type of behavior, including opposite styles of responsivity. Thus, a hostile impulse could spawn either irascibility or sweetness. The theory was not only shrouded in conceptual fog, but the proposed causal structures were essentially indeterminant and strewn with loopholes. Such theories were used mainly as post hoc explanatory devices.

Experimental efforts to verify the basic tenets of psychodynamic theory were like tilting at windmills. Proponents of psychodynamic theory dismissed experimental investigations as entirely unsuitable because the core determinants were not amenable to experimental variation. An Oedipal complex was not manipulatable. In their view, the theory could be tested only through clinical validation. In a letter to Freud, Rosensweing asked whether the interview content could be tainted by the therapists' influences. Freud argued that the therapist serves as a blank screen on which the psychic dynamics are projected. Therefore, the interview content remains uncontaminated. The claim of immaculateness of method had no foundation in fact. Interactional analyses showed that therapists were actively shaping the content through their suggestive interpretations and selective positive and negative reactions (Bandura, Lipsher, & Miller, 1960; Murray, 1956).

The second major feature of this approach was the adoption of a quasi-disease model of deviant behavior. Styles of behavior that diverged from prevailing norms were viewed as a symptom of an underlying pathology. However, the disease was psychic or metaphorical. Problems of living and unconventional patterns of behavior got labeled as symptomatic expression of a psychic pathology. We are now similarly witnessing a widespread medicalization of psychosocial problems.

The third distinguishing characteristic was the heavy reliance on the interview as the vehicle of personal change. It was assumed that by analyzing clients' reports of their recurrent conflicts and the problems they reenacted with their therapists they gain insight into their inner dynamics and develop better ways of behaving. Self-insight would promote change.

In the early 50's, Hullian theorists were translating the psychoanalytic doctrine into Hullian learning terms and processes to render it empirically testable. Dollard and Miller's (1950) publication, *Personality and Psychotherapy* became the bible for the times on which most of us were imprinted. Dollard and his Yale colleagues proposed a set of testable propositions concerning aggression cast in terms of a frustration-aggression model encompassing instigative drive forces and displacement processes governed by excitatory and inhibitory generalization gradients (Dollard, Doob, Miller, Moirer, & Sears, 1939). Whiting and Child (1953), and Sears and his colleagues extended the theory to the developmental sphere (Sears, Whiting, Nowlis, & Sears, 1953).

The psychodynamic theories fared poorly when subjected to close empirical scrutiny. They lacked predictive power. Self-appraisals and actuarial systems proved to be better predictors of future behavior than psychodynamic predictions, which supposedly had privileged access to the unconscious determinants (Dawes, Faust, & Meehl, 1989; Shrauger & Osberg, 1982).

Many outcome studies conducted in the 60's showed that it is difficult to change human behavior by talk alone. People gained all kinds of insights but exhibited little change in behavior. It is easier to alter people's beliefs about the causes of their behavior than to change their behavior enduringly. For example, alcoholics can be more readily persuaded that they drink because of fixated orality than to get them to give up booze. Interview modes of treatment showed limited gains in actual behavioral functioning, but some benefits on self-ratings of change. However, such measures exaggerate the level of behavioral change (Williams & Rappoport, 1983). On self-ratings even most nontreated controls report gains.

Each theoretical approach had its own favored brand of insight. One could reliably predict the types of insights and inner dynamics clients would find in the course of therapy from knowledge of their therapists' theoretical orientation. Conversational therapies seemed to be promoting conversion to belief systems in the guise of self-discovery. One could also predict whether the clients would find an unconscious mind and what is in it. A Freudian unconscious is different from a Jungian one, and Rogerians never unearthed an unconscious mind. Given the arbitrariness of the self-insights, it was hardly surprising that they were usually unaccompanied by behavior changes. Although people who underwent such treatments often reported some benefits, they usually did not change any more than comparable cases who received no formal treatment. Eysenck (1952) did a thorough demolition job on the efficacy of psychodynamic therapies.

Following the old adage that one should light a candle rather than curse the conceptual darkness, Dick Walters and I set forth an alternative view of human behavior in the book, *Social Learning and Personality Development* (Bandura & Walters, 1963).

It underscored the influential role of modeling and direct consequential experiences in the acquisition of behavior patterns, and their regulation through the complex interplay of contextual, incentive, and self-regulatory influences rooted in personal standards.

During this period, I was teaching the psychotherapy courses at Stanford. I became intrigued by cases in which direct modification of problem behavior not only produced lasting improvements in people's lives, but often had positive spillover effects on their nontreated areas of functioning. Once alcoholics were helped to gain sobriety, for example, the quality of their lives changed dramatically for the better. I spent several months tracking down such treatments published in obscure journals housed in the musty catacombs of the university library. In 1960, I emerged bleary-eyed but inspired from the catacombs to publish an analysis of psychotherapy in terms of acquisitional and regulatory mechanisms in the Psychological Bulletin entitled, *Psychotherapy as a Learning Process*. The conceptual scheme and accompanying psychosocial applications were organized around six basic principles of behavioral change (Bandura, 1961). The time was apparently ripe for a new direction in the conceptualization and treatment of behavior. I was flooded with reprint requests from home and abroad.

Based on this article, Eysenck invited me to contribute a chapter to a volume he was editing on behavior therapy. The chapter kept enlarging until it outgrew the assigned page allotment. Instead, it turned into a voluminous book in the making under the title, *Principles of Behavior Modification* (1969). The volume addressed the influential role of symbolic, vicarious, and self-regulatory mechanisms in human adaptation and change.

While working on these projects, I was invited to join the study section at the National Institute of Mental Health that reviewed grant proposals in developmental psychology, personality, and psychotherapy. Proposals for research on behavior therapy were being routinely rejected. They were dismissed as simply removing symptoms rather than treating their underlying causes. Moreover, it was claimed that they risked spawning more serious symptom substitution. Apocryphal stories were floated about the potential dangers of such approaches. In one of the more fanciful scenarios, a behavior therapist allegedly got a husband to quit grinding his teeth while sleeping, only to murder his wife the next week! This turned out to be a conceptual rather than a material homicide because inquiries never produced a spousal body.

I negotiated an understanding with my colleagues on the study section that the quality of a research proposal should be judged against the tenets of the theory on which it is founded rather than by the causal models favored by theoretical rivals. My first primary reviews and site visit reports upon joining the study section were Bijou and Baer's project at the University of Washington, and Ivar Lovaas' autism project at UCLA. Both were approved and funded. Behaviorally-oriented studies were now receiving a fair hearing based on the conceptual, methodological, and social merits of the proposals.

There were other paths of involvement in the growing network of proponents of the alternative theories and psychosocial practices. Wolpe (1958) submitted his manuscript on *Psychotherapy By Reciprocal Inhibition* to the Stanford Press for consideration. The Press sent it to me for advisory evaluation. In my supportive review I predicted that it will have modest sales at the outset, but continue to garner significant sales in years to come in the evolving field of behavior therapy. I invited Arnold Lazarus to Stanford during my sabbatical leave, which greased his relocation from South Africa.

For their dissertations, Gerald Davison (1968) verified the facilitative role of relaxation in the desensitization mode of treatment, and Bernard Perloff (1970) demonstrated that positive imagery works better than muscular relaxation in modifying phobic behavior. Both of these well crafted experiments, which underscored the influential role of symbolic and imagery processes, received dissertation awards. Wolpe (1974) cast the rationale for this treatment in terms of conditioning relaxation responses to anxiety cues. People who had been thoroughly desensitized to phobic threats in imagery, nevertheless varied in their actual coping behavior. In microanalysis of possible mechanisms governing therapeutic change, we found that symbolic desensitization enhances coping behavior to the extent that it raises perceived self-efficacy (Bandura & Adams, 1977).

The 60's ushered in radical changes in the explanation and modification of behavior. Causal analysis shifted from unconscious psychic dynamics to transactional social dynamics. Troublesome behavior was viewed as divergent rather than diseased behavior. Functional analysis of human behavior replaced diagnostic labeling that categorized people into psychopathologic types. Laboratory and controlled field studies of the determinants and mechanisms of behavioral functioning replaced content analyses of interviews.

The modes of treatment were altered in the content, locus, and agents of change. With regard to *content*, therapeutic efforts were directed mainly at modifying the actual problems for which people sought help through mastery experiences rather than conversing about their problems and their psychodynamic origins. In the transactional models that were adopted, the determinants of human behavior do not reside solely in the individual. People are both products and producers of their life conditions. The model of bidirectional causation had implications for the *locus* of change. Efforts were also directed at changing social practices that contribute to aversive and dysfunctional styles of behavior. Many human problems are institutional not simply individual. Collective problems require social solutions. A major issue for science and practice of psychosocial change was whether efforts should be centered mainly in treating the casualties of adverse social practices, or also altering the social practices producing the casualties.

A comprehensive approach of high social utility also requires prevention as well as remediation. As another aspect of the locus of change, to enhance successful results, treatments were typically carried out in the natural settings in which the problems arise. Some of the corrective practices were conducted in homes, schools, workplaces, or in the larger community, depending upon the sources of the contributing determinants. With regard to the *agents* of change, behaviorally-oriented approaches did not view professionals as the exclusive dispensers of treatments. By drawing on the vast resources of people to implement change programs under professional guidance, practitioners greatly expand the scope of their impact. If professionals had to implement every aspect of their treatments, their contribution would be but a tiny ripple in the vast sea of human problems.

Not all the behaviorally-oriented folks worshipped at the same theoretical alter. Some went the operant route as providing the best glimpse of the promised land. Others went the sociocognitive route. Vigorous epistemological battles were fought over cognitive determinants and the legitimacy of alternative forms of scientific inquiry (Bandura, 1995). Scientific advances are promoted by two kinds of theories (Bandura, 1996). One form seeks to identify relations between directly observable events, but shies away from the underlying mechanisms governing the observable events. The second form seeks to elucidate the mechanisms that explain the relations between observable events. Operant analysts took the view that the only legitimate scientific enterprise is one that links directly observable events.

In commenting on the issue of observability in scientific inquiry, Nagel (1961) explains that some of the most powerful theories of the natural sciences are not about factors that are "observable." Physicists, for example, have done remarkably well with atomic theory even though atoms are not given to public view. The major issues in contention regarding cognitive determinants were not about the legitimacy of inner causes, but about the types of inner determinants that are given favored status. Operant analysts dismissed internal determinants in the form of cognitions as explanatory fictions or functionally merely epiphenomena of conditioned responses. But they increasingly placed the explanatory burden within their own scheme on determinants inside the organism, namely the implanted history of reinforcement. Like other internal determinants, ontogenic history is neither observable nor directly accessible.

Multifaceted Applicability of Social Cognitive Theory

Social cognitive theory lends itself readily to social applications. The factors it posits are anchored in indices of functioning and are amenable to change. The determinants and mechanisms through which the influences operate are spelled out, so the theory provides explicit guidelines on how to promote personal and social change. The models of change we developed drew heavily on our knowledge of modeling, self-regulatory, and self-efficacy mechanisms.

Guided Mastery Treatments

The initial applications of modeling to the treatment of phobic disorders eventually evolved, with the creative contributions of Ed Blanchard and Bruni Ritter, into a powerful guided mastery treatment (Bandura, Blanchard, & Ritter, 1969). It relied on mastery experiences as the principal vehicle of change. When people avoid what they dread, they lose touch with the reality they shun. Guided mastery quickly restores reality testing in two ways. It provides disconfirming tests of phobic beliefs by convincing demonstrations that what the phobics dread are safe. Even more important, it provides confirmatory tests that phobics can exercise control over what they fear.

Intractable phobics, of course, are not about to do what they dread. Therapists must, therefore, create environmental conditions that enable phobics to succeed, despite themselves. This is achieved by enlisting a variety of performance mastery aids. Threatening activities are repeatedly modeled to demonstrate coping strategies, and to disconfirm people's worst fears. Intimidating tasks are reduced to graduated subtasks of easily mastered steps. Treatment is conducted in this stepwise fashion until the most intimidating activities are mastered. Joint performance with the therapist enables frightened people to do things they would refuse to do on their own. Another method for overcoming resistance is to have phobics perform the feared activity for only a short time. As they become bolder the length of engagement is extended. Protective conditions can also be introduced to weaken resistances that retard change.

Initially, therapists use whatever mastery aids are needed to restore coping behavior. As treatment progresses, supportive aids and protective controls are faded until clients manage the most intimidating activities on their own. After bold functioning is fully restored, self-directed mastery activities are arranged in which clients manage different versions of the threat on their own under varying conditions.

Self-directed mastery was designed to serve three purposes. By affirming the participants' personal capabilities, self-directed accomplishments would eliminate any misattribution of the successes to the mastery aids. By this means, misattribution problems can be easily eliminated without sacrificing the substantial benefits of powerful mastery procedures. Self-directed mastery experiences further strengthen and generalize restored coping capabilities. Moreover, multiple diverse successes serve as a vehicle for building resilience to the negative effects of adverse experiences. The capacity of an aversive experience to reinstate dysfunctions depends, in part, on the pattern of experience in which it is embedded rather than on its properties alone. A lot of neutral or positive experiences can neutralize the negative impact of an aversive event and curtail the spread of negative effects (Hoffman, 1969). For example, if after treatment, a dog phobic has no contact with dogs, an aversive encounter will quickly reinstate the phobia. But if the phobic had many neutral and positive experiences with different varieties of dogs, an aversive encounter is likely to produce a circumscribed effect – avoidance of the threatening animal without phobic generalization to the other canine types.

The initial tests of the efficacy of guided mastery showed it to be an unusually powerful treatment (Bandura, et al., 1969; Bandura, Taylor, Williams, Mefford, & Barchas, 1985). It eliminated severe snake phobias in everyone within a couple of hours. It eradicated experienced anxiety, autonomic reactivity, and secretion of stress-related hormones. It changed attitudes toward the phobic objects from loathing to more positive ones. The phobics had been plagued by recurrent nightmares for 20 or 30 years. The mere sight or mention of reptiles activated perturbing ruminations that the phobics felt helpless to turn off. Guided mastery wiped out their nightmares and aversively intrusive ruminations. The transformation of dream activity was fascinating to observe. As clients gained mastery, the phobic object changed from pursuing and terrorizing them in their dreams to beneficent creatures. As one woman gained mastery over her snake phobia, she dreamt that the boa constrictor befriended her and was helping her to wash the dishes. Eventually reptiles faded from her dreams and ruminative activity ceased. In comparative outcome studies, for phobics who achieved only partial improvement with desensitization, modeling alone, or cognitive behavior therapy, guided mastery eradicated the phobia in everyone in a short time (Bandura & Adams, 1977; Bandura, et al., 1969; Biran & Wilson, 1981; Thase & Moss, 1976). Follow-up assessments five years later found participants just as bold and unperturbed as they were at the end of treatment.

I was invited to present our program of research to the Langley Porter Clinic in San Francisco, a stronghold of psychodynamic adherents. It began with an inhospitable introduction to the effect that this young upstart is going to tell us seasoned pros how to cure phobias! While my host was proclaiming the virtues of the psychodynamic approach and flogging a behavioristic caricature, I was trying to figure out how to begin my sermonette with acknowledgment of the inimical atmospherics. I explained that my host's "generous" introduction reminded me of a football contest between Iowa and Notre Dame in South Bend. Iowa scored a touchdown, which tied the score. As the player ran on the field to kick the extra point, coach Evashevski turned to his assistant coach and remarked, "*Now there goes a brave soul, a Protestant attempting a conversion before 50,000 Catholics!*"

Powerful treatments are typically multifaceted. The next analytic task was to evaluate the contribution of the various components to the therapeutic outcomes. In experiments conducted with Bob Jeffery, we demonstrated that the mastery-aids component accelerated the rate of therapeutic change, and the self-directed mastery component enhanced the generality and durability of the changes (Bandura, Jeffery, & Gajdos, 1975; Bandura, Jeffery, & Wright, 1974).

The next phase in this program of research was to test the generalized utility of this mode of treatment across different types of dysfunctions. In an extended series of studies, Lloyd Williams showed that guided mastery was similarly powerful with one of the most incapacitating anxiety disorders, agoraphobia (Williams, 1990;

1992). Guided mastery proved more powerful than the exposure treatment in vogue, in which phobics repeatedly confront threatening situations without the benefit of mastery performance aids (Williams, Dooseman, & Kleifield, 1984; Williams, Turner, & Peer, 1985; Williams & Zane, 1989).

Self-Efficacy Theory

Self-efficacy theory was an outgrowth of our research described earlier designed to build resilience to adversity. In follow-up assessments, we were discovering that the participants not only maintained their therapeutic gains, but made notable improvements in domains of functioning quite unrelated to the treated dysfunction. Thus, for example, after mastering an animal phobia, participants had reduced their social timidity, became bolder in public speaking, expanded their competencies in various spheres of their lives, and boosted their venturesomeness in a variety of ways. Success in overcoming, within a few hours of treatment, a phobic dread that had constricted and tormented their lives for twenty or thirty years produced a profound change in participants' beliefs in their personal efficacy to exercise better control over their lives. They were acting on their belief, putting themselves to test and enjoying their successes much to their pleasant surprise.

I redirected my research efforts to gain a deeper understanding of personal efficacy. To guide this new mission, I formulated a theory that addressed the key aspects of human efficacy (Bandura, 1977). These aspects include the origins of efficacy beliefs, their structure and function, their diverse effects, the psychosocial processes through which they produce these effects, and the modes of influence by which they can be created and strengthened for personal and social benefit.

This belief system is the foundation of human agency. Unless people believe they can produce desired effects by their actions they have little incentive to act or to persevere in the face of difficulties. Whatever other factors serve as motivators, they are rooted in the core belief that one has the power to effect changes by one's actions. Using diverse methodologies converging evidence from causal tests demonstrated that, indeed, efficacy beliefs play a determinative role in human functioning. In one approach (Bandura, Reese, & Adams, 1982), perceived self-efficacy was raised in phobics to differential levels simply by having them observe modeled coping strategies until the preselected level of perceived efficacy is attained. Higher levels of perceived self-efficacy were accompanied by higher performance accomplishments.

A number of experiments were conducted in which self-efficacy beliefs are altered by bogus feedback unrelated to one's actual performance. Using this type of induction procedure, Weinberg, Gould and Jackson (1979) raised the self-efficacy beliefs of one group by telling them that they had triumphed in a competition of muscular strength, and lowered the self-efficacy beliefs of another group by telling them that they were outperformed by their competitor. The higher the instilled illusory beliefs of physical strength, the more physical endurance the participants displayed during competition on a new task measuring physical stamina. Failure in a subsequent competition spurred those with a high sense of perceived self-efficacy to even greater physical effort, whereas failure further impaired the performance of those whose perceived self-efficacy had been undermined.

Bogus normative feedback was another variant on the social comparative mode of altering beliefs of personal efficacy. Individuals were led to believe that they performed at high or low percentile ranks of a reference group, regardless of their actual performance. Those whose perceived efficacy was heightened by this means outperformed the individuals whose perceived efficacy was lowered (Litt, 1988; Jacobs, Prentice-Dunn, & Rogers, 1984).

Another approach to the test of causality is to control, by selection, level of ability but to vary perceived self-efficacy within each ability level. Collins (1982) selected children who judged themselves to be of high or low mathematical efficacy at each of three levels of mathematical ability. They were then given difficult problems to solve. Within each level of mathematical ability, children who regarded themselves as efficacious were quicker to discard faulty strategies, solved more problems, chose to rework more of those they failed, and did so more accurately. Perceived self-efficacy thus exerted a substantial independent effect on performance. A fifth approach to causality is to introduce a trivial factor devoid of information to affect competency, but that can alter perceived self-efficacy. Cervone and Peake (1986) used arbitrary anchor values to influence self-appraisals of efficacy. Self-appraisals made from an arbitrary high starting point biased students' perceived self-efficacy in the positive direction, whereas an arbitrary low starting point lowered students' appraisals of their efficacy. The higher the instated perceived self-efficacy, the longer individuals persevered on difficult and unsolvable problems before they quit. Mediational analyses revealed that the anchoring influence on performance motivation was entirely mediated by perceived self-efficacy.

Still another approach to the verification of causality employed a contravening experimental design in which a procedure that can impair functioning is applied, but in ways that raise perceived self-efficacy. Holroyd and his colleagues (Holroyd, et al., 1984), used this mode of verification with sufferers of tension headaches. In biofeedback sessions, they trained one group to become good relaxers. Unbeknownst to another group, they received feedback signals that they were relaxing whenever they tensed their muscles. They became good tensors of facial muscles, which, if anything, would aggravate tension headaches. Regardless of whether people were tensing or relaxing their musculature, bogus feedback that they were exercising good control over muscular tension instilled a strong sense of efficacy that they could prevent the occurrence of headaches in different stressful situations. The higher their perceived self-efficacy, the fewer headaches they experienced. The actual amount of change in muscular activity achieved in treatment was unrelated to the incidence of subsequent headaches.

The final way of verifying the contribution of efficacy beliefs to human functioning is to test the multivariate relations between relevant determinants and subsequent performances using structural equation modeling. Such analyses indicate how much of the variation in performance is explained by perceived self-efficacy when the influence of other determinants, including past performance, is controlled. The results of numerous studies revealed that efficacy beliefs contribute to performance both directly and through their impact on other determinants (Bandura & Jourden, 1991; Locke, Frederick, Lee, & Bobko, 1984; Ozer & Bandura, 1990; Wood & Bandura, 1989).

These diverse causal tests conducted with different modes of efficacy induction, varied populations, using both interindividual and intraindividual verification designs, and all sorts of domains of functioning provided supporting evidence that perceived self-efficacy contributes significantly to level of motivation and performance accomplishments.

Other lines of research advanced understanding of the processes through which efficacy beliefs regulate human functioning. The results of these studies showed that they do so through their impact on cognitive, motivational, affective, and choice processes. Specifically, efficacy beliefs influence whether people think strategically, pessimistically or optimistically; how well they motivate themselves and their staying power in the face of obstacles; their emotional well-being; and the life choices they make.

We conducted a series of studies to test whether different modes of treatment work in part by instilling and strengthening beliefs of personal efficacy (Bandura & Adams, 1977; Bandura, Adams, & Beyer, 1977; Bandura, Adams, Hardy, & Howells, 1980). The results of these microanalytic studies were consistent in showing that the self-efficacy belief system is a common pathway through which diverse interventions effect changes.

Self-efficacy theory and its diverse personal and social applications are extensively reviewed in *Self-Efficacy: The Exercise of Control* (Bandura, 1997). It presents the structure of the theory, documents the centrality of control beliefs in people's lives, specifies how to build a resilient sense of efficacy, and analyzes the processes through which such beliefs affect human motivation and accomplishments. Efficacy beliefs promote successful adaptation and change throughout the life course. The theory lends itself readily to social applications because it provides explicit guides on how to effect change. These include applications to education, health, clinical dysfunctions (i.e., anxiety, phobias, depression, eating disorders, substance abuse), personal and team athletic attainments, organizational productivity, and people's collective efficacy to improve their lives through united effort. Meta-analyses amply document the influential role of perceived self-efficacy in human adaptation and change (Holden, 1991; Holden, Moncher, Schinke, & Barker, 1990; Multon, Brown, & Lent, 1991; Stajkovic & Luthans, 1998).

Self-Regulatory Mechanism

People are not only knowers and performers. They are also self-reactors with a capacity to motivate, guide, and regulate their activities (Bandura, 1986; 1991). Another line of research that I was pursuing was designed to advance understanding of self-regulatory mechanisms. Self-regulation operates through a set of psychological subfunctions that must be developed and mobilized for self-directed change. People have to learn to monitor their behavior and judge it against an adopted performance standard. The cognitive comparison sets the occasion for self-reactive influence. Self-reactions provide the mechanism by which personal standards regulate motivation and action.

Much human behavior is regulated anticipatorily by expected material and social outcomes. Social cognitive theory broadened this functionalism to include self-evaluative outcomes. After people adopt personal standards, they influence their own motivation and behavior by the positive and negative consequences they produce for themselves. They do things that give them satisfaction and a sense of self-worth, and refrain from actions that evoke self-censure. Studies conducted in collaboration with Mike Mahoney, Carol Kupers, Karen Simon, and Bernard Perloff shed light on how personal standards are acquired, documented the regulative power of self-administered consequences, and identified conditions under which self-evaluative outcomes override external ones (Bandura & Kupers, 1964; Bandura & Mahoney, 1974; Bandura, Mahoney, & Dirks, 1976; Bandura & Perloff, 1967; Mahoney & Bandura, 1972; Simon, 1979a, 1979b).

Self-Management Models with Social Utility

Our knowledge of self-regulatory and self-efficacy mechanisms was used to devise efficacious self-management models with high social utility. Applications to health promotion and disease prevention is but one such example.

The recent years have witnessed a major change in the conception of human health and illness, from a disease model to a health model. It is just as meaningful to speak of levels of vitality as of degrees of impairment. The quality of health is heavily influenced by lifestyle habits. By exercising control over a few health habits, people can live longer, healthier, and slow the process of biological aging. Exercise, reduce dietary fat, refrain from smoking, keep blood pressure down, and develop effective ways of coping with stressors. If the huge health benefits of these few lifestyle habits were put into a pill, it would be declared a spectacular breakthrough in the field of medicine.

Effective self-management of health behavior requires development of self-regulatory skills to influence one's own motivation and behavior. In such programs, people have to track their behavior and the social and cognitive conditions under which they engage in it; set proximal goals for guiding and controlling their behavior; draw from an array of coping strategies rather than rely on a single technique; create self-motivating incentives to sustain their efforts; and apply multifaceted self-influence consistently and persistently.

Efficacy beliefs play an influential role in every phase of personal change – whether people even consider changing their health habits; whether they enlist the motivation and perseverance needed to succeed should they choose to do so; their vulnerability to relapse; their success in recovering control after a setback; and how well they maintain the habit changes they have achieved (Bandura, 1997; 1998).

The self-regulatory subfunctions and their self-efficacy underpinning were built into a self-management model devised by DeBusk and his colleagues to reduce health risks and promote health (DeBusk, et al., 1994). It equips participants with the skills and personal efficacy to exercise self-directed change. They are provided with guidelines on how to change detrimental health habits. To motivate and regulate their actions, they monitor their health habits, set explicit proximal goals, and apply self incentives to sustain their efforts. They receive periodic feedback of progress toward their goals, and instructive guides on how to manage troublesome situations.

Self-efficacy ratings identify areas in which self-regulatory skills must be developed and strengthened if desired changes are to be achieved and maintained.

The productivity of this self-management system is vastly expanded by combining self-regulatory principles with the power of computer-assisted implementation. A single implementer, assisted with a computerized coordinating and mailing system, provides intensive individualized training in self-management of large numbers of people simultaneously.

In tests of this system, employees in the workplace lowered high cholesterol levels by altering eating habits high in saturated fats (Bandura, 1997). They achieved even larger reductions if their spouses participated. The greater the room for dietary change, the greater the reduction in plasma cholesterol. A single nutritionist implemented the entire program at minimal cost for large numbers of employees. Sodium intake is linked to hypertension in people who are sensitive to this mineral, a sensitivity that increases with age as the body loses some of its efficiency. West and his colleagues demonstrated with patients suffering from heart disease that the self-management system enhances their self-regulatory efficacy and gets them to cut back on their level of sodium intake to desired levels and to maintain the low sodium diet stably over time (West, et al., 1999). At each successive point in the self-change program, the stronger the perceived self-regulatory efficacy, the greater the reduction in sodium intake.

Haskell and his colleagues used this system to promote lifestyle changes in patients suffering from coronary artery disease, which places them at high risk of heart attacks (Haskell, et al., 1994). At the end of four years, those receiving medical care by their physicians showed no change or a worsening of their condition. In contrast, those aided in self-management of health habits achieved large reductions in risk factors. They lowered their intake of fat, lost weight, lowered their bad cholesterol, raised their good cholesterol, exercised more, and increased their cardiovascular capacity. The program also altered the physical progression of the disease. Those receiving the self-management program had 47% less plaque on artery walls, and a higher reversal of arteriosclerosis. They also had fewer hospitalizations for coronary heart problems, and fewer deaths.

The success of this self-management system is currently being compared against the standard medical post-coronary care to reduce morbidity, and mortality in patients who have already suffered a heart attack (DeBusk, et al., 1994). The self-regulatory system is more effective in reducing risk factors, and increasing cardiovascular functioning than the standard medical care.

The self-management system is very well received by patients because it is individually tailored to their needs; provides continuing personalized guidance and informative feedback that enables them to exercise considerable control over their own change; it is a home-based program that does not require any special facilities, equipment, or attendance at group meetings that usually have high drop-out rates; can serve large numbers of people simultaneously under the guidance of a single implementer; is not constrained by time and place; combines the high individualization of the clinical approach, with the large-scale applicability of the public health approach; and provides valuable health-promotion services at low cost.

Linking the interactive aspects of the self-management model to the Internet can vastly expand its availability for preventive, and promotive guidance. Moreover, this model lends itself readily to a triage strategy of application that further enhances its scope and productivity. Many people may succeed with enabling interactions through the mail alone that provide them with sufficient structured guidance to accomplish the changes they seek. Successful self-changers with minimal guidance have a high sense of efficacy that they can get themselves to adopt healthful habits and to stick to them. Those who distrust their ability to succeed give up trying when they run into difficulties. They need additional support and guidance via telephone contact to see them through tough times. And finally, those who believe that their health habits are beyond their personal control need a great deal of guidance in a stepwise mastery program. Graduated successes build belief in their ability to exercise control and bolster their staying power in the face of difficulties and setbacks.

The self-management of chronic diseases provides another example of translation of self-regulatory and self-efficacy theory to highly cost-effective implementation models with high social utility. Chronic disease is the dominant form of illness and the major cause of disability. This is a growing health problem because, with people living longer, there is more time for detrimental health habits to spawn chronic diseases. The treatment of chronic disease must focus on self-management of physical conditions over time. The goal is to retard the biological progression of impairment to disability and to improve the quality of life of people with chronic disease.

Holman and Lorig (1992) devised a prototypic model for the self-management of chronic diseases. People are taught cognitive pain control techniques, self-relaxation, and proximal goal setting combined with self incentives as motivators to increase level of activity. They are also taught problem solving and self-diagnostic skills for monitoring and interpreting changes in their health status, skills in locating community resources and managing medication programs. The way health care systems deal with clients can alter their sense of efficacy in ways that support or undermine their restorative efforts (Bandura, 1998). Clients are, therefore, taught how to take greater initiative for their health care and dealings with health personnel.

These capabilities are developed through modeling of self-management skills, guided mastery practice, and informative feedback.

In a four-year follow-up of arthritic patients, the self-management program retarded the biological progression of disease, raised perceived efficacy to exercise some control over one's condition, reduced pain and substantially decreased the use of medical services, and improved the quality of life (Lorig, 1990). Perceived self-efficacy predicted the health benefits four years later. The self-management program produced similar health benefits for people suffering from other types of chronic diseases (Lorig, et al., 2000).

Macrosocial Applications

Social modeling also plays a paramount role at the society-wide level in enabling people to improve their lives and social conditions. Modeling is not only an important component in most modes of change, but an essential one. It shortcuts the tortuous process of competency development. The revolutionary advances in the communications technologies have vastly expanded the power of symbolic modeling. In modern day life, the electronic media, feeding off the communications satellites, are shaping lifestyles worldwide, transforming institutional practices, and serving as a major vehicle of sociopolitical change (Bandura, 1997; Braithwaite, 1994).

Symbolic modeling is readily applicable to macrosocial applications through creative use of the electronic media. The soaring population growth and the environmental devastation it produces is the most urgent global problem. The world population is doubling at an accelerating rate. It will seriously strain the earth's carrying capacity and degrade the quality of life if left unchecked (Ehrlich, Ehrlich, & Daily, 1995).

Sabido (1981) creatively translated several social cognitive principles into engrossing and influential radio and television dramatic serials that are being applied internationally with notable success in raising the status of women and in stemming the massive population tide. Culturally admired television models exhibit the beneficial styles of behavior. Social attraction increases the impact of modeling influences. Characters representing different segments of the viewing population are shown adopting the beneficial attitudes and behavior patterns. Seeing people similar to oneself succeed enhances the power of modeling. The episodes include positive models exhibiting beneficial lifestyles, negative models exhibiting detrimental lifestyles, and transitional models changing from detrimental to beneficial styles of behavior. Contrasting modeling highlights the personal and social effects of different lifestyles. Viewers draw inspiration from seeing others change their lives for the better. Vicarious motivators, in the form of the benefits of favorable practices and the costs of detrimental ones, are vividly depicted. Depicted benefits provide incentives for change. Melodramatic and other emotional devices are used to sustain high attentional involvement in the dramatic presentations. Epilogues and summarization of the modeled messages are used as symbolic coding aids to underscore the importance of the social practices that are enacted and to enhance their recallability.

It is of limited value to motivate people for change if they do not have the needed resources and environmental supports to realize those changes. Environmental guides and supports are therefore provided to expand and sustain the changes promoted by the media. This format informs people, enables them with strategies and sustaining self-beliefs, and motivates them for personal and social change. The story lines model family planning, women's equality, beneficial health practices, and a variety of effective life skills.

Worldwide applications of this creative format in Africa, Asia, and South America are raising people's efficacy to exercise control over their family lives, enhancing the status of women, and lowering the rates of childbearing (Brown & Cody, 1991; Singhal & Rogers, 1989; Vaughan, Rogers, & Swalehe, 1995). A controlled study in Tanzania compared changes in family planning and contraception use in parts of the country that received a radio dramatic series with the rest of the country that did not. The radio series significantly increased perceived efficacy to exercise control over family size. Families in the broadcast area adopted family planning and contraceptive methods at a higher rate.

Some of the story lines centered on safer sexual practices to prevent the spread of AIDS, where infection rates are high among long-distance truckers and prostitutes at truck stops. Responding to increased demand, the National AIDS Control Program distributed considerably more condoms in the broadcast region than in the control region. Those in the broadcast area also reduced the number of sexual partners. The greater the exposure to the modeled patterns, the stronger the effects on perceived efficacy to control family size and risky sexual practices.

Kenya provides another example of the impact of mass communications on reproductive behavior (Westoff & Rodriguez, 1995). The heavier the exposure to media messages, the stronger the preference to limit family size, and the greater the use of contraceptives. The relationship remains after multiple controls for demographic and socioeconomic factors. These macrosocial applications illustrate how a small collective effort can make a huge difference in an urgent global problem.

Concluding Remarks

The present article traces the evolution of social cognitive theory from a chilly tributary to part of the mainstream. The value of a psychological theory is judged by three criteria. It must have explanatory power; predictive power and, in the final analysis, it must demonstrate operative power to improve the human condition. Well-founded theory provides solutions to human problems. This brief retrospective report addresses some of the facets of an agentic sociocognitive approach to human understanding and betterment, and documents some of the applications of this theory at both individual and macrosocial levels.

References

Bandura, A. (1961). Psychotherapy as a learning process. *Psychological Bulletin, 58*, 143-159.

Bandura, A. (1977). Self-efficacy: Toward a unifying theory of behavioral change. *Psychological Review, 84*, 191-215.

Bandura, A. (1986). *Social foundations of thought and action: A social cognitive theory.* Englewood Cliffs, NJ: Prentice-Hall.

Bandura, A. (1991). Self-regulation of motivation through anticipatory and self-reactive mechanisms. In R. A. Dienstbier (Ed.), *Perspectives on motivation: Nebraska symposium on motivation* (Vol. 38, pp. 69-164). Lincoln, NE: University of Nebraska Press.

Bandura, A. (1995). Comments on the crusade against the causal efficacy of human thought. *Journal of Behavior Therapy and Experimental Psychiatry, 26*, 179-190.

Bandura, A. (1996). Ontological and epistemological terrains revisited. *Journal of Behavior Therapy and Experimental Psychiatry, 27*, 323-345.

Bandura, A. (1997). *Self-efficacy: The exercise of control.* New York: Freeman.

Bandura, A. (1998). Health promotion from the perspective of social cognitive theory. *Psychology and Health, 13*, 623-649.

Bandura, A., & Adams, N. E. (1977). Analysis of self-efficacy theory of behavioral change. *Cognitive Therapy and Research, 1*, 287-308.

Bandura, A., Adams N. E., & Beyer, J. (1977). Cognitive processes mediating behavioral change. *Journal of Personality and Psychology, 35*, 125-139.

Bandura, A., Adams, N. E., Hardy, A. B., & Howells, G. N. (1980). Tests of the generality of self-efficacy theory. *Cognitive Therapy and Research, 4*, 39-66.

Bandura, A., Blanchard, E. B., & Ritter, B. (1969). Relative efficacy of desensitization and modeling approaches for inducing behavioral, affective, and attitudinal changes. *Journal of Personality and Social Psychology, 13*, 173-199.

Bandura, A., Jeffery, R. W., & Gajdos, E. (1975). Generalizing change through participant modeling with self-directed mastery. *Behaviour Research and Therapy, 13*, 141-152.

Bandura, A., Jeffery, R. W., & Wright, C. L. (1974). Efficacy of participant modeling as a function of response induction aids. *Journal of Abnormal Psychology, 83*, 56-64.

Bandura, A., & Jourden, F. J. (1991). Self-regulatory mechanisms governing the impact of social comparison on complex decision making. *Journal of Personality and Social Psychology, 60*, 941-951.

Bandura, A., & Kupers, C. J. (1964). Transmission of patterns of self-reinforcement through modeling. *Journal of Abnormal and Social Psychology, 69*, 1-9.

Bandura, A., Lipsher, D. H., & Miller, P. E. (1960). Psychotherapists' approach-avoidance reactions to patients' expression of hostility. *Journal of Consulting Psychology, 24*, 1-8.

Bandura, A., & Mahoney, M. J. (1974). Maintenance and transfer of self-reinforcement functions. *Behaviour Research and Therapy, 12*, 89-97.

Bandura, A., Mahoney, M. J., & Dirks, S. J. (1976). Discriminative activation and maintenance of contingent self-reinforcement. *Behaviour Research and Therapy, 14*, 1-6.

Bandura, A., & Perloff, B. (1967). Relative efficacy of self-monitored and externally-imposed reinforcement systems. *Journal of Personality and Social Psychology, 7*, 111-116.

Bandura, A., Reese, L., & Adams, N. E. (1982). Microanalysis of action and fear arousal as a function of differential levels of perceived self-efficacy. *Journal of Personality and Social Psychology, 43*, 5-21.

Bandura, A., Taylor, C. B., Williams, S. L., Mefford, I. N., & Barchas, J. D. (1985). Catecholamine secretion as a function of perceived coping self-efficacy. *Journal of Consulting and Clinical Psychology, 53*, 406-414.

Bandura, A., & Walters, R. H. (1963). *Social learning and personality development*. New York: Holt, Rinehart & Winston.

Biran, M. & Wilson, G. T. (1981). Treatment of phobic disorders using cognitive and exposure methods: A self-efficacy analysis. *Journal of Counseling and Clinical Psychology, 49*, 886-899.

Braithwaite, J. (1994). A sociology of modeling and the politics of empowerment. *British Journal of Sociology, 45*, 445- 479.

Brown, W. J., & Cody, M. J. (1991). Effects of a prosocial television soap opera in promoting women's status. *Human Communication Research, 18*, 114-142.

Cervone, D., & Peake, P. K. (1986). Anchoring, efficacy, and action: The influence of judgmental heuristics on self- efficacy judgments and behavior. *Journal of Personality and Social Psychology, 50*, 492-501.

Collins, J. L. (1982, March). *Self-efficacy and ability in achievement behavior*. Paper presented at the annual meeting of the American Educational Research Association, N.Y.

Davison, G. C. (1968). Systematic desensitization as a counterconditioning process. *Journal of Abnormal Psychology, 73*, 91-99.

Dawes, R. M., Faust, D., & Meehl, P. E. (1989). Clinical versus actuarial judgment. *Science, 31*, 1668-1674.

DeBusk, R. F., Miller, N. H., Superko, H. R., Dennis, C. A., Thomas, R. J., Lew, H. T., Berger III, W. E., Heller, R. S., Rompf, J., Gee, D., Kraemer, H. C., Bandura, A., Ghandour, G., Clark, M., Shah, R. V., Fisher, L., & Taylor, C. B. (1994). A case-management system for coronary risk factor modification after acute myocardial infarction. *Annals of Internal Medicine, 120*, 721-729.

Dollard, J., Miller, N. E., Doob, L. W., Mowrer, O. H., & Sears, R. R. (1939). *Frustration and aggression*. New Haven, CT: Yale University Press.

Ehrlich, P. R., Ehrlich, A. H., & Daily, G. C. (1995). *The stork and the plow: The equity answer to the human dilemma*. New York: Putnam.

Eysenck, H. J. (1952). The effects of psychotherapy: An evaluation. *Journal of Consulting Psychology, 16*, 319-325.

Haskell, W. L., Alderman, E. L., Fair, J. M., Maron, D. J., Mackey, S. F., Superko, H. R., Williams, P. T., Johnstone, I. M., Champagne, M. A., Krauss, R. M., & Farquhar, J. W. (1994). Effects of intensive multiple risk factor reduction on coronary atherosclerosis and clinical cardiac events in men and women with coronary artery disease. *Circulation, 89*, 975-990.

Holman, H., & Lorig, K. (1992). Perceived self-efficacy in self-management of chronic disease. In R. Schwarzer (Ed.), *Self-efficacy: Thought control of action* (pp. 305-323). Washington, D.C.: Hemisphere.

Holroyd, K. A., Penzien, D. B., Hursey, K. G., Tobin, D. L., Rogers, L., Holm, J. E., Marcille, P. J., Hall, J. R., & Chila, A. G. (1984). Change mechanisms in EMG biofeedback training: Cognitive changes underlying improvements in tension headache. *Journal of Consulting and Clinical Psychology, 52*, 1039-1053.

Hoffman, H. S. (1969). Stimulus factors in conditioned suppression. In B. A. Campbell & R. M. Church (Eds.), *Punishment and aversive behavior* (pp. 185-234). New York: Appleton- Century-Crofts.

Holden, G. (1991). The relationship of self-efficacy appraisals to subsequent health related outcomes: A meta-analysis. *Social Work in Health Care, 16*, 53-93.

Holden, G., Moncher, M. S., Schinke, S. P., & Barker, K. M. (1990). Self-efficacy of children and adolescents: A meta-analysis. *Psychological Reports, 66*, 1044-1046.

Jacobs, B., Prentice-Dunn, S., & Rogers, R. W. (1984). Understanding persistence: An interface of control theory and self-efficacy theory. *Basic and Applied Social Psychology, 5*, 333-347.

Litt, M. D. (1988). Self-efficacy and perceived control: Cognitive mediators of pain tolerance. *Journal of Personality and Social Psychology, 54*, 149-160.

Locke, E. A., Frederick, E., Lee, C., & Bobko, P. (1984). Effect of self-efficacy, goals, and task strategies on task performance. *Journal of Applied Psychology, 69*, 241-251.

Lorig, K. (1990, April). *Self-efficacy: Its contributions to the four year beneficial outcome of the arthritis self- management course.* Paper presented at the meeting of the Society for Behavioral Medicine, Chicago, IL.

Lorig, K. R., Holman, H. R., Sobel, D. S., Laurent, D. D., Minor, M. M., & Gonzalez, V. M. (2000). *Living a healthy life with chronic conditions: Self-management of heart disease, arthritis, diabetes, asthma, bronchitis, emphysema and others.* Palo Alto, CA: Bull Publishing Company.

Lorig, K. R., Sobel, D. S., Stewart, A. L., Brown, Jr., B. W., Bandura, A., Ritter, P., Gonzalez, V. M., Laurent, D. D., & Holman, H. R. (1997). *Evidence suggesting that a chronic disease self-management program can improve health status while reducing health care utilization and costs: A randomized trial.* Submitted for publication.

Mahoney, M. J. & Bandura, A. (1972). Self-reinforcement in pigeons. *Learning and Motivation, 3*, 293-303.

Multon, K. D., Brown, S. D., & Lent, R. W. (1991). Relation of self-efficacy beliefs to academic outcomes: A meta-analytic investigation. *Journal of Counseling Psychology, 38*, 30-38.

Murray, E. J. (1956). A content-analysis method for studying psychotherapy. *Psychological Monographs, 70*, (13, Whole No. 420).

Nagel, E. (1961). *The structure of science*. New York: Harcourt, Brace and World.

Ozer, E. M., & Bandura, A. (1990). Mechanisms governing empowerment effects: A self-efficacy analysis. *Journal of Personality and Social Psychology, 58*, 472-486.

Perloff, B. (1970). *Influence of muscular relaxation, positive imagery, and neutral imagery on extinction of avoidance behavior through systematic desensitization*. Unpublished doctoral dissertation, Stanford University.

Sabido, M. (1981). *Towards the social use of soap operas*. Mexico City, Mexico: Institute for Communication Research.

Sears, R. R., Whiting, J. W. M., Nowlis, V., & Sears, P. S. (1953). Some child-rearing antecedents of aggression and dependency in young children. *Genetic Psychology Monographs, 47*, 135-234.

Shrauger, J. S., & Osberg, T. M. (1982). Self-awareness: The ability to predict one's future behavior. In G. Underwood & R. Stevens (Eds.), *Aspects of consciousness (Vol. 3). Awareness and self-awareness* (pp. 267-330). New York: Academic Press.

Simon, K. M. (1979a). *Effects of self comparison, social comparison, and depression on goal setting and self-evaluative reactions*. Unpublished manuscript, Stanford University, Stanford, CA.

Simon, K. M. (1979b). *Relative influence of personal standards and external incentives on complex performance*. Unpublished doctoral dissertation, Stanford University, Stanford, CA.

Singhal, A., & Rogers, E. M. (1989). Pro-social television for development in India. In R. E. Rice & C. K. Atkin (Eds.), *Public communication campaigns* (2nd ed., pp. 331-350). Newbury Park, CA: Sage.

Stajkovic, A. D., & Luthans, F. (1998). Self-efficacy and work-related performance: A meta-Analysis. *Psychological Bulletin, 124*, 240-261.

Thase, M. E., & Moss, M. K. (1976). The relative efficacy of covert modeling procedures and guided participant modeling on the reduction of avoidance behavior. *Journal of Behavior Therapy and Experimental Psychiatry, 7*, 7-12.

Vaughan, P. W., Rogers, E. M., & Swalehe, R. M. A. (1995). *The effects of "Twende Na Wakati," an entertainment-education radio soap opera for family planning and HIV/AIDS prevention in Tanzania*. Unpublished manuscript, University of New Mexico, Albuquerque.

Weinberg, R. S., Gould, D., & Jackson, A. (1979). Expectations and performance: An empirical test of Bandura's self-efficacy theory. *Journal of Sport Psychology, 1*, 320-331.

West, J. A., Bandura, A., Clark, E., Miller, N. H., Ahn, D., Greenwald, G., & DeBusk, R. F. (1999). *Self-efficacy predicts adherence to dietary sodium limitation in patients with heart failure*. Unpublished manuscript, Stanford University.

Westoff, C. F., & Rodriguez, G. (1995). The mass media and family planning in Kenya. International *Family Planning Perspectives, 21*, 26-31.

Whiting, J. W. M., & Child, I. L. (1953). *Child training and personality*. New Haven: Yale University Press.

Williams, S. L. (1990). Guided mastery treatment of agoraphobia: Beyond stimulus exposure. In M. Hersen, R. M. Eisler, & P. M. Miller (Eds.), *Progress in behavior modification* (Vol. 26, pp. 89-121). Newbury Park, CA: Sage.

Williams, S. L. (1992). Perceived self-efficacy and phobic disability. In R. Schwarzer (Ed.), *Self-efficacy: Thought control of action* (pp. 149-176). Washington, D.C.: Hemisphere.

Williams, S. L., Dooseman, G., & Kleifield, E. (1984). Comparative power of guided mastery and exposure treatments for intractable phobias. *Journal of Consulting and Clinical Psychology, 52*, 505-518.

Williams, S., L., & Rappoport, A. (1983). Cognitive treatment in the natural environment for agoraphobics. *Behavior Therapy, 14*, 299-313.

Williams, S. L., Turner, S. M., & Peer, D. F. (1985). Guided mastery and performance desensitization treatments for severe acrophobia. *Journal of Consulting and Clinical Psychology, 53*, 237-247.

Williams, S. L., & Zane, G. (1989). Guided mastery and stimulus exposure treatments for severe performance anxiety in agoraphobics. *Behaviour Research Therapy, 27*, 238-245.

Wolpe, J. (1958). *Psychotherapy by reciprocal inhibition*. Stanford: Stanford University Press.

Wood, R. E., & Bandura, A. (1989). Social cognitive theory of organizational management. *Academy of Management Review, 14*, 361-384.

Chapter 9

The Rise of Cognitive Behavior Therapy

Albert Ellis
Albert Ellis Institute for Rational Emotive Behavior Therapy

Biographical Introduction

I can't say that I originated cognitive behavior therapy because you can always find some ancient sage who practiced a form of it many hundreds of years ago. Thus, Gautama Buddha became enlightened and founded Buddhism more than 2500 years ago; and to his cognitive teachings were soon added the behavioral exercises of the Zen Buddhists and other groups. Hindu Yoga practices are also definitely cognitive behavioral, as are the combinings of religious philosophies with various behavioral rituals of the ancient Hebrews and the early Christians.

Indeed, many religious groups intent on creating what might be called therapeutic change in their members seem to use a combination of philosophic education, emotional exercises, and behavioral practices in order to encourage their adherents to devoutly follow their precepts. We might speculate that their combination of cognitive, emotive, and behavioral methods tends to show that in order to make and maintain profound personality changes, humans often have to strongly and persistently follow these combined methods. Combined cognitive, emotional, and activity procedures are almost essential to basic personality change.

When I started to regularly practice psychotherapy in 1943, I was already prejudiced in favor of cognitive behavior therapy. Unlike the vast majority of psychologists, I was well on my way to being a sexologist; and, in addition, I was very interested, not only in marriage and family relationships, but I had made a special study of love relationships. Since 1939 I had trained myself in these areas by reading thousands of books and articles on sex, love, and marriage and by voluntarily counseling my friends and relatives on their problems in these areas.

As a clinical sexologist, I followed the procedures of the early twentieth century practitioners – especially Iwan Bloch (1908), August Forel (1922), Havelock Ellis (1936), and W. F. Robie (1925), who were physicians and who practiced what could be called cognitive-behavior sex therapy. They educated their patients sexually, helped minimize their shame and guilt, and gave them practical in vivo homework assignments. Following their procedures, I found that I could help my early clients to overcome their sex problems, as well as many of their love and marital difficulties, often in just a few active-directive sessions.

I practiced this kind of cognitive behavior therapy from 1943 to 1947 and then mistakenly thought that I could do a deeper and more intensive kind of treatment by getting trained in liberal psychoanalysis, and practicing it for six years. I was really an existentialist analyst, since my supervisor and trainer, Richard Hulbeck, was a training analyst of the Karen Horney Institute and was also a leading existentialist (Hoellen, 1993). Moreover, on my own I was opposed to Freudian analysis, since I thought that Freud (1965) was exceptionally unscientific, knew very little about the origin of people's sex and love problems, and wrote brilliant fiction which he presented as scientific non-fiction. So I mostly followed the neo-Freudian views of Alfred Adler (1929), Franz Alexander and Thomas French (1946), Erich Fromm (1955), Karen Horney (1950) and Harry Stack Sullivan (1953).

I found that even this kind of liberal psychoanalysis was exceptionally inefficient and superficial, because it was passive, little educational, and lacking behavioral elements which I had effectively used as a sex therapist and love and marriage therapist. So I abandoned it in 1953, did an intensive study of many techniques of therapy in the next two years (Ellis, 1955a, 1955b) and started formulating a more efficient form of psychotherapy.

In January 1955, I started to do what I called rational psychotherapy (Ellis, 1957a, 1957b, 1958a, 1958b), later called rational-emotive therapy (Ellis, 1962b; Ellis & Harper, 1961), and finally retitled rational emotive behavior therapy (REBT) (Ellis, 1993). Although there were a few cognitive behavior therapies before REBT – such as those of Herzberg (1945) and Salter (1949) – they were highly unpopular in 1955. Freudian therapy ruled the roost (Freud, 1965) especially in the United States, and Rogerian Therapy, which I had been trained in while in graduate school (Rogers, 1943, 1951) was immensely popular.

Why was REBT, right from its start, heavily behavioral? Mainly because I had used behavior therapy on myself before I even thought of becoming a therapist; and because I had used it successfully for a dozen years in my specialty of sex, love, and marriage therapy. I first used it when I was 19 years of age and had a severe phobia of public speaking. I was the youth leader of a radical political group, but never dared give a public speech. But by reading the early experiments of John B. Watson and his associates (Jones, 1920; Watson, 1919; Watson & Raynor, 1920), I learned that they deconditioned young children in a few sessions to overcome their fears of animals by in vivo desensitization. So I forced myself, very uncomfortably, to speak and speak in public and within ten weeks got completely over my phobia – and since that time, as I frequently tell my workshop audiences, you can't keep me away from the public speaking platform!

Thrilled by my success in getting almost a hundred percent over my panic about public speaking, I soon tackled my second paralyzing phobia – social anxiety. I could talk to young women comfortably after being introduced to them by a friend, but panicked at the thought of approaching them by myself and starting up a conversation. I never did so, just as I had avoided all public speeches up to the time I used exposure to rid myself of this fear. So I gave myself the homework assignment, in the month of August when I was on vacation from college, of sitting next to every young woman I saw sitting alone on a bench in Bronx Botanical Gardens and giving myself no more than one minute – yes, one lousy minute – to start a conversation with her. No nonsense, Albert – *one minute*!

I actually, in one month, sat next to 130 young women – which I had practically never done in my life before, so afraid was I of being rejected. Whereupon 30 out of the 130 immediately got up and walked away. But that left me an even sample of 100 – good for research purposes! Nothing daunted, I opened a conversation with the remaining 100 women – for the first time, again, in my entire young life. I spoke about the weather, the birds and the bees, the flowers and the trees, the book they were reading – truly, about everything and anything.

As I have often related, I got absolutely nowhere with my efforts to befriend, to date, and perhaps even to marry a few of these women with whom I conversed. If Fred Skinner, who was then teaching at Indiana University, had known of my futile efforts, he would have predicted that I would have been extinguished. Of the hundred women I talked to, I only made one date – and she didn't show up for it. She kissed me in the park, promised to meet me again later in the evening, and didn't appear. Being a novice at this kind of dating, I forgot to take her telephone number. So I never did discover what happened to her. Thereafter, I always took the phone number of the women I arranged to date!

Anyway, I found out that nothing terrible happened when I got rejected by 100 women in one month. No one took out a stiletto and cut my balls off. Women only do that these days! No one vomited and ran away. No one called a cop. I had many interesting and pleasant conversations. I found out a great deal about women. And I got so relaxed about talking to strange women in strange places that I got good at conversing, and with my next hundred tries, I actually made three dates. Better yet, I got completely over my fear of approaching women for the rest of my life and have espoused the pickup technique of meeting new partners to hundreds of my clients over the years.

Well, in vivo desensitization really worked for me at the age of 19. So when I started to practice psychotherapy in 1943, when I was 30 years old, I used it, with much success, with many anxious and phobic clients. Some of them achieved remarkable cures of long-standing panic disorders in just a few sessions. So my attempts to use this behavioral technique were nicely reinforced; and REBT has used it more than the other cognitive behavioral therapies, which followed it about a decade after I started to use REBT in 1955.

Important Developments in the Rise of Cognitive Behavioral Therapies

As I have noted, the use of cognitive behavioral methods in personality change is centuries old. Modern therapy, which started to become popular in the late 18th century with the experiments of Franz Anton Mesmer, was almost always cognitive behavioral. Hypnotists like James Braid, Jean Martin Charcot, and Hippolyte Bernheim used educational-persuasive and emotive methods to put their clients into trances and then often gave them activity homework assignments to help them work against their disturbed symptoms. Bernheim (1897/1947) was quite cognitive, in that he realized that hypnotism worked mainly because clients took the suggestion of the hypnotist and decided to follow it. Emile Coué (1923) developed the cognitive aspects of hypnotism in the early years of the 20th century by realizing that suggestion was not only at the heart of hypnotic therapy, but also that people's negative self-suggestion – or what he called autosuggestion – was a prime element in creating neurotic disturbance and that they could consciously choose to replace it with positive autosuggestion to solve many of their emotive and behavioral problems. Coué also invented positive visualization to help disturbed people improve their psychophysical functioning. So he was definitely a cognitive behavioral therapist.

When did cognitive behavior therapy (CBT) start to be used? Probably in 1953, when I abandoned psychoanalysis and started to develop REBT. After several futile attempts to reform psychoanalytic thinking and to make it more scientific – in a series of articles I wrote from 1947 to 1953 (Ellis, 1950, 1956) – I abandoned it and looked for an alternative system of psychotherapy. I went back to philosophy, especially the philosophy of human happiness, which had been one of my main hobbies since the age of 16, and rediscovered the ancient Asian and Greek and Roman philosophers. I was particularly taken with Epicurus, who preached the philosophy of disciplined hedonism, and with Epictetus (1899), who brought the stoic philosophy from Greece to Rome in the first century A. D. Most of these ancient writers were constructivists who differed from the Freudian idea that childhood traumas caused early and later emotional disturbance. They were also opposed to the somewhat similar idea of Watson (1919), who stated that if he trained or conditioned a child during its first five years to behave in a certain way it would take on that personality pattern for the rest of its life.

On the contrary, the ancient philosophers were constructivists. They largely maintained, along with Epictetus (1899), who wrote in *The Enchiridion* or *Manuel* in the first century, "People are disturbed not by things, but by the views which they take of them." This philosophy gives humans some *choice* in making themselves disturbed and undisturbed; and it was solidly reiterated by the existentialist philosophers – such as Kierkegaard (1953), Heidigger (1962), Sartre (1968), and Tillich (1953) – in modern times.

Taking this constructivist or choice theory to heart, I created and started practicing REBT in January, 1955. I was not influenced by George Kelly (1955), whose brilliant *Psychology of Personal Constructs* appeared later in 1955 and which I didn't read until 1957. But I was thrilled to see, when I read it, how much his theory of personal choice overlapped with that which I had already incorporated in rational emotive behavior therapy.

REBT, as I noted in my first paper on it at the American Psychological Association Convention in Chicago in August 1956 (Ellis, 1958a), went beyond the previous cognitive therapies of Janet (1898), Dubois (1907), and Adler (1929), all of whom worked to change what Janet called the *ideés fixe* – the fixed ideas – of disturbed people. REBT specifically described twelve common irrational or dysfunctional beliefs – which I derived from my clients' formulations of their problems during the first year and a half that I used it. It hypothesized that these and related irrational beliefs (IBs) almost invariably accompanied and helped to instigate people's neurotic feelings and behavior. As its main cognitive method, it actively-directively showed clients how to empirically, logically, and pragmatically dispute these IBs. This was much more specific than the previous cognitive therapies, and was largely adopted by most of the other cognitive behavioral systems that originated about a decade later, such as those of Glasser (1965), Beck (1967), Meichenbaum (1974, 1977), and Mahoney (1974).

Moreover, my hypothesized irrational or dysfunctional Beliefs – which I soon raised to about 50 common IBs – were put into paper and pencil questionnaires. More than 1,000 research studies using these questionnaires have now been published that tend to confirm my hypothesis that when people hold more irrational or dysfunctional beliefs, and hold them strongly, they are more seriously disturbed than those who hold fewer of them and hold them weakly (Beck, 1991; Clark, 1997; Ellis, 1979; Glass & Arnkoff, 1997; Hollon & Beck, 1997).

Moreover, well over a thousand empirical studies have been published by REBT and CBT researchers that tend to show that when clients are shown their irrational and dysfunctional beliefs, and are taught how to use cognitive behavioral methods of changing them, they tend to become less neurotic and even less afflicted with severe personality disorders (Beck, 1991; Hollon & Beck, 1994; Lyons & Woods, 1991; McGovern & Silverman, 1984; Meichenbaum, 1977; Silverman, McCarthy, & McGovern, 1992).

So the REBT theories of emotional-behavioral disturbance and their cognitive behavioral treatment have been backed by many empirical studies.

What about REBT and its place in behavior therapy? I also clearly stated in my first presentations on REBT (Ellis, 1957a, 1958a, 1958b, 1960, 1962) that it is both highly emotive-evocative and behavioral; and I changed its name in 1961 from rational therapy (RT) to rational emotive therapy (RET). In the 1960's, following the work of Perls (1969) and Shutz (1967), I also added many experiential exercises to REBT, including my famous shame-attacking exercises (Ellis, 1973). So, from the start, REBT differed from most other therapies in its regular use of many cognitive, many emotive, and many behavioral methods; and in this respect it has always been, to use Arnold Lazarus' (1989) term, multimodal (Kwee & Ellis, 1997).

This is an important aspect of cognitive behavioral therapy: In theory as well as practice, it is eclectic and integrationist. I said in my first paper on REBT (Ellis, 1958a) that thinking, feeling and behaving overlap and are interrelated. The second and third paragraphs of this article state:

> The human being may be said to possess four basic processes – perception, movement, thinking, and emotion – all of which are integrally interrelated. Thus, thinking, aside from consisting of bioelectric charges in the brain cells, and in addition to comprising remembering, learning,

> problem-solving, and similar psychological processes, also is, and to some extent has to be, sensory, motor, and emotional behavior. Instead, then, of saying, 'Jones thinks about this puzzle,' we should more accurately say, 'Jones perceives-moves-feels-THINKS about this puzzle.' Because, however, Jones' activity in relation to the puzzle may be *largely* focused upon solving it and only *incidentally* on seeing, manipulating, and emoting about it, we may perhaps justifiably emphasize only his thinking.
>
> Emotion, like thinking and the sensorimotor processes, we may define as an exceptionally complex state of human reaction which is integrally related to all the other perception and response processes. It is not *one* thing, but a combination and a holistic integration of several seemingly diverse, yet actually closely related, phenomena (Ellis, 1958, p. 35).

I think that all behavior therapy is really cognitive behavioral, since even in its purest form it consists of teaching, educating, and persuading clients to experiment with new behaviors. In pointing this out in a discussion I had with Joe Wolpe in 1995, I got Wolpe to state:

> There is an important point that Al Ellis made about cognitive events in therapy. Yes, cognition enters into everything we do. When we have a conversation, there is cognition on both sides. When Al Ellis and I are talking to you now, we are thinking that you are thinking, and all this is cognition. When I am telling a person to assert himself in certain situations, I am using his intellect, he is taking on what I say cognitively, and will later by using his judgment in carrying out assertive action (Ellis & Wolpe, 1997, p. 116).

Behavior Therapy, then, is just about always cognitive behavioral; and cognitive-behavior therapy practically always tends to be integrational, because its theory and practice hold that there are many roads to treating disturbed individuals, and these include various psychodynamic, interpersonal, person-centered, and other therapeutic methods (J. Beck, 1992; Ellis, 1958, 1962, 1998, 1999; Goldfried 1980, 1985). Even the radical behaviorists, such as Hayes (1994; Hayes, Strosahl, & Wilson, 1999) have fairly recently included distinctly cognitive and emotive methods in their form of behavior therapy and seem to be increasingly headed in that direction. So today, more than ever before, behavior and cognitive behavior therapy are following REBT and Lazarus' multimodal therapy in becoming wide-ranging in their therapeutic procedures.

Case Study of Reactions to Rational Emotive Behavior Therapy

My most cited publication on REBT was my book *Reason and Emotion in Psychotherapy* (Ellis, 1962). The reactions to it by leading therapists all over the world were almost uniformly negative. Fritz Perls carried on a feud with me for many years, contending that the book was boringly intellectual and completely omitted any emotional element. Carl Rogers never mentioned it publicly but, according to his intimates, was solidly against it. Several leading psychoanalysts called it superficial and made snippy remarks about it.

Psychologists were much kinder. Francis Ilg and Louise B. Ames, prominent child psychologists, called it "a most important, unusually interesting, and at times terribly amusing book." The unorthodox psychoanalyst, Harry Bone, a leading Sullivanian, was quite enthusiastic about it, and wrote:

> Aside from his contributions to therapy, Ellis has made many important thoroughly scholarly researches which do not have as many readers as they deserve. I unhesitatingly recommend his unique contribution to psychotherapy and his excellent exposition of his highly original system. It seems to me that Ellis's basic principle of *complete absence of blame* of not "blaming *anyone* for *anything* at *any time*," is essentially identical with Carl Rogers' principle of *unconditional positive regard*. The *thoroughness* with which they espouse this principle and its *implications* together with their respective ways of effectively *implementing* it, distinguishes their systems from other systems. This is the source of their potency and economy. I consider Ellis' *Reason and Emotion in Psychotherapy* the most important contribution to the field since Carl Rogers' contribution (Bone, 1968, p. 174).

Reviews of *Reason and Emotion in Psychotherapy* were almost nonexistent; and *Contemporary Psychology* only reviewed it when John Gullo, already a practicing psychologist who used REBT, convinced the editors to review it and gave it a very favorable review. Otherwise, the book would have been ignored by this journal – as it was by all the other professional journals. Despite this fact, *Reason and Emotion* sold more copies over the years than almost any other professional book of its day and a number of therapists learned how to do REBT mainly by reading it. To my surprise, although clearly written for the psychological profession, it became popular in the self-help field and I have many endorsements of it by readers who found it more helpful than some of my other books for the public.

Speaking of my popular books, they have been much more widely reviewed than my professional ones. *A Guide to Rational Living* (Ellis & Harper, 1997) first published in 1961, has sold almost two million copies, has been largely praised highly, and has been one of the books that therapists have recommended most to their clients. It has received very favorable reviews by many mental health professionals, including Cyril Franks, Daniel Wiener, Thomas W. Allen, Harold Greenwald, and Rowena and Heinz Ausbacher. Frank Richardson said that "It is still perhaps the single best 'self-help' book available to lay persons and psychotherapy clients" (1977, p. 271). Sol Gordon noted, "Still, in my judgment, the most sensible *and* usable of the self-help books" (1980, p. 203).

My popular books which applied REBT methods to sex, love, and marriage problems have sold very well, but been heavily criticized for their liberal views. Conservative professionals and critics have often objected to them strongly and have sometimes objected to the cognitive behavioral techniques they presented, often for the first time, to the public (Ellis, 1958b, 1960). They have been influential in the field of sex therapy, and have encouraged William Masters and Virginia Johnson, Helen Kaplan, Joseph LoPicolo, Lonnie Barbach, Bernie Zilbergeld and other authorities to adopt cognitive behavioral methods. But they also have prejudiced some professionals against REBT theory and practices in non-sexual areas, because of their objections to my sexual liberalism. On the other hand, my forthright sex writings have influenced many members of the public and mental health professionals to favor general CBT theory and practice. Prejudice, apparently, goes both ways!

Possible Object Lessons for the Future of Cognitive Behavior Therapy

Cognitive behavior therapy has come a long way since I first started to do REBT in 1955. It is perhaps the most common form of psychological treatment that therapists actually do today, no matter what system of therapy they say they follow. Many of its common procedures – such as cognitive restructuring and in vivo shame-attacking exercises – are widely used by many different kinds of therapists.

Moreover, in subtle or conscious ways, the use of various kinds of cognitive instruction restructuring is commonly employed in various forms of CBT (such as the constructivist therapies of Mahoney [1991] and Neimeyer [Neimeyer & Mahoney, 1995], in fairly pure behavior therapy (such as that of Wolpe 1990), and in radical behavior therapy (such as that of Hayes (Hayes, Stroshahl & Wilson, 1999)). So, again, important elements of CBT are almost universally used today in most psychotherapies (Alford & Beck, 1997; Ellis, 1987, 1994, 1999a, 1999b, 1999c).

This is exactly, I think, what preferably should happen in the future. Cognitive behavior therapies had better be tested for their effectiveness in their own right – though, actually, this is difficult to do, since they include a number of different cognitive, emotive, and behavioral techniques. But they also can be at least partially integrated with methods derived from psychodynamic, interpersonal, person-centered, and other schools of therapy.

This kind of integration has always been experimentally tried by many therapists. Even Freud (1965) gave occasional activity homework assignments; and REBT practitioners have at times used pollyannaish, unrealistic, and irrational methods, to which normally they are allergic (Ellis, 1994, 1996, 1999a, 1999b, 1999c). Whatever works works! Though as Hayes (1994) and I (Ellis, 1999c) have pointed out, some workable methods can also interfere with clients' using deeper and more elegant methods of treatment.

Cognitive behavioral therapy is probably here to stay – and to be constantly revised and improved. That is the way of scientific endeavor, and therefore the way to continue to go!

References

Adler, A. (1929). *The science of living.* New York: Greenberg.
Alford, B. A., & Beck, A. T. (1997). *The integrative power of cognitive therapy.* New York: Guilford.
Alexander, F., & French, T. M. (1946). *Psychoanalytic therapy.* New York: Ronald.
Beck, A. T. (1967). *Depression.* New York: Hoeber-Harper.
Beck, A. T. (1991). Cognitive therapy: A 30-year retrospective. *American Psychologist, 46,* 382-389.
Bernheim, H. (1987/1947). *Suggestive therapeutics.* New York: London Book Company.
Bloch, I. (1908). *The sexual life of our time.* New York: Rebman.
Bone, H. (1968). Two proposed alternatives to psychoanalytic interpreting. In E. Hammer (Ed.), *Use of interpretation in treatment* (pp. 169-196). New York: Grune and Stratton.
Clark, D. A. (1997). Twenty years of cognitive assessment: Current status and future directions. *Journal of Consulting and Clinical Psychology, 65,* 946-1000.
Cove, E. (1923). *My method.* New York: Doubleday.
Dubois, P. (1907). *The psychic treatment of nervous disorders.* New York: Funk and Wagnalls.
Ellis, A. (1950). An introduction to the scientific principles of psychoanalysis. *Genetic Psychology Monographs, 41,* 147-212.
Ellis, A. (1955a). *New approaches to psychotherapy techniques.* Brandon, VT.
Ellis, A. (1955b). Psychotherapy techniques for use with psychotics. *American Journal of Psychotherapy, 9,* 452-476.
Ellis, A. (1956). An operational reformulation of some of the basic principles of psychoanalysis. In H. Feigl & M. Scriven (Eds.), *The foundations of science and the concepts of psychology and psychoanalysis* (pp. 131-154). Minneapolis: University of Minnesota Press. (Also: *Psychoanalytic Review, 43,* 163-180).
Ellis, A. (1957a). *How to live with a neurotic: At home and at work* (Rev. ed.). Hollywood, CA: Wilshire Books.
Ellis, A. (1957b). Outcome of employing three techniques of psychotherapy. *Journal of Clinical Psychology, 13,* 344-350.
Ellis, A. (1958a). Rational psychotherapy. *Journal of General Psychology, 59,* 35-49.
Ellis, A. (1958b). *Sex without guilt.* North Hollywood, CA: Wilshire Books.
Ellis, A. (1960). *The art and science of love.* New York: Lyle Stuart & Bantam.
Ellis, A. (1962). *Reason and emotion in psychotherapy.* Secaucus, NJ: Citadel.
Ellis, A. (Speaker). (1973). *How to stubbornly refuse to be ashamed of anything* (Cassette recording). New York: Albert Ellis Institute.
Ellis, A. (1979). Rational-emotive therapy: Research data that support the clinical and personality hypotheses of RET and other modes of cognitive-behavior therapy. In A. Ellis & J. M. Whiteley (Eds.), *Theoretical and empirical foundations of rational-emotive therapy* (pp. 101-173). Monterey, CA: Brooks/Cole.

Ellis, A. (1987). Integrative developments in rational-emotive therapy (RET). *Journal of Integrative and Eclectic Psychotherapy, 6*, 470-479.
Ellis, A. (1993). Changing rational-emotive therapy (RET) to rational emotive behavior therapy (REBT). *Behavior Therapist, 16*, 257-258.
Ellis, A. (1994). *Reason and emotion in psychotherapy* (Rev. ed.). Secaucus, NJ: Carol Publishing Group.
Ellis, A. (1996). *Better, deeper, and more enduring brief therapy.* New York: Brunner/Mazel.
Ellis, A. (1999a). *How to make yourself happy and remarkably less disturbable.* San Luis Obispo, CA: Impact Publishers.
Ellis, A. (1999b, May 29). The importance of cognitive processes in facilitating accepting in psychotherapy. Invited address to the 25th Anniversary Annual Convention of the Association for Behavior Analysis, Chicago.
Ellis, A. (2000). A continuation of the dialogue on counseling in the postmodern era. *Journal of Mental Health Counseling, 22*, 97-106.
Ellis, A., & Harper, R. A. (1997a). *A guide to successful marriage* (Rev. ed.). North Hollywood, CA: Wilshire Books. 1997.
Ellis, A., & Harper, R. A. (1997b). *A guide to rational living.* North Hollywood, CA: Wilshire Books.
Ellis, A., & Wolpe, J. (1997). Discussion by Albert Ellis and response by Joseph Wolpe. In J. K. Zeig (Ed.), *The evolution of psychotherapy. The third conference* (pp. 115-119). New York: Brunner/Mazel.
Ellis, H. (1936). *Studies in the psychology of sex* (2 vols). New York: Random House.
Epictetus. (1890). *The works of Epictetus.* Boston: Little Brown.
Forel, A. (1922). *The sexual question.* New York: Physician's and Surgeon's Book Company.
Freud, S. (1965). *Standard edition of the complete psychological works of Sigmund Freud.* New York: Basic Books.
Fromm, E. (1955). *The sane society.* New York: Rinehurst.
Glass, C. R., & Arnkoff, D. B. (1997). Questionnaire methods of cognitive self-statement assessment. *Journal of Consulting and Clinical Psychology, 65*, 911-927.
Glasser, W. (1965). *Reality therapy.* New York: Harper & Row.
Goldfried, M. R. (1980). Toward the delineation of therapeutic change principles. *American Psychologist, 35*, 991-999.
Goldfried, M. R. (1995). *From cognitive-behavior to psychotherapy integration.* New York: Springer.
Gordon, S. (1980). *The new you.* Lafayette, NY: Ed. U Press.
Hayes, S. C. (1994). Content, context and the types of psychological acceptance. In S. C. Hayes, N. S. Jacobson, V. M. Follette, & M. J. Dougher (Eds.), *Acceptance and change: Content and context in psychotherapy* (pp. 13-32). Reno, NV: Context Press.
Hayes, S. C., Strosahl, K., & Wilson, K. G. (1999). *Acceptance and Commitment Therapy.* New York: Guilford.
Heidegger, M. (1962). *Being and time.* New York: Harper & Row.

Herzberg, A. (1945). *Active psychotherapy.* New York: Grune & Stratton.

Hoellen, B. (1993). Richard Huelsenbeck und Albert Ellis. *Zeitschrift fur Rational-Emotive Therapie und Kognitive Verhaltens Therapie, 4,* 5-37.

Hollon, S. D., & Beck, A. T. (1994). Cognitive and cognitive-behavior therapies. In A. E. Bergin & S. L. Garfield (Eds.), *Handbook of psychotherapy and behavior change* (pp. 428-466). New York: Wiley.

Horney, K. (1950). *Neurosis and human growth.* New York: Norton.

Janet, P. (1898). *Neuroses et idée fixes.* Paris: Alcan.

Jones, M. C. (1920). The elimination of children's fears .*Journal of Experimental Psychology, 7,* 383-390.

Kelly, G. (1955). *The psychology of personal constructs.* New York: Norton.

Kierkegaard, S. (1953). *Fear and trembling* and *The sickness unto death.* New York: Doubleday.

Kwee, M. G .T., & Ellis, A. (1997). Can multimodal and rational emotive behavior therapy be reconciled? *Journal of Rational-Emotive and Cognitive-Behavior Therapy, 15* (2).

Lazarus, A. A. (1989). *The practice of multimodal therapy.* Baltimore, MD: Johns Hopkins.

Mahoney, M. J. (1974). *Cognition and behavior modification.* Cambridge, MA: Ballinger.

Mahoney, M. J. (1991). *Human change processes.* New York: Basic Books.

McGovern, T. E., & Silverman, M. S. (1984). A review of outcome studies of rational-emotive therapy from 1977 to 1982. *Journal of Rational-Emotive Therapy, 2*(1), 7-18.

Meichenbaum, D. (1974). Self instructional training: A cognitive protheses for the aged. *Human development, 17,* 273-280.

Meichenbaum, D. (1977). *Cognitive-behavior modification.* New York: Plenum.

Neimeyer, R. A., & Mahoney, M. J. (1995). *Constructivism in psychotherapy.* Washington, DC: American Psychological Association.

Perls, F. (1969). *Gestalt therapy verbatim.* New York: Delta.

Richardson, F. (1977). Basic Ellis revised. *Journal of Individual Psychology, 33,* 270-271.

Robie, W. F. (1925). *The art of love.* Ithaca, NY: Rational Life Press.

Rogers, C. R. (1943). *Counseling and psychotherapy.* Boston: Houghton Mifflin.

Rogers, C. R. (1951). *Client-centered therapy.* Boston: Houghton Mifflin.

Salter, A. (1949). *Conditioned reflex therapy.* New York: Creative Age.

Sartre, J. (1968). *Being and nothingness.* New York: Washington Square.

Schutz, W. (1967). *Joy.* New York: Grove.

Silverman, M. S., McCarthy, M., & McGovern, T. (1992). A review of outcome studies of rational-emotive therapy from 1982-1989. *Journal of Rational-Emotive and Cognitive-Behavior Therapy, 10*(3).

Sullivan, H. S. (1953). *The interpersonal theory of psychiatry.* New York: Norton.

Tillich, P. (1953). The courage to be. Cambridge: Harvard University Press.

Watson, J. B. (1919). *Psychology from the standpoint of a behaviorist.* Philadelphia: Lippincott.

Watson, J. B., & Rayner, R. (1920). Conditioned emotional reactions. *Journal of Experimental Psychology, 3*, 1-14.

Wolpe, J. (1990). *The practice of behavior therapy* (4th. ed.). Needham Heights, MA: Allyn and Bacon.

Chapter 10

From Psychodynamic to Behavior Therapy: Paradigm Shift and Personal Perspectives

Cyril M. Franks
Distinguished Professor Emeritus, Rutgers University

"No wind blows in favor of a ship that has no direction."
Essays, Michael Eyquem de Monte (Montaigne 1533 - 1592).

"The times they are a changin.'"
Bob Dylan, circa 1964.

Introduction

The value of an intellectual biography lies in tracing the connection between events and thoughts. This intellectual autobiography spans some 50 years, 3,000 miles and the greatest adventure of all, a journey of the mind from the birth of behavior therapy to its coming of age on the threshold of a new millennium. My early years are likely to be of only historic interest to the general reader and alien to most American psychologists. Nevertheless, a description of these formative years might clarify the manner in which my thinking about behavior therapy evolved. The basic ingredients include: a classical education stressing language and literature; training in both the technology and methodology of applied science; my wartime experiences; my growing disappointment with psychoanalysis, at best a pseudo-scientific model with a total unawareness of outcome evaluation, accountability and the like; the cavalier treatment of psychologists in medical facilities; the self-satisfied medical establishment's unawareness that any therapy other than Freudian could be either possible or necessary. Half a century ago, most clinical psychologists seemed to tolerate their exclusion as therapists and see little that was wrong with this situation. Inspired by the work of Hans Eysenck and his associates, such factors sparked my desire to establish a new, and eventually accepted, behavioral paradigm. To the best of my knowledge, these matters have not been described elsewhere.

Formative Years

I was born in 1923 in a primarily English – rather than Welsh – speaking resort town in South Wales. Until war came my childhood was pleasant and uneventful. As with all children of promise, my education was fully subsidized from kindergarten through postgraduate university levels by the British regional department of education. I attended an elitist high school for boys from ages 11 through 17 where selection for a strictly academic education was determined by high scores on a rigorous screening examination. Intellectually qualifying girls received a similar education in a separate school. My earliest recollection was of Dylan Thomas, a then unknown one-of-the-crowd aspiring writer several years ahead of me in school, striving to instill the elements of Chaucer into my unappreciative head. In this rarefied setting, typing and woodwork were out of the question and sports and physical training were compulsory after-school activities in addition to a demanding homework schedule. Nevertheless, morale and teacher/student camaraderie were high despite continuing academic pressures.

French or German, plus Latin, were compulsory and, in addition, my family expected me to attend after-school Hebrew classes and Jewish cultural studies three times a week. Furthermore, all students had to go to weekly Welsh-language classes where Welsh was of little interest to many of us and of even less utility. All in all, I acquired an excellent education and a lasting ability to express myself effectively in speech and writing, both of which stood me in good stead over the years.

In 1939 the long-expected war came to the UK But, despite severe vicissitudes, my formal education continued surprisingly smoothly until repeated nationwide Nazi bombing razed our impressive 300-year-old school building to the ground and killed several classmates. Understandably, war curtailed what was previously an idyllic education. Nevertheless, morale remained high as we tried to cope as best we could. After four years of general education and searching school examinations I opted, as was the custom in those days, to specialize in three subjects for two more years: applied mathematics, physics and electronics (premature school specialization has been long since discontinued) where, despite wartime disruptions, two years later I managed to pass all school examinations. But, by then, my technical interest in both physics and electronics had began to wane. As the war intensified, at 18 years of age I was directed, because of my specialization subjects, to become a full-time student at the nearby University of Wales and complete an intensive, accelerated four-year degree program in two years, continuing with the same three high school subjects. It was too late to change and, in any event, I had no say in the matter. Time was not on the British side and, despite the Soviet Union's valiant war effort, we were still very much alone. Fortunately, things changed when America entered the war. Two years later I obtained my expected B.S. degree as planned and, despite a still declining interest in applied physics and electronics, once again I was drafted, this time to a top-secret government facility for electronic "hot shots" who, for painfully obvious reasons, soon turned out not to include me.

I was directed to work on the development of an urgently needed infrared device for military truck driving in convoy at night in total darkness where both sides were striving to perfect this device prior to the imminently expected second front. By this time, my technical deficits becoming increasingly apparent, I was ignominiously reassigned to a leading, but less pressured, electronics company in London. The area turned out to be one of the most dangerous and stressful regions in the hard-pressed British Isles. Here, German rocket bombs, known as V2s, indiscriminately and unpredictably rained down sudden death by day and night. Without warning, several fellow workers were blown to fragments in the coming months.

Fortunately, the war in Europe ended soon after and I was free, subject to college acceptance, to study whatever and wherever I chose, again at government expense. Although by then vastly more interested in the methodology of science than the technology of electronics, my love of literature and writing remained. At the same time, my interest in people and whatever made them "tick" blossomed. So, as a compromise, I enrolled in a 16-month teacher-training program at London University, specializing in teaching applied sciences and elementary electronics at technical high school levels.

The Search

My first, and last, school job was teaching general science to Merchant Service cadets at the London Nautical School. Classes ending in the early afternoon left me ample time to take numerous university courses in general and clinical psychology. These under my belt, four years later I was eligible to apply for admission both to what is now known as a clinical internship and a Ph.D. program in psychology. Then came the daunting task of finding an acceptable university base. Even at this early stage I knew that "acceptable" meant a broadly behavioral climate and a stringent questioning of Freudian theory and practice which, even then, I regarded as a pseudoscience. Freudian psychotherapy went unchallenged by all mental health practitioners and necessities such as control groups, validation, outcome evaluation, follow-up and patient satisfaction were unheard of.

For three months I briefly visited and rejected most of the few university departments in Western Europe offering training in clinical psychology at that time. Another requirement, then thought out of the question for non-physicians, was that fully-trained clinical psychologists be permitted to serve as therapists in medically controlled settings. I felt that this situation would never change in the foreseeable future. Fortunately, I was wrong but, at the time, I had no idea how change might come about.

The next step was to make an extended visit to the University of London Institute of Psychiatry, Maudsley Hospital, where Hans Eysenck and his staff offered both an internship-type program in clinical psychology and a related Ph.D. program after completion of the former. So I looked no further after making a second visit to the Maudsley, where Eysenck, becoming well-known, endorsed my decision to apply for admission to both programs. Eysenck's Ph.D. program offered a combination of clinical and experimental psychology, which was just what I wanted. But even at the Maudsley, clinically trained psychologists were expected and permitted only to give psychological tests, write reports, do some occasional vocational guidance and interviewing, and engage in non-threatening, physician sanctioned research. Most curious of all, or so it seemed to me, virtually all clinical psychologists, outside the Maudsley, subscribed unconditionally to a Freudian model.

What especially irked me was that, despite four years of study, most clinical psychologists disregarded their training, fully accepting Freudian dogma, and never thinking seriously about an alternative. They also seemed to tolerate a demeaning, hospital status. Thus, on my second Maudsley visit, I knew where I wanted to spend the next few years as a student. What I did not know at the time was that this experience was to determine my career path for the rest of my professional life.

Maudsley Days

Eysenck, then at the beginning of his career and already department head, even in those early days, was a favorite target of criticism. Prominent in psychology circles, Eysenck had astutely gathered around him a coterie of loyal but, at times, critical students and junior faculty periodically reinforced by an infusion of visiting colleagues from around the world. Our first, and long-term-goal, then regarded by the mental health community as an impossible dream, was to supplement the ubiquitous, and then only, model of Freudian therapy with an, as yet, undetermined data-based learning theory approach. In effect, this involved a paradigm shift from a psychodynamic to a behavioral model and in which the two paradigms were expected initially to co-exist with gradually diminishing psychodynamic influence.

The notion of a paradigm, applied initially only to the social sciences by Kuhn (1970), was later extended to psychology to meet our needs. By a paradigm shift we meant a sweeping, significant, and hopefully lasting, change in a prevailing, comprehensive, explanatory system. For example, when Galileo courageously announced his data-based explanation of the locations and orbits of heavenly bodies in our solar system, there was a gradual shift from the then literally heretical, church-ordained dogma about the central positions of the sun and earth, away from the old to the new observation-based paradigm, much akin to the eventual replacement of Freudian dogma with data.

Under Eysenck's leadership, the second goal was to gather enough data to validate an appropriate personality structure in terms of two factorially determined orthogonal dimensions, first neuroticism and introversion-extraversion followed, much later, by psychoticism (the latter remaining more a hope than a reality). To advance these goals a soundproof classical conditioning laboratory had to be constructed, using primarily eyeblink and GSR conditioning.

Program research, nothing new and offering many tactical advantages, was the favored strategy. Thus, being familiar with program research and, when my incorrectly presumed technological skills also became known, I was invited to join Eysenck's department as an unpaid student member of his research group and put in charge of the construction and development of the new conditioning laboratory. Accepting this invitation with alacrity I enrolled in both programs, first the 12-month clinical internship following approval of my carefully scrutinized psychology training and, second, enrollment in the at least three-year full-time Ph.D. research program.

Unfortunately, Monte Shapiro, Eysenck's distinguished colleague, directed the internship program. If my memories of long-past events do not lead me too far astray, the clinical internship presented a major dilemma. Most projective techniques, correctly judged invalid, were not taught and exclusive reliance was placed upon relatively more objective assessment tests such as neuropsychology procedures, intelligence testing, certain multiple-choice questionnaires, the MMPI and structured interviews. Consequently, students untrained in everyday bread-and-butter projective techniques, such as the Rorschach, were unable to gain employment as clinicians virtually anywhere. Fortunately, this total ban on training in projective techniques was relaxed soon after even though they were always used sparingly and with caution.

Reinforced by group enthusiasm and stimulating weekly discussion in Eysenck's home, I successfully, but not enthusiastically, completed this fragile internship and began my Ph.D. research in earnest as well as active participation in the ongoing search for a new paradigm. The new conditioning laboratory continued to be my responsibility by virtue of a rashly presumed electronic expertise, laying the groundwork for a series of published drug and personality conditioning studies involving both normal and clinically abnormal populations. Publication of an invited article about our new laboratory in the prestigious journal *Nature* further provided a timely and heartwarming boost to morale (Franks 1955).

After much investigation and thought various field models were examined and found wanting in one way or another. Eventually we settled on a combination of Hullian and Pavlovian S-R learning theory and the methodology of behavioral science adapted to meet our clinical requirements, such as empirical validation, outcome evaluation, follow-up and client satisfaction. Having found what then seemed to be the only exclusively "behaviorally correct" formula, it took me many years to realize that, without abrogating rigid behavioral principles, I was as intolerant as our despised Freudian counterparts. My thinking began to change with the pioneering and influential text *Behavior Therapy and Beyond* (Lazarus, 1971).

The Dawn of Behavior Therapy

Having agreed that our new approach to therapy would stem from the notions of Pavlov and Hull, if only because there was really no feasible alternative, we set out to develop some behaviorally valid theory-based innovative procedures, a task, which turned out to be more arduous than anticipated. At first, laboriously we produced little more than a few novel, but validated, parent-training reinforcement techniques, some phobia extinction and anxiety reduction strategies and unimaginative aversion conditioning training for the mentally retarded. Not knowing better, initially we focused exclusively on the presenting problem and none of this could even remotely be called behavior therapy. This was around the time that Eysenck (1959) coined the term behavior therapy in Europe, Wolpe and Lazarus (1958) in South Africa and Lindsley, Skinner and Solomon in the USA (1958), all working independently. Regrettably, we overlooked the operant conditioning of Skinner and his associates, perhaps because we viewed Skinner as primarily an animal psychologist and not a clinician.

My initial focus on trying to develop a conditioned aversion to alcohol abuse seemed a feasible beginning but, as we soon discovered, this was still not behavior therapy. All treatments of alcoholism were notoriously unsuccessful to-date and, consequently, to our surprise, some physicians were willing to let lay therapists "have a try." At first, I focused exclusively on the development of a conditioned aversion to alcohol. In so doing, never talking to the patient or looking into anything meaningful in the patient's life other than the alcohol abuse, I never looked into relevant life circumstances. This procedure, still unworthy of the name behavior therapy, or any therapy for that matter, failed dismally, as we might have expected. Slowly, I became more sophisticated and learned from experience, publishing a few exploratory studies of the behavioral treatment of alcoholism and achieving no real success until I updated my thinking. Anticipating the trail-blazing multimodal therapy of Lazarus (1971), I went beyond conditioned aversion *per se*, began to talk to the patient about seemingly significant concerns in addition to presenting problems and started to explore multi-level situations, real life settings and multi-stimulus approaches, including the development of a conditioned aversion, trying to modify the patient's self-defeating life-style. Although our short-term success rates were modestly better, but far from spectacular, for me this was the beginning of primitive behavior therapy (Franks, 1963), a tiny crack in the physician's Freudian superstructure.

When Dollard and Miller's (1950) pioneering American text tried to explain psychoanalytic practices and S-R learning theory principles under one cover, I believed that things were beginning to change for the better but, alas, I soon learned that this was premature, merely wishful thinking! In essence, what these two forward-looking mental health professionals had unwittingly produced was a scholarly exercise in translating the limited language of learning theory into psychoanalytic gospel and vice versa in order to facilitate communication. Both distinguished authors, one more learning theory-oriented than the other, made the tacit assumption that psychoanalytic theory and practice were unassailable truths. What they had really produced was a sophisticated dictionary. So, discouraged again, having completed my internship, I took a year off to take an M.A. degree at the University of Minnesota where primarily, I learned that everyone "did his or her own thing." Few had heard of behavior therapy whereas, at the University of Minnesota, everyone knew all about the MMPI!

A year later I returned to London with my American wife, Violet, now a leading feminist behavior therapist, and I completed my Ph.D. in 1954, eventually becoming a tenured junior faculty member of Eysenck's department. Meanwhile, the name Eysenck had justifiably become a byword throughout British psychology and elsewhere. Parenthetically, Eysenck's published autobiography was provocatively called *Rebel With a Cause!* Over the years Eysenck reveled in specious arguments and outrageous statements. Two years after his 1998 death the debate continues – was Eysenck a brilliant scientist or a controversial provocateur? Probably both.

Move to the USA, Start of the AABT, and Subsequent Developments

In 1958, Wolpe's groundbreaking desensitization text, already well-known to our Maudsley group in manuscript form appeared in print, first in the USA then worldwide. For the first time there was, at last, a viable behavioral alternative to psychodynamic therapy which could be readily applied to treating the sorts of patients and problems that make up the bulk of general psychiatric practice. Thus, still disappointed with Dollard and Miller but encouraged by Wolpe's book, I decided to relocate to the USA in the naïve hope that American therapists would offer better opportunities in a more friendly climate. Once again I was disappointed.

Nevertheless, in 1957 I accepted a position as Director of Psychology at the Neuropsychiatric Institute, Princeton, NJ where my first goal, with the help of an NIMH grant, was to establish an American counterpart of our British conditioning laboratory. Gradually this became a reality and the publication flow went across both sides of the Atlantic. With Eysenck, my second and equally important goal, facilitated by Wolpe's text, was to make a behavioral mental health paradigm a meaningful reality. Unfortunately, I soon found that the climates in both the USA and the UK, among psychiatrists and clinical psychologists alike, were much the same. In this frame of mind, discouraged again, I came across few kindred spirits until a chance meeting occurred, a meeting which would lead eventually to the creation of the Association for Advancement of Behavior Therapy (AABT).

Dorothy Susskind, then a graduate student at New York's Yeshiva University, was in the final stages of a Ph.D. dissertation examining certain aspects of Eysenck's work. Soon I learned not only more about Susskind's dissertation but also about our common dissatisfaction with mental health training and therapy in both countries and, even more to the point, we talked extensively about what might be done about it. I also learned that Susskind was both a knowledgeable clinical psychologist and an experienced administrator and organizer. As a first step we set up several meetings with a few carefully selected participants and soon we were convening regularly to explore the possibilities of forming our own organization. Eventually, about 40 seriously interested professionals formed the nucleus of what later became AABT. These individuals include such luminaries as Paul Brady, Edward Dengrove, Andrew Salter, Arthur Staats, Leonard Ulmann, Leonard Krasner, Arnold Lazarus, Joseph Cautela and Joseph Wolpe in addition to Dorothy Susskind and myself. We constituted the initial planning group, with Stuart Agras and Eysenck offering periodic support from afar. Sadly, Salter, Wolpe, Eysenck and Cautela are no longer with us and we continue to miss them. On a happier note, three founding fathers are still professionally active; Staats, Lazarus, and myself.

Our first task was to settle on an appropriate name for our fledgling association. Having been actively involved with the British Association for Advancement of science for several years, my first name suggestion was unanimously accepted and our organization briefly became the Association for Advancement of the Behavioral Therapies. From the start, the word "advancement" was meant to imply scholarly rather than personal advancement. An equally important goal was to develop behavior therapy as a conceptual unity and, by general consent, the name of the AABT was changed to its present singular form and the name, Association for Advancement of Behavior Therapy has remained this way ever since.

In 1966, I was elected first President of the AABT, probably because no one else was willing to take on this demanding chore and, probably for similar reasons, I also agreed to become the first Editor of the Association's newly formed Newsletter and first Program Chair for a half-day meeting held in parallel with the Annual Convention of the American Psychological Association. In those early months, Susskind and I carried out much of the slog work, including such mundane chores as stuffing envelopes and folding and mailing announcements. It was around this period, 1970, that I became Professor of Psychology at Rutgers University.

Later, for nine years, I also served as founding Editor of the AABT's first journal, *Behavior Therapy*, including choosing and negotiating with a suitable publishing house. Throughout this period my blinkered vision of behavior therapy gradually matured. It took many years for me to appreciate that there is no such thing as an interaction involving behavior alone, making me wonder how so-called cognitive behavior therapy could be paradigmatically different from behavior therapy. And, though not well developed as yet, a similar argument applies to affect.

The Times They are Indeed a Changin'

In 2001, the AABT, now firmly launched, has a membership approaching 6,000. Behavior therapy and its now probably dominant offshoot, cognitive behavior therapy, exceed most optimistic expectations as far as numbers alone (a flawed criterion) are concerned. Perhaps some two dozen behavior therapy, cognitive behavior therapy and behaviorally related journals of one kind or another, mostly in English, are scattered around the globe. Nowadays, for the most part the behavioral and the Freudian paradigms, respectively, coexist in mutual tolerance if not always in mutual peace and harmony. With maturity and security the early need of some behavior therapists to adopt an I-am-better-than-you attitude is no more. More important, especially in the USA and UK, the occasional pockets of resistance, still encountered from some physicians, are becoming fewer and fully-qualified nonmedical behavior therapists are now free to practice in most psychiatric facilities on almost equal footings–a remarkable index of progress in a comparatively short time.

While this is not the place to write a needed history of behavior therapy, if I may be indulged at this point I would like to mention, by way of history, a few personal accomplishments which continue to give me gratification. First, there is my continuing Editorship of the quarterly journal *Child and Family Behavior Therapy*, now in its 25th year. Second, with different collaborators at various times, Terry Wilson and I produced the *Annual Review of Behavior Therapy* for 12 years, gaining in size and substance and serving as a continuing chronicle of significant behavioral happenings from year to year. The series continued without interruption until the growth of the behavioral literature, some written in languages other than English, made it impossible to maintain this pace. Reluctantly, the series had to be discontinued. Hopefully, someone, or some group, will eventually take on this daunting task.

Third and fourth are two earlier texts, both "firsts" in their respective ways. The first, *Conditioning Techniques in Clinical Practice and Research* (Franks, 1964), focused on the limited behavior therapy literature of that time. The second, an overview of the still limited behavioral literature in 1969, consists primarily of an appraisal of what I then considered to reflect the overall status of behavior therapy, written by others and myself. Appropriately, the title *is Behavior Therapy: Appraisal and Status* (Franks, 1969). Since the field changes so rapidly, both books are now of primarily historic interest.

In terms of more recent developments, the rapid rise of cognitive behavior therapy and its impact upon behavior therapy at large is remarkable. With little doubt, cognitive behavior therapy, for better or worse, probably both, is now the dominant influence in our field. But I am still unclear what is meant by cognitive behavior therapy, a term used in diverse ways. In this regard, one may speculate, perhaps uncharitably, about the needs of a few cognitive behavior therapists to achieve professional visibility as soon as possible even if this sometimes entails taking a few shortcuts. Other cognitive behavior therapists sincerely perceive many of the early, painstaking methodological exactitudes as now unnecessary and, perhaps, never were necessary. I now recognize that both positions have merit and Krasner's verdict (in this book) that cognitive behavior therapy is the "oxymoron of the century" may be unwarranted. In any event, regardless of validity and long-term outcome, a variety of appealing and creative new cognitive behavior therapy techniques emerge regularly. Part of the problem is that the original, precise notions about the nature of a stimulus and response sometimes become unrecognizable and, in so doing, cognitive behavior therapy is in danger of becoming nonexclusive, thereby blurring the once unique identity of behavior therapy.

At first, the combination of changing times and the many new faces of behavior therapy made me feel very uneasy, so much so that, in 1981, I wrote an article with the self-explanatory title "2081: Will we be many, or one–or none?" (Franks, 1981). It seemed to me, at that time, that my vision of the unity of behavior therapy was rapidly falling apart. Until the 1990's my still lingering belief in the unity of behavior therapy seemed feasible and that, somehow, even the unity of psychology at large was at hand, so much so that, in 1993, I became President of Arthur Staats' now defunct organization SUNI: the Society for Studying Unity Issues. Now, however, recent events force me to reconsider my position both with respect, on the one hand, to the desirability of the notion of unity in behavior therapy and, on the other hand, the probability that diversity rather than unity in behavior therapy adds vitality to our movement. After all, not surprising, if long-established disciplines such as physics and medicine continue to fall far short of unity how can the relatively new discipline of behavior therapy expect to succeed? Regrettably, Staats' lifelong attempt to generate a comprehensive system of clinical/behavioral psychology has not received the recognition it merits.

As I now see it, behavior therapy is becoming, at least, bi-modal. There is the declining minority of hard-core, card-carrying behavioral diehards who still conform faithfully to a strict, behavioral foundation and there is the freewheeling, growing majority of loosely behavioral psychologists, especially the self-styled cognitive behavior therapists, and there is a spectrum of positions in between. I still favor some form of behavioral orientation and some form of recognizable S-R learning theory but I no longer regard changes in the perceived nature of behavior therapy with apprehension. Consequently, I am now prepared to consider seriously most novel interpretations of behavior therapy. But there is one proposed innovation that I find hard to stomach and that is the proposal to combine behavior therapy and psychodynamic therapy in one way or another. For reasons obvious to me I find this curious notion totally unacceptable. Behavior therapy and psychodynamic therapy are two incompatible systems and both, in my book, would probably fare better to go about their respective ways (Franks, 1984).

Behavior therapy began as an exclusively behavioral protest against the prevailing psychodynamic regime. Originally a hard-nosed entity, behavior therapy is now confronted with a panoply of bewildering behaviorally-related acronyms: CT, BT, RECBT, ACT, DBT, and more. There are probably a dozen varieties of CBT alone. Conditioning, Dialectical, Cognition, Behavior, and Affective are vying with each other for their share of the limelight.

My journey has come a long way in the past 50 years, from closed-minded notions about the nature of behavior therapy to tolerance and cautious acceptance. As I continue my journey I hope one day to see something which, so far, has not occurred, the emergence of some new and fundamental behavioral concept. Since the eras of Pavlov and Skinner, no new generally accepted concept of significance relating to conditioning/behavior therapy has emerged. The impressive accomplishments and "busy work" of behavior therapists are gratifying but I hanker for a new Pavlov or Skinner to emerge. Maybe I am expecting too much. Meanwhile, I have reached the present stage of my journey, a stage still in formation, with a growing awareness of alternate behavioral models, different than the one to which I have long been accustomed.

Decades ago, during an extended visit to what was then known as the U.S.S.R., my Soviet colleagues explained politely but firmly that behavior therapy, well-developed in the West, could legally be neither practiced nor studied anywhere in the then Communist world regardless of the fact that my brand of behavior therapy stems largely from the work of Pavlov. In all Communist countries, behavior therapy, said the Soviets, is a regressive product of S-R learning theory built upon a "false and simplistic" 19th century mechanistic materialism. Patiently, my Soviet colleagues tried, with no success, to correct my faulty thinking to reflect a "politically correct" dialectical materialism rather than my "primitive" mechanistic materialism.

It was not until very recently that I admitted that, as far as the differences between mechanistic and dialectical materialism are concerned, the Soviets had a point, but, of course, I never could accept the Marxist overtones. Only recently did I begin to appreciate contemporary developments in operant conditioning, applied behavior analysis and their, as yet largely unrealized clinical potentials. Gradually I became aware of very different behavioral models couched in functional dynamic, operant conditioning and contextual terms involving notions still new to me, such as integrative couples therapy, dialectical behavior therapy and more. It is time to take into account more than an exclusively mechanistic behavior therapy, models hitherto neglected by most therapists, models not, as yet, well-developed clinically in sharp contrast to their mechanistic, classical conditioning-based predecessor.

It was not until late 1999 that Hayes and Toarmino clearly pinpointed two very different, and rarely interacting, traditions in behavior therapy, thereby sharpening my fuzzy thinking about such matters, two compartmentalized traditions with few points of interaction, the first popular and well-established clinically and the second clinically not well-developed and yet to show what it could accomplish; the first tradition, still largely mechanistic and based upon classical conditioning, the second less mechanistic, stemming, in large part, from operant conditioning, and applied behavior analysis.

For the time being, while recognizing the virtues of both traditions and the many impressive accomplishments of the first, I will continue to work within both traditions while learning more about the second. As yet I am more comfortable with, and more knowledgeable about, mainstream traditional behavior therapy. Meanwhile, the second tradition waits in the wings ready to move to center stage. Meanwhile I will work with interest and curiosity towards what the future of behavior therapy may bring.

Postscript

In 1970 I became Professor of Psychology at Rutgers University in its clinical Ph.D. program. From time to time my positions have included Clinical Director and Director of post-Doctoral Training. In 1974 the Rutgers Graduate School of Applied and Professional Psychology came into being, offering a full-time doctorate in applied and professional psychology (Psy.D.) for clinicians, the first of its kind anywhere. My active involvement with both programs continued until retirement as Distinguished Professor Emeritus in 1991.

The evening of retirement festivities began with a merciless, but lovingly crafted, "roasting" engineered by half a dozen longtime associates in the presence of several hundred colleagues and friends from the USA and abroad. The evening concluded with a quite different, totally unexpected, event, the annual "Cyril M. Franks' Award for Excellence in Research." A small committee would meet annually to select what, in the committee's opinion, was the most outstanding doctoral dissertation of the year at Rutgers in professional psychology. As part of the graduation ceremony, held at the end of each academic year, the award-winning new doctor is presented with an appropriately inscribed plaque and his or her name added to an annual, wall-mounted list. The recipient also receives a modest honorarium, a procedure followed ever since.

Following retirement, other than formal teaching and tedious committee meetings I did almost as much as usual until, in 1997, I suffered a major stroke which still severely curtails most professional activities other than an occasional address on special occasions and the editorship of my journal *Child and Family Behavior Therapy*. This brings my chronicle up-to-date, a culmination of half a century of endeavor. At the AABT's 34th Annual Convention, in November, 2000, I became the recipient of the Association's Lifetime Achievement Award, presented at a formal Awards ceremony. I will always be receptive to new ideas as long as I am able. As Gertrude Stein is alleged to have said on her deathbed after a life of characteristic bombast, "I will continue to ask questions and seek answers until better questions and better answers come along."

References

Dollard, J., & Miller, N. D. (1950). *Personality and psychotherapy*. New York: McGraw-Hill.

Eysenck, H. J. (1959). Learning theory and behaviour therapy. *Journal of Mental Science, 195*, 61-75.

Franks, C. M. (1955). A conditioning laboratory for the investigation of personality and cortical functioning. *Nature*, 175, 984-985.

Franks, C. M. (1963). Behavior therapy, the principles of conditioning and the treatment of the alcoholic. *Quarterly Journal of Studies of Alcohol, 24*, 511-529.

Franks, C. M. (1964). *Conditioning techniques in clinical practice and research*. New York: Springer Publishing Company.

Franks, C. M. (Ed.). (1969). *Behavior therapy: Appraisal and status*. New York: McGraw-Hill.

Franks, C. M. (1981). 2081: Will we be many, or one, or none? *Behavioural Psychotherapy, 9*, 287-290.

Franks, C. M. (1984). On conceptual and technical integrity in psychoanalysis and behavior therapy: Two fundamentally incompatible systems. In H. Arkowitz & S. B. Messer (Eds.), *Psychoanalytic therapy and behavior therapy* (pp. 223-247). New York: Plenum Press.

Hayes, S. C., & Toarmino, D. (1999). The rise of clinical behaviour analysis. *The Psychologist, 12*, 105-108.

Kuhn, T. S. (1970). *The structure of scientific revolutions* (2nd ed.). Chicago: University of Chicago Press.

Lazarus, A. A. (1971). *Behavior therapy and beyond*. New York: McGraw-Hill.

Lindsley, O. R., Skinner, B. F., & Solomon, H. C. (1953). *Studies in behavior therapy* (Status report I). Waltham, MA: Metropolitan State Hospital.

Staats, A. (1996). *Behavior and personality: Psychological behaviorism*. New York: Springer Publishing Company.

Wolpe, J. (1958). *Psychotherapy by reciprocal inhibition*. Stanford, CA: Stanford University Press.

Chapter 11

Cognitive Behavior Therapy: The Oxymoron of the Century

Leonard Krasner
Stanford University

Introduction

The topics I plan to cover are the rationale for the topic of the paper "Cognitive Behavior Therapy – The Oxymoron of the Century," a history of "behavior therapy," "behavior modification" and the Unabomber, some views and the joining of the label of "cognitive," of cognitive therapy, with "behavior therapy" and a quick touch on the future of "behavior therapy."

I begin my paper with a confession that I suffer from a very serious mental disorder called "throw nothing away-itis." So in preparing this paper, I tried to go through the cartons of articles, papers, and correspondence on "Behavior Therapy" that I have in my house, as well as dozens of books, journals and magazines I have on "Behavior Therapy." Since there are page limitations, I apologize in advance for omitting any relevant references.

In effect, the contentions of this paper are that both behavior therapy and cognitive therapy are helpful procedures in alleviating health and mental health problems, although my own bias makes me prefer behavior therapy. I am not precluding a therapist using both procedures, cognitive therapy and behavior therapy to help a troubled client. However, the major theme of the paper is that the label "cognitive behavior therapy" is an "oxymoron."

Behavior Therapy

As for the history of behavior therapy, I will start with a paper I wrote on "Behavior Therapy." It was in volume 22 of the *Annual Review of Psychology,* 1971, and it was the first paper on this topic in the *Annual Review.*

In this 1971 article of 28 years ago, I cited 397 publications, which included publications by almost all of the speakers in this week's conference: Sidney Bijou, Leo Reyna, Ogden Lindsley, Albert Bandura, Stewart Agras, Walter Mischel, Leonard Krasner, Cyril Franks, Donald Baer, Todd Risley, Arnold Lazarus, Montrose Wolf, Gordon Paul, Gerald Davison, and the father of Julie Vargas, a gentlemen named Fred Skinner.

The first paragraph of the 1971 article:

> In recent years most authors start their chapters in the *Annual Review of Psychology* with a declaration that the task of reviewing their particular

> field is overwhelming because of the literature explosion. We can do no less, especially in view of the fact that this is the first *Annual Review* chapter on behavior therapy. In preparing the material for this chapter we have compiled a bibliography of over 4000 items, most of which should be included in any comprehensive review of this field. Needless to say, space limitations in this volume and the finiteness of the author's life preclude full justice being done to all.

In this article, I noted that there were 15 streams of development that have come together in the last part of the 1960's to form a distinctive approach to helping individuals with behavior socially labeled as deviant. These 15 streams were:

> Perhaps the most important general stream is that of *experimental psychology* and within it the concept of "behaviorism." A recent definition of behaviorism by Kantor (1969) captures the spirit of this viewpoint.
>
> What is behaviorism? ... it is a renunciation of the doctrines of soul, mind, and consciousness. Positively expressed, behavioristic psychology is the study of the behavior of organisms interaction with their surroundings.
>
> The field of *instrumental conditioning* tracing back to Thorndike and overwhelmingly influenced by the research and philosophical views of Skinner (1938, 1953, 1957, 1961, 1966, 1969) has represented the most influential stream in the development of behavior therapy as exemplified by the volume of research and application reported in the current literature.
>
> A major influence on current behavior therapy has been the research, clinical work, and writings of the psychiatrist Wolpe (1958, 1968, 1969), who in turn was influenced by the psychologists James Taylor and Leo Reyna. Wolpe introduced the technique of reciprocal inhibition, basing it in part on the classical conditioning research of Pavlov and Hull.
>
> A group of psychologists and psychiatrists, working within the framework of experimental psychology primarily influenced by Hullian learning concepts, practiced at the Maudsley Hospital in London under the general direction of Eyseneck (1960, 1964).
>
> There was a stream of investigators and practitioners in the United States, frequently working in educational institutions, who were applying behavioral, conditioning, and learning concepts to various problem behaviors. Influenced by J. B. Watson, this stream can be traced through the works of Mary Cover Jones, Burnham, Dunlap, Mowrer (1938), Hollingworth (1968), Guthrie, and more recently Phillips (1968) and Pascal (1959). In effect, these investigators can be retroactively labeled as behavior therapists.
>
> There has been a group of investigators attempting to interpret psychoanalysis in learning theory terms (Hullian). The most influential work has been the Dollard & Miller (1950) book and the papers of Shoben and Shaw of that same period.

An important stream is that tracing directly to the applications of the research of Pavlov. Treatment procedures in the Soviet Union and to a lesser extent in this country have been directly influenced by Pavlovian classical conditioning.

The *social psychology* laboratory has contributed a psychology of social influence which is being increasingly incorporated into a behavior therapy framework.

The field of *developmental and child psychology* has offered us a stream of research exemplified by the contributions of Sears, Miller & Dollard, Bijou, Baer, Gewirtz, N. Ellis, and Stevenson. The current emphasis is on vicarious learning via modeling such as the research of Bandura (1968).

Investigations of the parameters of the social influence process have brought within its framework a series of human interactions previously seen as unique or discrete phenomena. This has included research on such clinical experimenter bias, subject and patient expectancy, and the effects of non-verbal cues in interviews.

It is now clear that there are available behavioral, social learning alternatives to the traditional disease model of psychopathology as developed in the mid-nineteenth century. Every one of the current books on behavior therapy presents such alternative behavioral models. More than any other point, this change in the conceptualization of the target behavior is the key to modern behavior therapy.

In tracing the streams of development of behavior therapy, it is of importance to include one negative stream. That is, the apparent failure of psychodynamic and psychoanalytic psychotherapies as indicated by outside critiques and internal dissatisfaction. It is not a question of denigrating an opposing point of view but rather of becoming aware of the broader paradigm clashes that are involved. Behavior therapy grew, in large part, out of dissatisfaction with traditional psychotherapy techniques.

The training of clinical psychologists has traditionally been within the so-called "Boulder model" which conceived of the professional role of the clinical psychologist both as a research scientist and as a professional person who *applies* that science. Behavior therapy opens up the possibility of finally being able to successfully achieve the spirit of this training, demonstrating that the researcher and the clinician are *not* separate but are integral parts of one role.

Cognizance must be taken of a stream of influence from psychiatrists who have stressed the importance of observation of behavior and human interactions such as Adolph Meyer, H. S. Sullivan, and those therapists who attempted environmental manipulation in ward milieu programs and in some community programs.

There is an increasingly important stream that can be labeled *utopian* in its emphasis on planning the social environment to elicit and maintain the best of man's behavior. It includes an ethical concern for the social implications of behavior control, as well as offering blueprints for a better life such as Skinner's *Walden Two* (1948). This stream can of course be traced from Plato's *Republic* to the setting up of a token economy on a psychiatric ward or in a community setting.

These historical streams of development are now converging into the field of *behavior therapy*. Thus behavior therapy is more than a series of techniques or the application of learning theory; it is a broad conceptualization of human behavior. Unless we view behavior therapy in this context, its applications and implications will be irrelevant.

A major integrating theme of the early post-World War II group of behavior therapy investigators was a broad model of human behavior which emphasized social/environmental causation. The basic theoretical framework of the emerging "behavior therapy" movement of the 1960's was its social learning alternative to the then current pathology oriented medical school (Ullmann & Krasner, 1965).

The issues in very broad terms of clashing conceptual models of human nature, oversimplified perhaps, by calling them "inner" and "outer" explanations of locus of causation of behavior (the perennial "nature" vs. "nurture" controversy, which has been with us as a society for a very long period of time). There are theorists and investigators who conceptualize in terms of inner concepts, variables or metaphors, such as disease, pathology, traits, personality, mind, cognitions, and mind-body, health-illness dichotomies. Others, primarily but not exclusively, identified as behaviorists, focus on the outer, environmental, social consequences, social learning emphasis, and a "utopian" stream–the planning of social environments to elicit and maintain the best of human behavior.

Thus, we are arguing that behavior therapy developed in the 1960's, and that it represented a clear alternative paradigm in the mental health industry to the then predominant paradigm with its focus on inner processes. This is, of course, not to say that there were no usage of inner concepts and terminology in behavioral thinking, such as awareness, self, anxiety, phobia, conditioning, bias, expectancy, etc. However, the major focus was on outer environmental concepts.

The first use of the term behavior therapy in the literature was in a 1953 status report by Lindsley, Skinner, and Solomon, referring to their application of operant conditioning (of a plunger pulling response) research with psychotic patients. Lindsley suggested the term to Skinner, based on it simplicity and linkage to other treatment procedures.

Independently of this early usage, Lazarus (1958) used the term to refer to Wolpe's application of reciprocal inhibition techniques to neurotic patients, and Eysenck (1959) used the term to refer to the application of what he termed "modern learning theory" to the behavior of neurotic patients based in large part on the procedures of a group of investigators then working at the Maudsley Hospital in London.

Cyril Franks, in his 1969 volume on *Behavior Therapy: Appraisal and Status*, pointed to the disagreements then among self-identified behavior therapists as to the definition of behavior therapy. He pointed out that "Responses alone are the data available to the student of human behavior, and all else is a matter of inference and construct." Franks noted and attributed theoretical importance to the base of a "common, explicit, systematic and priori usage of learning principles to achieve well-defined and pre-determined goals."

During this period of the 1960's there were considerable publications about, discussions of, and drawing up of lists of the ways in which behavior therapy differed from traditional psychotherapy. These lists ranged from those having a dozen or more clear differences (pointing to behavior therapy as a clear alternative model) to those de-emphasizing the differences or even calling for a *bridging* of the two approaches. Whether it is possible, or even desirable to combine the two approaches was a controversy of the period. Eysenck (1969), for example, took the position that bridging between behavior therapy and psychoanalysis was undesirable. My own position on this issue is that the bridging of two paradigmatic models which have historically developed as clear *alternatives* to each other would generally show a misunderstanding of the basic principles of both.

A unifying factor in behavior therapy was its basis in derivation from experimentally established procedures and principles. The specific experimentation varied widely but had in common all of the attributes of scientific investigation including control of variables, presentation of data, replicability, and a probabilistic view of behavior.

A more encompassing framework comes from those who viewed behavior therapy in the broader context of *social learning* terms. (The authors: Bandura, 1969; Eysenck and Rachman, 1968; Franks, 1969; Kanfer and Phillips, 1970; Krasner and Ullmann, 1965; Staats, 1962; Ullmann and Krasner, 1965; and Wolpe, 1969). My opinion, and I stress the word "opinion," was that the disciplinary matrix and exemplars manifested in these books did indeed represent a new paradigm that was a clear *alternative* to that then current in the healing professions focusing on inner pathologies.

Another succinct descriptive statement about behavior therapy comes from the first editorial in the first issue of a new journal *Behavior Therapy* in 1970, by the first editors of the journal Cyril Franks and John Paul Brody – "Behavior therapy did not arise from a single source but resulted from the confluence of several diverse streams of thought, each of which entailed more or less original ways of thinking about and approaching clinical problems."

Behavior Modification

Next we move on to the label of "behavior modification" and its impact on an individual who has become quite infamous in our society, the Unabomber.

We adopted the description of *behavior modification* offered by Watson (1962). In presenting a historical introduction to Bachrach's (1962) collection of research on the experimental foundations of clinical psychology, Watson used the term *behavior modification* to cover a multitude of theoretical approaches:

It includes behavioral modification as shown in the structured interview, in verbal conditioning, in the production of experimental neuroses, and in patient-doctor relationships. In a broader sense, the topic of behavior modification is related to the whole field of learning (Watson, 1962, p. 19).

The field of behavior modification itself was a major illustration of learning theory applied in the environment. In their introduction to this field, Ullmann and Krasner (1965) defined the then emerging field in the framework of applied learning theory: "In defining behavior modification we follow the work of Robert Watson...who noted that behavior modification included many different techniques, all broadly related to the field of learning, but learning with a particular intent; namely; clinical treatment and change" (p. 1).

Bandura (1969), in a most influential and widely cited book, placed "the principles of behavior modification" within the conceptual framework of social learning....By requiring clear specification of treatment conditions and objective assessment of outcomes, the social learning approach...contains a self-corrective feature that distinguishes it from change enterprises in which interventions remain ill-defined and their psychological effects are seldom objectively evaluated (p. v).

Bandura integrated the investigations, by then greatly expanded, that were derived from the influence of Skinner, Wolpe, and the British group (e.g., Eysenck).

On April 26, 1995, the *New York Times* published on the front-page excerpts from a letter received from the Unabomber. The first three sentences were:

> We have nothing against universities or scholars as such, all the university people whom we have attacked have been specialists in technical fields. (We consider certain areas of applied psychology, such as behavior modification to be technical fields.)

Reading that article in the *New York Times* was disturbing because it was 1995 and by then the term "behavior modification" had pretty much disappeared from the literature replaced by "behavior therapy" and the first books which had the term "behavior modification" in the title "Case Studies in Behavior Modification" and "Research in Behavior Modification" were written and edited by Leonard Ullmann and myself in 1965. My first thought on seeing that *New York Times* article was – could the Unabomber have been a graduate student of mine? In fact, I got several phone calls from graduate students saying "watch your mail." However, within the next year, Ted Kaczynski was arrested as the Unabomber and on the list of people he had sent bombs to, in 1985, was James McConnell, a psychology professor at the University of Michigan, who had written articles on "behavior modification." McConnell did not open the package but his secretary did and was badly hurt.

Kaczynski had been a graduate student at the University of Michigan and obtained a doctorate degree in math there. Thus, he may have taken a psychology course with McConnell or read of his research. My own surmise is that Kaczynski correctly interpreted the consequences of the behavioral modification model, being able to train people in changing their environment could and should lead to a better and more ideal world as symbolized by the utopian book *Walden Two* written by one of the major founders of "behavior therapy" and "behavior modification," a gentlemen named Fred Skinner.

It may be that Kaczynski was determined to prevent this utopian society since he would not be in control of such a society. Anyway, keep alerted to any new information that may emerge about the Unabomber.

Cognitive Behavior Therapy

Having disposed of the Unabomber, I hope we now come to the section of this paper which elaborates on "cognitive behavior therapy as an oxymoron." We start with dictionary definitions of "cognition," "behavior," and "oxymoron."

Cognition: "The mental process or faculty by which knowledge is acquired. That which comes to be ***known*** as through perception, reasoning or intuition; knowledge" (American Heritage Dictionary).

Behavior: "Manner of conducting oneself, manners, conduct, course of action" (American Heritage Dictionary).

Oxymoron: "A rhetorical figure by which contradictory terms are cojoined so as to give point to the statement or expression; a contradiction in terms" (Oxford Universal Dictionary).

In presenting the dictionary definitions of "cognition" and "behavior" we are presenting the basis of two contradictory models. We can simplify the models by labeling them as "inner" and "outer," cognition is an inner and behavior is an outer model. In terms of applying these models to working with human beings, in systematic research or in helping with problems in life. These two models should be labeled "cognitive therapy" and "behavior therapy." We are not saying which is more effective or desirable. We are not even contending that both models should not be applied to the same individual. What we are contending is that the label of "cognitive behavior therapy" is an oxymoron since the two terms "cognitive" and "behavior" are contradictory.

As behavior therapy developed and became successful in terms of attracting adherents to the paradigms, the very nature of the model began to shift and there developed a merger with the model to which it had been a genuine alternative. In oversimplified terminology, behavior therapy was an "outer" (social/environmental) model of human nature as against the then predominant "inner" (personality/biological/mental/cognitive/disease) model. Behavior therapy has, to a large extent, been co-opted by and merged into the inner model, thus it would no longer represent the paradigm in which many of its early adherents believed. The term "cognition" has returned to a predominant position in psychology. We view these developments not as another paradigm shift but rather as a *paradigm lost*.

Skinner's relevance to the behavior therapy movement was always central as one of the founders, having coined the term "behavior therapy" to describe early work that extended animal laboratory findings to human patients in the Metropolitan State Hospital in Waltham, Massachusetts (Lindsley, Skinner, & Solomon, 1953). The title of Skinner's paper in the August, 1987 issue of the *American Psychologist*: "Whatever Happened to Psychology as the Science of Behavior?" expressed his disenchantment with the current scene in behavior therapy and psychology more generally. His chief complaint was about how the entire field had been swept away with enthusiasm for cognitive psychology.

A curve showing the appearance of the word *cognitive* in the psychological literature would be interesting. A first rise could probably be seen around 1960; the subsequent acceleration would be exponential. Is there any field of psychology today in which something does not seem to be gained by adding that charming adjective to the occasional noun? The popularity may not be hard to explain. When we became psychologists, we learned new ways of talking about human behavior. If they were "behavioristic," they were not very much like the old ways. The old terms were taboo, and eyebrows were raised when we used them. But when certain developments seemed to show that the old ways might be right after all, everyone could relax. Mind was back. Cognitive psychologists like to say that "the mind is what the brain does," but surely the rest of the body plays a part. The mind is what the *body* does. It is what the *person* does. In other words, it is behavior, and that is what behaviorists have been saying for more than half a century.

In looking back over his half century of developing the experimental analysis of behavior, Skinner was not sanguine about how the field of psychology had developed. In his introduction to his paper on "Why I am not a cognitive psychologist," Skinner (1977) nicely summarizes the outer/environmental model:

> The variables of which human behavior is a function lie in the environment. We distinguish between (1) the selective action of that environment during the evolution of the species, (2) its effect in shaping and maintaining the repertoire of behavior which converts each member of the species into a person, and (3) its role as the occasion upon which behavior occurs. Cognitive psychologists study these relations between organism and environment, but they seldom deal with them directly. Instead they invent internal surrogates which become the subject matter of their science (p. 1).

A more encompassing framework comes from those who viewed behavior therapy in the broader context of *social learning* (Bandura, 1969). Ullmann and Krasner (1965) described behavior therapy as "treatment deducible from the sociopsychological model that aims to alter a person's behavior directly through application of general psychological principles." This was contrasted with "evocative psychotherapy" which was "treatment deducible from a medical or psychoanalytic model that aims to alter a person's behavior indirectly by first altering intrapsychic organizations."

As major contributor to and founder of the behavior therapy movement, Wolpe expressed his disenchantment in a 1986 paper in *Comprehensive Psychiatry* entitled "Misrepresentation and Underemployment of Behavior Therapy." This was also a bitter paper in which Wolpe reviewed current psychiatry, psychology, and psychotherapy literature to demonstrate his contention that "Despite its well-documented record of success in the treatment of the neuroses, behavior therapy is little taught in departments of psychiatry because of an inaccurate image based on misinformation" (p. 192). He documented and illustrated with research reports and literature reviews the claim that "Misinformation about behavior therapy has a long history. The earliest reports elicited a great deal of scorn from the psychiatric establishment" (p. 192). For example, Wolpe referred to a review of his 1958 book *Psychotherapy by Reciprocal Inhibition* which had many factual errors, and he noted that "Misreporting, often with pejorative overtones, has been the rule ever since" (p. 192). Similar to Skinner's lament about the rise of cognitive ideas, Wolpe noted that:

> More harmful of late have been allegations by the cognitivists that revive in a new way the idea of behavior therapy being simple and mechanistic. In promoting a number of idiosyncratic cognitive techniques that they claim (without justification) to have improved the results of behavior therapy, they also assert that standard behavior therapy overlooks thoughts and feelings (p. 193).

In effect according to Wolpe, the theoretical and practical roots of behavior therapy were deviated from, misunderstood, and misrepresented.

Before concluding, I will cite passages from four recent, from the late 1990's, articles which offer succinct summaries of the topics I have been discussing. These are by Albert Ellis, David Reitman, Albert Bandura, and Stewart Agras:

> For the past half century, traditional behavior therapy has done a credible job of helping clients to alleviate their dysfunctional feelings and behaviors and to maintain this improvement. Rational Emotive Behavior Therapy (REBT), and some other forms of cognitive behavior therapy (CBT), have added to behavior therapy's record of success by including cognitive and philosophic restructuring techniques that aim to help some clients not only to *feel* better, but to become less disturbed and less disturb*able*. Unlike more traditional forms of behavior therapy, REBT and CBT often lead to profound and more lasting attitudinal change in clients that include anti-*must*urbation, unconditional self-acceptance, unconditional other-acceptance, high frustration tolerance, anti-awfulizing, and minimal overgeneralizing. Such lasting attitudinal changes, and understanding the processes and mechanisms by which they are achieved, may enhance and extend the goals of behavior therapy into the next millennium (Ellis, 1997).

Ellis (1997) describes how Rational Emotive Behavior Therapy (REBT) can be distinguished from Behavior Therapy (BT) and, perhaps more significantly, "adds" to BT. Among the issues raised by Ellis is the suggestion that traditional BT may lead only to temporary or superficial behavior changes, and that the goals of BT should be extended to include more comprehensive and enduring "personality change." In this commentary, I discuss the underlying medical model adopted by cognitive therapists, the empirical data that bear on the issue of "adding" to BT, and an alternative framework to evaluate clinical practice. It is suggested that there are more similarities among therapists, and their therapies, than differences. Thus, as Charles Ferster (1972) suggested 25 years ago, more effort should be devoted to studying what successful therapists do, and less to arguing the merits of therapists' theoretically informed explanations for success (Reitman, 1997).

The present commentary discusses the scientific legitimacy of theories confined to correlations of observables and those that specify the mechanisms governing the relations between observable events. Operant analysts frame the theoretical differences misleadingly when the operant approach is portrayed as addressing environmental influence for affecting change but cognitive approaches are depicted as disembodied from environmental influences and thus can only provide correlates with action. In point of fact, both approaches encompass environmental influences. The major issues in contention are whether human thinking is entirely or only partially shaped by environmental influences (Bandura, 1996).

If the central aim of behavior therapy is to help people overcome clinical problems in order to improve their lives, then the field has been a remarkable success. Although there were a few examples of controlled outcome studies in the psychotherapy literature when behavior therapy emerged, there was little evidence that any form of psychotherapy was efficacious (Eysenck, 1952). Behavior therapy has changed all that by adding hundreds of controlled treatment trials to the literature in the intervening years. The major advances in the treatment of anxiety disorders, depression, eating disorders, alcohol dependence, and the many applications within the field of behavioral medicine all attest to the remarkable success of behavior therapy. The field has brought experiment to the clinic, has refined the methodology for such studies, and has developed the standards for determining the efficacy and effectiveness of psychosocial treatments. Non-behavioral therapies must now meet the same standards, and some of them, for example, interpersonal therapy (Weissman & Markowitz, 1994), are beginning to do so. Such trends bring us precariously close to a purely empirical approach to therapeutic behavior change, but that is what is needed if our aim is to understand the mechanisms by which all effective psychosocial treatments work in order to understand how best to change behavior (Agras, 1997).

Behavior Therapy in the Year 2001

We have not yet completed data collection on the third generation of behavior therapists. In our framework, this includes those who completed degrees in the period 1976 to 1995. What has been rather remarkable about the first two generations has been the relative consistency of the values of behavior therapists as compared to their non-behavior therapist contemporaries. Behavior therapy was and remains a movement unified by some philosophical and theoretical foundations. In this sense, behavior therapy has not lost its identity even though one can readily identify controversies and disagreements that have occurred within the behavior therapy movement.

One such controversy between first and second-generation behavior therapists was about whether or not to include the word "cognitive" as a description of what was done by behavior therapists. Although opinions on this matter differed sharply in the 1970's and 1980's, our investigations suggest that most of what made behavior therapy unique remained in tact. Even though the oxymoron, "cognitive behavior therapy," was introduced into the literature, the fear that this would lead to the abandonment of basic scientific assumptions did not materialize. Behavior therapists, even "cognitive" behavior therapists, did not turn to mysticism, and they did not denounce empiricism.

We are optimistic about behavior therapy and the future, not only because we can foresee the continuation of the influence of the behavior therapy movement on the mental health field, but also because being hopeful about the future has always been a major feature of behavior therapy as a distinct community of behavioral scientists. The optimism of behavior therapy was given classic expression in Skinner's *Walden Two* (1948).

References

Bandura, A. (1968). Modeling approaches to the modification of phobic disorders. In R. Poner (Ed.), *The role of learning in psychotherapy* (pp. 201-16). London: Churchill.

Bandura, A. (1969). *Principles of behavior modification.* New York: Holt, Rinehart & Winston.

Dollard, J., & Miller, N.E. (1950). *Personality and psychotherapy.* New York: McGraw Hill.

Eysenck, H. J. (1959). Learning theory and behaviour therapy. *Journal of Mental Science, 195*, 61-75.

Eysenck, H. J. (1960). *Behaviour therapy and the neuroses.* London: Pergamon.

Eysenck, H. J. (Ed.). (1964). *Experiments in behaviour therapy.* New York: Pergamon.

Eysenck, H. J. (1969). The two faces of behaviour therapy. *Association for the Advancement of Behavioral Therapy, 4*, 1-2.

Eysenck, H. J. (1969). Relapse and symptom substitution after different types of psychotherapy. *Behaviour Research and Therapy.* 7, 287-88.

Franks, C. M. (Ed.). (1969). *Behavior therapy: Appraisal and status.* New York: McGraw-Hill.

Kanfer, F. H., & Phillips, J. S. (1970). *Learning foundations of behavior therapy.* New York: Wiley.

Kantor, J. R. (1969). *The scientific evolution of psychology* (Vol. 2). Chicago: Principia.

Krasner, L. (1971). Behavior therapy. In P. H. Mussen (Ed.), *Annual Review of Psychology* (Vol. 22). Palo Alto, CA:Annual Reviews.

Krasner, L., & Ullmann, L. P. (Eds.). (1965). *Research in behavior modification: New developments and implications.* New York: Holt, Rinehart & Winston.

Lazarus, A. A. (1958). New methods in psychotherapy: A case study. *South African Medical Journal, 33*, 660-64.

Lindsley, O. R., Skinner, B. F. & Solomon, H. C. (1953). *Studies in behavior therapy. Status report 1.* Waltham, MA: Metropolitan State Hospital.

Mowrer, O. H. (1938). Apparatus for the study and treatment of enuresis. *American Journal of Psychology, 51*, 163-66.

Pascal, G. R. (1959). *Behavioral change in the clinic. A systematic approach.* New York: Grune & Stratton.
Phillips, E. L. (1968). Achievement place: Token reinforcement procedures in a home-style rehabilitation setting for "pre-delinquent" boys. *Journal of Appliued Behavior Analysis, 1,* 213-23.
Skinner, B. F. (1938). *The behavior of organisms.* New York: Appleton-Century-Crofts.
Skinner, B. F. (1948). *Walden two.* New York: Macmillan.
Skinner, B. F. (1953). *Science and human behavior.* New York: Macmillan.
Skinner, B. F. (1957). *Verbal behavior.* New York: Appleton-Century-Crofts.
Skinner, B. F. (1961). *Cumulative record.* New York: Appleton-Century-Crofts.
Skinner, B. F. (1966). Contingencies of reinforcement in the design of a culture. *Behavioral Science, 11,* 159-66.
Skinner, B. F. (1968). *The technology of teaching.* New York: Appleton-Century-Crofts.
Skinner, B. F. (1969). *Contingencies of reinforcement: A theoretical analysis.* New York: Appleton-Century-Crofts.
Skinner, B. F. (1997). Why I am not a cognitive psychologist. *Behaviorism, 5,* 1-10.
Ullmann, L. P., & Krasner, L. (Eds.). (1965). *Case studies in behavior modification.* New York: Holt, Rinehart & Winston.
Watson, R. I. (1962). The experimental tradition and clinical psychology. In A. J. Bachrach (Ed.), *Experimental foundations of clinical psychology.* New York: Basic Books.
Wolpe, J. (1958). *Psychotherapy by reciprocal inhibition.* Stanford: Stanford University Press.
Wolpe, J. (1968). Psychotherapy by reciprocal inhibition. *Conditional Reflex, 3,* 234-40.
Wolpe, J. (1969). *The practice of behavior therapy.* New York: Pergamon.
Wolpe, J. (1969). Basic principles and practices of behavior therapy of neuroses. *American Journal of Psychiatry, 125,* 1242-47.
Wolpe, J. (1969). How can "cognitions" influence desensitization? *Behaviour Research Therapy, 7,* 219.

Chapter 12

The Development of Behavioral Medicine

W. Stewart Agras
Stanford University School of Medicine

Why, in the late-fifties, would a psychiatrist be attracted to behavior therapy? I had decided in medical school that I wanted to follow a research career, and realized that research in psychiatry was underdeveloped and would undoubtedly expand greatly in the future, a guess that turned out to be correct. When I began my career in psychiatry, formal residency training in that specialty was in its infancy. For example, the Institute of Psychiatry in London did not offer a structured residency training program at that time. Hence, I moved from London to Montreal in 1956 because McGill University was one of the few centers offering a structured three year residency program in psychiatry. American psychiatry (Canada not excepted) partly because of the influence of European psychiatrists who had emigrated to North America in the wake of World War II, was dominated by psychoanalytic thinking and the use of psychodynamic therapy. It should be remembered that psychiatry had few therapies to offer at that time, comprising a few medications with limited effectiveness, electroshock therapy, and insulin coma treatment. However, the era of psychopharmacology, namely antidepressants (first in the crude form of izoniazid, an antitubercular medication that had been noted to enhance the mood of patients with tuberculosis) and antipsychotics (in the form of chlorpromazine) was dawning. The problem with psychodynamic therapy, to one who was trying to learn how to do it, was that its procedures were not formalized. Moreover, as Eysenck pointed out in his detailed review in 1952, there was little evidence that psychotherapy as then practiced was effective (Eysenck, 1952).

Introduction to Behavior Therapy and the Experimental Analysis of Behavior

In 1958, Wolpe published his seminal book, Psychotherapy by Reciprocal Inhibition, while at the Center for Advanced Study in the Behavioral Sciences at Stanford. Having read the book, I visited Wolpe, then Professor of Psychiatry at the University of Virginia, to observe his treatment of phobics with systematic desensitization. He was an enthusiastic teacher and a kind colleague, I was after all a very junior person, just finishing my Fellowship in psychiatry at McGill. His influence led me to formulate a model for psychotherapy research, with phobia as a distinct and measurable disorder, and systematic desensitization, as a simple treatment, the procedures of which were straightforward, well documented, and easily learned. At the same time I read much of what Skinner had published and could see how applicable operant conditioning might be to mental illness.

All this may have come to nothing had I not moved to the University of Vermont, to a newly formed Department of Psychiatry headed by Tom Boag, a faculty member from McGill. Until that time, psychiatry had been a division of the department of medicine, rather than being a department in its own right. Here, fortuitously, Harold Leitenberg, with a Ph.D. in experimental psychology from the operant program at Indiana, arrived as an assistant professor in the Department of Psychology at the same time. I was looking for an experimental psychologist to work with, and he was looking for an entree to the clinic to apply operant procedures. Together we worked with two different experimental methods to identify effective therapeutic procedures for the treatment of phobia. Following Lang's work using snake phobics as an analogue of clinical phobia (Lang & Lazovik, 1963; Lang, Lazovik, & Reynolds, 1965), we examined the hypothesized therapeutic ingredients in desensitization in randomized controlled studies, eventually demonstrating that none of the hypothesized procedures such as a hierarchy or pairing imagined feared scenes with relaxation, appeared critical to the outcome (Agras, Leitenberg, Barlow, Curtis, Edwards, & Wright, 1971; Barlow, Leitenberg, Agras, & Wincze, 1969). In a complementary approach with phobic patients, we took an operant approach to phobias of various types, examining the effects of reinforcement, informational feedback, and exposure to the feared situation, in a series of single case controlled research studies. We were fortunate in being able to admit these patients to the University of Vermont Clinical Research Center (CRC), where they could be studied using single case experimental designs, in a controlled environment free of charge. We were also fortunate to attract an excellent group of graduate students in psychology, the first of which was David Barlow. With this group, we examined other disorders in similar ways: anorexia nervosa (Agras, Barlow, Chapin, Abel, & Leitenberg, 1974; Leitenberg, Agras, & Thompson, 1968), tics (Agras & Marshall, 1965), hysterical paralysis (Agras, Leitenberg, Barlow, & Thompson, 1969), and even delusional speech (Wincze, Leitenberg, & Agras, 1972). In each case demonstrating experimental control over these difficult to manage behaviors.

An Example of Early Research

The single case research on phobia published in a series of papers forms an excellent example of early work in the application of the experimental analysis of behavior to clinically relevant behaviors. With very few patients we were able to discover much of importance. This work was influenced by Lindsley's pioneering applications of Skinner's findings to psychiatric patients, as well as the studies of Ayllon and Azrin in schizophrenia (Ayllon & Michael, 1959; Ayllon & Azrin, 1965). In our first study, the participants were three severely agoraphobic individuals, with numerous fears including: fear of leaving home by themselves, traveling alone, crowds, illness, and death (Agras, Leitenberg, & Barlow, 1968). Two of the three patients were unable to leave their homes alone, while the third was just able to manage a five-minute drive to work. In each case the patient's central difficulty, walking any distance from a "safe place" by themselves, was assessed by distance walked alone from the clinical research center. To assess this behavior, a course was laid out from the CRC to downtown Burlington Vermont, a distance of about one mile. Landmarks were identified at 25-yard intervals and the patient was asked what point they had reached when they returned. Because much of the course was observable, frequent checks of the patient's behavior were made throughout the study, confirming the accuracy of their reports. Following a baseline phase in which the patient was told to walk as far as they could alone, praise for progress in walking further was given in a shaping schedule. As can be seen in Figure 1, distance walked increased steadily while being reinforced, declined dramatically when no reinforcement was given, showing first a typical extinction burst, and then quickly recovered when reinforcement was reinstated, with the patient being able to walk downtown alone, something she had not done for many years.

Having had little success with psychodynamic psychotherapy for such patients, this degree of experimental control was remarkable to me. The patient's maladaptive behavior improved, relapsed, and improved again, depending on the reinforcement schedule. The reactions of contemporaries to these data were mixed. The paper was published in the Archives of General Psychiatry denoting acceptance by the more scientifically minded psychiatric community. On the other hand during presentations to psychiatric audiences comments such as "this type of treatment is immoral. . .because it is superficial and does not deal with the underlying problems" were also common. Similar objections were raised concerning the use of psychopharmacological agents by many psychoanalysts. Our findings were accepted with much interest by the then small behavior therapy community, and particularly by the growing group of individuals engaged in the rapidly burgeoning field of Applied Behavior Analysis.

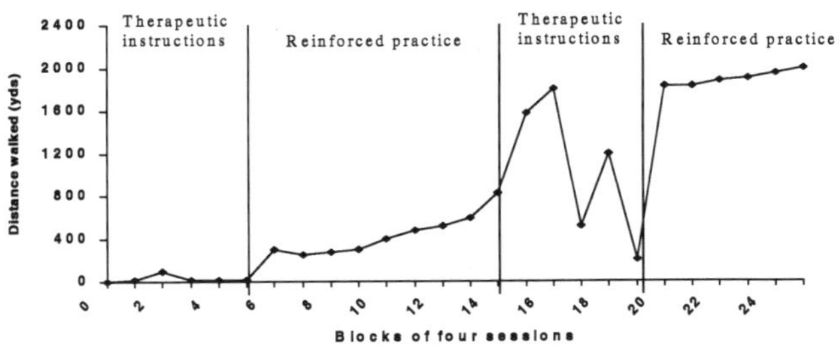

Figure 1.

In the next study, which involved two phobic patients, we examined the effects of feedback of progress in single case experiments (Leitenberg, Agras, Thompson, & Wright, 1968). The first patient was a severe claustrophobic whose phobia dated back to childhood when she was locked in a small cupboard by some friends, one of the rare occasions when a specific trauma is reported as leading to a phobia. The fears became increasingly incapacitating and were much worsened when her husband died about seven years before admission to the CRC. Briefly the experiment consisted in giving the patient a stopwatch and asking her to record the amount of time she was able to remain in a small dimly lit room. This provided her with feedback as to her progress. After 22 sessions in which she was able to increase her time in the room, the stopwatch was removed, with the excuse that it was broken. Under this condition her progress slowed and then picked up again when the stopwatch was reintroduced. Similar results were found for the second case. Parenthetically, the close relationship to animal studies is revealed in this paper by the detailed description of the experimental environment, e.g. "A room 4 ft. wide and 6 ft. long, illuminated by a 100W shaded bulb, provided a situation in which the patients claustrophobia could be measured."

So far then, both positive reinforcement and feedback as to progress had been shown to be therapeutic in cases of phobia. However, when we examined the baseline behavior of three agoraphobics simply given the instruction to walk as far as you can without undue anxiety, varying responses were found, from no response, to a modest increase in distance walked with some relapse, to steady improvement. It appeared that externally provided positive reinforcement and/or feedback was not always needed. The likely suspect was exposure to the phobic situation, which led to the next series of single case experiments.

Five patients took part in these experiments, although only one of these patients who participated in two studies will be discussed here (Leitenberg, Agras, Edwards & Thompson, 1970). The patient was a knife phobic. Her problem had begun some seven years before the experiment. While using a kitchen knife she suddenly thought that she might kill one of her grandchildren who were running around the kitchen making a noise. This very frightening intrusive thought recurred and during the next year her obsessive thoughts increased so that she became unable to use a knife. She was admitted to a psychiatric unit and treated with various medications and systematic desensitization and was discharged improved. Eighteen months later her husband died, precipitating a marked depression that required further hospitalization and treatment with electroshock therapy, again improving. However, her fear of knives slowly returned, and once more she was unable to handle or even look at a sharp knife, and had been unable to cook or work in her kitchen.

In the first experiment with this patient, a sharp knife was placed in a box. On a signal the patient opened the box and looked at the knife until she could look no longer. A timer recorded the duration of each trial. In the first phase of the experiment the patient's ability to look at the knife gradually increased. Then exposure to the knife was stopped for several days, a period matched to the preceding exposure treatment. No improvement occurred during this phase of the experiment. When the patient again began practice she again began to improve. A second no-exposure phase showed the same result of no progress, while the final exposure phase again resulted in continued progress. It can be argued, however, that the lack of progress in the no exposure phase was due to the patient perceiving that she was not being treated. Hence, in the next series of trials, psychotherapy was alternated with exposure practice, with a positive expectancy engendered for both treatments. Again, however, no progress occurred during the no exposure (psychotherapy) phases, while continued progress occurred during exposure trials. This result was confirmed in our other work using randomized controlled experiments with snake phobic individuals (Barlow, Leitenberg, Agras, & Wincze, 1969; Leitenberg, Agras, Barlow, & Oliveau, 1969; Oliveau, Agras, Leitenberg, Moore, & Wright, 1969). It was clear that exposure to the actual phobic situation was far superior to imagined exposure as would occur in systematic desensitization.

I suspect that Wolpe knew this. During my visit to him I was struck by the fact that he insisted on his patients practicing in the phobic situation following each desensitization session. As time has gone on, exposure therapies have become the standard approach to the treatment of phobia, displacing systematic desensitization. This does not detract from Wolpe's seminal contribution to the field. Systematic desensitization provided an enormous stimulus to psychotherapy research, led to the analog psychotherapy experiment with snake and spider phobics, which in turn allowed for a dissection of those aspects of desensitization that worked in reducing phobic behavior.

It may be of interest to note that the University of Vermont CRC was located one floor above the psychiatric unit. But these were very different milieu's and it was difficult to transfer the results of our research one floor down. This was an early introduction to the enormous problem of disseminating new psychotherapeutic procedures, a problem that remains with us today.

The Underpinnings of Behavioral Medicine

In 1969, I moved to the University of Mississippi Medical Center as Chair of the Department of Psychiatry, accompanied by David Barlow who became Director of Psychology training. The Dean of the Medical School was interested in improving the Department and giving it a new direction and was, therefore, most supportive of a behavioral approach to psychiatric disorders. The idea behind the move was to integrate the new psychology and psychiatry within an academic medical center giving equal power to both disciplines. In line with this, Barlow used the name Psychology Residency for the psychology internship training program. Fortunately, others shared this vision and we were joined by Michel Hersen, Edward Blanchard, Peter Miller, Leonard Epstein, Tom Sajwaj, Gene Abel, and Matig Mavissakalian (the latter two being psychiatrists) amongst others, all of whom went on to become well known researchers. Moreover, the psychology residency attracted many outstanding individuals. Within this new environment it was easier to transfer effective behavior change procedures to the clinic. However, the intellectual basis of the Department was the investigation of disordered human behavior based on theories and procedures derived from psychology. Soon we had three research rounds a week, yet were unable to present all the ongoing research.

It should be noted that the introduction of behavioral science teaching in medical schools began in 1958 at the University of Kentucky. At the time of my move to Mississippi there were some 17 Departments of Behavioral Science in schools of medicine. Hence the need to introduce the findings of modern behavioral science to medical students and residents in various disciplines was well recognized. Yet much of this teaching was not viewed as relevant by medical students and other physicians in training. This was probably because nothing was taught about the application of behavioral science to the treatment of medical conditions. Mainly, of course, because very little was known about such applications at the time.

I also became more deeply involved in the Society for the Experimental Analysis of Behavior, first as Associate Editor, and then as Editor of the Journal of Applied Behavior Analysis. Our research enterprise was deeply influenced by the field of applied behavior analysis, and particularly by the findings of researchers such as Montrose Wolfe, Ted Allyon, Nathan Azrin, and John Paul Brady, to name just a few. Yet it was also integrated with the broader field of behavior therapy, and was becoming integrated into psychiatric practice.

The scientist practitioner model proved very appealing within the medical school environment, not only within psychiatry but also with other disciplines. For here were researchers who could apply behavior change procedures that were known to work and effectively care for patients with difficult problems. It is my view that the integration of the psychologist scientist practitioner into medical school departments where they were treated as equals, with the opportunity to apply behavior change procedures first to psychiatric problems, and then to medical problems, was one of the important prerequisites for the later development of behavioral medicine.

The Rise of Behavioral Medicine

What were the other prerequisites for the development of behavioral medicine? The first, in terms of historical sequence, was the development of *Psychosomatic Medicine*. This field had begun to grow in the thirties, and the journal *Psychosomatic Medicine* was begun in 1939. One of the primary hypotheses underlying psychosomatic medicine was that many physical ailments were caused by intrapsychic conflict interacting with organ predisposition, presumably stemming from either genetic or environmental causes, and specific personality patterns, for example, dependent personality. Understanding these patterns would lead, it was thought, to better treatment of patients with disorders such as asthma, peptic ulcer, and ulcerative colitis. It was regarded as a field of much promise for medicine. Yet, in 1979 the President of the Psychosomatic Society noted in his Presidential address that "Psychosomatic medicine has by no means had the influence. . .that was predicted for it 30 years ago" (Graham, 1979). I have previously argued that the main reason for this lack of influence on the practice of medicine was due to the lack of intervention research (Agras, 1982). Comparing a random sample of papers published in the journals *Psychosomatic Medicine* and *Behavior Therapy*, an equal number of articles (about half in each journal) were clinically focused. Hence, psychosomatic medicine was clearly a clinical field. However, 15% to 20% of all articles in *Behavior Therapy* reported controlled intervention research compared with only 3% of the papers published in *Psychosomatic Medicine* during the same period. Nonetheless, the basic psychological research stemming from the psychosomatic medicine field, as it moved back to the laboratory away from psychoanalytic theory, was an important prerequisite for the development of behavioral medicine.

A further influence was the realization that many of the risk factors for chronic disabling disease, for example cardiovascular disease and some cancers, were behaviors. These behaviors included: inactivity, overeating, high fat consumption, high alcohol consumption, cigarette smoking, and risk taking in various forms. Moreover, procedures deriving from behavior therapy could be used to modify some of these behaviors and enhance self-control. At the same time there was a growing realization that disease prevention and health promotion were needed to delay, ameliorate, or even prevent the onset of various diseases, to improve the nations health and reduce the growing health care costs. These influences, combined with pertinent biologic research, came together in the mid-70's, a catalytic confluence, from which behavioral medicine emerged. There are various definitions of the field, some focusing on intervention or prevention, others on the etiology or risk factors for medical disorders, in which case the interaction between environment and biologic variables becomes the focus of interest.

In 1973, I moved to Stanford and began to consider these issues and develop a new research program influenced not only by my previous research background but also by the pioneering work of Jack Farquar at Stanford who was taking a community behavior change approach to cardiovascular disease prevention (Farquar, et al., 1977; Leventhal, Safer, Cleary, & Gutman, 1980). In 1975 the Laboratory for the Study of Behavioral Medicine was founded at Stanford under my direction. Simultaneously, demonstrating that the notion of behavioral medicine was in the air at the time, Ovid Pomerleau and Paul Brady opened a behavioral medicine program at the University of Pennsylvania (Pomerleau, 1975; Pomerleau, 1979). Both programs were focused on clinical research using theories and procedures from the experimental analysis of behavior and from behavior therapy. At this time Bandura's formulation of social learning theory formed the theoretical background to our work (Bandura, 1965). Researchers from the Stanford program became consultants to the Coronary Primary Prevention Project, bringing their expertise to the recruitment of the large number of participants needed for this study, and later to the problem of providing help to the participants in adhering to the medication regimen in this long-term study. Hence, adherence research became one focus of the Stanford program, followed in the next few years by studies on the treatment of obesity, and the use of non-pharmacological methods to reduce blood pressure. The program produced basic psychological research pertinent to the clinical problems being investigated, identified behavioral risk factors for these disorders, and carried out both preventive and intervention research. In addition to the research focus, an outpatient clinic for the treatment of stress disorders, obesity, and other medical problems for which behavior change procedures seemed justified, was opened, followed by an inpatient unit specializing largely in eating disorders, pain problems, and other medical disorders with accompanying psychological problems. The close linkage between research and the clinic was important because it allowed reciprocal feedback from the two different worlds, on the one hand informing research, and on the other informing clinical practice.

In 1977, the Yale Conference on behavioral medicine sponsored by the National Heart Lung and Blood Institute (NHLBI) brought together an interdisciplinary audience to consider theoretical models, definitions for the field, the elements constituting the field, and the possible futures of such a field (Schwartz & Weiss, 1977). The NHLBI at the National Institutes of Health, with the prompting of Steven Weiss, became one of the first Institutes to provide continuing support to the field of behavioral medicine, leading eventually to a behavioral medicine grants review committee at the National Institutes of Health, which in turn provided a funding mechanism for much of the research in behavioral medicine.

By 1978, it had become clear that a more specialized academic society than the Association for the Advancement of Behavior (AABT) was needed. Until that time AABT had been home to the burgeoning field of behavioral medicine. The Academy for Behavioral Medicine Research was founded at a meeting at the Institute of Medicine in 1978. However, that society was limited to senior researchers in the field. It was clear that a society structured similarly to AABT was needed, a society that would attract researchers and clinicians, to keep the field moving forward. At the 1978 meeting of AABT various individuals and groups interested in such a society were brought together, and with the help of AABT, the Society for Behavioral Medicine (SBM) was founded, and I was elected the first President of this interesting new organization. In my view the key purpose of the Society was to facilitate communication among the various disciplines involved in behavioral medicine. To this end the *Abstracts of Behavioral Medicine* was begun, a journal that provided selected abstracts of pertinent studies. The notion was that primary research papers should be published in the scientific journal most relevant to that research and not in a specialized behavioral medicine publication with limited readership. This step was aimed at better disseminating the results of research from this new field. The *Abstracts* was aimed at cross-disciplinary communication.

Both the Academy and SBM successfully pursued their somewhat different paths, eventually forming a linkage between the two societies, such that Fellows of SBM are members of the Academy. Most medical schools have divisions or groups focused on behavioral medicine research and clinical work, and similar developments have occurred in other countries. Apparently, the time was right for such a development, one that appears to have been accepted by other medical disciplines.

From Single Case to Multisite Studies

In the late 1970's the remarkable increase in the number of cases of eating disorders, particularly bulimia nervosa, presenting in our clinic led me to return to an earlier interest in the eating disorders. Previously we had used single case experiments to isolate some of the therapeutic procedures leading to weight gain in patients with anorexia nervosa. Among these were positive and negative reinforcement, informational feedback, and the serving of large meals. (Agras et al., 1974; Leitenberg, Agras, & Thompson, 1968). Each of these procedures led to increased caloric intake and weight gain in patients with anorexia nervosa and were used in the treatment of such patients (Agras & Werne, 1977). The research with bulimia nervosa began somewhat differently, eventually following the research flow described in more detail elsewhere (Agras & Berkowitz, 1980). The first step was to treat a series of cases of bulimia nervosa treated with a version of cognitive-behavior therapy (CBT) reported by Fairburn, (1981). The results reported by Fairburn were replicated with a reasonable proportion of bulimics recovering by the end of treatment (Schneider & Agras, 1985). The treatment was based on the hypothesis, deriving from clinical observation, that extreme dieting caused by severe weight and shape concerns, was the driving force behind binge eating and purging. Later studies carried out in our laboratory demonstrated that when bulimics were deprived of food by not serving them breakfast and lunch, and were then served a buffet, they would eat more at the buffet than a non-deprived control group of bulimics. However, the number of calories eaten over the whole laboratory day were not statistically significantly different between groups (Telch & Agras, 1996). This suggests that the caloric regulation of bulimics is normal. However, because they restrict food intake and then eat a large amount of food at one sitting, they perceive this to be a binge. Later studies suggested that mood was likely to alter the perception of a feeding episode. In a negative mood bulimics were more likely to classify an eating episode as a binge (Agras & Telch, 1998).

The primary goal of cognitive-behavioral therapy was to help the patient attain a regular eating pattern with lessened dietary restriction. Self-monitoring became the primary tool to determine the ongoing eating, binge eating, and purging patterns, at to guide the therapist and patient in selecting goals for treatment, as well as providing monitoring of progress. Weight and shape concerns and other cognitive and emotional distortions were addressed with behavioral experiments and cognitive therapy in the second half of treatment.

The next step in the research program was to compare the new treatment with a psychotherapy that did not contain any of the key procedures comprising cognitive-behavioral therapy, but that engendered an equal expectancy of success in the patient. Cognitive-behavioral therapy was more effective than a placebo (non-directive) psychotherapy (Kirkley, Schneider, Agras, & Bachman, 1985). This led to a series of controlled outcome studies both with bulimics and the later defined syndrome "binge eating disorder" further documenting the effectiveness of CBT and defining some of the critical elements comprising the treatment package (Agras, 1995; Wilson & Fairburn, 1997). In addition, CBT was compared to antidepressant medication, the latter having been found more effective than placebo in a series of controlled outcome studies (Agras et al., 1992). CBT appeared to be more effective than antidepressant medication, and adding medication to CBT was only marginally beneficial.

When a research field accrues sufficient single site controlled studies it may become necessary to conduct larger scale studies to increase study power. Two such studies appeared important to pursue. The background to the first study was the finding that a form of interpersonal therapy (IPT) although slower to achieve its effects was as effective at follow-up as CBT (Fairburn, Jones, Peveler, Hope, & O'Connor, 1993). In order to compare two active treatments, a large sample size was necessary, leading to the first multisite study. The background to the second study was the question as to what treatment to offer patients who fail CBT. The two potential candidates were antidepressant medication and IPT both of which had proved useful in controlled trials. In order to have sufficient subjects for such a comparison, i.e. treating only the CBT failures (about 45% of those treated) a large sample size was again needed, leading to the second multisite trial. The conduct of multicenter trials is of necessity more complex than the conduct of a single site trial. There are, however, many advantages besides the large sample size that such trials are able to accrue. The involvement of several investigators leads to improvements in all aspects of the study including: assessment procedures, therapist training, data acquisition and analysis, as well as writing up the results of the study.

Some Lessons for the Future

What can we learn from the development of behavior therapy and behavioral medicine? It is clear that one cannot forecast the development of a scientific field because developments in science interact with the changing needs of society, in turn altering the course of the scientific field. For a clinically oriented field to gain acceptance in medicine it must develop effective therapeutic procedures based on well designed studies. Unlike behavioral medicine, psychosomatic medicine failed to do this, and gained little general acceptance as a clinical field. Hence, the first lesson for a clinical field is that it must develop treatments that have been shown to be effective in controlled trials. To do this the field must attract a cadre of researchers. Apparently, a new theoretical approach such as behavior therapy that begins to demonstrate efficacy in its therapeutic procedures will attract innovative researchers who will move the field forward. It may often be the case that the early findings, seminal to the development of the field, will later be found wanting. But such studies provoke new research which is best served if it can utilize findings and theories from basic science. After all, Wolpe described animal experiments in his book, but did not provide any controlled studies with human behavior problems.

Another important lesson has been the flexibility of the field of behavior therapy and the Association for the Advancement of Behavior Therapy in accepting and tolerating a range of viewpoints useful to the advancement of the field. Arguments have been solved by the data accrued by proponents of one viewpoint or another, rather than leading to schisms within the field. For example, it is to the credit of many of the early workers in applied behavior analysis that they joined AABT rather than having a separate society, adding a great deal to the scientific discourse. The ability to include and tolerate different views is of extraordinary importance to the development of a new field. Behavior therapy, and following in its footsteps, behavioral medicine, were able to do this, and both fields prospered because of this ability.

But there have been some relative failures along the way. The notion of prevention has not penetrated clinical medicine as much as might have been hoped. It is true that the prevalence of cigarette smoking has dropped as have the rates of lung cancer. But the prevalence of overweight and obesity has steadily increased over the years, even among children, forecasting a rise in the diseases comorbid with obesity. For behavioral medicine to advance prevention efforts it is clear that scientists must ally themselves with political activists so that changes can be made at the societal level. Altering the ways in which cigarettes can be advertised can do more than individual physicians can do in their efforts to help someone stop smoking.

A field with much to offer the public has to position itself correctly. Behavior modification was not a term acceptable to the public, with its overtones of George Orwell's *1984*. Other words had to be used. Similarly, the remarkable popularity of "alternative medicine," even though many of the procedures used have not been shown to be effective, should remind us that what is attractive to science is not necessarily attractive to the public. Luckily, science is being injected into alternative medicine, and I would regard it as another frontier for behavioral medicine.

Finally, there are often long delays in translating the findings of applied research to the clinical domain. Behavior change procedures are often complex and need to be sensitively applied to each individual. Unlike new medications, for which large budgets for disseminating the use of the drug exist, psychosocial research has no such money. Although workshops can be helpful in introducing a new therapeutic procedure, more is required for therapists to attain a reasonable level of expertise. For example, as is done in controlled clinical trials, ongoing supervision of a number of cases is often necessary for therapists to gain the necessary expertise. Even more problematic is the fact that the practice of many psychotherapists is comprised of a mix of patients with different behavior problems, not allowing the therapist to gain sufficient expertise through continued practice with particular diagnostic entities. One solution to this would be to introduce different levels of therapy for use in different locales, simpler modes for the solo practitioner, more complex modes for the specialty clinic, where a particular kind of case would form a substantial proportion of therapists time. An example of a simpler therapeutic mode is the use of self-help manuals with brief therapist support. More sophisticated self-help treatments are also available in computerized form, and would be easily accessible via the internet.

The future of behavioral medicine is uncertain. Enormous structural changes are occurring in the health system and will likely continue for some time to come. These changes will eventually shape the direction of behavioral medicine, from science to applications. Hopefully the changes will be rational with a greater emphasis on healthful living from infancy through old age.

References

Agras, W. S. (1982). Behavioral medicine in the 1980's: Nonrandom connections. *Journal of Consulting and Clinical Psychology, 50*, 797-803.

Agras, W. S. (1995). Treatment of the obese binge eater. In K. D. Brownell & C. G. Fairburn (Eds.), *Eating disorders and obesity: A comprehensive handbook* (pp. 531-535). New York, NY: The Guilford Press.

Agras, W. S., Barlow, D. H., Chapin, H. N., Abel, G. G., & Leitenberg, H. (1974). Behavior modification of anorexia nervosa. *Archives of General Psychiatry, 30*, 2799-286.

Agras, W. S., & Berkowitz, R. I. (1980). Clinical research in behavior therapy: Halfway there? *Behavior Therapy, 11*, 472-487.

Agras, W. S., Leitenberg, H., & Barlow, D. H. (1968). Social reinforcement in the modification of agoraphobia. *Archives of General Psychiatry, 19*, 423-427.

Agras, W. S., Leitenberg, H., Barlow, D. H., Curtis, N., Edwards, J., & Wright, D. (1971). The role of relaxation in systematic desensitization. *Archives of General Psychiatry, 225*, 511-514.

Agras, W. S., Leitenberg, H., Barlow, D. H., & Thompson, L. E. (1969). Instructions and reinforcement in modification of neurotic behavior. *American Journal of Psychiatry, 125*(10), 1435-1439.

Agras, W. S., & Marshall, C. (1965). The application of negative practice to spasmodic torticollis. *American Journal of Psychiatry, 122*(5), 579-582.

Agras, W. S., Rossiter, E. M., Arnow, B., Scheider, J. A., Telch, C. F., Raeburn, S. D., Bruce, B., Perl, M., & Koran, L. M. (1992). Pharmacologic and cognitive-behavioral treatment for bulimia nervosa: A controlled comparison. *American Journal of Psychiatry, 149*, 82-87.

Agras, W. S., & Telch, C. F. (1998). The effects of caloric deprivation and negative affect on binge eating in obese binge-eating-disordered women. *Behavior Therapy, 29*, 491-503.

Agras, W. S., & Werne, J. (1997). Behavior modification in anorexia nervosa: Research foundation. In R. Vigersky (Ed.), *Anorexia nervosa. A monograph of the National Institute of Child Health and Development* (pp. 181-195). New York, NY: Raven Press.

Ayllon, T., & Azrin, N. H. (1965). The measurement and reinforcement of behavior of psychotics. *Journal of the Experimental Analysis of Behavior, 8*, 357-369.

Ayllon, T., & Michael, J. (1959). The psychiatric nurse as a behavioral engineer. *Journal of the Experimental Analysis of Behavior*, *2*, 323-334.

Bandura, A. (1965). *Principles of behavior modification*. New York, NY: Holt, Rhinehart, & Winston.

Barlow, D. H., Leitenberg, D., Agras, W. S., & Wincze, J. P. (1969). The transfer gap in systematic desensitization: An analogue study. *Behavior Research and Therapy*, *7*, 191-197.

Eysenck, H. J. (1952). The effects of psychotherapy: An evaluation. *Journal of Consulting and Clinical Psychology*, *16*, 319-324.

Fairburn, C. G. (1981). A cognitive-behavioral approach to the management of bulimia. *Psychological Medicine*, *11*, 707-711.

Fairburn, C. G., Jones, R., Peveler, R. C., Hope, R. A., & O'Connor, M. (1993). Psychotherapy and bulimia nervosa. Longer-term effects of interpersonal psychotherapy, behavior therapy, and cognitive-behavior therapy. *Archives of General Psychiatry*, *50*, 419-428.

Farquar, J. W., et al. (1977). Community education for cardiovascular health. *Lancet*, *1*, 1192-1195.

Graham, D. T. (1979). What place in medicine for psychosomatic medicine? *Psychosomatic Medicine*, *41*, 357-362.

Kirkley, B. G., Schneider, J. A., Agras, W. S., & Bachman, J. A. (1985). A comparison of two group treatments for bulimia. *Journal of Consulting and Clinical Psychology*, *53*, 43-48.

Lang, P. J., & Lazovik, A. D. (1963). Experimental desensitization of a phobia. *Journal of Abnormal and Social Psychology*, 519-525.

Lang, P. J., Lazovik, A. D., & Reynolds, D. J. (1965). Desensitization, suggestibility, and pseudotherapy. *Journal of Abnormal Psychology*, *70*, 395-402.

Leitenberg, H., Agras, W. S., Barlow, D. H., & Oliveau, D. C. (1969). The contribution of selective positive reinforcement and therapeutic instructions to systematic desensitization therapy. *Journal of Abnormal Psychology*, *74*(1), 113-118.

Leitenberg, H., Agras, W. S., Edwards, J. A., & Thompson, L. E. (1970). Practice as a psychotherapeutic variable: An experimental analysis within single cases. *Journal of Psychiatric Research*, *7*, 215-225.

Leitenberg, H., Agras, W. S., & Thompson, L. (1968). A sequential analysis of the effect of selective positive reinforcement in modifying anorexia nervosa. *Behavior Research and Therapy*, *6*, 211-218.

Leitenberg, H., Agras, W. S., Thompson, L. E., & Wright, D. E. (1968). Feedback in behavior modification: An experimental analysis in two phobic cases. *Journal of Applied Behavior Analysis*, *1*, 131-137.

Leventhal, H., Safer, M. A., Cleary, P. D., & Gutmann, N. (1980). Cardiovascular risk modification by community based programs for life-style change. Comments on the Stanford study. *Journal of Consulting and Clinical Psychology*, *48*, 150-158.

Oliveau, D. C., Agras, W. S., Leitenberg, H., Moore, R. C., & Wright, D. E. (1969). Systematic desensitization, therapeutically oriented instructions, and selective positive reinforcement. *Behavior Research and Therapy*, *7*(1), 27-35.

Pomerleau, O. F. (1975). Role of behavior modification in preventive medicine. *New England Journal of Medicine*, *292*, 1277-1282.

Pomerleau, O. F. (1979). Behavioral medicine: The contribution of the experimental analysis of behavior to medical care. *American Psychologist*, *34*, 654-663.

Schneider, J. A., & Agras, W. S. (1985) A cognitive behavioral group treatment of bulimia. *British Journal of Psychiatry*, *146*, 66-69.

Schwartz, G. E., & Weiss, S. M. (1977). *Proceedings of the Yale conference on behavioral medicine* (NIH Publication No. 78-1424). Washington, DC: U.S. Department of Health, Education, & Welfare.

Telch, C. F., & Agras, W. S. (1996). The effects of short-term food deprivation on caloric intake in eating disordered subjects. *Appetite*, *26*, 221-234.

Wilson, G. T., & Fairburn, C. G. (1998). Treatments for eating disorders. In P. E. Nathan & J. M. Gorman (Eds.), *Guide to treatments that work* (pp. 501-530). New York, NY: Oxford University Press.

Wincze, J. P., Leitenberg, H., & Agras, W. S. (1972). The effects of token reinforcement and feedback on the delusional verbal behavior of chronic paranoid schizophrenics. *Journal of Applied Behavior Analysis*, *5*, 247-262.

Chapter 13

Toward a Cumulative Science of Persons: Past, Present, and Prospects

Walter Mischel
Columbia University

After an early childhood in Vienna, I migrated as an eight-year old with my family, fleeing as Jewish refugees from the Nazis in 1938, and ultimately settling in New York City. Deciding reluctantly not to become a painter, and after part-time jobs as a social worker in New York's Lower East side (while attending – more or less – college) I entered psychology in the 1950's. I was fortunate to have stumbled by pure chance into an especially exciting time in the clinical psychology program at Ohio State University where I was trained in research and exposed to the clinical psychology of the time. Jules Rotter, whose pioneering 1954 book brought the social learning approach to clinical psychology, was one of my mentors there. My second mentor was George Kelly, whose two-volume book in the same year started the "cognitive revolution" at least in clinical psychology and ultimately more widely. And B. F. Skinner, who gave a breathtaking colloquium at Ohio State – the only one I can remember – was a third influence that left an indelible impact. In retrospect, much of my work in the almost half century since then seems an attempt to integrate and transform these three influences into a new perspective – a viewpoint that would help me to make sense of two fundamental issues central for understanding human behavior and personality that have intrigued me consistently.

1968 Revisited: The Paradigm Challenge

The first of these issues took shape for me slowly over the first ten years of my career. It led me to fundamentally question and ultimately reject the reigning paradigm of personality and clinical psychology that defined the mainstream at the time, and indeed since the beginnings of the field of personality. My concerns about that paradigm grew as I tried to find my bearings in psychology, first teaching at the University of Colorado from 1956 to 1958, and then in four years on the faculty of Harvard University's Department of Social Relations. In 1962 I moved to Stanford University's Psychology Department which provided an ideal scholarly context. In that supportive intellectual setting I could concentrate on trying to make sense of a number of paradoxes that became increasingly disconcerting as I looked more closely at the data of the field and at my own research findings.

Early Hopes

This was a time when, beginning in the mid-1950's, the field of clinical psychology and personality had a giant growth spurt, both as a profession and as a science. It was stimulated on the one hand by demands for clinical psychologists in new health care facilities for millions of World War II veterans, and on the other by the opening of the Sputnik-launched space race, which fueled federal support for science in the United States. In this context, a new generation of clinically-schooled psychologists was trained to dedicate themselves to two-pronged careers as "scientist/practitioners." Most of us tried to straddle both roles; scientists devoted to invalidating our favorite hypotheses in research, and clinicians eager to apply the findings of what promised to become the new psychological science to improve the human condition.

A vast research literature sprouted rapidly, which tried to demonstrate the reliability and validity of an array of techniques that claimed to be analogous to X-rays of the human mind – from Rorshachs and Thematic Apperception Tests to Minnesota Multiphasic Personality Inventories and interviews – inherited from an earlier generation of practitioners. It was widely hoped, and often claimed, that these methods at a minimum would yield psychometrically sophisticated, reliable ways to capture the essentials of what the person "is really like," stably over time and across situations. This mission was guided by the "classic" view of human dispositions. Shared both by trait and psychodynamic approaches, these traditional assumptions about personality arose from a self-evidently true observation. On practically any dimension of human behavior, there are substantial, distinctive differences in the response of different persons within the same social situation: Obviously, *within* the same objective stimulus situation, there often are also large differences *between* individuals. Second it is assumed that individuals are characterized by *stable* and *broadly generalized* dispositions that endure over long periods of time and that generate consistencies in their social behavior across a wide range of situations. With this belief, assessors tried to predict behavior in many domains and contexts from a variety of personality indicators or "signs" from which they inferred these dispositions.

As an example, working as an assessment consultant at the beginnings of the Peace Corps in Washington DC, while still teaching at Harvard, the goal was to predict the probable success of Peace Corps teachers in Nigeria on the basis of a battery of measures while they were still in training. The project, as well as the finding, was representative of the expectations and assessment strategies of that time (Mischel, 1965). What was learned highlighted both the typical data obtained and the concerns that grew from them. Briefly, global ratings of the trainees made by the faculty, by the assessment board for the project, and by an interviewer were significantly intercorrelated. For example, the assessment board and the interview ratings correlated .72, showing that the assessors had similar impressions of the candidates' personalities in training. Independently, field performance of the Peace Corps teachers when they were on their assignments in Nigeria was assessed on six criterion subscales (which also were highly intercorrelated), and these were aggregated into a multiple scale criterion. To illustrate the major findings, simple self-reports and self-ratings, as on anxiety-relevant items and attitudes to authority, yielded modest but often statistically significant correlations with outcome criteria, accounting for small but significant amounts of variance. On the other hand, more global and indirect measures failed even to reach significance. For example, behavior in the interviews, one of the favorite global methods, predicted total criterion performance in Nigeria with a correlation of .13, accounting for a trivial percentage of the variance.

A three-person subcommittee of the assessment board based its pooled recommendations of each candidate on their discussion and review of all data from all observer sources during training. They thus integrated information from faculty evaluations, academic records, peer ratings, and interviews. A larger final assessment review board discussed these recommendations, considering each candidate individually. None of the separate predictions made by the training staff correlated significantly with criterion performance, to the dismay of those who were so confident in the power of their procedures. Especially notable is that even when the data were aggregated to enhance reliability, the resulting combined evaluations of each candidate by the total assessment board predicted aggregated performance outcomes in the field with a nonsignificant correlation of .20.

1968 Challenges to Classic Dispositional Assumptions

Findings like these were startling at a time when even small samples of behavior had seemed to promise a diagnostic X-ray to illuminate the core of personality – to allow rapid inferences from a few subtle signs observed by experts to broad generalizations about what the individual was like "on the whole," and then from these inferences about generalized global dispositions to predict specific outcomes. Were such predictive failures anomalies?

By the late 1960's I had scrutinized and sifted through the findings emerging from the voluminous investigations of the preceding years. These data – which seemed consistently to undermine and contradict the most central beliefs about the nature of personality consistency and coherence – led me to a thorough reexamination of the traditional global trait and psychodynamic approaches to personality, challenging its core assumptions (Mischel, 1968). Probably neither the findings nor the challenge were surprising to Skinnerians, given that Skinner had dismissed the mainstream of personality and clinical psychology altogether thirty years earlier. But whereas Skinner's critique could be rejected within personality psychology as arbitrary and from an outsider who had not taken the data of the field seriously, my 1968 challenge traumatized the established paradigm and its guardians.

To recapitulate the essentials, considerable evidence was found that cognitive constructions about oneself and the world, including other people, are often extremely stable and highly resistant to change. Self-concepts, and the impressions of other people including clinical judgments – the theories that we have about ourselves and each other – these phenomena and many more of the same type were found to have consistency and even tenacious continuity (Mischel, 1968). Indeed, our constructions about other people are often built quickly and on the basis of little information (e.g., Bruner, Olver, & Greenfield, 1966), and soon become difficult to disconfirm. An impressive degree of continuity and consistency also was found for another aspect of cognition: namely, cognitive or information-processing styles. These styles are often closely related to measures of intelligence and cognitive competence and, like "intelligence" itself, they tend to have higher consistency relative to more social dimensions of behavior (e.g., "conscientiousness," "honesty," "friendliness").

Apart from cognitive and intellective dimensions, the domain of social dispositions and interpersonal behavioral consistency proved much harder to document. In fact, a surprisingly reliable degree of behavioral specificity or "discriminativeness" (Mischel, 1973) was found regularly in the behavioral referents for such character traits as rigidity, social conformity, dependency, and aggression; for attitudes to authority; and for virtually any other nonintellective personality. In some readings of the literature, noncognitive personality dispositions began to seem much less global than traditional psychodynamic and trait positions had assumed them to be, with response patterns even in highly similar situations typically failing to be strongly related.

> Individuals show far less cross-situational consistency in their behavior than has been assumed by trait-state theories. The more dissimilar the evoking situations, the less likely they are to produce similar or consistent responses from the same individual. Even seemingly trivial situational differences may reduce correlations to zero. Response consistency tends to be greatest within the same response medium, within self-reports to paper-and-pencil tests, for example, or within directly observed nonverbal behavior. Intraindividual consistency is reduced drastically when dissimilar response modes are employed. Activities that are substantially associated with aspects of intelligence and with problem solving behavior – like achievement behaviors, cognitive styles, response speed – tend to be most consistent (Mischel, 1968, p. 177).

Evidence of this sort, in smaller amounts, had been noted for many years (e.g., Hartshorne & May, 1928; Newcomb, 1929) indicating instability and lack of consistency across situations in domains of behavior expected to reflect generalized and stable traits. In the past, however, such data were interpreted to reflect the imperfections of tests and tools and the resulting unreliability and errors of measurements; the fallibility of clinical judges; and other similar methodological problems. The new criticisms also noted that these methodological sources constituted serious constraints, but took another step, suggesting that the observed inconsistency so often found in studies of noncognitive personality dimensions may reflect the state of nature and not just the noise of measurement. Of course, this need not imply a capriciously haphazard world, but it did suggest a world in which personality consistencies seem greater than they are and in which the organization of behavior seems simpler than it is (Mischel, 1969, pp. 1014-1015).

The Psychodynamic-Clinical Alternative

At the same time that global traits were challenged in their core assumptions, I – along with many others (e.g., Peterson, 1968) – also questioned, but on different grounds, the dispositional paradigm of psychodynamic approaches. In contrast to the neglect of situational variables for which classic trait approaches were being criticized, psychodynamic approaches to personality dispositions had long recognized both the specificity and complexity of behavior, rejecting the idea of broad, overt behavioral consistencies across situations at the "surface" level. They believed that the observed inconsistencies in the individual's overt behavior could be understood as merely superficial diversities that masked the fundamentally consistent, underlying dispositions and dynamics (Mischel, 1971a, p. 153). Thus, psychodynamic theories at an abstract level could readily deal with the facts of inconsistencies in the person's behavior. But they were subject to another problem. The embarrassment for them was in the failure to provide compelling empirical evidence that the inferences they generated about the underlying or genotypic dispositions were useful either for the prediction of behavior or for its therapeutic modification, especially when compared to simpler, less inferential, and less costly alternatives.

Perhaps the most serious challenges to classic dispositional approaches, both of the trait and of the psychodynamic type, arose primarily from the clinical experiences of the 1950's and early 1960's with clients seeking help. It was in that clinical context, not in the laboratory, that many clinicians came to doubt the value both of the psychodynamic and of the trait-dispositional portraits to which they were devoting most of their effort (e.g., Peterson, 1968; Vernon, 1964). Skepticism about the utility of such global assessments arose not from any lack of interest in the client's dispositions nor from a neglect of individual differences. Instead, it arose from a growing anxiety that psychodynamic and trait "personality diagnostics," too often generated without close attention to the clients' own views of their lives and specific behaviors, might be exercises in stereotyping that missed the uniqueness of individuals and pinned the persons instead on a continuum of clinician-supplied labels, as George Kelly (1955) had charged years earlier.

Many empirical studies had investigated the utility of clinicians' efforts to infer broad dispositions indirectly from specific symptomatic signs and to unravel disguises in order to uncover the hypothetical dispositions that might be their roots. The results on the whole threw doubt on the utility of clinical judgments even when the judges were well-trained, expert psychodynamicists, working with clients in clinical contexts and using their own preferred techniques (Bandura, 1969; Mischel, 1968; Peterson, 1968). Clinicians guided by concepts about underlying genotypic dispositions did not seem better able to predict behavior than the persons' own direct and simple self-report, demographic variables, or in some cases the clinicians' secretaries (e.g., Mischel, 1968). The disappointments of expert clinical judgment were especially disconcerting when contrasted with evidence for the predictions possible from indices of directly relevant past behavior, such as an individual's past record of maladjustment and hospitalization (Lasky, et al., 1959). A correlation of .61 was found, for example, between the weight of a patient's file folder and the incidence of rehospitalization. As results like these illustrate, even a simple measure of a person's past can sometimes powerfully predict relevant aspects of the future, in sharp contrast to more complex, indirect, costly efforts. It should be equally evident that the simple fact that one cannot predict well from some previously favored measures and strategies denies neither the importance of individual differences nor the potential value of all sorts of assessments for all sorts of purposes (e.g., Mischel, 1983). It does not mean that individual differences are necessarily unpredictable, but it does indicate that the nature and locus of that predictability may be quite different from what had been assumed.

When concerns with clinical practice were combined with the evidence from empirical studies of global traits, the challenge in 1968 both to trait and to psychodynamic approaches to personality became considerable. After review of the utility of psychometrically measured traits, as well as of psychodynamic inferences about states and traits, I was led to the following conclusion:

> Responses have not served very usefully as indirect signs of internal predispositions. Actuarial methods of data combination are generally better than clinical-theoretical inferences. Base rates, direct self-reports, self-predictions, and especially indices of relevant past behavior typically provide the best as well as the cheapest predictions. Moreover, these predictions hold their own against, and usually exceed, those generated either clinically or statistically from complex inferences about underlying traits and states. In general, the predictive efficiency of simple, straightforward self-ratings and measures of directly relevant past performance has not been exceeded by more psychometrically sophisticated personality tests, by combining tests into batteries, by assigning differential weights to them, or by employing more complex statistical analyses involving multiple-regression equations. The conclusions for personality measures apply, on the whole, to diverse content areas including the prediction of college achievement, job and professional success, treatment outcomes, rehospitalization for psychiatric patients, parole violations for delinquent children, and so on. In light of these findings it is not surprising that large-scale applied efforts to predict behavior from personality inferences have been strikingly and consistently unsuccessful. . . . (Mischel, 1968, p. 145-146).

Finally, beyond the empirical challenge questioning the utility of global traits was the practice of endowing such dispositions with causal powers in theoretical explanations of behavior. Allport (1937) had most articulately argued that behind the confusion of trait terms, the disagreement of judges, and the errors of empirical observation, trait terms ultimately refer to "bona fide mental structures" (p. 289) that generate (i.e., produce) consistencies in behavior not only over time, but also across situations. To the degree that traits also were commonly used as causal entities in explanation of the determinants of behavior, they became vulnerable to criticisms of circularity (Mischel, 1968; Peterson, 1968; Skinner, 1953; Vernon, 1964). If descriptions of behavior are used to invoke traits, which in turn are offered as explanations of the same behavior from which they were inferred in the first place, the circularity of the reasoning becomes embarrassing.

The critiques of traditional dispositional approaches that emerged at this juncture were first read by many as "situationist" attacks on personality itself and as unjustified denials of the importance of individual differences. Reactions of this type were understandable, given a long tradition of dichotomizing the person and the situation and contrasting the relative importance of the two sources of variance, rather than clarifying how they interact psychologically. But while the challenge to traditional dispositional paradigms called attention to the significance of situations or contexts in the study of persons, my basic message was not a negation either of personality as a field or of individual differences as a phenomenon. On the contrary, the focus was on the idiographic nature of each person interacting with the specific contexts of his or her life and on the need to revise some favorite assumptions of traditional personality theories to take those unique interactions into account seriously. Far from denying individual differences in personality, the criticisms were largely motivated to defend individuality and the uniqueness of each person against the tendency, prevalent in 1960's clinical and diagnostic efforts, to use a few ratings or few behavioral signs to categorize people into categories on an assessor's favorite nomothetic trait dimensions. It was common practice to assume in the 1960's that such assessments were useful to predict not just "average" levels of individual differences, but a person's specific behavior on specific criteria as well as "in general." It was not uncommon to undertake decision making about a person's life and future on the basis of a relatively limited sampling of personological "signs" or "trait indicators." It was this type of practice that I challenged:

> Global traits and states are excessively crude, gross units to encompass adequately the extraordinary complexity and subtlety of the discriminations that people constantly make. Traditional trait-state conceptions of man have depicted him as victimized by his infantile history, as possessed by unchanging rigid trait attributes, and as driven inexorably by unconscious irrational forces. This conceptualization of man, besides being philosophically unappetizing, is contradicted by massive experimental data. The traditional trait-state conceptualizations of personality, while often paying lip service to man's complexity and to the uniqueness of each person, in fact lead to a grossly oversimplified view that misses both the richness and the uniqueness of individual lives (Mischel, 1968, p. 301)

In sum, the dissatisfactions that crystallized two decades ago were wide in range, reflecting many concerns. Global dispositional approaches were faulted as not useful for the planning of specific individual treatment programs, for the design of social change programs, or for the prediction of the specific behavior of individuals in specific contexts. Perhaps most troubling theoretically, they also were criticized for not yielding evidence of cross-situational consistency and for failing to provide a theoretically compelling analysis of the basic psychological processes that underlie the individual's cognition, affect, and actions (e.g., Mischel, 1973).

Aftermath of the Challenge: Toward a Theoretical Integration

These challenges fueled a period of prolonged and heated controversy about personality dispositions and the construct of personality itself that dominated thinking in the area throughout the 1970's and early 1980's (e.g., reviewed in Magnusson & Endler, 1977). The debate was multifaceted – engaging many segments of the field, spilling into adjacent areas, and spanning from one extreme that exaggerated the dilemma to another that trivialized it. The claims ranged from contentions that personality was a largely fictitious construction in the mind of the perceiver (e.g., Shweder, 1975), to counterarguments intended to prove that global dispositions as traditionally conceptualized were "alive and well" if one simply employed a more reliable measurement strategy to find them (e.g., Epstein, 1979). In the same period, social psychologists amassed evidence for the power of situational variables, and proposed that humans have a persistent tendency to invoke dispositions as favorite (albeit erroneous) explanations of social behavior (e.g., Nisbett & Ross, 1980; Ross & Nisbett,1991). In that sense, Skinner's focus on the importance of the situation and of stimulus control in the regulation of social behavior, although never acknowledged within social psychology, was at last echoed within it.

In the abstract and as a general framework, "person/situation interactionism" was easily and widely given lip service and even embraced in the 1970's within social and personality psychology. Indeed it was prematurely hailed as yielding a solution to the long-standing controversy and the growing confusion. The continuing challenge, however, still awaited answers: how to reconceptualize dispositions to take such interactions into account incisively, *a priori* in the form of specific predictions, and not just in post hoc attempts to deal with unpredicted and perhaps basically unpredictable higher-order interactions after they are found in the data. My efforts to address this challenge and to provide a theoretical framework for understanding and predicting individual differences in the interactions of persons and situations have been spelled out in detail over the years elsewhere (e.g., Mischel, 1973, Mischel & Shoda, 1995, 1998).

Briefly, a set of person variables was proposed in the early 1970's (Mischel, 1973), based on theoretical developments in the fields of social learning and cognition that had been bypassed or ignored by personality theory at that juncture. In light of the complexity of the interactions between the individual and the situation that was emphasized by the critics of global trait assumptions, the focus in the search for person variables shifted. This shift called attention away from inferences about what broad traits a person *has* to focus instead on what the person *does* in particular conditions in the coping process. Of course, what people do encompasses not just motor acts, but what they do cognitively and affectively, including the constructs they generate, the projects they plan and pursue, and the self-regulatory efforts they attempt in light of long-term goals (to illustrate from the vast array). Moreover, it was argued that these descriptions of what persons *do* must include the specific psychological conditions in which they do it, thus providing more condition-qualified, "local," contingent, and specific characterizations of persons in contexts, in contrast to context-free traits.

The cognitive-social learning approach to personality (Mischel, 1973) shifted the unit of study from global traits inferred from behavioral signs to the person's cognitions, affect, and action assessed in relation to the particular psychological conditions in which they occur. The focus thus changed from describing situation-free people with broad trait adjectives to analyzing the interactions between conditions and the cognitions and behaviors of interest. In the 1960's much personality research on social behavior was undertaken to study the processes of cognition and social learning through which potential behaviors are acquired, evoked, maintained, and modified (e.g., as reviewed in Bandura, 1969; Mischel, 1968). Less attention had been devoted to the psychological products within the person of these processes in the course of development. The cognitive-social learning reconceptualization of personality was intended to identify a set of interrelated person variables that capture these "products" of the individual's psychological history and that in turn mediate the manner in which new situations are interpreted.

The person variables that were proposed consisted of such constructs as the person's expectations, goals, values, and self-regulatory competencies. Although the proposed variables overlap and interact, each yields distinctive information about the probable specific interaction between the individual and any given psychological situation. Each may be assessed objectively. Most important theoretically, each is also amenable to study in two distinct but complementary ways. Each may be conceptualized as a person variable that is the *product* of the individual's social-cognitive development and on which individuals differ. Each also may be conceptualized in terms of the psychological *processes* relevant to understanding the operations of that variable and its psychological meaning. Thus, each variable has both a structural and a functional aspect in an emerging theory of personality. More recent versions of this approach address the specific nature of the organization of the person variables, their interactions within the mediating system (the Cognitive Affective Personality System, or CAPS), and the stimulus features in the social environment that activate them. These interactions have been analyzed and modeled in detail, including as computer simulations (Mischel & Shoda, 1995; Shoda & Mischel, 1998).

A Conditional Approach to Dispositions

Historically, the failure to find strong support for cross-situational consistency at the behavioral level, given the widespread assumption that personality consists of traits, expressed across many different situations as generalized, global behavior tendencies, was read originally as a basic threat to the construct of personality itself. As noted above, the effect was an unfortunate and prolonged "person versus situation" debate, and a paradigm crisis in the area.

Aggregating over situations to remove them. After years of debate, consensus was reached about the state of the data: The average cross-situational consistency coefficient is nonzero but not by much (Bem, 1983; Epstein, 1983; Mischel & Peake, 1982a, b). But there was and still is deep disagreement about how to interpret the data and proceed in the study of personality (e.g., as discussed in Mischel & Shoda, 1995, 1998; Pervin, 1994). The most widely accepted strategy used by the classic dispositional or trait approach currently acknowledges the low cross-situational consistency in behavior found from situation to situation: It then systematically removes the situation by aggregating the individual's behavior on a given dimension (e.g., "conscientiousness") over many different situations (e.g., home, school, work) to estimate an overall "true score," treating the variability across situations as "error."

An alternative conception of stability: Incorporating the situation into the search for consistency. In the traditional approach to behavioral dispositions, the observed variability within each person on a dimension is seen as "error" and averaged out to get the best approximation of the underlying stable "true score," so the question simply becomes: Is person A different overall in the level of helpfulness than person B? This question is important, and perhaps the best first question to ask in the analysis of personality invariance. But it may also be its premature end if we ignore the profile information about when and where A and B differ in their unique pattern with regard to the particular dimension of behavior. What if person A's helping behavior occurs mostly with people from whom he can expect a "return," while person B's helping behavior is correlated with the perceived level of need for help, irrespective of the possibility of future returns? These differences in their pattern of variability in relation to situations may be a possible key to understanding individuality and personality coherence and their underlying motivations and personality systems. In that case, these patterns are potential "signatures" of personality that need to be identified and harnessed rather than deliberately removed.

Evidence for the conditional (contextualized) expression of dispositions. Many of the results of my research program on the structure of consistency in social behavior were based on behavior observed intensively and extensively at a well-controlled field laboratory site. The long-term, intensive observational field laboratory developed in this research program was located within a 6-week summer residential camp setting and treatment program for troubled children, called Wediko (e.g., Mischel, 1990; Shoda, et al., 1993a, 1993b, 1994). This setting provided an exceptional opportunity to examine behavior in vivo as it unfolds across situations and over time under unusually well-controlled research conditions that assured the reliability and density of measurement.

We found a type of stability that was seemingly contradictory to earlier assumptions about the consistency and structure of dispositions and that was systematically bypassed, rather than harnessed. Consistent with – and predicted by – the Cognitive Affective Personality System (CAPS) model developed with Yuichi Shoda (Mischel & Shoda, 1995, 1998; Shoda & Mischel, 1998), individuals may be characterized by distinctive and stable patterns of variability in their prototypic behavior in relation to different significant psychological situations, as will be described below. Thus, although findings showing the variability of behavior and the importance of the situation in the past have been interpreted as evidence against the utility of the personality construct, our work has shown that this need not be the case (Mischel & Shoda, in press; Shoda, et al., 1994). On the contrary, at least some of this variability is intra-individually stable and meaningful: Indeed it seems to reflect some of the essence of personality coherence and to provide a potential window into the underlying social cognitive and affective processes and system that generate it (e.g., the individual's construals, goals, and motivations).

Distinguishing nominal and psychological situations: Finding the "active ingredients" (psychological features) within situations. To test for the existence and meaningfulness of the hypothesized, stable *if/then* situation-behavior relations, everyday social behavior was observed as it unfolded over the course of each summer in the Wediko residential camp setting, yielding an exceptionally large and comprehensive set of systematic observations for each participant (Shoda, et al., 1989, 1993a, b, 1994; Shoda, 1990). The first requirement in the Wediko field study was to identify the situations in which the behavior occurred (Shoda, et al., 1994). But which situations? In studies of the consistency of behavior across situations, the situations usually have been defined in nominal terms, as places and activities in the setting, for example, as woodworking activities, arithmetic tests, dining halls, or school playgrounds (e.g., Hartshorne & May, 1928; Newcomb, 1929). Individual differences in relation to such specific nominal situations, even if highly stable, necessarily would be of limited generalizability. On the other hand, if situations are redefined to capture their basic psychological features then information about a person's behavior tendencies specific to those situation features (Kelly, 1955; Mischel, 1973) might be used to predict behavior across a broad range of contexts that contain the same psychological features (Shoda, et al., 1993a). For example, situations that include criticism or lack of attention from a partner might be those in which individuals hypersensitive to rejection in intimate relations become consistently more upset than others (e.g., Downey & Feldman, 1996; Mischel & Shoda, 1995). The key for achieving generalizability, therefore, is to identify psychological features of situations that (1) play a functional role in the generation of behaviors, and (2) are contained in a wide range of nominal situations.

It was thus important to identify the relevant psychological features – the "active ingredients" (if we make the analogy with the potent aspects of a chemical substance) as opposed to the inactive, filler elements that exert a significant impact on the behavior of the person. These active ingredients may occur within many different nominal situations (Shoda, et al., 1994). Individual differences in response to nominal situations, such as the daily activities within a camp, then may be understood in terms of the person's stable responses to the encoded active psychological features within the nominal situations. These psychological features, in turn, may consist of combinations of even more specific features and may be analyzed in terms of their overlap and similarity.

As predicted, we found that individual differences in behavior were relatively inconsistent across different types of psychological situations. However, they were significantly more consistent across the same types of psychological situations, i.e., those that contain the same active ingredients even when they were embedded within different nominal situations (Shoda, et al., 1994). Further, cross-situational consistency increased substantially in the individual's behavior as the number of shared features increased. In short, the situation specificity of individual differences in behavior found repeatedly over the years has often been seen as limiting the generalizability and utility of personality descriptions, prompting repeated paradigm crises in the field. Our results suggest a very different possibility: If the distinctive and stable *if/then* contingencies for the individual are defined in relation to the basic psychological ingredients or features that occur in many different nominal situations, then it may be possible to understand and predict behaviors in a novel situation given that its psychological ingredients are known. Moreover, to the degree that particular sets of such active ingredients or psychological features for an individual (or for a personality type) are imbedded in diverse nominal situations (e.g., at woodworking in camp, on playground at school, at mealtime at home), it may become possible to predict behavior across those seemingly different situations and contexts, allowing much broader predictability even for quite specific behavioral manifestations (Mischel & Shoda, 1995, 1998; Shoda, et al., 1994).

Resolving the Consistency Paradox

It was in the 1970's that the so-called "consistency paradox" (e.g., Bem & Allen, 1974) was articulated, and it proposed a possible resolution to the paradigm crisis produced by the evidence for the lack of cross-situational consistency within the individual's behavior. This now classic paradox refers to the notion that while intuition seems to support the belief that people are characterized by broad dispositions resulting in extensive cross-situational consistency, the research in the area (as discussed above) has persistently failed to support this intuition. To resolve this paradox, Daryl Bem predicted that behavioral cross-situational consistency would be demonstrable at the level of specific situations, but only for that subset of people who view themselves as consistent on the particular dimension and for whom that dimension is thus personally relevant (Bem & Allen, 1974).

To test this proposition, my studies of the consistency paradox (Mischel & Peake, 1982, 1983) were conducted with a sample of Carleton College undergraduates who volunteered to participate in extensive self-assessments relevant to their conscientiousness and friendliness. Directly contradicting Bem's prediction, we found that the students' perceptions of their own overall consistency or variability on conscientiousness were not related closely to the observed cross-situational consistency of their actual behavior directly observed as it occurred in vivo across diverse daily situations. Although inter-judge agreement was greater for those students who saw themselves overall as consistent in conscientiousness, their average behavioral consistency across the measures was not significantly greater than that of students who saw themselves as variable. In short, in this study, people who saw themselves as consistent on a dimension were seen with greater interjudge agreement by others, but their overall behavior was not necessarily more consistent cross-situationally.

If, as the Carleton data suggest, the self-perception of consistency is unrelated to the level of cross-situational consistency in the referent behaviors, in what is it rooted? To try to answer this question, we proposed that consistency judgments rely heavily on the observation of central (prototypic) features, so that the impression of consistency will derive not from average levels of consistency across all the possible features of the category, but rather from the observation that some central features are reliably (stably) present. This perspective suggests that extensive cross-situational consistency may not be a basic ingredient for either the organization or the perception of personal consistency in a domain.

We hypothesized that the impression that a person is consistent with regard to a trait is not based mostly on the observation of average cross-situational consistency in all the potentially relevant behaviors (e.g., punctuality for classes, punctuality for appointments, desk neatness, etc.). Instead, we proposed that when people try to assess their variability (vs. consistency) with regard to a category of behavior, they scan the temporal stability of a limited number of behaviors that for them are most relevant (prototypic) to that category. That is, it was hypothesized that the impression of consistency is based extensively on the observation of *temporal* stability in those behaviors that are most relevant to the prototype. No relationship was expected between the impression of high consistency versus variability and overall cross-situational consistency. The results supported these expectations (Mischel & Peake, 1982). Those students who saw themselves as highly consistent in conscientiousness were significantly more temporally stable on these prototypic behaviors than were those who viewed themselves as more variable from situation to situation – an effect that was replicated in the domain of friendliness by Peake within the same sample of students (Peake, 1982). In contrast to the clear and consistent differences in temporal stability for the prototypic behaviors, the self-perceived low and high variability groups did not differ in mean temporal stability for the less prototypic behaviors. Finally, also as expected, self-perceived consistency and behavioral cross-situational consistency were unrelated in Mischel and Peake's (1982) study.

These findings suggested that peoples' intuitions of their cross-situational consistency are not illusory: they are based on data, but these data are not highly generalized cross-situational consistencies in their behaviors on the whole. Intuitions about one's consistency seem to arise, instead, from the observation of temporal stability in prototypical behaviors. This would certainly not be a fictitious construction of consistency. The "error" simply would be to confuse the temporal stability of key behaviors with pervasive cross-situational consistency, and then to overestimate the latter.

Condition-Behavior Stabilities: In Search of Local Predictability

The classic trait strategy essentially treats situations as if they were error, and seeks to cancel their effects by aggregating across them to eliminate their role and to demonstrate stable individual differences. The approach my associates and I favor, in contrast to the classic route, seeks consistencies by linking the behavior of interest to a circumscribed set of contexts, thus pursuing consistency on a more local, condition-bound, contingent, and specific (rather than global) level. Both approaches seem to accept the fact that average levels of consistency in behavior from situation to situation tend to be modest, even after aggregation over multiple occasions. Advocates of the traditional trait strategy propose circumventing this constraint by abandoning attempts to predict behavior from situation to situation altogether. Instead, they confine their predictive efforts to aggregates over multiple situations (e.g. Epstein, 1979). Such a strategy can enhance the resulting coefficients dramatically (as the Spearman-Brown formula has long recognized). But it bypasses rather than resolves the classic problems found in the search for coherences from situation to situation by "averaging out" the situation rather than predicting behavior in it. And, of course, it places a low ceiling on the accuracy possible for predicting behavior in specific situations.

We have continued to explore the view that personality coherences involve prototypic features of behavior that are cross-situationally discriminative but meaningful, temporally stable dispositional indicators when they occur in certain diagnostic contexts. Instead of pursuing high levels of overall consistency from situation to situation for many aggregated behaviors in a wide range of aggregated contexts, the goal is to identify the distinctive "bundles" or sets of temporally stable prototypic condition-behavior relations that characterize the individual under predictable circumstances (e.g., Mischel, 1973; Wright & Mischel, 1987). Although these *if/then* condition-behavior relations may occur only some of the time, they may figure crucially both in the perception of personality and in its organization (e.g., Mischel & Peake, 1982; Wright & Mischel, 1987, 1988).

In this vein, we developed a conditional approach to dispositions in which dispositional constructs are viewed as clusters of *if/then* propositions. Rather than construing dispositions as generalized response tendencies aggregated over diverse situations, we view them as propositions summarizing contingencies between categories of conditions and categories of behavior. A basic unit in the analysis of dispositions, then, becomes the conditional frequency of acts that are central to a particular behavior category in circumscribed, "diagnostic" conditions (Wright & Mischel, 1987, 1988). This type of *if/then* proposition contrasts with the traditional focus on the overall frequency of dispositionally relevant behaviors aggregated across a wide range of situations. It calls explicit attention to inextricable specific links between conditions and actions in determining the implications of people's behavior for dispositional judgments about them (e.g., Mischel & Shoda, 1995, 1998, 1999; Shoda, Mischel, & Wright, 1989). It equally highlights the interactive nature of the person-situation relations that characterize social behavior.

To summarize, although context sensitivity and discriminativeness across situations may be the rule rather than the exception for most social behavior, it is also possible to find specific coherences that differentiate individuals and that can be identified under predictable contingencies for at least some people and behaviors, suggesting "local" areas of relative predictability without resorting to aggregation across situations. Such local coherences seem to occur at least in situations requiring cognitive and self-regulatory competencies that make high demands and strain people's available competence, at least with regard to some categories of disadvantageous behavior (aggression, withdrawal). Moreover, we have found significant links between ratings on these dimensions and individuals' actual behavior in difficult situations at relatively molecular episodic levels of observation, even without benefit of aggregating across different behavioral features.

Beyond Stimulus Control: Why I Became a Cognitive Social Psychologist

The fact that the situation plays an enormously powerful role in the often automatic activation and regulation of complex human social behavior was of course central to my critique of traditional approaches to clinical and personality psychology. I saw the power of the situation convincingly in my own work on the willingness and ability of young children to delay gratification by continuing to wait for two little treats later as opposed to settling for one right now. We found that such a seemingly trivial change in the situation as whether the rewards remain exposed on the plate facing the preschool child or are placed under it can change the average delay time from less than a minute to more than ten (e.g., Mischel, Shoda & Rodriguez, 1989). Thus whether or not the young child finds delay of gratification excruciatingly difficult or easily achievable hinges on the subtleties of the situation, and when these *IF*s are properly understood and introduced the *THEN*s that follow can become highly predictable.

Overcoming Stimulus Control Through Self-Regulation

The same set of studies also generated a second set of findings, however, that led me to join the cognitive revolution but without abandoning my focus on behavior and its determinants (e.g., Mischel, 1973). Most compelling for me was the finding that regardless of the objective stimulus facing the subject, it was its mental representation, as primed by suggestions on how to think about the rewards, that controlled the delay of gratification behavior, regardless of the actual rewards present in the situation. Namely, when these representations focused on the "hot" consummatory features of the stimulus (e.g., "while you're waiting you can think about the pretzel's salty, crunchy taste") the frustration of continued delay of gratification became unbearable for most children even when the external stimulus facing the subject was completely controlled. Conversely, when the mental representation focused on the "cool," informative cue properties (e.g., "you can think about the pretzels as if they were little sticks") , sustained, goal-directed delay of gratification and "willpower" became manageable, again regardless of the external stimulus in the situation (Mischel, 1974, 1996; Mischel, Shoda & Rodriguez, 1989). Thus the way the child represented the stimuli cognitively during the delay period profoundly transformed their impact: the power thus resides in the head, not in the external stimulus.

Likewise, even in the presence of the rewards, which makes delay difficult for children, delay was easily sustained when the children self-distracted (e.g., by imagining that they were playing with a toy, or by thinking about pleasant activities such as swinging on a swing at the birthday party). If the crucial process is in the head, individuals should be able to influence it through self-generated strategies to influence the mental representations of the reward objects, just as it is influenced by the strategies that the situation suggests.

In fact, in the same research program we found impressively stable individual differences in the ability to overcome stimulus control pressures in the purposeful pursuit of long-term goals (e.g. Mischel, Shoda, & Peake, 1988; Shoda, Mischel, & Peake, 1990). For example, in laboratory situations in which individual differences in such strategies were activated, those 4-year-old children who delayed longer became more socially and cognitively competent young adults, also achieving higher levels of scholastic performance, as reflected in their SAT verbal and quantitative scores (e.g., Shoda, Mischel, & Peake, 1990). In short, behavior in the delay situation was a function not only of the characteristics of the situation but also of the individuals in it. The fact that these distinctively human efforts also require the strategic utilization and support of situations undermines neither the role of the person nor of the situation, but requires attention to their reciprocal interaction. These interactions have been conceptualized more recently in a theoretical two-system "hot/cool" framework that takes account both of the automatic, stimulus-response aspects of functioning and of the more reflective, cognitive mediating system, focusing on the specifics of their interplay (Metcalfe & Mischel, 1999). The findings from this research also make the common distinction between the power of the situation and of the person fuzzy. For example, does the fact that attention is focused away from the rewards in the delay situation (e.g., by covering the rewards or avoiding them cognitively) demonstrate the power of situational variables in self-control? It does in the sense that they show how specific changes in the situation can make delay either very difficult or very easy. But the same results also show that even young children can and do increase their own mastery and personal ability to control the effects of stimuli on them by modifying how they think about those stimuli, by "reframing" them cognitively, or by distracting themselves and focusing on other aspects of the situation while continuing in their goal-directed behavior.

Empirically, it by now seems undeniable: in everyday life, as well as in the laboratory, people can and do modify and transform the power and impact of the stimuli that they encounter and create, persisting in pursuit of long-term difficult goals even in the face of potent barriers and temptations along the route (e.g., Mischel, Cantor & Feldman, 1996). These phenomena (as when the habitual smoker gives up tobacco, and the difficult new year's resolution to exercise is actually executed) may be the rare events, but it is their importance for being human, not their frequency, that is at issue, and surely it is part of what psychologists must explain in a comprehensive account of what is significant in everyday life.

In sum, the prevalence and significance of automaticity of *if/then* links in everyday life and of the power of the situation is not diminished (it may be enhanced) by the concurrent recognition of the field's other major conclusion: regardless of its frequency, humans do engage at least some of the time and under some circumstances in self-regulatory behavior in pursuit of their long-term goals and values. In these moments they manage to purposely modify, transform, and even overcome the power of the immediate stimulus, interjecting their own personal agendas between the external IF and the observable external THEN, in ways that reveal their distinctive personality signatures.

References

Allport, G. W. (1937). *Personality: A psychological interpretation.* New York: Holt, Rinehart, & Winston.

Bandura, A. (1969). *Principles of behavior modification.* New York: Holt, Rinehart, & Winston.

Bem, D. J. (1983). Further Déjà vu in the search for cross-situational consistencies in behavior: A response to Mischel and Peake. *Psychological Review, 90,* 390-393.

Bem, D. J., & Allen, A. (1974). On predicting some of the people some of the time: the search for cross-situational consistencies in behavior. *Psychological Review, 81,* 506-520.

Bruner, J. S., Olver, R., & Greenfield, P. (1966). *Studies in cognitive growth.* New York: Wiley.

Downey, G., & Feldman, S. (1996). Implications of rejection sensitivity for intimate relationships. *Journal of Personality and Social Psychology, 70,* 1327-1343.

Epstein, S. (1979). The stability of behavior: On predicting most of the people much of the time. *Journal of Personality and Social Psychology, 37,* 1097-1126.

Epstein, S. (1983). Aggregation and beyond: Some basic issues on the prediction of behavior. *Journal of Personality, 51,* 360-392.

Hartshorne, H., & May, A. (1928). *Studies in the nature of character: Studies in deceit* (Vol. 1). New York: MacMillan.

Kelly, G. A. (1955). *The psychology of personal constructs* (Vols. 1-2). New York: Norton.

Lasky, J. J., Hover, G. L., Smith, P. A., Bostian, D. W., Duffendack, S. C., & Nord, C. L. (1959). Post-hospital adjustment as predicted by psychiatric patients and their staff. *Journal of Consulting Psychology, 23,* 213-218.

Magnusson, D., & Endler, N. S. (Eds.). (1977). *Personality at the crossroads: Current issues in interactional psychology.* Hillsdale, NJ: Erlbaum.

Metcalfe, J., & Mischel, W. (1999). A hot/cool system analysis of delay of gratification: Dynamics of willpower. *Psychological Review, 106,* 3-19.

Mischel, W. (1965). Predicting the success of Peace Corps volunteers in Nigeria. *Journal of Personality and Social Psychology, 1,* 510-517.

Mischel, W. (1968). *Personality and assessment.* New York: Wiley.

Mischel, W. (1973). Toward a cognitive social learning reconceptualization of personality. *Psychological Review, 80,* 252-283.

Mischel, W. (1974). Cognitive appraisals and transformations in self-control. In B. Weiner (Ed.), *Cognitive views of human motivation* (pp. 33-49). New York: Academic Press.

Mischel, W., Shoda, Y., & Peake, P. K. (1988). The nature of adolescent competencies predicted by preschool delay of gratification. *Journal of Personality and Social Psychology, 54,* 687-699.

Mischel, W. (1969). Continuity and change in personality. *American Psychologist, 24,* 1012-1018.

Mischel, W. (1971). *Introduction to personality.* New York: Holt, Rinehart, & Winston.

Mischel, W. (1983). Alternatives in the pursuit of the predictability and consistency of persons: Stable data that yield unstable interpretations. *Journal of Personality* [special issue on prediction], *51,* 578-604.

Mischel, W. (1990). Personality dispositions revisited and revised: A view after three decades. In. L. Pervin (Ed.), *Handbook of personality psychology* (pp. 111-134). New York: The Guilford Press.

Mischel, W. (1996). From good intentions to willpower. In P. M. Gollwitzer & J. A. Bargh (Eds.), *The psychology of action: Linking cognition and motivation to behavior* (pp. 197-218). New York: Guilford Press.

Mischel, W., Cantor, N., & Feldman, S. (1996). Principles of self-regulation: The nature of willpower and self-control. In E. T. Higgins and A. W. Kruglanski (Eds.), *Social psychology: Handbook of basic principles* (pp. 329-360). New York: Guilford.

Mischel, W., & Peake, P. K. (1982). Beyond Déjà vu in the search for cross-situational consistency. *Psychological Review, 89,* 730-755.

Mischel, W., & Peake, P. (1982). In search of consistency: Measure for measure. In M. P. Zanna, E. T. Higgins, & C. P. Herman (Eds.), *Consistency in social behavior: The Ontario Symposium* (Vol. 2, pp. 187-207). Hillsdale, NJ: Erlbaum.

Mischel, W., & Peake, P. K. (1983). Analyzing the construction of consistency in personality. In M. M. Page (Ed.), *Nebraska Symposium on Motivation, 1982: Personality-Current theory and research* (Vol. 30, pp. 233-262). Lincoln: University of Nebraska Press.

Mischel, W., & Shoda, Y. (1995). A cognitive-affective system theory of personality: Reconceptualizing situations, dispositions, dynamics, and invariance in personality structure. *Psychological Review, 102(2),* 246-268.

Mischel, W., & Shoda, Y. (1998). Reconciling processing dynamics and personality dispositions. *Annual Review of Psychology, 49,* 229-258.

Mischel, W., & Shoda, Y. (1999). Integrating dispositions and processing dynamics within a unified theory of personality: The cognitive affective personality system (CAPS). In L. Pervin & O. John (Eds.), *Handbook of personality: Theory and research* (pp. 197-218). New York: Guilford Press.

Mischel, W., Shoda, Y., & Rodriguez, M. L. (1989). Delay of gratification in children. *Science, 244,* 933-938.

Newcomb, T. N. (1929). *Consistency of certain extrovert-introvert behavior patterns in 51 problem boys.* New York: Columbia University, Teachers College, Bureau of Publications.

Nisbett, R. E., & Ross, L. D. (1980). *Human inference: Strategies and shortcomings of social judgment.* Englewood Cliffs, NJ: Prentice Hall

Peake, P. K. (1982). Searching for consistency: The Carleton Student Behavior Study. Doctoral Dissertation, Stanford University. *Dissertation Abstracts, 43,* Pt. B, Section 8, p. 2746. (University Microfilms No. AAD 83-01259).

Peterson, D. R. (1968). *The clinical study of social behavior.* New York: Appleton-Century-Crofts.

Pervin, L. A. (1994). A critical analysis of current trait theory. *Psychological Inquiry, 5,* 103-113.

Ross, L., & Nisbett, R. E. (1991). *The person and the situation: Perspectives of social psychology.* New York: McGraw-Hill.

Shoda, Y., Mischel, W., & Peake, P. K. (1990). Predicting adolescent cognitive and self-regulatory competencies from preschool delay of gratification: Identifying diagnostic conditions. *Developmental Psychology, 26,* 978-986.

Shoda, Y., Mischel, W., & Wright, J. C. (1989). Intuitive interactionism in person perception: Effects of situation-behavior relations on dispositional judgments. *Journal of Personality and Social Psychology, 56,* 41-59.

Shoda, Y., Mischel, W., & Wright, J. C. (1993). The role of situational demands and cognitive competencies in behavior organization and personality coherence. *Journal of Personality and Social Psychology, 65,* 1023-1035.

Shoda, Y., Mischel, W., & Wright, J. C. (1993). Links between personality judgments and contextualized behavior patterns: Situation-behavior profiles of personality prototypes. *Social Cognition, 11,* 399-429.

Shoda, Y., Mischel, W., & Wright, J. C. (1994). Intraindividual stability in the organization and patterning of behavior: Incorporating psychological situations into the idiographic analysis of personality. *Journal of Personality and Social Psychology, 67,* 674-687.

Shweder, R. A. (1975). How relevant is an individual difference theory of personality? *Journal of Personality, 43,* 455-485.

Skinner, B. F. (1953). *Science and human behavior.* New York: Macmillan.

Vernon, P. E. (1964). *Personality Assessment: A critical survey.* New York: Wiley.

Wright, J. C., & Mischel, W. (1987). A conditional approach to dispositional constructs: The local predictability of social behavior. *Journal of Personality and Social Psychology, 53,* 1159-1177.

Wright, J. C., & Mischel, W. (1988). Conditional hedges and the intuitive psychology of traits. *Journal of Personality and Social Psychology, 55,* 454-469.

Chapter 14

A Small Matter of Proof

Donald M. Baer
University of Kansas

Intellectual Biography

My parents were immigrants who had to work rather than finish high-school educations. Appraising their new country, they saw two ways up for their children: business and education. They sent me to school with very clear instructions: It was the most important part of my life; I should learn everything that was taught; and I should cause no trouble. I was a compliant child; it would be a long time before I disobeyed any of those instructions.

Massachusetts and Pennsylvania public schools made me literate, grammatical, and able to calculate. They also taught me how a few parts of the world worked. They called that Science. I loved knowing how any part of the world worked; I do not know why. Kantor might have labeled it maximizing an ecological reinforcer (Kantor, 1924/1926), but a label is not an explanation.

Science was not taught in the public schools then as if it were interesting, glamorous, all-explanatory, or crucial to the future of our society. Instead, it was taught as if this was what we could *prove* about how some part of the world worked. I found that something called "understanding" or "explanation" was already one of my most potent reinforcers, and I was taught implicitly that it always came wrapped in experimental proof.

When I studied at the University of Chicago, my teachers promptly displayed the diversity of activities people call Science. I found that proof was supremely important only in what they called Natural Science. Other paradigms of Science depended much more heavily on something called theory.

Theory came in at least two kinds. One kind guessed that what had been proven true in many particular cases, almost without exception, would remain true in all or most future cases. For example, if the three-term contingency had proven demonstrably analytic for a long list of behaviors and stimuli, why not assume, as an act of theory, that it always would? Especially if subsequent experience required us only to change the three-term contingency to the N-term contingency? This, I was taught, was a legitimate but minor use of theory, and quite typical of Natural Science.

The second kind of theory was a way of seeming to understand, explain, or predict what you could not prove. For example, if people behaved in a remarkable variety of ways, why not invent an Id to motivate all those ways, an Ego to learn how to let the real world regulate the maximal overall satisfaction of the Id, and a Superego to explain exceptions to apparent maximal satisfaction? This, I was taught, was a legitimate and major form of theory. It was the kind of theory that was prized, honored, battled over, disseminated, and turned into show business and profit. In its best forms, its major terms were verbal inventions; by definition, they were immune to direct proof or disproof. That put proof in its properly small place, which was to confirm or disconfirm any observable deductions from the inventions. Confirmations meant the inventions were good; disconfirmations meant the inventions were even better, because disconfirmation was much too harsh a term for this event. It really was a rich encounter, one that allowed the theorist to "discover" certain details in the inventions not appreciated before. Given an apparent disconfirmation, theorists did not drop their disconfirmed theory and build a better one; instead, they "discovered" that there was more to the original theory than they had appreciated before. Explaining away disconfirmations let them claim an even greater "understanding" than before.

The only abstainers to that kind of theory were people who defined understanding as something both explanatory and proven. For them, their major reinforcer, understanding, required the conditioned establishing operation (Michael, 1995), proof.

I thanked the University of Chicago for showing me all the wonderful ways people could behave and call it Science. Again, but this time by choice, I endorsed Natural Science. My best teachers then, Leo Nedelsky, Jacob Gewirtz, and Howard Hunt, affirmed that choice, as would my next best teacher, Sidney Bijou. I was content to do the minor theory that characterized Natural Science, and to use inference only with foreboding. The dictionary definition of foreboding is an apprehension of coming misfortune.

An epiphany led me to behaviorism. I was studying mathematics and physics in graduate school, and not liking them. One day a friend in psychology asked me to explain an equation in one of his textbooks. The equation was Weber's Law. I was astounded that psychology could use differential calculus. My undergraduate brush with psychology had offered it as psychodynamic, and the media I had consumed equated it to the rather bizarre forms of insight that allowed a happy ending.

I borrowed my friend's textbook, which was on experimental psychology. It presented a natural science of behavior: It offered an experimental proof of almost everything it asserted, and labeled any unproven assertions as possibly wrong. I could not imagine anything more fascinating. I stayed up all night to read it through. With the perfect symbolism of the dawn, I decided to transfer to psychology and study the natural science of behavior, especially human behavior.

Of everything psychology subsequently showed me, the approach that most depended on natural science was that form of behaviorism called operant conditioning then, and behavior analysis later. Of all I had seen so far, operant psychology and psychophysics were the only ones constantly wedded to proof, and the subsequent behavior analysis had ambition – it aimed for scope. It tried for scope by proceeding from what it had proven to what it had not yet proven, but might. The rest of psychology did the reverse, as if the greatest honor was to arrive at something unprovable.

So to speak, I had not been raised to be a behaviorist; I had been raised to be a proof consumer. Behavior analysis apparently valued proof more than any other approach, so I joined.

A related intellectual epiphany occurred much later. In a faculty bar after a colloquium, a professor of psychology told me, with the intensity that only a very drunk academic can muster, that Hullian theory had never been disproven. I realized immediately that he was correct: it had not been disproven, because it could not be disproven. It had merely extinguished, and had left behind some betrayed subscribers. It was not their theory that had betrayed them. When they were embarrassed momentarily by some fact, they could always "discover" another fractional antedating goal response in the theory, and so explain away the fact. The betrayal had been by a shallow Science audience that simply could not commit to an ever more complex relationship. I began then to suspect that major theorists would ultimately want not research but marital therapy.

A Case Study of Two Articles by Baer, Wolf, and Risley

In 1968, Montrose Wolf, Todd Risley, and I published an article in the new *Journal of Applied Behavior Analysis*. I had the privilege of writing the first draft, and the pleasure of discovering that my coauthors largely agreed with it. The article was entitled "Some current dimensions of applied behavior analysis." It proposed and elaborated seven generative dimensions of this new discipline: The discipline should be applied, behavioral, analytic, technological, conceptual, effective, and capable of producing appropriately generalized behavior changes.

In 1987, in response to an invitation by Jon Bailey, then editor of that journal, we published another version of it. Bailey's argument was that 20 years of relevant experience might or might not change some of its arguments, and that either case would be interesting. Again, I had the privilege of writing the first draft, and the pleasure of discovering that my coauthors largely agreed with it. We postulated the same seven generative dimensions. As Bailey had supposed, their basic meanings remained the same as in 1968, but their ramifications were more elaborate and more realistic in 1987. (Bailey's proposal was wise and prudent. Any discipline that can ever state its generative dimensions should do so, and review them every 20 years to see if they have changed, and how, and argue whether that is good or bad.)

In my opinion, then and now, there were not really seven generative principles of applied behavior analysis; basically, there were only three. Those three were that the discipline be capable of producing generalized behavior changes, be capable of explaining how it did that, and be capable of proving its power and its explanations. The most urgent of these capabilities was proof. In support of that thesis, consider the seven dimensions more or less in order, to see their underlying allegiances.

Applied

The surface meaning of "applied" was that the target behavior changes would have considerable social significance and importance. Subsequent experience elaborated that surface meaning into two kinds of reasons for changing behavior: one was to find out how it could be changed; the other was that someone did not like the behavior the way it was, and did like some other way it could be. The first connoted basic science; the second connoted application, depending on the social importance of that someone.

But "applied" could have an underlying meaning as well. It could be an acid test of proof. Behavior analysis had proven the power of its principles to change convenient behaviors of convenient organisms in well controlled laboratories. Could it prove that those principles were similarly powerful for the complicated behaviors called problems in people in real trouble in real-world settings? While some applied behavior analysts were trying to be useful to their society, others were asking for a better proof of these principles. Analogous to the conceit that if you can make it in New York you can make it anywhere was the premise that if these principles work in application they work anywhere. Whatever else application was, it was a proof technique.

Behavioral

One reason for a science of behavior is that behavior exists, therefore deserves analysis, and under analysis proves lawful. But another reason is that "behavior" usually denotes something observable, and hence something in which changes are amenable to direct proof rather than inference. Proof consumers will of course prefer a psychology of directly measurable behaviors to a psychology of necessarily inferred behavioral "constructs." Whatever else behaviorism is, it is a proof technique.

Analytic and Conceptual

In 1968, "analytic" meant experimental analysis: We could prove what had caused the behavior change. "Conceptual" meant that we not only could prove what had changed the behavior, we also could explain why that technique should have changed that behavior in that way. As Skinner had daringly proved by his book, *Verbal Behavior* (1958), behavior analysis could pursue conceptual analysis quite extensively without a shred of direct proof. However, the applied behavior analysis proposed by Baer, Wolf, and Risley could not. In it, conceptual analysis might follow a proof of what had changed behavior, or might precede a proof of what would change behavior, but it never was divorced from proof. Yet proof could be divorced from it, and still be proof.

For many psychology audiences, this wedding of conceptual analysis and proof was the worst disadvantage of applied behavior analysis; for those audiences, flights of conceptual analysis should never be seriously restrained by anything as mundane as proof. But for proof consumers, this constraint was of course the greatest recommendation of this kind of applied behavior analysis. It also made clear that the proper question was about our reinforcers. For me, the question was, if I could have a natural science of behavior, why would I want an unnatural one?

Technological

A technology is a set of recipes for reliably accomplishing some outcome. The term "technological" implies forcefully that these recipes always work. Technology is therefore a body of completely described procedures accompanied by complete descriptions of the parameters necessary and sufficient for them to work reliably. That requires a lot of proof. Whatever else the development of a technology is, it is the result of a great deal of proof. Applied behavior analysis tried to develop and accumulate a behavioral technology, so it had to prove what was necessary to yield a recipe that should always work, and then prove the extent to which it did.

Effective

In 1968, the basic way to be effective was to state a measurable goal and then demonstrate how closely the procedures applied to a problem attained that goal. That was essentially a problem in proof. We usually chose the goal to be a behavior change other than a client's statement that things were better now. We knew that the relation between what people said and how they behaved otherwise could be anything; we simply did not trust their statements about behavior changes to be true, unless we had programmed them to be true – and we were not sure we could do that in a thoroughly, permanently generalized way. It seemed better to measure goal attainments directly, and to prove that they were attainments of the procedures that had been applied.

By 1987, effectiveness also meant that the goal was worth the cost of attaining it the way we had attained it. Cost meant the costs of the procedures that accomplished the goal, and any costs of everything else those procedures caused, if anything. Both were problems in proof, because it was safer to prove what were and what were not the systematic consequences of the procedures, than to infer that things must be better now and that nothing could have gone wrong.

But 20 years had shown a use for clients' statements that things were or were not better now. Sometimes behavior was changed in ways the clients or other audiences did not like. That could result in countercontrol, which severely diminished anything that could be called effectiveness, and was bad for our reputation. We began asking all relevant audiences if they liked the procedures, their outcomes, and the personnel; we meant to assess something called the social validity (Kazdin, 1977; Wolf, 1978) of our programs. We did that not just for the pleasure of positive answers, but also because negative answers might predict countercontrol. The old problem of proof arose even more severely: If we allowed unhappy audiences to lie to us about liking our procedures, we would fail to predict the subsequent countercontrol, and effectiveness and reputation would be lost. Experience suggests that audiences easily lie about what has just happened to them.

Suddenly we were in the ironic position of needing truthful talk about behavior from the very people we earlier had not trusted to talk truthfully about behavior.

Thus, to be effective had become an urgent problem in increasingly complex and difficult proofs. Those proofs required measuring everything that happened, attributing it correctly to our procedures or elsewhere, and knowing the relation between what our audiences said and what they would do later.

Capable of Appropriately Generalized Behavior Changes

Whatever else the production of *appropriately* generalized behavior changes may be, it is, if the term "appropriately" is deserved, a technology. So it must be based on a large body of proof, which is the only way to produce any technology. In 1968, it was sufficient to prove how we accomplished appropriate generalizations; in 1987, it was imperative to prove as well that our choices of "appropriate" were in fact appropriate. It also seemed reasonable to acknowledge that "generalization" was a pragmatic term, and "stimulus control" was its analytic obverse.

Overview

Of the seven generative dimensions proposed to define applied behavior analysis, six of them are essentially proof techniques or proof demanders. The 1968 "Current Dimensions" paper had been written to formalize what we were teaching our students then. The simple part of what we taught them was whatever was known then about how to change behavior. That was a mixture of procedures, a conceptualization that gave the procedures meaning, and a conceptualization about how to match procedures to problems. The complex and difficult parts of what we taught were what we and our students had to prove in the process, if our adventures were to be part of a scientific discipline. The essence of the argument was the primacy of proof.

That argument seemed worth publishing in the first issue of the *Journal of Applied Behavior Analysis*. Twenty years later, it seemed worth reaffirmation and elaboration, but mainly reaffirmation.

Important Developments in the Rise of the Behavior Therapies

For those of us who saw applied behavior analysis primarily as the acid test of the power and generality of behavior analysis, the decades after 1968 were very informative. Behavior analysis passed instance after instance of this test, and continues to pass more instances of it today. Most of us saw that some problems of people and society arose from the behavior of those people and their society. The final significance of applied behavior analysis might well be that it would show how to solve some of those problems.

Thus applied behavior analysis took a place among the already existing behavior therapies. The behavior therapies had been doing very nicely with some problems that seemed suitable for the logic of classical conditioning and its extinction, inhibition, and disinhibition. The targets of those procedures were sometimes directly observable behaviors, and sometimes were inferred internal behaviors. The inferred, internal behaviors were considered the explanation of the success seen with the external, directly observable behaviors. In that sense, these behavior therapies hardly seemed different from the psychodynamic therapies against which they were a rebellion. But because the procedures applied were conditioning-relevant procedures, and since those procedures had in the past always been applied to behaviors, using them in this clinical way must be "behavior therapy."

Sometimes those behavior therapists measured how well they had done with the measurable parts of their approach, and sometimes they proved how well they had done with those parts. They did not prove anything about their inferred internal behaviors, because they could not; they merely inferred that these internal behaviors mediated their observable success, and thereby explained it.

That practice of course attracted criticism from natural-science adherents. Rather than give up those internal explanatory events, these practitioners coined the term, "cognitive-behavior therapy." That denoted that they considered the inferred "cognitive" construct (1) explanatory; (2) either necessary or at least useful; (3) real, in that we all know that we do behave privately at times; and (4) still essentially behavioral, because the inferred behavior was presumably being controlled by procedures that traditionally controlled observable behaviors.

To solve more of the clinical problems presented, the cognitive-behavior therapists needed not that kind of explanation, but the addition of operant logic. It is easier to generate applications, especially skill-building applications, from the N-term contingency than to strain Pavlovian mechanisms, observable or not, into those pursuits. That argument is perhaps only pragmatic. But behavior analysis also offered a world view – if anyone wanted one.

So, cognitive-behavior therapies came increasingly to use techniques from the operant or subsequent behavior-analytic realm. These cognitive-behavior therapies paid applied behavior analysis one immense compliment and one casual insult. The compliment was to adopt some of its procedures. The insult was to impose an internal cognitive argument on the behavior-analytic thesis. The behavior-analytic thesis was that a complete analysis of the external environment would show when those procedures would be effective and when they would not. When the cognitive-behavior therapies gave primacy to cognitions instead, they allowed, and perhaps encouraged, a neglect of the crucial details of environmental control.

An example may be instructive: time out. Time out is probably a widely used and largely misused procedure in our society today. It is often prescribed as an acceptable way to reduce undesirable behavior, and the behavior therapies often package it with an attempt at cognitive reorganization. But behavior-analytic logic teaches that time out has no necessary or fixed function for behavior. If the reinforcement and punishment schedules of the time-out environment are worse than those of the time-in environment, time out will weaken the behavior on which it is systematically contingent, but only if the contingency is managed well. If the reinforcement and punishment schedules of the time-out environment are equal to those of the time-in environment, time out will not change the behavior on which it is systematically contingent, other than continue to detract from the time available for good programming. If the reinforcement and punishment contingencies of the time-out environment are better than those of the time-in environment, time out will strengthen the behavior on which it is systematically contingent, but only if the contingency is managed well.

A booklet is needed to explain thoroughly what those three statements mean and why they are unavoidably true. Another booklet is needed to describe how to manage a time-out contingency, or any contingency, well or badly. Another booklet is needed to describe how to assess the reinforcement and punishment schedules naturally operative in the two environments. Another booklet is needed to describe how to change those schedules to make and keep the time-out contingency effective. Another booklet is needed to describe how to record everything relevant and graph it, so as to reveal whether progress is being made, and how much; and if no progress is being made, to explain how to best choose the next procedures. Another booklet is needed to explain convincingly to the potential user of time out that the user's behavior of using it, even ineffectively, is subject to quite powerful reinforcement, especially when time out frees the user for a while from living with the behavior of the timed-out person. Another booklet is needed to explain that no behavior problem is solved merely by eliminating an undesirable behavior: The behaver needs desirable ways of gaining the reinforcers and avoiding the punishers that the undesirable behavior gained and avoided. Those desirable ways may not already exist in the behaver's repertoire. Then they will have to be taught. Many booklets are needed to describe the relevant teaching processes well enough to get them done effectively.

Usually, when time out is stolen from applied behavior analysis, its many booklets are not stolen as well. Instead, hapless parents are told that whenever their child misbehaves, they should shut the child in a room alone until the child behaves better. They are often told what lessons their child will learn from this, as if that explained why the child would behave better.

Sometimes, that painfully incomplete recommendation actually reduces the undesirable behavior; sometimes it does not. Most often, we will never know which is true, because most often, the people who recommend the technique rely on the parents' report of how well it worked. Like all behaviors, parent report is subject to control by many contingencies. Sometimes one of those contingencies is to reassure the therapist that the problem has been solved, not because it has, but because the parents want a graceful way to leave this therapist and find a different one. When you give up proof, you give up knowing.

In general, the cognitive-behavior therapies find the causation or mediation of behavior change in the cognitions of the behaver. Consequently, they target those cognitions when change is necessary, on the premise that if the cognitions change, so will the relevant behaviors. They give little attention to a second possibility, which is that if only the behaviors are targeted for change, and are changed, cognitions about them will change as well, and exactly as the therapist would like. And the usual cognitive-behavior therapy gives very little attention to a third possibility, which is, in metaphor, that behaviors and cognitions about those behaviors can lead perfectly independent lives. In only one of those three cases is the cognition a reasonable target for intervention, because only in that case is it the explanatory mediation of the change.

The need to explain what is true creates most of the arguments among the cognitive-behavior therapists and the applied behavior analysts. Their difference seems to lie primarily in where they seek explanation. Perhaps nothing is more destructive of peace among scientists than disagreements on how to explain what they know is true. Behavior analysts will look for "why" in the organism's environment; cognitive scientists will look for it inside the organism (even as they agree that its now far-distant early origins probably were in the external environment).

Some cognitive-behavior therapies use a few putative behavior-change techniques, minus their booklets, for a secondary role. They use whatever putative behavior-change techniques the therapist knows or likes for the primary behavior-change role; but they still target changes in cognitions first. They do not see the cognitive changes as behavior-change techniques; they see them as what will make the behavior-change techniques powerful. It is as if clients must first (in one notable example) accept themselves and their world as they are, and then commit themselves to some goal, because only after that will the differential reinforcement available to a therapist change their behavior in a useful, dependable way.

When applied behavior analysis is informed by the principles of radical behaviorism, it is not hostile to the notion of private behaviors, which may be all that is meant by "cognition." It is, however, congenitally cautious about inference, and extremely skeptical of the premise that inferred cognitions have any autonomy – that they are first causes. In radical behaviorism, cognitions are seen as behaviors – private behaviors, for the most part, meaning only that they are not directly measurable. But private behaviors, like observable behaviors, may play any of three roles in a problem-solving chain: (1) One chain is that a problem is presented and evokes the unobservable behaviors called cognitive processing, which in turn evoke a problem solution. In such chains, teaching or repairing the cognition should prove quite effective. (2) A second chain is that a problem is presented and evokes a solution, which in turn evokes cognitive processing of the solution and its problem. In this chain, there is very little to be gained by targeting the cognition; it is not the cause of the solution, but the result of the solution. (3) A third chain is that a problem is presented, and it simultaneously evokes a solution and cognitive processing of the problem. In this chain, the cognitive processing and the solution have no relation to each other; each is an independent response to the problem. Then targeting the cognition will again have little value in promoting a solution.

Most cognitive-behavior therapies package what their practitioners will call cognition-change techniques with what applied behavior analysts will call behavior-change techniques. When those packages succeed, the presumed cognition changes are seen as crucial, or at least functional. Yet there is no proof of that. True, in the world of practice, packages are seen as highly desirable: an addition of one kind of strength to another kind of strength, which presumably will most benefit the maximal number of clients. But in the world of proof, packages are seen as confoundings: There may well be a proof that the package is effective, but there probably is not a proof of which of its components contributed what, if anything, to that effectiveness. The experimental analysis of therapy packages is rarely done, probably because it is forbiddingly expensive and probably not cost-effective, as will be seen below.

If the three chains postulated above all can be real, then applied behavior analysts cannot logically dismiss the cognitive-behavior therapies for wasting time and effort on cognitions of unproven function in the effective package. One of those three causal chains is almost exactly what the cognitive-behavior therapists postulate is the general case. So, the question is, in the problems with which we all work, how prevalent is each of these three causal chains?

And the next question is, predictably, is the first question amenable to proof?

Perhaps many applied behavior analysts who consider that question will be reminded of an unfinished bit of proof the field still requires, namely, the possibility of a placebo effect. The problem is crystal-clear in medical research. In the evaluation of new medical therapies, a placebo control is now mandatory. Any medical procedure usually is delivered to patients with a good bit of theater: the distinctiveness of the clinic or hospital setting; the formidable equipment on every side; the white coat; the societal role; the past personal cures remembered; the promise, belief, or hope by patients, clinicians, and observers alike that this will work; the general successes steadily celebrated in the media, especially the entertainment media; the authoritative manner of medical personnel; and the extraordinary costs. Once medical researchers discovered that good theater could "cure" certain ailments by itself, they had to distinguish forevermore between medical cures on the one hand, and drama cures on the other – i.e., placebo cures that deliver all the theater but without any medical agent.

The alternative is to recognize good theater as not a placebo but as simply another medical agent, useful in some cases but not in others.

The parallel question remains unanswered for the behavior therapies and for applied behavior analysis: How much of our effectiveness is attributable to good theater, and how much to the procedures our science said should have been the effective agents? Perhaps this question has been neglected by applied behavior analysis so long because we quietly suspect that we are very bad theater. We put causation in the environment, when almost every client knows it surely must well up from within. Thereby, we are bad theater. In that context, what cognitive-behavior therapies add to applied behavior analysis looks, at least, exactly like much better theater: Cognitions are processes welling up from within! *There* is a therapy worth the ticket price.

So, one proof problem is to ask if the explicit targeting of cognitions is the appropriate placebo control for applied behavior-analytic interventions. And if, as in medical research, this presumed placebo turns out to be effective for the behavior changes we target, then once again, an alternative is to consider it not a placebo but a behavior-analytic agent, specifically, a bit of conditional-stimulus control or a conditioned establishing operation (Michael, 1995).

The question still begging for a proof is the separate contributions, if any, of what are called the cognitive and what are called the behavioral components of the typical cognitive-behavior therapy package. If that is the question, we can of course, as always, answer it at the level of theory, ideology, business, or rhetoric. But we might also consider it a problem for proof.

What would a proof require? First, it needs a null hypothesis. That hypothesis could assign priority to the cognitive procedures of the package, and ask if the behavior-change techniques add anything to them; or it could give priority to the behavior-change procedures of the package, and ask if the cognitive techniques add anything to them. I argue here that the procedures of applied behavior analysis are well known to me as behavior-change procedures, whereas the procedures of cognitive reorganization seem to me to be much less dependable, as I look back on my own education. Thus I will for myself phrase the null hypothesis as if applied behavior analysis had the priority: my null hypothesis is that the addition of cognitive procedures to behavior-analytic procedures does not alter the effectiveness of the behavior-analytic procedures. Anyone else may recast the null hypothesis to give priority to the cognitive procedures: the alternative null hypothesis is that the addition of behavioral procedures adds nothing to the effectiveness of cognitive procedures. Either way, the problem for proof is much the same; we shall either compare cognitive-only to cognitive-plus-behavioral, or compare behavioral-only to behavioral-plus-cognitive. (If we are well funded, which we never are, we can compare cognitive-only, behavioral-only, and cognitive-plus-behavioral.)

This question is about the comparative effectiveness of some therapies for a population of potential clients. That makes it an actuarial question. Actuarial questions require actuarial designs, i.e., well sampled group designs. In the most rudimentary design, we need to compare a group of clients receiving a package of behavior-change and cognition-change procedures to a group of clients receiving only the behavior-change procedures (or only the cognition-change procedures). Fortunately, or perhaps unfortunately, many research professionals have for several decades considered the proof requirements for the comparison of any Therapy A to any Therapy B. Here is a summary of what they have shown the problem requires:

- Agreement on common outcome measures, which should always include social-validity assessments made by the clients and the therapists, and procedural-fidelity assessments made of the therapists' behavior.
- A very large sample of cases representative of the populations of interest.
- Random assignment to Therapy A and Therapy B of very many cases from a homogeneous sample.

- Alternatively, matched assignment to Therapy A and Therapy B of very many cases from a heterogeneous sample, according to the variables that define them as heterogeneous.
- Assessment of each case's pleasure or resentment with the assignment, so as to analyze the degree to which any unequal distribution of these reactions across the two groups could bias the outcome.
- Random assignment to Therapy A and Therapy B of very many therapists from a homogeneously skilled population of such therapists.
- Alternatively, matched assignment to Therapy A and Therapy B of very many therapists from a heterogeneously skilled population of such therapists, according to the variables that define them as heterogeneously skilled.
- Assessment of each therapist's pleasure, resentment, confidence, or hesitation with the assignment, so as to analyze the degree to which any unequal distribution of these reactions across the two groups could bias the outcome.
- Assessment of what therapies, if any, each case has had previously, and with what effectiveness, so as to analyze the possibility that Therapy A or Therapy B does best if preceded by some Therapy X or worst if preceded by some Therapy Y, and so as to analyze the degree to which any unequal distribution of these histories across the two groups could bias the outcome.
- Assessment of the correlates of attrition of cases from each group, so as to analyze the degree to which an unequal distribution of attrition, or of reasons for attrition, across the two groups could bias the outcome.

This list of the requirements for an accurate comparison of some Therapy A to some Therapy B is not complete; it is only a good beginning.

Object Lessons for the Future

Until this kind of extraordinarily expensive proof is in hand, which would seem to be never, there is small good reason to debate the relative merits of applied behavior analysis and the cognitive-behavior therapies. There is even less reason to attempt literature-based meta-analyses of what each is best and worst at doing. Such analyses are almost inevitably full of, or susceptible to, the seriously misleading biases just listed, which a proper proof would either prevent or assess for some form of covariance analysis.

We might better simply note that each discipline has found an evolutionary niche in which it prospers and reproduces, a little, and that each probably will continue to do so for many years to come. What we cannot afford to prove about our variety can always be observed, not to see what is true, but to see what survives. And if survival (rather than correctness) is of interest, then we might well remember an old rule of evolution: A population with some diversity has a better chance of surviving some sudden change in the survival contingencies than a population with little diversity.

Are the behavior therapists and the applied behavior analysts a population? To decide that, we should first compare our disciplines to the theories, size, power, and entrenchment in our society of all the disciplines and therapies we are not. That comparison will show that, despite our diversity in where we seek explanation, we are, compared to our alternatives, very much alike, and very different from them. Similarly, simple politics will show that if we behave as one population, we will survive much better than if each of our subdivisions secedes because it considers itself the lone fraction of the population that is doing our discipline correctly.

Being scientists as well as practitioners and survivors, we probably will continue seeing small differences in where to seek explanation as crucial differences, until proof or extinction decides the matter. But to continue being survivors, we should remember to forget those differences at all survival-relevant moments.

References

Baer, D. M., Wolf, M. M., & Risley, T. R. (1968). Some current dimensions of applied behavior analysis. *Journal of Applied Behavior Analysis, 1*, 91-97.

Baer, D. M., Wolf, M. M., & Risley, T. R. (1968). Some still-current dimensions of applied behavior analysis. *Journal of Applied Behavior Analysis, 20*, 313-327.

Kantor, J. R. (1924/26). *Principles of psychology* (Vol. 1-2). Chicago: Principia Press.

Kazdin, A. E. (1977). Assessing the clinical or applied significance of behavior change through social validation. *Behavior Modification, 1*, 427-452.

Michael, J. (1995). What every student of behavior analysis ought to learn: A system for classifying the multiple effects of behavioral variables. *The Behavior Analyst, 18*, 273-284.

Skinner, B. F. (1957). *Verbal behavior.* New York: Appleton-Century-Crofts.

Wolf, M. M. (1978). Social validity: The case for subjective measurement, or how applied behavior analysis is finding its heart. *Journal of Applied Behavior Analysis, 11*, 203-214.

Chapter 15

Do Good, Take Data

Todd R. Risley
University of Alaska

The Origins of Applied Behavior Analysis

In the late 1950's, **Jack Michael**[1], a bright but irritating young psychology instructor, moved from the Universities of Kansas to Houston to Arizona State. Along the way he befriended two nontraditional students, protected them through their Ph. D. programs, and turned them loose on the world: **Teodoro Ayllon**, who produced a series of unprecedented field studies at a mental hospital in Saskatchewan for his dissertation in the late 1950's (Ayllon, 1959); and **Montrose Wolf** who proceeded to set the parameters of Applied Behavior Analysis at the Institute for Child Development at the University of Washington in 1962-64. The methods they modeled are now so universal in Applied Behavior Analysis that their origins go unnoticed:

- Systematic observation and recording by people;
- with checks for the bias and drift that are likely when people are involved.
- Repeated observations within sessions and across days, weeks and months;
- with experimental designs that go with observation and recording over time.

But their most important "breakthrough" contribution was the demonstration that naively simple immediate things were actually powerfully important in the real lives of people. You see, at the time we were all talking about the principles of learning and behavior but we thought they would be actually expressed only in complex, multiply-interactive combinations in the ongoing actions of people in real life. (In this respect, we were all "Hullians.") We assumed that their role could only be isolated and analyzed after carefully designed histories in specially arranged settings – in other words, in laboratories. And laboratory work, both 'neohullian' and 'human operant,' was flourishing in the early 1960's. It was certainly flourishing at the University of Washington. (My master's thesis research [Risley, 1964] was an example.)

(At this point, we will leave Ayllon to his own affairs, with the reminder that he was recruited by **Nathan Azrin**, an established leader in experimental psychology at the time and the most prolific contributor of good research on many topics to the experimental analysis of behavior. At Anna State Hospital Azrin and Ayllon started [Ayllon & Azrin, 1964], and Azrin developed, arguably the most productive and important program of problem-solving field research that has yet existed [cf. Azrin, 1977]).

Montrose Wolf arrived at Washington as a post-doc in the summer of 1962. There he found a flourishing setting that had been deliberately and bravely created by **Sidney Bijou**. Bijou was a full professor of psychology and was responsible for the child clinic, the preschools and the experimental-child laboratory at the Institute of Child Development, (ICD) and had established a research lab at Rainier State School. He had recruited **Donald Baer** and **Jay Birnbrauer** as new assistant professors in developmental psychology and filled the post-doc position of child clinic director with successively, **Ivar Lovaas, Ralph Wetzel**, and **Robert Wahler**. On his research and training grants, Bijou had recruited and supported a cadre of graduate students including me. (I had finished my undergraduate work at San Diego State, where **Virginia Voeks**, who had studied with both Hull and Guthrie, taught the learning and child psychology courses. She sent me to the University of Washington in 1960 where I was offered an assistantship at ICD.)

When he arrived, Wolf was assigned to teach the preschool teachers an introductory course in learning principles. The four class projects designed by Wolf and carried out by the teachers constituted the discovery of the power of social attention in real life. We had never seen or imagined such power! We were all amazed at the speed and magnitude of the effects of simple adjustments of such a ubiquitous variable as adult attention. Thirty-five years later, positive attention, praise, and "catch them being good" have become the foundation of most American advice and training for parents and teachers – making this the most influential discovery of modern psychology.

We were also enthused by the methodology that was evolving as the studies progressed: direct observation with interval recording, interobserver reliability, reversals of conditions, and concurrent multiple measures – this at a time when the only real-time data being collected were from automatic recorders in laboratory settings, and the few real-world efforts were being documented only with field notes (excepting the hospital studies of Ayllon and associates, 1959, 1962, 1963).

Among Wolf's other duties at Washington was the task of building an experimental classroom for children with mental retardation at Rainier State School, 40 miles away. He had brought from Arizona State the first seed of a system of symbolic reinforcers that he cultivated into a durable motivational system to maintain academic behavior, a system now called a *point system* or *token economy*. (He also helped design an ingenious curriculum of reading comprehension.) (See Risley, 1997 for a list of the publications from Wolf's 1962-64 work at Washington.)

Wolf also modeled ease and enthusiasm in directly interacting with the preschool children at ICD and the institutionalized people at Rainier School. There-to-fore everyone seemed to avoid such direct contact – ostensibly "to avoid research contamination," but also because no one was very good at talking to children. (I have seen many, many academics who are so obviously uncomfortable and clumsy at direct contact with the people they study that they only deal with them through graduate student proxies.)

At the same time, Montrose Wolf accepted the task of getting a vision-impaired 3-year-old boy with autism, who displayed tantrums and self-injury and who resided in a psychiatric hospital 50 miles distant, to wear his glasses. I assisted him with this little chore. Thus began a year of weekly drives that culminated in the premier study of behavior modification (Wolf, Risley, & Mees, 1964). That study introduced the procedure of contingent social isolation, labeled it *time-out* (to note the vague similarity to the laboratory procedure), and demonstrated its power with a reversal design. Thirty-five years later, and now recommended by the American Academy of Pediatrics (1998), half the parents and teachers in the United States use this nonviolent practice and call it "time-out," which makes it a social invention unmatched in modern psychology.

That work and related work over the next year (Risley & Wolf, 1964, 1967; Wolf, Risley, Johnston, Harris, & Allen, 1967) are also noteworthy in that they introduced the direct reinforcement of verbal imitation and the shaping of meaningful speech. It is amusing to recollect the exclamations of amazement from professionals – even behavioral professionals working with children with autism – at the sight of Wolf or me matter-of-factly using bites of food to shape functional speech with children with autism and mental retardation. (Ferster gave us credit for our procedures, but did not use them. Lovaas used them.)

In 1963, I had decided to pursue the deliberate development of functional speech in children with severe speech deficits as my dissertation project and, with Bijou's support, started working with a dozen children with various diagnoses (autism, retardation, aphasia). In Bijou's laboratory, I had been using the Wisconsin General Test Apparatus (a tray with choices that was pushed through a curtain when the subject was sitting with quiet hands and looking at the tray front). This I adapted into the now familiar face-to-face "discrete trial" procedure – after much reluctance because it was a "restricted operant" and not a "pure" free-operant procedure. Reflecting this preference for free-operant (initiated) behavior, I alternated periods of offering (or "baiting" the environment with) attractive things or activities and waiting for the child to initiate, before prompting a more elaborate request – the germ of the procedure Betty Hart and I later elaborated into "incidental teaching."

With Montrose Wolf's demonstrations that the things we were studying and discussing could actually be powerfully influential in simple ways in real life, the Institute of Child Development became caught up in a remarkable time of discovery and excitement. The Institute's research meeting was the high point of our week. People came from miles around to listen, to question and to present their work. It seemed that everything anyone innovated was immediately adapted by everyone else.

A steady stream of visitors came from around the world to see Bijou and the work at the Institute. Wolf and I would take them on our twice-a-week rounds to the classrooms (and labs) at Rainier State School, then to the mental hospital near Olympia and then back to Seattle. All the while we would be "double teaming" them with descriptions, argument, and excited discussions. After another day at ICD –

observing my speech shaping sessions, preschool teachers taking data and using adult attention, and Wahler's clinic staff exploring functional analyses of children's problem behaviors; and after attending one of the Institute's research meetings – most visitors departed as enthusiasts and many became active colleagues.

The Journal of Applied Behavior Analysis

Now, let us skip ahead a few years to 1966, after Baer and Richard Schiefelbusch had recruited some of us together again to the University of Kansas. The combination of field research methods and problem-solving strategies that Ayllon and Wolf modeled for us had now evolved in sophistication and example and had proliferated across the country (except peculiarly in those places where operant laboratory research was strongest). By this time, books of readings (such as Ullman & Krasner, 1965, or Ulrich, Stachnik, & Mabry, 1966) were not enough to handle the studies being generated. We needed a journal. Wolf campaigned for a journal and Sage and Academic Press each responded favorably. But by then we had convinced the Society for the Experimental Analysis of Behavior to sponsor an applied companion to the *Journal of the Experimental Analysis of Behavior* (JEAB). With the wise guidance of Azrin, the Society selected Montrose Wolf as the first editor, and he designed and named the *Journal of Applied Behavior Analysis* (JABA).

The Baer, Wolf and Risley (1968) article was written, primarily by Baer, as an attempt to differentially prompt certain types of submissions. Wolf and I intended that article to be heuristic ("Some Current") rather than definitive ("Dimensions of Applied Behavior Analysis"). He and I assumed that the enterprise of Applied Behavior Analysis would evolve – that findings would condense into knowledge and technology, and that new problems and opportunities would require and beget new research methodologies. Underlying all the suggestions in that article were the dimensions that most concerned Wolf and me:

The encouragement of field research;

- the insistence that you should seek lawfulness in the everyday activities of people; and
- the pursuit of the invention (and documentation) of new behavioral technology.

We wished to devote JABA's space and reviewing resources to the display and shaping of the analysis of those variables that actually influence what people actually do – not analogs to what people do, and not derived variables that may or may not account for what people do. Laboratory research had other outlets and audiences, such as JEAB.

We did not think that laboratory research findings are unimportant to human affairs – quite the contrary. It is just that one must study and directly analyze human affairs to know what derived principles and findings might, in fact, be relevant in any instance. We saw too many examples of behavioral researchers behaving like other psychologists and casually extrapolating their findings to account for things they actually knew little or nothing about. To quote the wisdom of Sidney Bijou,

"Before you try to explain something be sure that it, in fact, exists." As a matter of intellectual honesty or scientific integrity, if you are going to claim a relationship between laboratory findings and human affairs you need to know a great deal about both of them. And if you are going to propose some new and better way of doing something, you need to demonstrate the utility of your proposal. We saw too many studies, even behavioral studies, whose importance to human affairs were highlighted in their introduction and discussion sections but absent in their procedures and results sections.

And Wolf and I saw the exciting possibility of experimentally analyzing human affairs rather than simply passively observing them as other applied psychologists were doing. We were sure that a new era of natural science would emerge that would directly explore more and more of human affairs – and through field (and laboratory) analysis, account for that reality in progressively fewer terms. And we were sure that a new era of behavioral and social invention and technology would flourish – and through cultural insertion, continually improve human kindness and productivity. I leave it to you to judge whether we are succeeding. In the field or in the laboratory, let me remind you of our common grounds in Behavior Analysis:

Realism: There is a reality that exists independent of our perspective of it.
Natural History: The reliable description of that reality.
Natural Science: The description of reality in progressively fewer terms.
Experimental Analysis: You can understand best when you intervene ("to carve reality at its joints").
Empiricism: It is best to derive our concepts from description and analysis of reality. To paraphrase the author of Walden (one): "How much virtue there is to simply see, and to fasten words again to visible things."

My Version of Applied Behavior Analysis

Within Applied Behavior Analysis there was (and is) a diversity of emphases from *religious* to *philosophical* to *empirical*: for some, *B. F. Skinner* was the final word and their task was to defend and interpret his writings; for others, *Radical Behaviorism* was a philosophical worldview for logical analysis, explanation and debate; for many of us, *Methodological Behaviorism* was an attempt to import the simplest precepts of natural history and experimental analysis into the slow, incremental process of observing, accounting for, and improving human affairs. If allowed to oversimplify it might be said that Bijou and Baer were mostly interested in *explaining* the world, and Wolf was mostly interested in *fixing* the world. I think I was mostly interested in *exploring* the world.

I was most influenced by Skinner's urgings for the development of behavioral and social technology to overcome our genetic predilections and our cultural superstitions. In the first three chapters of *Science and Human Behavior* (1953), Skinner had outlined an agenda for an inductive, empirical approach to a science of human behavior. (Which was followed by 26 chapters of a deductive, logical explanation of uninvestigated human behavior.) In *Walden Two* (1948), Skinner had envisioned an experimenting community, constantly monitoring and redesigning itself. (Without, however, envisioning much effort to document and demonstrate the resultant technology and inventions.)

Murray Sidman's *Tactics of Scientific Research* (1960) gave me an experimental, inductive model of science that assumed that one should strive to discover things and invent technology in the largely uncharted world of behavior. And Donald Campbell (1957, 1963, 1969) gave me both the mission and the methodology to pursue reforms as experiments.

John F. Kennedy and the civil rights movement convinced me that it was not only acceptable to act on social problems – it was imperative to act. And act I have.

Although speech and language development has been a predominant theme in my career, a parallel theme has been to be a "social entrepreneur" – pursuing "openings of opportunity" to find out how the world really works by taking responsibility and trying to intervene in human problems that presented themselves to me.

After applying my molecular technology for shaping and strengthening and generalizing behaviors, I usually found myself complaining about and blaming teachers, parents, and attendants who were not doing all day long what I advised them to do. I soon found that even those who were skillful and willing often could not divert the time or attention from their other tasks – and that those other tasks, often badly designed and orchestrated, consumed more time and attention than they should. I therefore became most interested in ***human organizations***, ***human settings*** – and ***human crises***.

Organizations are arrangements of people which have activities and goals that persist though the participants may change. Organizations provide predictable establishing operations and contingencies of social and material reinforcers across all participants, and provide predictable curricula of models, prompts, instruction and reinforcement criteria for each participant. The organizations in which a person participates provide the infrastructure of predictable schedules, discriminative stimuli, contingencies and reinforcers of most of her or his daily life. People suffer when their family, social, community and work organizations are disrupted or incompetent.

Settings are the physical environments in, on, and around which human activities occur. Settings facilitate or impede human actions across every occupant by the antecedent, response effort or consequence effects of their designs. Everyone passes through many settings each day and they are at risk of failure or even injury when the settings that make up their homes, neighborhoods, streets, markets, schools, playgrounds, and work or recreation places are badly designed for their activities.

Crises are opportunities. Although many human organizations and human settings are poorly suited to the activities intended in them, there is little opportunity to explore and intervene and understand them, and to invent appropriate organizational technologies and physical designs, until a crisis comes. A crisis improves the social acceptance of *any* change. (Change is stressful and is usually resisted by affected people.) A crisis improves the political and resource support for *large* changes. (Without crisis, only small aspects of organizations and settings can be explored, probed, understood, and changed.) And a crisis provides the ethical basis for taking personal and professional responsibility and for making assertive interventions.

The following is an account of the human organizations and settings where I have taken responsibility for people in some significant aspects of their lives – with the intent of making their lives better and contributing knowledge and technology for use for others. I have omitted several projects that are too complicated or sensitive to describe, and many more where aspects of peoples' lives were not at stake (see endnote 1 for some of these), or where someone else was primarily responsible (endnote 2 names most of those people). In each of the following projects I was personally at social, political and professional risk for the conduct of the project, and ethically responsible to ensure benefits to the people being served. Although there were several other participants in each project (partially reflected in the authorship of resultant publications), **I have named only those persons who shared the risks and responsibilities of starting a project**. The term 'created' indicates a service where none previously existed; and 'begun' indicates the conversion of an existing service. In the references, the publications are listed by project.

The Child Speech-Shaping and Behavior Lab at Florida State University where parents (and graduate students and colleagues) were taught to shape and reinforce skills of severely impaired children. Created in 1964, it served a dozen children and their mothers, and was turned over to Bill Hopkins and Jack May in 1965. It was funded out-of-pocket except for space. No publications were generated although speech-shaping refinements made here were included in Risley & Wolf, 1967.

The Turner House Language Development Preschool, where welfare children attended a half-day preschool to enhance their language development. Created with **Betty Hart** in 1965, it served 200-250 children and closed in 1981 when our longitudinal study of children's everyday language experience (Hart & Risley, 1992, 1995, 1999) began. It was funded by NICHD grants. Seventeen publications were generated.

The Parent Cooperative Preschool where welfare mothers came to learn to teach their own and each other's children. Created in 1966, it served 50-60 mothers and their children and was turned over to Rodney Hammond and Don Bushell in 1969. It was funded by OEO and NICHD grants. Three publications were generated.

The Turner House Urban Recreation Project where we assumed program responsibility for an existing very problematic evening recreation center serving older children and adolescents in a high-crime neighborhood. This recreation center occupied the same building as our preschool and we took it over more or less in self-defense. Begun with **Charles Pierce** in 1970, it served several hundred children and youth (about 40 any evening) and was relocated in 1971. It was funded by the Episcopal Church and a NICHD graduate student stipend. Two publications were generated.

The Day Care Environments Project where we assumed management responsibility for the operation of two existing, typically problematic day care centers serving children of the working poor. Begun in 1970, it served about 150 children and ended in 1973. It was funded by NICHD grants and parent fees. Seven publications were generated.

The Juniper Gardens Tenant's Association Project where residents of a low-income, high-crime housing project were organized to decide on community rules and operate a community security patrol. Created in 1970 with **Edward Christophersen,** it served about 1500 residents living in 420 apartments and ended in 1974. It was funded by NIMH grants. Three publications were generated.

The Lawrence Infant Day Care Center, which provided full day care for babies, 6-weeks-old to walking. Created in 1970, it served over 300 babies, 20 at any one time, and closed in 1984. I started this program with my own son and 10 other babies and was the supervisory caregiver for much of the first summer to design the program. It was funded by USOE grants and parent fees. Five publications were generated.

The Juniper Gardens Community Recreation Center that was open each weekday after school for children from the housing project and surrounding low-income, high-crime neighborhood. Created in 1971 with **Robert Quilitch,** it served over 500 3-16 year old children, about 50 on any one day, across two years. It was funded by an NIMH grant and a USOE graduate student stipend. Two publications were generated.

The Nursing Home Activities Project that provided daily leisure activities for the aged residents of a nursing home. Begun with **Lynn McClannahan** in 1971, it served all of the ambulatory residents in a 100-bed private nursing home for 2 years. It was funded by an NIMH grant and a USOE graduate student stipend. Six publications were generated.

The Roadrunner Project that adapted the Infant Day Care operations manual into the active-treatment day program in an institution, for a group of people who were profoundly retarded and non-ambulatory. Begun with **Jim Favell** in 1971 with a 2-week working retreat by me with the team of graduate students and post-docs from my Kansas projects, the project continued to serve the 16 residents of the Roadrunner 'cottage' until 1982. With **Judy Favell,** portions of the Toddler Day Care manual were also adapted and institution-wide quality assurance systems were developed to improve services to the other 300 institutionalized residents during that time. It was funded by the State of North Carolina and NICHD grants. Ten publications were generated.

Guidelines for Behavioral Procedures in Programs for Persons with Mental Retardation was a multi-year effort to clarify behavioral procedures and their use, and suggest client protection systems to enable State programs to confidently use behavioral programming. This project started as a rational response by a State Director of Mental Retardation to real and rumored abuses in Florida institutions. In 1972, I participated in a resident abuse investigation; then throughout 1973 I site visited all Florida MR institutions; I then co-chaired and orchestrated a blue-ribbon task force of behavioral and legal experts to construct guidelines in 1974; and finally I designed professional procedures for human rights and peer review panels and coordinated their implementation from 1975-1980. This effort was variously funded by the State of Florida, the National Association of Retarded Citizens, and the Association for the Advancement of Behavior Therapy. Eight publications were generated.

The Lawrence Toddler Day Care Center that provided full day care for children from walking to 30 months old. Created with **Mike Cataldo** in 1972, it served about 150 toddlers, 20 at any one time, and closed in 1986. It was funded by USOE and Maternal and Child Health grants and parent fees. Eight publications were generated.

The Johnny Cake Child Study Center; a residential treatment program for dependent-neglected children with 3 group homes, a school, a recreation center, an office building, four houses and 10 apartments for staff (and our own fire engine) around a private lake in the mountains of Arkansas. A private philanthropy of a wealthy man, I converted the center's primary mission into developing, testing and disseminating child-rearing technology for the problems normal middle-class families would be facing in the future. In 1973, Mike Cataldo, Rusty Clark, 2 other post-docs, 7 graduate students, and 11 employees were recruited to create a large research program while serving 18 children in residential care. When business reverses ended the philanthropy of the sponsor, the Center was closed in 1976. Four publications were generated.

The Nashville Police Operations Project that developed and tested new procedures for problematic areas in the daily duties of patrol officers. Begun with **Robert Kirchner** in 1974 as an adaptation of the mechanical monitoring developed for the Juniper Gardens security patrol, the project expanded to include six graduate students (including 2 police captains in key positions) and one post-doc. The supervision, patrol, and case preparation routines of about 500 police officers serving a city of a half-million people were rationalized, refined, manualized and implemented when the project ended in 1979. It was funded by the Nashville Metropolitan police Department and DOJ and DOT grants. **Five publications were generated.**

The Nursing Home Operations Project where we assumed responsibility for the daily care routines of a 100-bed private nursing home and the meal service of a 100-bed county nursing home; adapting the engagement measures and the staff management and nutrition systems from our child day care centers. Begun in 1975 with a one-week working retreat by me and my students working as nursing aides, it served about 300 fragile elderly people over four years. It was funded by USPHS Health Services Research grants. Three publications were generated.

Individualized services for People with Mental Health or Developmental Disabilities where severely disturbed children and people with developmental disabilities in a State were provided access to care and treatment services designed for each individual. The effort began in 1984 when I arranged for some new DD funds to be targeted to serve difficult clients in individual homes – to begin building Alaska's capacity to do without a MR institution. It advanced in 1985 with **Karen Ward** and **Theda Ellis** with a statewide effort to convert all sheltered workshops into supported employment programs. It advanced in 1986 with **John VanDenBerg** and the Alaska Youth Initiative to bring back from out-of-state institutions all Alaskan children and youth and one-by-one create heavily supported homes and community lives for each of them. In 1988, to protect and extend these initiatives I temporarily became the Director of Alaska's Division of Mental Health and Developmental Disabilities. With **Mike Renfro** approximately 300 people had been provided complex services in individual arrangements when I returned to the University in 1991 – and the State's MR institution was closed, on schedule, in 1996. This effort was funded with NIMH, ADD, and VR grants and State of Alaska general funds. Two publications were generated.

Alaska's Autism Intensive Early Intervention Project where young children with autism throughout Alaska are provided state-of-the-art treatment in their homes by their parents and teams of family volunteers. Created in 1993, the project has trained the parents and volunteer teams, and orchestrated the treatment of over 50 children. With **Cheryl Risley** the program is now, finally, able to reliably ensure full-dosage treatment (pervasive assertive parenting, plus 40 hours/week of direct instruction and incidental teaching for two years, and a final year of self-control training). It is now starting 6 new children per year into a 36-month treatment regimen. Pilot work for national field trials are scheduled to begin next year. (This will probably be the last service project I will start.) It is funded by State of Alaska DD services, USDOE and ADD grants. One publication has been generated so far.

I live at 'Risley Mountain,' the homestead of four generations of my family where I was born in 1937. My strongest impression from childhood is of my mother's long hours of energetic toil at the tasks of homestead living without electric lights, indoor plumbing and central heating. To wash a load of clothes, she had to have hauled about 40 gallons of water from the spring 200 yards behind the cabin – 10 gallons at a time with a child's wagon in the summer and a sled in the winter. She had to have hand-sawn about 10 rounds of wood off of logs skidded in by horse – and split them into hand-size stove wood with a double-bitted axe. She heated the water in copper boilers on the wood stove, and dipped it into a washing machine that was powered by a gasoline engine that crankstarted and ran somewhat dependably. With a stick, she would fish out the washed clothes, garment by garment, and feed each through the motor-driven wringer into a first and then into a second tub of rinse water beside the washing machine. After a final wring, she would clothespin each garment on an outdoor clothesline and take it down when it was dry or when it began to rain, whichever came first. In the winter the clothes would freeze stiff as boards, but would slowly dry anyway even if it snowed. (We used cloth diapers then so I was probably toilet trained early.) My mother weighed 90 pounds so her approach to the heavy labors of homestead living was of small loads and many trips all day long. (But mother also read for self-improvement every evening by lamplight and talked to me of 'bookish' things. With me in tow, she would stop by to see her "school marm" friends whenever she arranged a ride into town for groceries, or to the Sunday afternoon gathering of school teachers and other educated people at the government doctor's house to listen to classical music on his victrola. And I would hear talk of foreign things like wine or sidewalks and foreign lands like France or California.)

Fortunately, when I became old enough to use a handsaw and axe, we moved closer to town and had oil for heat and propane for cooking; and I was liberated from hour-a-day firewood chores. Next we acquired a small diesel-powered 'light plant' and had electric lights to read by; thus liberating us from the daily chore of cleaning and servicing kerosene lamps and Coleman lanterns. Then rural electrification came, enabling indoor plumbing which liberated us from trips to a cold outhouse; and liberated me from my duties of hand pumping and carrying from the neighborhood well all the water used by two households. (The neighborhood joke was that we had 'walking water' that was slowly carried by a boy with his nose in a book and his head in the clouds. My fourth grade teacher wrote to me last year: "What a dreamer you were. When we had your attention you did excellent work.") From direct experience I have a favorable view of invention and technology and am less enthusiastic than most about the benefits of getting back to the 'simple' life. The simple life was simple because waking hours were consumed by hard, thoughtless, simple chores. Since I was a child on a primitive homestead, the world population has tripled – and more people than ever live lives that are harder, more stupefying, and more time demanding than my family's homestead life. And as populations grow, as people migrate and become strangers, as economies shift and work skills become obsolete, as physical inventions and technologies change the nature of daily life, the need for new behavioral and social inventions and technologies is accelerating.

In reality, we don't know much about *what* people actually do in their everyday lives. And in theory, we only know a little about *why* they do what they do. But, we do have some *tools* for finding out what people do and some *tools* to influence what people do – and so we can invent some ways to help. In the process we will learn and pass on some things that apply to other people with other problems in other circumstances – and thus add to our knowledge about what people do, why they do it, and how to help. Do *you* have enough tools to see reality clearly and change it for the better? You will never know unless you try.

References

Turner House Language Development Preschool

Greenwood, C. R., Hart, B., Walker, D., & Risley, T. R. (1994). The opportunity to respond revisited: A behavioral theory of developmental retardation and its prevention. In R. Gardner, III, D. M. Sainato, J. O. Cooper, T. E. Heron, W. L. Howard, J. W. Eshleman, & T. A. Grossi (Eds.), *Behavior analysis in education: Focus on measurably superior instruction.* Pacific Grove, CA: Brooks Cole.

Hart, B. M., & Risley, T. R. (1968). Establishing use of descriptive adjectives in the spontaneous speech of disadvantaged preschool children. *Journal of Applied Behavior Analysis, 1*, 109-120.

Hart, B. M., & Risley, T. R. (1974). Using preschool materials to modify the language of disadvantaged children. *Journal of Applied Behavior Analysis, 7*, 243-256.

Hart, B. M., & Risley, T. R. (1975). Incidental teaching of language in the preschool. *Journal of Applied Behavior Analysis, 4*, 411-420.

Hart, B. M., & Risley, T. R. (1976). Community-based language training. In T. D. Tjossem (Ed.), *Intervention strategies for high risk infants and young children.* Baltimore, MD: University Park Press.

Hart, B. M., & Risley, T. R. (1978). Promoting productive language through incidental teaching. *Education and Urban Society, 10*, 407-429.

Hart, B. M., & Risley, T. R. (1980). In vivo language intervention: Unanticipated general effects. *Journal of Applied Behavior Analysis, 13*, 407-432.

Hart, B., & Risley, T. R. (1980). *Incidental teaching of language.* Austin, Texas: PRO-ED.

Hart, B., & Risley, T. R. (1981). Grammatical and conceptual growth in the language of psychosocially disadvantaged children. In M. Begab, R. Barber, & C. Haywood (Eds.), *Psychosocial influences in retarded performance* (pp.181-198). Baltimore, MD: University Park Press.

Hart, B., & Risley, T. R. (1983). Incidental strategies. In R. L. Schiefelbuch (Ed.), *Communicative competence: Acquisition and intervention.* Baltimore, MD: University Park Press.

Reynolds, N. J., & Risley, T. R. (1968). The role of social and material reinforcers in increasing talking of a disadvantaged preschool child. *Journal of Applied Behavior Analysis, 1*, 253-262.

Risley, T. R. (1972). Spontaneous language and the preschool environment. In J. C. Stanley (Ed.), *Preschool programs for the disadvantaged: Five experimental approaches to early childhood education*. Baltimore, MD: John Hopkins University Press.

Risley, T. R. (1977). The social context of self-control. In R. B. Stuart (Ed.), *Behavioral self-management: strategies, techniques and outcome*. New York: Brunner/Mazel.

Risley, T. R. (1978). Behavior modification perspective and bilingual/bicultural education models. *Bilingual Resources, 1*, 8-10.

Risley, T. R., & Hart, B. (1968). Developing correspondence between the non-verbal and verbal behavior of preschool children. *Journal of Applied Behavior Analysis, 1*, 267-281.

Risley, T. R., Hart, B., & Doke, L. A. (1971). Operant language development: The outline of a therapeutic technology. In R. L. Schiefelbusch (Ed.), *The language of the mentally retarded*. Baltimore, MD: University Park Press.

Risley, T. R., & Reynolds, N. J. (1970). Emphasis as a prompt for verbal imitation. *Journal of Applied Behavior Analysis, 3*, 185-190.

Parent Cooperative Preschool

Jacobson, J. M., Bushell, D. B., Jr., & Risley, T. R. (1969). Switching requirements in a Head Start classroom. *Journal of Applied Behavior Analysis, 2*, 43-47.

Risley, T. R. (1968, January). Jenny Lee: Learning and lollipops. *Psychology Today*, 25.

Risley, T. R., Reynolds, N. J., & Hart, B. (1970). The disadvantaged: Behavior modification with disadvantaged preschool children. In R. Bradfield (Ed.), *Behavior modification: The human effort*. Palo Alto: Science and Behavior Books.

Turner House Urban Recreation Project

Pierce, C. H., & Risley, T. R. (1974). Recreation as a reinforcer: Increasing membership and decreasing disruptions in an urban recreation center. *Journal of Applied Behavior Analysis*, 7, 403-411.

Pierce, C. H., & Risley, T. R. (1974). Improving job performance of neighborhood youth corps aides in an urban recreation program. *Journal of Applied Behavior Analysis, 7*, 204-215.

Day Care Environments Project

Doke, L. A., & Risley, T. R. (1972). The organization of day care environments: Required versus optional activities. *Journal of Applied Behavior Analysis, 5*, 405-420.

Krantz, P., & Risley, T. R. (1977). Behavioral ecology in the classroom. In K. D. O'Leary & S. G. O'Leary (Eds.), *Classroom management: The successful use of behavior modification* (2nd ed.). New York: Pergamon Press.

LeLaurin, K., & Risley, T. R. (1972). The organization of day care environments: "Zone" versus "man-to-man" staff assignments. *Journal of Applied Behavior Analysis, 5*, 225-232.

Montes, F., & Risley, T. R. (1975). Evaluating traditional day care practices: An empirical approach. *Child Care Quarterly, 4,* 208-215.
Risley, T. R., & Twardoz, S. (1976). The preschool as a setting for behavioral intervention. In H. Leitenberg (Ed.), *Handbook of behavior modification and therapy*). Englewood Cliffs, NJ: Prentice Hall.
Risley, T. R. (1977). The ecology of applied behavior analysis. In A. Rogers-Warren & S. Warren (Eds.), *Ecological perspectives in behavior analysis.* Baltimore, MD: University Park Press.
Twardosz, S., & Risley, T. R. (1982). Behavioral-ecological consultation to day care centers. In A. Jager & R. Slotnick (Eds.), *Community mental health and behavioral ecology.* New York: Plenum Press

Juniper Gardens Tenant's Association Project

Chapman, C., & Risley, T. R. (1974). Anti-litter procedures in an urban high-density neighborhood. *Journal of Applied Behavior Analysis, 7,* 377-383.
Christophersen, E. R., Doke, L. A., Messmer, D. O., & Risley, T. R. (1975). Measuring urban problems: A brief report on rating grass coverage. *Journal of Applied Behavior Analysis, 8,* 230.
Kloss, J. D., Christophersen, E. R., & Risley, T. R. (1976). A behavioral approach to supervision. *Security Management, 20,* 48-49.

Lawrence Infant Day Care Center

Cataldo, M. D., & Risley, T. R. (1974). Infant day care. In R. Ulrich, T. Stachnik & J. Mabry (Eds), *Control of human behavior* (Vol. 3). Glenview IL: Scott Foresman.
Herbert-Jackson, E., O'Brien, M., Porterfield, J., & Risley, T. R. (1977). *The infant center: A complete guide to organizing and managing infant day care.* Baltimore, MD: University Park Press.
Risley, T. R. (1975). Day care as a strategy for social intervention [Introduction]. In E. Ramp & G. Semb (Eds.), *Behavior analysis: Areas of research and application.* Englewood Cliffs, NJ: Prentice Hall.
Twardosz, S., Cataldo, M. F., & Risley, T. R. (1974). Infants' use of crib toys. *Young Children, 29,* 271-276.
Twardosz, S., Cataldo, M. F., & Risley, T. R. (1974). Open environment design for infant and toddler day care. *Journal of Applied Behavior Analysis, 7,* 529-546

Juniper Gardens Community Recreation Center

Quilitch, H. R., & Risley, T. R. (1973). The effects of play materials on social play. *Journal of Applied Behavior Analysis, 6,* 573-578.
Quilitch, H. R., Christophersen, E. R., & Risley, T. R. (1977). The evaluation of children's play materials. *Journal of Applied Behavior Analysis, 10,* 401-502.

Nursing Home Activities Project

McClannahan, L. E. (1973). Therapeutic and prosthetic living environments for nursing home residents. *Gerontologist, 1*, 33-41.

McClannahan, L. E. (1973). Recreation programs for nursing home residents: The importance of patient characteristics and environmental arrangements. *Therapeutic Recreation, 2*, 26-31.

McClannahan, L. E., & Risley, T. R. (1973, June). A store for nursing home residents. *Nursing Homes*, pp. 8-12.

McClannahan, L. E., & Risley, T. R. (1974). Design of living environments for nursing home residents: Recruiting attendance at activities. *Gerontologist, 14*, 236-240.

McClannahan, L. E., & Risley, T. R. (1975). Design of living environments for nursing home residents: Increasing participation in recreational activities. *Journal of Applied Behavior Analysis, 8*, 261-268.

McClannahan, L. E., & Risley, T. R. (1975). Activities and materials for severely disabled geriatric patients. *Nursing Homes, 24*, 10-13.

Roadrunner Project

Cataldo, M. F., & Risley, T. R. (1974). Evaluation of living environments: the MANIFEST description of ward activities. In P. O. Davidson, F. W. Clark, & L. A. Hamerlynck (Eds.), *Evaluation of social programs in community, residential and school settings.* Champaign IL: Research Press.

Favell, J. E., Risley, T. R., Wolfe, A. F., Riddle, J. I., & Rasmussen, P. R. (1981). The limits of habilitation: How can we identify them and how can we change them? *Analysis and Intervention in Developmental Disabilities, 1*(1), 37-43.

Favell, J. E., & Cannon, P. R. (1976). Evaluation of entertainment materials for severely retarded persons. *American Journal of Mental Deficiency, 81*, 357-361.

Favell, J. E., Favell, J., Riddle, J. L., & Risley, T. R. (1983). Promoting change in mental retardation facilities: Getting services from the paper to the people. In W. P. Christian, J. Hannah & T. J. Glahn (Eds.), *Programming effective human services.* New York: Plenum

Hart, B., & Risley, T. R. (1976). Environmental programming: Implications for the severely handicapped. In H. J. Prehm & S. J. Deitz (Eds.), *Early intervention for the severely handicapped: Programming and accountability* [Monograph No. 2]. University of Oregon: Severely Handicapped Learner Program.

Jones, M. L., Favell, J. E., & Risley, T. R. (1983). Socioecological programming of the mentally retarded. In J. L. Matsen & F. Andrasik (Eds.), *Treatment issues and innovations in mental retardation.* New York: Plenum Press.

Jones, M. L., Risley, T. R., Favell, J. E. (1983). Ecological patterns. In J. L. Matson, & S. E. Breuning (Eds.), *Assessing the mentally retarded.* New York: Grune & Stratten.

Jones, M. L., Favell, J. E., Lattimore, J., & Risley, T. R. (1984). Improving independent engagements of nonambulatory multihandicapped persons through systematic analysis of leisure materials. *Analysis and Intervention in Developmental Disabilities, 4*, 313-332.

Jones, M. L., Lattimore, J., Ulicny, G., & Risley, T. R. (1985). Programming for engagement. Environmental design. In R. P. Barret (Ed.), *Treatment of severe behavioral disorders: Contemporary approaches with the mentally retarded.* New York: Plenum.

Lattimore, J., Stephens, T. E., Favell, J. E., & Risley, T. R. (1984, April). Increasing direct care staff compliance to individualized physical therapy body positioning prescriptions: Prescriptive checklists. *Mental Retardation, 22*(2), 79-84.

Guidelines for Behavioral Procedures in State Programs for Persons with Mental Retardation

Azrin, N. H., Risley, T. R., Stuart, R. B., & Stolz, S. B. (1977). Ethical issues for human services. *Behavior Therapy, 8*, v-vi.

Favell, J., Favell, J. E., Riddle, J. I., & Risley, T. R. (1981). A quality-assurance system for ensuring client rights in mental retardation facilities. In G. T. Hannah, W. P. Christian, & H. B. Clark (Eds.), *Preservation of client rights: A handbook for practitioners providing therapeutic, educational, and rehabilitative services* (pp. 345-346). New York: The Free Press Publishing Co.

Favell, J. E., & Risley, T. R., et al. (1982). The treatment of self-injurious behavior (AABT Task Force Report.) *Behavior Therapy, 13*, 529-554.

May, J. G., Jr., Risley, T. R. Twardosz, S., Friedman, P., Bijou, S. W., Wexler, D., et al. (1976). *Guidelines for the use of behavioral procedures in state programs for retarded persons.* Arlington Texas: National Association for Retarded Citizens.

Risley, T. R. (1975). Certify procedures not people. In W. S. Wood (Ed.), *Issues in evaluating behavior modification.* Champaign, IL: Research Press.

Risley, T. R., & Sheldon-Wildgen, J. (1980). Suggested procedures for human rights committees of potentially controversial treatment programs. *The Behavior Therapist, 3*(2), 9-10.

Risley, T. R., & Sheldon-Wildgen, J. (1982). Invited peer review: The AABT experience. *Professional Psychology.*

Sheldon-Wildgen, J., & Risley, T. R. (1983). Balancing clients' rights: Establishing human rights and peer review committees. In A. Bellack, M. Herson, & A. Kazdin (Eds.), *International handbook of behavior modification.* New York: Plenum Press.

Lawrence Toddler Day Care

Herbert-Jackson, E., Cross, M. Z., & Risley, T. R. (1977). Milk types and temperatures – what will young children drink? *Journal of Nutrition Education, 9*, 76-79.

Herbert-Jackson, E., & Risley, T. R. (1977). Behavioral nutrition: consumption of foods of the future by toddlers. *Journal of Applied Behavior Analysis, 10*, 407-413.

O'Brien, M., Porterfield, J., Herbert-Jackson, E., & Risley, T. R. (1979). *The toddler center: A practical guide to day care for one and two-year olds.* Baltimore, MD: University Park Press.

O'Brien, M., Herbert-Jackson, E., & Risley, T. R. (1978; 1979). Menus for toddlers in day care: A toddler taste test turns up nutritious foods suited to young preschoolers [Four part series]. *Day Care and Early Education, 6*(1), 48-53; *6*(2), 49-54; *6*(3), 49-54; *6*(4), 48-53.

O'Brien, M., Houston, A. C., & Risley, T. R. (1983). Sex typed play of toddlers in a day care center. *Journal of Applied Developmental Psychology, 4*, 19.

O'Brien, M., & Risley, T. R. (1983). Infant-toddler day care: practical considerations and applications to children with special needs. In E. M. Goetz & K. E. Allen (Eds.), *Early childhood education.* Rockville, MD: Aspen Systems.

Porterfield, J. K., Herbert-Jackson, E., & Risley, T. R. (1976). Contingent observation: An effective and acceptable procedure for reducing disruptive behaviors of young children in group settings. *Journal of Applied Behavior Analysis 9*, 55-64.

Twardosz, S., Cataldo, M. F., & Risley, T. R. (1975). Menus for toddler day care: Food preference and spoon use. *Young Children, 30*, 129-144.

Johnny Cake Child Study Center

Clark, H. B., Green, B. F., Macrae, J. W., McNees, M. P., Davis, J. L., & Risley, T. R. (1977). A parent advice package for family shopping trips: Development and evaluation. *Journal of Applied Behavior Analysis, 10*, 605-624.

Dineen, J. P., Clark, H. B., & Risley, T. R. (1977). Peer tutoring in elementary students: Educational benefits to the tutor. *Journal of Applied Behavior Analysis, 10*, 231-238.

Greene, B. F., Clark, H. W., & Risley, T. R. (1978). *Shopping with children: Advice for parents.* San Rafael, CA: Academic Therapy Publications.

Risley, T. R., Clark, H. B., & Cataldo, M. F. (1976). Behavioral technology for the normal middle-class family. In E. J. Mash, L. C. Handy, & L. A. Hamerlynck (Eds.), *Behavior modification and families* (pp. 34-60). New York: Brunner/Mazel.

Nashville Police Operations Project

Carr, A. F., Larson, L. D., Schnelle, J. F., Kirchner, R. E., & Risley, T. R. (1980). Effective police field supervision: A report writing evaluation program. *Journal of Police Science and Administration*, *8*(2), 212-219.

Currey, G. H., Carr, A. F., & Schnelle, J. (1979). Juvenile warning citations: A diversion from Juvenile Court. *FBI Law Enforcement Bulletin, 48* (12).

Domash, M. A., Schnelle, J. F., Stromatt, E. L., Carr, A. F., Larson, D., Kirchner, R. R., & Risley, T. R. (1980). Police and prosecution systems: An evaluation of a police criminal case preparation program. *Journal of Applied Behavior Analysis, 13*, 397-406.

Larson, L. D., Schnelle, J. F., Kirchner, R. E., Carr, A. F., Domash, M. A., & Risley, T. R. (1980). Reduction of police vehicle accidents through mechanically-aided supervision. *Journal of Applied Behavior Analysis, 13*, 571-582.

McNees, M. P., Egli, D. S., Marshall, R. S., Schnelle, J. F., & Risley, T. R. (1976). Shoplifting prevention: Providing information through signs. *Journal of Applied Behavior Analysis, 9*, 399-405.

Nursing Home Operations Project

Risley, T. R. (1978). Toward a system of nursing home organization and management. In T. Glynn & S. McNaughton (Eds.), *Behavior Analysis in New Zealand* (pp. 1-25). Auckland, New Zealand: University of Auckland.

Spangler, P. F., Risley, T. R., & Bigelow, D. D. (1984). The management of dehydration and incontinence in nonambulatory geriatric patients. *Journal of Applied Behavioral Analysis, 17*, 397-401.

Traughber, B., Erwin, K. E., Schnelle, J. F., & Risley, T. R. (1983). Behavioral Nutrition: An evaluation of a simple system for measuring food and nutrient consumption. *Behavioral Assessment, 5, 263-280.*

Individualized Services for People with Mental Health or Developmental Disabilities

MacFarquhar., L. W., Dowrick, P. W., & Risley, T. R. (1993). Individualizing services for seriously emotionally disturbed youth: A nationwide survey. *Administration and Policy in Mental Health, 20*(3), 165-174.

Risley, T. R., (1996). Get a Life! Positive behavioral intervention for challenging behavior through life arrangement and life coaching. In L. K. Koegel, R. L. Koegel, & G. Dunlap (Eds.), *Positive behavioral support: Including people with difficult behavior in the community.* Baltimore, MD: Paul Brookes.

Alaska's Autism Intensive Early Intervention Project

Risley, T. R. (1997). Family preservation for children with autism. *Journal of Early Intervention, 21*, 15-16.

Other References Cited

American Academy of Pediatrics, Committee on Psychosocial Aspects of Child and Family Health (1998). Guidance for effective discipline. *Pediatrics, 101*, 723-728.

Ayllon, T. (1959). *The application of reinforcement theory toward behavior problems.* Unpublished doctoral dissertation, University of Houston.

Ayllon, T. (1963). Intensive treatment of psychotic behavior by stimulus satiation and food reinforcement. *Behavior Research and Therapy, 1*,53-61.

Ayllon, T., & Azrin, N. H. (1964). Reinforcement and instructions with mental patients. *Journal of the Experimental Analysis of Behavior*, 7, 327-331.

Ayllon, T., & Haughton, E. (1962). Control of the behavior of schizophrenic patients by food. *Journal of the Experimental Analysis of Behavior, 5*, 343-352.

Ayllon, T., & Michael, J. (1959). The psychiatric nurse as a behavioral engineer. *Journal of the Experimental Analysis of Behavior, 2*, 323-334.

Azrin, N. H. (1977). A strategy for applied research: Learning based but outcome oriented. *American Psychologist, 32*, 140-149.

Baer, D. M., Wolf, M. M., & Risley, T. R. (1968). Some current dimensions of applied behavior analysis. *Journal of Applied Behavior Analysis, 1*, 91-97.

Campbell, D. T. (1957). Factors relevant to the validity of experiments in social settings. *Psychological Bulletin, 54*, 297-312.

Campbell, D. T. (1969). Reforms as experiments. *American Psychologist, 24*, 409-429.

Campbell, D. T., & Stanley, J. C. (1963). *Experimental and quasi-experimental designs for research.* Chicago: Rand McNally.

Hart, B., & Risley, T. R. (1992). American parenting of language-learning children: Persisting differences in family-child interactions observed in natural home environments. *Developmental Psychology, 28*(6), 1096-1105.

Hart, B., & Risley, T. R. (1995). *Meaningful differences in the everyday experiences of young American children.* Baltimore, MD: Paul Brookes.

Hart, B., & Risley, T. R. (1999). *The social world of children learning to talk.* Baltimore, MD: Paul Brookes.

Kazdin, A. (1992). *Personal communication.*

Risley, T. R. (1964). Generalization gradients following two-response discrimination training. *Journal of the Experimental Analysis of Behavior, 7*, 199-204.

Risley, T. R. (1997). Montrose M. Wolf: The origin of the dimensions of Applied Behavior Analysis. *Journal of Applied Behavior Analysis, 30*, 377-381.

Risley, T. R., & Wolf, M. M. (1964). Experimental manipulation of autistic behaviors and generalization into the home. Paper read at American Psychological Association, Los Angeles.

Risley, T. R., & Wolf, M. M. (1967). Establishing functional speech in echolalic children. *Behaviour Research and Therapy, 5*, 73-88.

Sidman, M. (1960). *Tactics of scientific research.* New York: Basic Books.

Skinner, B. F. (1948). *Walden two.* New York: Macmillan.

Skinner, B. F. (1953). *Science and human behavior.* New York: Macmillan.

Wacker, D. P. (1998). Editorial. *Journal of Applied Behavior Analysis, 31*, 511.

Wolf, M. M., Risley, T. R., Johnston, M., Harris, F., & Allen, E. (1967). Applications of operant conditioning procedures to the behavior problems of an autistic child: A follow-up and extension. *Behaviour Research and Therapy, 5*, 103-111.

Wolf, M. M., Risley, T. R., & Mees, H. L. (1964). Applications of operant conditioning procedures to the behavior problems of an autistic child. *Behaviour Research and Therapy, 1*, 305-312.

Ullman, L. P., & Krasner, L. (Eds). (1965). *Case studies in behavior modification.* New York: Holt, Rinehart & Winston.

Ulrich, R., Stachnik, T., & Mabry, J. (Eds.). (1966). *Control of human behavior.* Glenview, IL: Scott Foresman.

Footnote

[1] The names of the co-risktakers have been made bold as I wish to mark my high value of such risk and responsibility taking.

Endnotes

***Endnote 1:* Some projects that did not serve specific people continue to serve our profession.**

The JABA editorial procedures system was developed and manualized with **Nancy Krompotich** in 1972 to make the young *Journal of Applied Behavior Analysis* less vulnerable to management inexperience of editors. The system remains pretty much intact across 8 generations of editors (Wacker, 1998) and has spread to other journals (Kazdin, 1992).

The journal *Behavior Therapy* had been published by Academic Press in an ambiguous relationship with the Association for Advancement of Behavior Therapy (AABT) which was responsible for its content. As the journal had grown, the publisher's extra page charges had become a financial drain on the Association. In 1975, with **Elizabeth Kovacs,** I set up AABT's in-house publishing capacity and carefully extracted the journal from a surprised Academic Press. *Behavior Therapy* has contributed 50-100 thousand dollars to AABT every year since then.

In 1976 the area of behavior & medicine was dominated by psychopharmacology and other emphases on "biological intervention with behavior outcomes." With the acquiescence of the AABT board, I allocated my AABT president's discretionary resources and the new journal income to found the Society of Behavioral Medicine (SBM) with **Elizabeth Kovacs** and **Mike Cataldo,** and to operate it from the AABT offices until it could support itself. SBM's primary emphasis was and continues to be "behavioral interventions with health outcomes."

When I returned to Alaska, I found that the University of Alaska in Anchorage had no experience or administrative structure for providing direct services in the community. With **Karen Ward** and **John VanDenBerg,** I obtained office space in the community and a funding appropriation from the State, and in 1986 created the Mental Health Services Training Center that was later renamed the Center for Human Development (CHD). With space and funding, the Center was able to become a University Affiliated Program on Developmental Disabilities when UAPs were funded for new states in 1991. I created a separate non-profit arm of the CHD:UAP in 1994 to insulate the University from liability, and thereby enable the development of risky services needed in the State. These organizations continue to expand the size and number of innovative programs they provide to people with disabilities in Alaska.

Endnote 2: **Beyond my own projects, I have been invited to consult and collaborate on projects where others were responsible and were striving to create or improve services to people.**

I contributed to and learned from one or more projects not otherwise mentioned in this chapter with each of the following: (* are now deceased) **Deborah Allness, Roy Anderson, Michael Baring-Gould*, Thomas Bellamy, Susan Berenz, Howard Bess, Jay Birnbrauer, Donald Bushell, Michael Cataldo, Walter Christian, David Clugston*, Jan Coulter, Thomas Creer, Rick Crowley, George Currey*, Norman Dinges, Peter Dowrick, Marie Doyle*, S. K. Dunn, Carl Dunst, Siegfried Engelmann, Stephen Fawcett, James Favell, Judith Favell, Dee Foster, David Giles, Thomas Glennan, E. L. Glynn, Michael Graf*, Robert Gregovitch, June Groden, Vance Hall, Betty Hart, Leo Hamerlynck, Gerald Hannah, Barbara Henjum, Jaime Hermann, John Hess, Robert Horner, Michael Jones, Kiyo Kitahara*, Elizabeth Kovacs, Martha Kramer, Patricia Krantz, Albert Kushlick, Charles Lester, Robert Liberman, Ivar Lovaas, Kayleen Lowe, John Lutzker, Louis Malenfant, Ken Mazik, Jack McCallister, Lynn McClannahan, Gail McGee, Hugh McKenzie, Stuart McNaughton, Pat McNees, Terry Olson, Linda O'Neall, John Ora*, Maris O'Rourke, Mike Renfro, Iverson Riddle, Todd M. Risley, Fred Robrecht, Thomas Sajwaj, Juan Jose Sanchez-Sousa, Matthew Sanders, Richard Schiefelbusch, Saleem Shah*, Jan Sheldon, James Sherman, Mike Strouse, Richard Stuart, Terry Trask, Dorothy Truran*, Sandra Twardosz, Gary Ulicny, John VanDenBerg, Karen Ward, Roger Weed, David Weikert, Bud Wetzel*, Montrose Wolf.**

Chapter 16

Application of Operant Conditioning Procedures to the Behavior Problems of an Autistic Child: A 25-Year Follow-Up and the Development of the Teaching Family Model

Montrose M. Wolf
University of Kansas

The first thing that I would like to describe is how I first got into the field of behavioral psychology. Jack Michael arrived at the University of Houston in 1957. The first description of Jack by a fellow student was, "He obviously can't be a very good teacher because he dresses so badly." I had also heard the student rumor that Jack had been asked to leave Kansas University because he was teaching Skinner. Then Jack arrived in his strangely colored short pants and flip-flop sandals. And, to make matters worse, Jack announced that the course would concentrate on animal research! I began looking through my timetable for a course more in line with my neo-Freudian interests. But, Learning Theory was a required course for psychology majors. However, I did arm myself with drop slips in case the course became too painful. I was already thinking about changing my major to philosophy, anyway.

Jack, rather than choosing something interesting like Carl Jung, assigned Keller and Schoenfeld's *Principles of Psychology* (1950) as our textbook. The first few chapters did turn out to be fascinating. By the third chapter I was converted. I converted not because they had all the answers. But, because their natural science approach seemed to hold the greatest promise among the psychological systems for achieving the answers. In addition, Jack was also excited about the application of behavioral principles to important human problems. Jack described Ted Ayllon's pioneering research at Saskatchewan Hospital. At Jack's suggestion, I read Skinner's newest book *Science and Human Behavior* (1953) which made a strong case for the application of behavioral principles to human problems.

I described my conversion to my girlfriend, Sandra, who was also a psychology major. She was horrified! But, she sat in on some lectures and became a convert, too.

Others became Jack's students. Ted Ayllon published with Jack the pioneering applied behavioral study: The Psychiatric Nurse as a Behavioral Engineer (JEAB, 1959). That paper was the model for applied research. It showed the use of mediators, in this case the Psychiatric Nurses, who were trained to apply the behavioral principles, working with the behavior analyst in the psychiatric institution. And, how mediators could be used in other settings like schools and institutions for other populations. Finally, others also became members of the group which met in Jack's living room and planned how to save the world through behaviorism, including John Mabry, Pat Corke, Leland Johnson, Jerry Short, Lee Meyerson, Nancy Kerr, Lloyd and Polly Brooks (both deceased), and Sam Toombs (deceased).

Jack shared his library with us, so we began reading more Skinner and the early issues of JEAB. We helped to celebrate the approval by APA of Division 25.

Jack also generously shared his research equipment. I built a rat box to study the effects of combined discriminative stimuli. Jack let us use the equipment at night. We were responsible for rewiring the equipment so it would be ready for Jack's research the next day. Unfortunately, there were times when we didn't rewire the equipment correctly. Jack would make cracks about our long line of serendipitous experiments.

One day Jack got a call from friends at Arizona State University. Their plan was to establish ASU as the first psychology department specializing in behavioral research, theory, and application. Some of us went to ASU as graduate students and helped to set up *Fort Skinner in the desert*. Unfortunately, the new chairperson began receiving criticism from other departmental heads about the ASU department being too narrow. The new chairperson began referring to us students as poorly trained *relay raconteurs*.

At ASU, during the good days, we had lots of exciting courses. For example, we got to read neat stuff like Bijou and Baer's *Child Development* (1961).

We also read a very interesting theoretical analysis by Charles Ferster (1961). He discussed how the behavior problems of childhood autism might be due to subtle positive reinforcement, punishment, and extinction contingencies. Ferster and DeMyer (1961) also published a very important laboratory study about autistic children. They showed that neutral stimuli could be conditioned in the laboratory.

We also read about the fascinating human operant research taking place in institutions. Few had made the leap from the lab to the other side of the one-way glass or to schools or to homes. In fact, some were of the opinion that such a leap was premature and unwise because we didn't know enough, that we needed to wait for more basic human operant research.

In 1962, Sidney Bijou visited ASU. He described to us his interest in taking this leap. Sid described his exciting programs and opportunities. For example, to teach a behavioral course to pre-school teachers who were asked to convert from a psychodynamic to a behavioral orientation. And, a research opportunity to work with Jay Birnbrauer on a new behavioral classroom at Rainier State School for the developmentally disabled. We described to Sid the token economy research that we had carried out with pre-school children (Staats, Staats, Schultz, & Wolf, 1962).

So, in 1962, Sid hired me on his NIMH grant. I arrived at the University of Washington on the first day of July. I had been there less than two weeks, when Sid called Todd Risley, a graduate student, and me into his office. Sid had just completed a conversation with Jerman Rose, the Director of the Childrens' Psychiatric Hospital at Fort Steilacoom, Washington. Jerman Rose wanted us to work with a child with the following characteristics.

A list of Dicky's Characteristics:

- He was 3 1/2 years old.
- He had developed normally until about nine months old.
- He was diagnosed as autistic.
- He developed a high rate of self-destructive temper tantrums ("He was a mess, all black and blue and bleeding." His parents reported after a typical tantrum.)
- No normal language (Echolalic).
- Not toilet trained.
- Did not go to bed at night. (Tantrumed unless a parent stayed up with him).
- Did not eat at the table (Grazed).
- Because his problems were so severe, permanent institutionalization had been recommended to the parents.
- Cataracts had been removed from the lenses of both eyes.
- The ophthalmologist predicted that unless he begins wearing glasses within the next six months he would permanently lose his macular vision.
- He had been hospitalized for three months and they had not taught him to wear his glasses.

No one had used behavioral clinical procedures before with autistic children. So, this looked like a tough case. Especially in the hostile environment of a psychoanalytic childrens' hospital. Todd and I pointed out these concerns to Sid. But, Sid kept replying that we should wait and see what was up before making a final decision.

And Sid was right, of course (Wolf, Risley, & Mees, 1964; Wolf, Risley, Johnston, Harris, & Allen, 1967).

You may be wondering what happened to the pre-school teachers in the behavioral course that I taught? Well, it went better than you might expect. Todd and I began our weekly trips to Dicky's hospital that summer. So, we took the pre-school teachers and others on our weekly trips and presented Dicky's data at every class session. The teachers began looking for opportunities to replicate the Dicky study by behaviorally analyzing the normal behavior problems of the pre-school children in their classrooms. They began with "regressed" crawling behavior (Harris, Johnston, Kelly, & Wolf, 1964). And, then they moved to isolate behavior (Allen, Hart, Buell, Harris, & Wolf, 1964), operant crying (Hart, Allen, Buell, Harris, & Wolf, 1964), and motor skills (Johnston, Kelly, Harris, & Wolf, 1966).

Because the teachers made the conversion we were able to provide Dicky with a strong behavioral treatment program for the next two years which made him ready for special education classes at school. And, we were later informed that he went into regular classes. He graduated from high school as well.

His IQ also changed. During his early years he was untestable. A Washington psychologist sent us a copy of a report in 1985 when Dicky was 26 years old that included an IQ test. According to that psychologist Dicky's WAIS Verbal IQ score was 98.

Todd has visited with Dicky in person and on the phone. Since high school he has lived independently and has had a series of jobs.

You may be wondering what happened at the new behavioral classroom at Rainier State School for the developmentally disabled with Jay Birnbrauer? It was also exciting. We were able to set up a powerful demonstration program (Birnbrauer, Bijou, Wolf, & Kidder, 1965; Birnbrauer, Wolf, Kidder, & Tague, 1965).

We can draw some conclusions about the impact of these studies. First, time-out has been widely disseminated. According to Hart and Risley (personal communication), about half the teachers and parents in their study use time-out as a non-violent disciplinary procedure. Furthermore, the American Academy of Pediatrics published an article in the journal *Pediatrics* encouraging pediatricians to recommend that parents use 'time outs' and positive reinforcement instead of spanking when children misbehave (*Pediatrics*, 1998).

Finally, the behavioral autism treatment program has been widely adapted by others.

The Development of the Teaching-Family Model

As one of the founders of the Teaching-Family model, I was honored for our team's contribution to the success of Boys Town's programs with the Boys Town's Father Flanagan Award for Service to Youth, 1996. We were also honored by our recent awards from The Society for the Advancement of Behavior Analysis Award for Distinguished Service to Behavior Analysis for 1998, and the American Psychological Association, Division 25, Award For Outstanding Applied Research – For innovative and important research on applications of behavioral principles to address socially significant human behavior, 1998.

We have described the history of the model's development in a couple of recent articles. One description appears in Wolf, Kirigin, Fixsen, Blase, & Braukmann (1995):

> A case study in program development and refinement is presented. We describe the Teaching-Family model and its history, the original research goal of developing a community-based program that was more humane, more effective in teaching community-living skills, and less expensive than the traditional large state institutions prevalent when we began. We present the research on the components of the model and the outcome research on the complete model.

We share the serious problems that occurred when we attempted to replicate the program in other communities. We argue that the subjective consumer feedback questionnaire (and the other components of the comprehensive quality refinement system that have evolved over the past 25 years) have played an important role in the survival and success of the model. We recommend that people interested in increasing the quality and survival rates of their human services programs may want to consider developing a similar technology driven by systematic reciprocal feedback from consumers and line staff instead of relying on unplanned consumer and staff feedback, as many programs do now. Such feedback helps us to continue improving the quality of the always evolving Teaching-Family model (p. 11-12).

References

Allen, K. E., Hart, B., Buell, J. S., Harris, F. R., & Wolf, M. M. (1964). A study of the use of reinforcement principles in a case of "isolate" behavior. *Child Development, 35*, 511-518.

Ayllon, T., & Michael, J. (1959). The psychiatric nurse as a behavioral engineer. *Journal of the Experimental Analysis of Behavior, 2*, 323-334.

Bijou, S. W., & Baer, D. M. (1961). *Child development*: A Systematic and Empirical Theory (Vol. 1). New York: Appleton-Century-Crofts.

Birnbrauer, J. S., Bijou, S. W., Wolf, M. M., & Kidder, J. D. (1965). Programmed instruction in the classroom. In L. P. Ullmann & L. Krasner (Eds.), *Case studies in behavior modification* (pp. 358-363). New York: Holt, Rinehart, & Winston.

Birnbrauer, J. S., Wolf, M. M., Kidder, J. B., & Tague, C. E. (1965). Classroom behavior of retarded pupils with token reinforcement. *Journal of Experimental Child Psychology, 2,* 219-235.

Ferster, C. B. (1961). Positive reinforcement and the behavioral deficits of autistic children. *Child Development, 32*, 437-456.

Ferster, C. B., & DeMyer, M. K. (1961). The development of performances in autistic children in an automatically controlled environment. *Journal of Chronic Diseases, 13*, 312-345.

Hart, B. M., Allen, K. E., Buell, J. S., Harris, F. R., & Wolf, M. M. (1964). Effects of social reinforcement on operant crying. *Journal of Experimental Child Psychology, 1*, 145-153.

Harris, F. R., Johnston, M. K., Kelly, C. S., & Wolf, M. M. (1964). Effects of positive social reinforcement on regressed crawling of a nursery school child. *Journal of Educational Psychology, 55*, 35-41.

Johnston, M. K., Kelly, C. S., Harris, F. R., & Wolf, M. M. (1966). An application of reinforcement principles to the development of motor skills of a young child. *Child Development, 37,* 370-387.

Keller, F. S., & Schoenfeld, W. N. (1950). *Principles of psychology: A systemic text in the science of behavior.* New York: Appleton-Century-Crofts.

Skinner, B. F. (1953). *Science and human behavior*. New York: Macmillan.

Staats, A. W., Staats, C. K., Schultz, R. E., & Wolf, M. M. 1961). The conditioning of textual responses using "extrinsic" reinforcers. *Journal of the Experimental Analysis of Behavior, 5,* 33-40.

Wolf, M. M., Kirigin, K. A., Fixsen, D. L., Blase, K. A., & Braukmann, C. J. (1995). The Teaching-Family model: A case study in data-based program development and refinement (and dragon wrestling). *Journal of Organizational Behavior Management, 15* (11-68).

Wolf, M. M., & Risley, T. R. (1965). Application of operant conditioning procedures to the behavior problems of an autistic child. *Behavior Research and Therapy, 1,* 302-312.

Wolf, M. M., Risley, T. R., & Mees, H. (1964). Application of operant conditioning procedures to the behaviour problems of an autistic child. *Behavior Research and Therapy, 1,* 305-312.

Wolf, M. M., Risley, T. R., Johnston, M. K., Harris, F. R., & Allen, K. E. (1967). Application of operant conditioning procedures to the behavior problems of an autistic child: A follow-up and extension. *Behavior Research and Therapy, 5,* 103-111.

Chapter 17

The Active Unconscious, Symptom Substitution, & Other Things That Went 'Bump' in the Night

Gordon L. Paul
University of Houston

Introduction and Overview

The title of this chapter signifies theoretical constructs that were relevant as my thinking gradually shifted from a psychoanalytic orientation to a behavioral point of view. The "active unconscious," "symptom substitution," and "other things that went 'bump' in the night" all refer to concepts and principles that I once believed were the way to understand human behavior and the best ways to go about changing it. They also reflect beliefs that had to be painfully abandoned in the face of firm evidence of their spuriousness and lack of utility.

Even though I now use behavioral conceptualizations and behavior therapy techniques, I do not call myself a behavior therapist. The functional analysis of behavior is a major part of what I now do, but I do not call myself a behavior analyst. The fact is that I abhor the categorical restrictions, frequent cult-like trappings, and pigeonholing of *any* "school" approach. This position has been personally costly in many ways. For example, I belong to neither the Association for the Advancement of Behavior Therapy (AABT) nor the Association for Behavior Analysis (ABA)–and some of my most respected friends have been key players in these organizations. Beyond missing the camaraderie, my failure to regularly network through such groups has resulted in fewer people being familiar with my work and that of my coworkers than otherwise would have been the case.

On the other hand, the lack of affiliation with any doctrinaire school has been professionally valuable for both research and clinical practice. It has allowed freedom to easily move between the classical and instrumental sides of the behavioral fence. It has allowed me to rationally select or combine principles and procedures with the greatest utility for the problems I address at any given time, including those problems that are called cognitive ones.

This chapter fulfills the editors' request for coverage of four topics: (1) an intellectual autobiography; (2) observations of developments during the "behavioral revolution;" (3) an historical case study of one of my publications; and (4) reflections on possible object lessons for the future. Rather than a linear sequence, the topics are blended as I describe a personal odyssey that combines reconstruction of my developmental autobiography with observations of my own paradigm shift.

For more than 30 years my work has emphasized institutionalized populations, observational assessment, and treatment of psychoses (e.g., Mariotto, Paul, & Licht, 1995; Paul, 1987b; Paul, 2000; Paul & Lentz, 1977, 2001). These efforts have drawn more heavily on the work of people identified with applied behavior analysis than did my earliest work on anxiety-related problems.

Rather than focus on more recent work, I selected for the case study the publication reporting an examination of insight versus desensitization in psychotherapy (Paul, 1966). The investigation was completed for my Ph.D. dissertation in 1964. This publication was chosen because of its developmental importance for me as well as for the field. Following the case study of the selected publication, I return to more autobiography with developmental significance before offering reflections and recommendations based on these experiences.

Intellectual Autobiography

Official Academic Genealogy

My official academic genealogy is presented in Figure 1. This is a lineage of major professors of which anyone could be proud – tracing back to William James. Surprisingly, these academic ancestors all demonstrate the approach to science that Nickles (2001) ascribes to James. I view Nickles' five points of contrast as continua of relative focus rather than mutually exclusive categories, but the group does share the following characteristics. All emphasized problem solving over abstract truth seeking as a goal. All emphasized pragmatic over foundational-epistemological

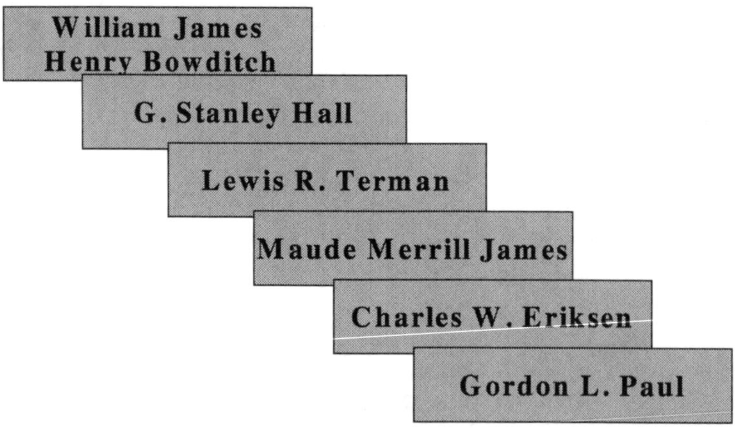

Figure 1. Official academic genealogy.

selection of problems for study. All made heavy use of heuristic rather than just epistemic appraisal of knowledge. All showed a forward-looking prospective focus rather than a backward-looking historical one. Science for this line of my academic ancestry was clearly an enterprise that should make a difference to societal problems and to the lives of real people. It is for me as well.

For his fifth point of contrast, Nickles (2001) also ascribes to James an emphasis on case-based thought and practice over thoroughgoing rule-based inquiry. (Usage of "case-based thought" and "case study" in this context does not include single-subject behavior analysis, which would be considered "rule-based inquiry.") This portrayal may characterize the majority of James's own work. However, the remainder of the group appears to have used both case-based and rule-based inquiry, depending on whether the task involved the context of discovery or the context of justification (Reichenbach, 1938). Within the context of discovery, ideas and hypotheses were derived from many sources, including traditional case studies. Such case studies have been used for generating novel concepts, for teaching, for clarification, and for casting doubt on widely accepted practices. (Ullmann & Krasner, 1965, p. 44-49, provide an excellent exposition on such use of case studies.) However, within the context of justification, my academic ancestors and I seem to be in agreement that data are an absolute requirement. Evidence from rule-based inquiry is necessary to separate facts from opinions and speculations.

Developmental Prelude

My academic genealogy shows a line of influence that is part of the public record. The more important aspects of an intellectual autobiography, of course, are not yet in the public domain. Newly entering professionals often seem to believe that the senior people in any discipline were born with a grand plan for accomplishment. That grand plan is further presumed to be one that was based on the senior person's current conceptual approach or research program. Senior people may be viewed as having always been as they currently appear. Obviously such notions are not true.

A broad range of developmental experience influences each person's intellectual approach, accomplishments, and ultimate status. These include nonacademic life experiences, chance events, choices based on irrelevant factors, and lucky or unlucky timing as well as formal academic influences. Ultimately, consequences interactively shape the approach that becomes a basis for some rational professional action. The following excursion is an attempt to summarize a number of these experiences that now seem important to my professional development.[1]

1940-1954: Public schools and community college in Marshalltown, IA. Elementary through high-school years and 1 year of community college were spent in the public schools of Marshalltown, IA – a town with less than 30,000 population. I had no notion that there were competing orientations and schools of psychology during this period. In fact, I was hardly aware that the discipline of psychology existed. I majored in life, love, and music – attending school full time while working part-time and summer jobs. Jobs included work as a paperboy, baby sitter, caddy, butcher's apprentice, warehouse and field laborer, construction worker, theatre usher and doorman, mechanic, truck driver, salesman, and musician.

Always taller than my peers, I achieved my adult height (6 ft. 4 in.) by the time I was 13 years old. This allowed me to pass as much older and work in travelling dance bands and jazz groups. That work provided many maturing experiences. I organized 5-piece and 7-piece combos and a 12-piece dance band during my last 2 years of high school and first year of college – booking whatever group the employers could afford. Family and friends were the most important developmental influences during this period.

My mother, Ione Hickman (Perry), taught piano and was the single teacher in a one-room school for 1st through 8th grades. She taught many years with a 2-year associate's certificate. While continuing to teach full time, she earned the B.A. degree in 1961, followed by advanced study, certification, and acclaim in special education and sex education. Her reluctant retirement from "going out" to work came in 1991, following a total of 54 years in the classroom and reaching the forced-retirement age in two separate school systems. Since her last formal retirement, she has continued to teach piano and tutor special-education students at home – being 89 years young at the time of this writing. This special lady provided a model of excellence and compassion for others that has been a major influence in everything I have tried to do.

My father, Leon D. Paul, ended formal schooling in the 6th grade when he was expelled for striking the principal during an argument about driving a car to class. His life was a troubled one involving hard work, fast cars, chain smoking, and heavy drinking as well as extremes of both hypermanic activity and severe depression. After losing the family farm in 1939, he worked group piecework in a local factory until his sudden death, under questionable circumstances, at age 40. He had difficulty expressing affection and was a strict disciplinarian who, under the influence of alcohol, often became physically abusive. He was fond of saying, "Do as I say, not as I do." When sober, he demonstrated a brilliant mind, natural leadership, charm, and a genuine concern for others. At those times, family and friends adored my father and it was fun to be with him. Friendships were far more important to him than career advancement or financial gain. He was an anti-snob for whom "being one of the guys" meant refusing elected offices and promotions to management positions. Explicit advice from my father came in a talk at the time of my parents' divorce. I was a sophomore in high school. "Always remember that your word is your bond," and, "Do whatever you want to do, but be the best damned one in town." I have tried to follow his advice in those regards. Unfortunately, we only became close after I could relate to him as an adult – just before his death in 1954.

Although an only child, I was raised in a large extended family of cousins, aunts, uncles, and maternal grandparents. Nobody had much money. Most were employed as tradesmen, factory workers, sales people, clerical workers, or sharecroppers. One uncle was a military pilot. Many were involved with music, some professionally. The family provided multiple models for hard work, assumption of personal responsibility, and helping one another. These ethics were so strongly shared that they seldom needed verbalization.

There were also extremes of values and behavior on many dimensions. Some family members were ministers, including a "hellfire and damnation" evangelical preacher. Some were outspoken atheists. Most were quiet Quakers, Christians, or agnostics. Politically they spanned the gamut from far left-wing liberals to arch right-wing conservatives. My grandmother was president of the Women's Christian Temperance Union while most in the following generations were heavy users of alcohol. Some banned playing cards from their homes while others were inveterate gamblers. The family had its share of folks who could be called "philanderers" and those who could be called "prudes." Large family reunions were enjoyable events that provided demonstrations of tolerance as well as multiple examples of conflict resolution. They also showed selective avoidance of problem topics, based on respect for others.

Several close family members endured chronic and painful physical conditions (e.g., cancer, arthritis, heart disease, surgeries). Many of us had to deal with premature deaths of family members from disease, accidents, and a suicide. There were a few known instances of serious child abuse, several failed marriages, and both an aunt and a close cousin whose emotional problems were severe enough that they were hospitalized with diagnoses of schizophrenia. The beneficial role of social support from family and friends was much in evidence here.

My experience with behavioral and emotional problems during this early developmental period resulted in a strong desire. I wanted to understand the distressing actions, thoughts, and emotions of troubled and troubling loved ones, in particular, as well as those of people in general. However, entering a profession to try to gain this understanding and to do something about it had not yet occurred to me. Rather, I was committed to a career as a professional musician.

1954-1958: U. S. Navy, music school, bands, and San Diego City College. A stint of military service was required in those days. After discovering that my height excluded me from becoming a fighter pilot, I auditioned for and gained admission to the U.S. Naval School of Music in Washington DC. This provided a way of jointly meeting my military obligation and furthering my career in music. I majored in music, minored in business, and discovered psychology as an avocation during my 4-year enlistment as a contract musician in the U. S. Navy. My last tour of duty helped to change career focus from music to psychology.

During my first leave, in-route from basic training to the music school, I renewed contact with a young woman in Marshalltown whom I briefly had met before entering the navy–Joan M. Wyatt. Following a whirlwind courtship, she became my wife on Christmas Eve, 1954, and returned with me to Washington. We lived off base in a one-room apartment, sharing the lone bathroom with no less than 15 other people. She worked in the post-exchange office, attended most of the duty jobs that I played, and made me the envy of every sailor on the station. For 46 years,

Jo Paul has been my lover, partner, and best friend – participating in most of the decisions that influenced my personal and professional development.

Familiarity with performance anxiety is the most memorable among many experiences in music school that had impact on my later work as a psychologist. At the music school, instruction, practice, rehearsals, and duty jobs with navy bands (concerts, parades, shows, and dances) entailed a complete immersion in music, 18 hours a day, 7 days a week (not unlike the commitment required of graduate school in psychology). A performance exam on each student's major instrument was required prior to graduation (tenor sax for me). This exam determined the quality of the next assignment and whether or not any choice was allowed among alternatives. It was conducted in a room that was accessible only by a spiral staircase to the third floor of the music school. Everyone called it the "ivory tower." The student performed prepared pieces to demonstrate virtuosity, followed by demonstration of whatever the examiners might request – such as transpositions, sight-reading, or riffs. Examiners included the commandant of the school and heads of the section (e.g., reeds) and groups (jazz, symphonic) as well as each student's individual instructor.

The context of this exam already maximized its threat value – especially when an outcome could be 2 years separation from my new bride in some foreign country with a foul climate. To make matters worse, a recent oral infection had been followed by extraction of four impacted wisdom teeth. I had been conducting and announcing instead of playing the saxophone for some time when my exam was scheduled – with only one week to prepare. I experienced the full rush of debilitating overarousal that I had seen others suffer. The week's preparation was a waste as I unsuccessfully tried to gain control with prescription drugs. The trip up the spiral staircase, trailing behind my examiners, produced an excruciating anxiety spiral, resulting in a total inability to perform. The damn horn would not make a sound!

Fortunately, my reed instructor was familiar with the circumstances. His "state-versus-trait" explanation for my failure was successful in getting the exam extended. I was able to practice, drug-free, and regain a level of instrumental proficiency sufficient to pass the exam and obtain my choice of duty stations. Ever after, I have had an empathic appreciation of the experience of anxiety and of its effects on performance. The experience also strengthened my desire for understanding these powerful emotions.

I was able to obtain one of the best assignments for anyone planning the musical career that Jo and I had envisioned. It was with the band assigned to the commander of cruisers and destroyers, Pacific fleet. This band was known for its top-quality jazz musicians and for its great USO show schedule. During my tenure with the group, musicians were recruited on discharge directly to the Lawrence Welk Orchestra (considered a sell-out) and to the Stan Kenton Orchestra (the epitome for big band jazz). Even though the assignment counted as sea duty, the admiral, his staff, and the band transferred among flagships such that sea duty involved a trip to Hawaii every 6 months. Otherwise, everyone lived on dry land in San Diego, CA. Jo and I lived in navy housing where there was an active social life. Both of our sons were born there.

Because we worked shows and dance jobs only a couple of nights a week, I was able to attend night school at San Diego City College. It was there that I took introductory psychology and became fascinated with the subject matter. Psychology, especially psychoanalytic theory, became an avocation. Playing in jazz clubs, observing drunken sailors, and other wild parties increased my interest in knowing about the unconscious bases of human motivations.

Additional time for self-directed study of psychology inadvertently came from an attempt to advance my future career in music. I was offered the opportunity to organize and direct a band on the cruiser that was to be the American flagship for the Australian Olympics. I was reluctant to accept such an offer as Jo had recently given birth to our first son, Dennis, and was pregnant with our second son, Dana. However, we decided that the publicity from leading the official American band at the Olympics – just a year before I was to be discharged – was such a great opportunity for our future in the music business that I could not refuse. I violated the well-known military taboo and volunteered for temporary duty on that flagship.

Unlike duty in San Diego, this ship regularly went to sea – typically 3 weeks out, followed by a weekend in port. The ship was based in Long Beach, CA. This required more than a 100-mile drive each way to join my family in San Diego. As the only rated musician on the flagship, I declined jobs other than working with the band, while the band members also had other shipboard duties. They could work with me only 3 hours per day. After about 3 days at sea, I had exhausted everything of interest on the ship (excluding gambling in the anchor locker). This left 14 or 15 hours a day for me to entertain myself.

I pursued my avocational interest in psychology as a way to escape excruciating boredom – pouring through the available psychology books. These were mostly by or about Freud. This self-directed education further strengthened my interest in Freudian theory. I became enamored with the deep and mysterious unconscious and with the hydraulic operation of libidinal energies.

After all the effort, I never did get to the Olympics. The duty radioman, a friend whose shipboard hammock was in the same area as mine, awaked me one night with some disturbing news. A military crisis had resulted in the cruiser's reassignment to the Suez Canal theatre of operations. Rather than serving as the flagship for the Australian Olympics, the cruiser was to depart for the Suez hotspot within 48 hours. I quickly arranged to terminate my temporary duty and returned to the admiral's band in San Diego.

The last year in the navy was spent at Great Lakes with a show band whose schedule regularly involved 3-week traveling stints. We lived in an off-base apartment in a "Little America" ghetto in Waukegan, IL. The band was great, but the travel schedule was not conducive to a good family life with Jo and our two sons. As this was a typical schedule for civilian bands as well, I again volunteered to try something different – the job of bandmaster for the Service School Command. In addition to training officers in parade procedures, this job entailed organizing 100 non-professional musicians to perform concerts and parades. I imagined that this would be very similar to teaching high school and college bands. That experience made it clear that a satisfying career in music for me was not to be found outside of big band jazz. Ten years as a professional musician was thus put on the shelf.

Undergraduate Major in Psychology – University of Iowa: 1958-1960

My decision to major in psychology was one of expedience. Avocational interests had resulted in more credits in psychology than in anything other than music. Psychology would take the least amount of time in which to complete a bachelor's degree. Jo was willing to work and take primary responsibility for the boys while I attended classes.

Because we were residents of the state, the University of Iowa, Iowa City, offered low-cost tuition and even lower-cost married student housing in "tin-hut" converted barracks. Tuition, rent, and utilities were cheap enough to be covered by the GI Bill. Jo would need to earn only enough to cover incidentals, such as food, clothing, and transportation. Iowa City was also close to our extended families. On these grounds – with no clue as to the nature of the psychology department – I applied to the University of Iowa and was accepted with junior-level standing.

Things are not always as anticipated. I majored in psychology and minored in mathematics at the University of Iowa. The impact of education at this institution on my development was recognized only later. The 2 years in Iowa City were not at all what we had planned – personally or academically.

On the personal side, we discovered that Jo was pregnant with our daughter, Joni, just before my discharge from the navy. Our family soon included three children. Jo continued with child rearing and emotional support as her primary jobs; for money, she did contract typing in our tin hut. I worked 30-40 hours weekly as a fitter and salesman at a local shoe store while attending classes full time. We did not do much for entertainment, but we were all together.

On the academic side, conflict among schools of psychology was evident from the first set of classes. Conflicts among competing theories of learning and among theories of personality seemed to drive most of the faculty's interests. In retrospect, the greatest genuine conflict was one of contrasting epistemologies. At the time, I mistakenly viewed it as a conflict of "basic research with rats" versus "clinical applications with people." The strong push for theory-driven laboratory research and apparent derogation of clinical work by the senior professors at Iowa had a paradoxical effect on my intellectual development. It solidified my commitment to the predominant psychodynamic approaches of the time and to a clinical career, in psychiatry or clinical psychology, rather than research.

Instructors and academic influences. Kenneth Spence, head of the psychology department, appeared to rule with an iron hand that left most faculty as well as students quivering. I was never enrolled in a course with him. He seldom spoke to undergraduates. However, the influence of "Spence-Hull" theory – as it was known there – was ubiquitous. An anti-clinical bias appeared prevalent among the senior faculty.

As an undergraduate, my classes exposed me to only two clinicians in the psychology department – young assistant professors, Charles VanBuskirk and Ron Wilson. I also received instruction from well-known senior faculty, including Jud Brown, I. E. Farber, Dee Norton, and Gustav Bergmann, the last member of the Vienna Circle. More applied courses were smuggled from the faculty at the Child Welfare Research Station, including Boyd McCandless, Charles Spiker, and Charles Truax, who was visiting for a year. John Knott ran the EEG lab at the medical school and taught my physiological psychology and anatomy courses – with both cats and human cadavers as resources. All were strong instructors.

Research methods, psychometrics, and statistics courses were required of psychology majors. I hated those courses. Rather than run rats to examine some theory-relevant principle for my undergraduate research project, I investigated acoustics – specifically, the overtones produced by different fingerings on the saxophone. It was not much related to psychological theory, but the findings had some practical use (musical arrangers should be careful where they score trills).

I liked the courses in abnormal psychology, personality theory, motivation, and physiology. Even the study of sensation and perception was interesting. This was the meat of my avocational interests, packaged in a formal discipline. Translating Freud's letters to Wilhelm Fliess to fulfill the foreign language requirement further enhanced my interest in Freudian theory. Ron Wilson semi-secretly guided additional clinical studies as special topics. From that, I found Anna Freud, Harry Stack Sullivan, and Eric Fromm all added embellishments to psychodynamic thought that seemed to make sense. Wilson also arranged for me to work briefly as an aide at the state mental hospital. That was my first exposure to institutionalized people with severe psychoses.

Learning theory was all right, particularly after I discovered ego-analytic theorists, such as Heinz Hartman, Ernst Kris, and Rudolph Lowenstein. Their notion of conflict-free spheres of functioning allowed understanding of unconscious motivations and of the mysterious active unconscious without stereotypically invoking libido theory. I always had a little trouble accepting the ubiquity of that. Hullian theory as applied by Dollard and Miller (1950) provided a translation of psychoanalytic principles that removed some of the mysticism from Freud while showing the applicability of learning theory to complex clinical problems.

Ideological commitment and career choice. I became committed, prematurely, to a neo-Freudian, ego-analytic approach. I also became committed to clinical practice – not research. The decision became, should it be psychiatry or clinical psychology? Both could take as long as 7 years before earning a living above the poverty level. We now had three children and only the GI Bill as a firm financial resource.

Jo again demonstrated her customary support. Either psychiatry or psychology was fine with her. I should focus, however, on things that *really* were of interest if we were going to endure the hard work and lengthy period of austerity entailed by either choice. On careful study, it was clear that I did not want to spend 3 years learning about cuts and bruises. Why spend years on material that appeared only tangentially related to understanding and ameliorating the distressing actions, thoughts, and emotions of troubled and troubling people? I wanted immediately to get to the real stuff of learning to understand the mysterious unconscious bases of human behavior. Clinical psychology seemed the route to follow.

We needed to find a university that would provide real clinical training. As money to move our family was in short supply, the distance from Iowa City was an important factor for consideration of any graduate program. Availability of financial support through a fellowship or assistantship, including a tuition waiver, was also of critical importance.

The University of Illinois at Urbana-Champaign and Ohio State University, Columbus, both advertised large and active clinical programs. I did some careful library work to verify the advertisements, the facilities available for clinical training, quality ratings, and the nature of faculty publications. It seemed that research training was a necessary evil to obtain clinical training in psychology. At least the research in these two departments had an applied focus with people. Ron Wilson concurred that both had good reputations. I applied to those two programs and was accepted at both places. Both also offered support with a tuition waiver for the first year. Continuing support would be dependent on my performance.

Before I responded to either offer, Jud Brown called me into his office to say that the Iowa faculty thought I would be throwing away my career by pursuing this "clinical business." Although I hadn't applied there, he said the faculty would like me to stay at Iowa for graduate school. He offered admission with a tuition waiver and guaranteed financial support. I was flattered by the Iowa offer. Guaranteed financial support in our situation was also very tempting. However, the University of Iowa did not provide the clinical emphasis that I was seeking.

Graduate School – University of Illinois at Urbana-Champaign: 1960-1964

Jo and I selected the doctoral program in clinical psychology at the University of Illinois at Urbana-Champaign for graduate training. This choice over Ohio State was based on factors that were as unrelated to professional issues as the earlier selection of the University of Iowa. The major reason for selecting Illinois rather than Ohio State was, again, one of expediency. Moving to Champaign-Urbana from Iowa City and visits to relatives in Iowa would be cheaper than corresponding travel to and from Columbus. Another factor that determined this choice was the quality of inexpensive married-student housing. Although still renovated barracks, instead of the Iowa-style tin huts with 6-foot high window sills, Illinois housing had frame walls with windows through which Jo and the kids could actually look. After Iowa City, ordinary windows and doors had become important.

Some things are as anticipated – and more! I majored in clinical psychology and minored in physiological psychology and educational psychology (group therapy) during our 4 years of graduate school at the University of Illinois. Homemaking continued as Jo's major job – rearing our three children and providing emotional support to all four of us. She added preschool daycare to her home typing to help with finances after our sons started school. My earnings now came from efforts in psychology rather than music or sales. I first worked as a half-time research assistant. Following initial clinical training, I also worked as an assistant in the department's training and research clinic, with added summer work at both the Student Counseling Bureau and the Veteran's Administration (VA) Hospital, Danville, IL. I obtained a predoctoral fellowship from the National Institute of Mental Health (NIMH) for support during the final year. Social activities and entertainment centered on the psychology department and the student housing project. Jo and the kids were regularly in close contact with other spouses and children who were in similar circumstances.

Our entering class at Illinois numbered about 60 graduate students, half of whom were clinical majors. We all shared proseminar, quantitative methods, and research design courses during the first year. The welcome by Lloyd Humphreys, head of the department, set the stage for a very stressful year. He noted a few "empirical facts." (1) Graduate students should become immersed in psychology as a discipline – successful students typically devoted **at least** 80 hours per week to classes, work, and study in psychology. (2) It had been documented that people could survive on 4 hours of sleep per night for the period of time we should plan to be in graduate school. (3) Two-thirds of the entering class would likely flunk or leave before earning doctorates. (4) Students were unlikely to be successful in both graduate school and in marriage. Clearly, this was going to take real effort in the interpersonal as well as academic arena.

Avoidance schedules produce a lot of behavior, but they do not feel good. The amount of work required was not much different from what Jo and I had done for the previous 2 years at Iowa, but it was more intense. The threat of flunking also made it much more anxiety laden. To add to the stress, we all had been used to being the top students in our undergraduate courses. Now we were told our competition came from the highest 5-10 % of the undergraduate population. Clinical students learned that only 6-8 of 30 entering students each year typically made it through qualifying exams for doctoral candidacy. We really thought it was a plan to weed-out those who could not work under pressure – a version of "trial by fire."

Now I tell my students that I not only had to walk 2 miles in the snow to get to graduate school, but it was uphill both ways! The proseminar course, as conducted in our first year, was a brutal experience. I generally favor the concept of a proseminar, in which faculty members each spend a week or two with the entire group of first-year students. Unfortunately, for our entering class, there were as yet no guidelines for the amount of material to be assigned. Each faculty member attempted to cover everything that was important in his own specialty. These assignments often exceeded 2000 pages of reading a week, with testing so comprehensive as to require recall of specific footnotes. The expected attrition in the first year class did occur, either from failure or from people's unwillingness to tolerate the required life style. Two students left to be admitted to acute psychiatric units. Unnecessarily stressful, indeed!

Graduate students organized into study groups as a way to deal with the massive amount of reading and to maintain some degree of interpersonal support. After a few abortive trials with other students, Tom D'Zurilla, Ron Krug, Rick Schulte, and I settled in as an effective working group. We continued to meet twice a week for study and review of all common course material throughout graduate school, including preparation for the doctoral qualifying exams. We became close friends who socialized with each other's families and friends, in the limited time available for those activities. The reviews, arguments, discussions, and mutual support within our study group were a major influence on my intellectual development during this period.

Instructors and academic influences. Those who successfully endured the "trial by fire" were rewarded by such intense education and training experiences that our horizons had to undergo major expansion. By the time I undertook my doctoral dissertation, I had received classroom or seminar instruction from what I later realized was an incredibly talented list of figures in the psychology department and affiliated labs or institutes. These influential instructors included Jack Adams, Wes Becker, Ray Cattell, Lee Cronbach, Don Dulany, Charles Eriksen, Fred Fiedler, Marty Fishbein, Ray Frankman, Bob Grice, Harry Hake, Lloyd Humphreys, Joe Hunt, Will Kappauf, Sam Kirk, Joe McGrath, Bill McGuire, Hobart Mowrer, Larry O'Kelly, Charles Osgood, Don Peterson, Hal Rosen, Don Shannon, Ivan Steiner, Larry Stolurow, Garth Thomas, Harry Triandis, Ledyard Tucker, Mort Weir, and Jerry Wiggins. Merle Ohlsen, Cecil Patterson, and Fred Proff taught courses in the educational psychology counseling program, where I completed a minor in group counseling and therapy.

I initially viewed research experience only as a way to earn money and as a necessary evil to obtain the doctoral degree. Incorporation of research and scientific method as natural problem-solving strategies developed only gradually. Practical training in applied research was continuous, through paid employment as a research assistant, class work, and required thesis and dissertation projects.

Based on my undergraduate work in acoustics, my first research assistantship was with Grant Fairbanks in the Speech Research Laboratory. My next assistantship was in the psychology department with Wes Becker. He was a "factor analyst" at that time, before his conversion to a "behavior analyst." That position included helping to build his garage as well as work on grant-supported projects. Roy Hamlin supervised research work at the VA Hospital. Charles Eriksen was advisor for both my master's and doctoral studies. He also encouraged incidental research to answer other questions of interest. Other members of my doctoral committee were Wes Becker, Lloyd Humphreys, Merle Ohlsen, Don Shannon, and Jerry Wiggins. All were devoted to the discipline and served as strong models for professional work.

The clinical facilities, supervision, and training were as rich as advertised. I overbooked to maximize my clinical experience. This included extra practica, special topics, and formal supervision for the clinical aspects of research assistantships as well as paid clinical service jobs. By tradition, students continued to carry clients in the departmental clinic throughout their tenure in the clinical program – even while collecting data and writing dissertations.

I received clinical supervision as part of course work and formal practica in assessment and psychotherapy from a number of well-known clinicians in several different facilities. Supervision through the department's Psychological Clinic came from Joe Becker, Wes Becker, Nate Eisen, Don Shannon, Jerry Wiggins, and Arnie Miller. Don Shannon also supervised my work in a paid position there as well as assessments in the public school system. Larry O'Kelly ran the EEG lab. O'Kelly and Wes Becker, along with Angela Folsom, from the Danville VA Hospital, supervised neuropsychological assessments in both clinic and hospital settings. Helaine Moody and Bill Ward supervised other clinical work at the VA Hospital, where they were full-time clinical staff. Bill Gilbert and Alice Jonietz were supervisors for clinical practica through the Student Counseling Bureau, while Tom Ewing and Mort Wagman supervised my paid clinical work there. Merle Ohlsen supervised my conduct of therapy groups through the Guidance and Counseling Center of the College of Education.

By the time other requirements for the Ph.D. degree were completed, I had accumulated more than 2000 hours of supervised clinical work beyond the minimum specified for graduation in the program. This was sufficient to successfully petition to bypass the predoctoral internship requirement and go directly to postdoctoral internship training.

Len Ullmann joined the clinical faculty at Illinois after my dissertation study was in progress. I informally audited some of his classes. He helped to reinforce changes in thinking that were already underway as my dissertation findings unfolded. He was especially influential in expanding my interest in the application of operant principles. However, his influence came after the data had already been collected for the focal publication. He guided me to Stanford University Press as a publisher for the monograph to report the study and its findings. He also introduced me to Len Krasner, who was instrumental in helping to arrange a postdoctoral internship at the VA Hospital in Palo Alto/Menlo Park, CA.

Upheaval and attempts at recovery. Most clinical training was based on Freudian, Rogerian, neo-Freudian or ego-analytic theories and associated insight-oriented approaches to psychotherapy. Sullivan, Rogers, Fromm, Dollard and Miller, and eclectic ego-analysts were the predominant affiliations of my clinical supervisors – and I loved it! However, the evidence-based content and research courses regularly failed to support the fundamental principles underlying the clinical training. I hated that! I became determined to demonstrate the basic truth of psychodynamic concepts.

As we all had to complete a master's thesis, I planned to use that project to document the operation of unconscious learning, through use of heat stress with cool-air reinforcement. Even though I had not enjoyed acquisition of the knowledge, my previous course work in quantitative methods and research design, from both Iowa and Illinois, had prepared me to critically evaluate the literature. Previous studies, I believed, had simply not involved variables or designs that were strong enough to demonstrate the phenomena of learning without awareness in a laboratory setting. I wanted to ensure that the quality of the research design was so strong that no alternative explanations could sully the conclusion that unconscious learning occurred.

Following his presentations in proseminar, I asked Charles (Erik) Eriksen to supervise my master's study. Beyond the fact that he was the expert in the topic area, Erik had a reputation as a strict methodologist. He also had been debunking many cherished principles of psychodynamic theory. In fact, the title of this chapter is fashioned after a presentation of his, entitled, "Subliminal perception, preconscious thought, and other things that go 'bump' in the night."

My master's research found quite the opposite of what I hoped to demonstrate. The study did not simply fail to document the operation of unconscious learning. Findings actually showed how reinforcement effects could produce different classes of "crazy behavior" that were explainable by correlated hypotheses regarding stimulus control – not psychodynamic principles (Paul, Eriksen, & Humphreys, 1962). This outcome – of my own investigation – created a major chink in my beliefs.

The next explicit effort to support psychodynamic concepts came in a literature review for a physiological course with Larry O'Kelly. I had tinkered some with hypnosis. Surely hypnotic phenomena demonstrated the active unconscious. The production of non-herpetic skin blisters by hypnotic suggestion should be a natural demonstration. I did a critical review of that literature, again drawing on my previous forced methodological training. Once more, my own efforts found better explanations for the phenomena, not support for the psychodynamic principles (Paul, 1963). This added another chink in my beliefs.

I was not the only one who was disturbed by the lack of evidence to support our practical clinical training. Several of the faculty and students were as well. Much ferment was present among advanced clinical students as well as among the remaining members of my class. A group of us convinced Erik to offer a seminar in which we could seriously examine Eysenck's (1952, 1961) outrageous claims that insight-oriented psychotherapy did not work and that this new approach called "behavior therapy" did. The behavior therapy literature was sparse enough at that time to be covered in a single semester. We concluded that Bandura's (1961) review article was essentially correct regarding the promise for that approach. However, we did not believe that the literature demonstrated ineffectiveness of the psychodynamic approach. We concluded that there was simply no good evidence regarding the effectiveness of insight-oriented psychotherapy – only a lot of flawed studies. Nevertheless, the absence of evidence to support my preferred approach added another disquieting chink in beliefs.

Concerted clinical efforts. Concurrently, I decided to personally treat a few cases with Wolpe's (1958) systematic desensitization to demonstrate to myself that the results were simply transference cures. Surely, anxiety was a symptomatic, distorted discharge of accumulated tension – a derivative of unconscious conflicts between contradictory impulses and defensive forces. Once I personally observed the superficial nature of client response to desensitization, I thought, I could comfortably discard Wolpe's uncomplicated counter-conditioning model for the more comprehensive psychodynamic approach.

The definitions in Wolpe's book and other publications were, unfortunately, not precise enough for me to replicate his procedures. Hal Johnson was a research assistant in Erik's lab at the time. Together, we used our knowledge of learning principles and of physiological responses to imaginal stimuli to develop procedures that should be followed, if Wolpe's hypotheses were true. We ran several subjects with polygraph monitoring to establish the timing parameters for progressive relaxation training and for presentation of hierarchically ordered stimuli for imaging.

Following our development of timing parameters, I arranged for clinical coverage and personally treated 10 or 11 clients with anxiety related problems. I was careful to limit my interventions to systematic desensitization – with no psychodynamic interpretations. This was especially difficult as some of the cases involved perfectly obvious symbolism. The reason for treating more than a handful of clients was that *every one* demonstrated clinical improvement! I continued to add more clients on the presumption that the next one would be unsuccessful. I knew enough to realize that these results could be more apparent than real, based as they were on uncontrolled case studies. Still, this created another chink in my beliefs.

I arranged to do a small comparison with 11 students who requested treatment for test anxiety, following their participation in a validity study of an anxiety scale (Paul & Eriksen, 1964). I treated five with individual systematic desensitization and compared their outcomes to six equated but untreated classmates. In contrast to the untreated group, the entire treated group showed improvement on self-reported anxiety and on course exam performance. We never published this study because of the obvious within-class confounding of therapist characteristics and lack of control for nonspecific treatment effects. Nevertheless, the findings were disquieting. They added another chink in my beliefs.

The Focal Study of Insight versus Desensitization (Paul, 1966)

The lack of adequate controls was the only reassuring aspect of my apparent and unanticipated successes with systematic desensitization. It was probable, I thought, that placebo responses and the nonspecific effects of psychological support, simply from undergoing treatment, had been operating. My application of systematic desensitization still could be merely producing transference cures. I had not followed these clients long enough to check on the occurrence of early relapse or symptom substitution. Yes, I thought. That was it! It really would take a well-controlled study to demonstrate these effects and the superiority of insight-oriented psychotherapy.

Background and Preparation

I had to complete a dissertation study anyway. If that amount of work was to be done, it ought to provide some answers to questions that were personally important. My thoughts were as follows. It was clear that previous real-life treatment studies were badly flawed. Both the "known," but undemonstrated, effectiveness of insight-oriented psychotherapy and the early relapse and symptom substitution expected from systematic desensitization should appear in an investigation with really good research design. An ideal design was needed.

I decided to undertake such a comparative study and, again, asked Erik to be my research advisor. Even though he was not actively involved in treatment research, if Erik approved a design, I was confident that the findings would be solid. He and I, together, identified other desirable faculty for my doctoral committee. I wanted critical expertise in measurement, quantitative methods, learning theory, and psychodynamic theory – including coverage by one or more of the participating insight-oriented therapists. This would ensure that the study surpassed the highest standards of all stakeholders. After I had outlined my overall plan and obtained agreement of potential therapists, I asked Wes Becker, Lloyd Humphreys, Merle Ohlsen, Don Shannon, and Jerry Wiggins to serve on the committee. All agreed.

Design principles. Before selecting the committee, I scoured the literature to determine the domains and classes of variables that needed to be measured, manipulated, or controlled in order to provide cause-effect evidence of effectiveness for **any** psychotherapeutic approach. The resulting principles and concepts were later expanded in two publications, where the "ultimate clinical question" was explicated. A paper on the strategy of outcome research in psychotherapy was published in the *Journal of Consulting Psychology* (Paul, 1967b). The recommendations were further elaborated in a chapter on design and tactics in Cyril Franks' edited book (Paul, 1969a). Before detailing this material in print, however, I had formulated what was needed to design a comparative study of treatment effectiveness that would allow unambiguous conclusions. My forced training in research methods at Iowa and Illinois again proved useful.

Target problem. I identified interpersonal-performance anxiety as a timely target for treatment research. Anxiety was the major component in most, if not all, theories of neurosis and the reduction of anxiety was a goal of nearly every psychotherapeutic approach. My experience in music school provided first-hand knowledge of the potential devastating effects of anxiety on performance. Epidemiological data showed interpersonal-performance anxiety to be a frequent emotional problem with a serious impact on functioning. Further, this was an anxiety problem that appeared delimited enough to allow rigorous experimental methodology, yet significant enough for broad generalization of findings – generalization that would not be possible with mere laboratory analogues of psychological difficulties. Public performance also provided prototypic stress conditions for the direct measurement of improvement or worsening. These situations would similarly allow assessment of the predicted effects from the conflicting theories on which competing treatments were based – generalization of improvement versus symptom substitution.

At that time, a course in public speaking was a graduation requirement for liberal arts students. Many found performance anxiety to be a major impediment to their successful completion of this requirement. People often delayed the course until their senior year. Large numbers sought treatment and a very large percentage was reported to simply drop out without graduating. Here was a population of young adults who should be essentially psychiatrically normal, but with a serious emotional problem that they were highly motivated to overcome. An ideal group, it seemed, with which to arrange multiple treatment and control conditions within the necessary partial-factorial research design.

Performance anxiety was a serious concern to the faculty and administration of the speech department as well. So much so that the faculty were eager to announce the availability of treatment and allow me to collect assessment data within their classes.

Insight-oriented therapists. Experienced practitioners were crucial if the superiority of psychodynamic principles and procedures were to be demonstrated. I solicited participation of only those insight-oriented therapists with the best reputations. Although I intended to obtain grant funding to pay therapists, the hourly rate would be nominal compared to their usual charges. Therapists also needed to be confident enough in their usual treatment approach to pit it against systematic desensitization and a stylized attention-placebo treatment. Further, to control for therapist attributes, nonspecific treatment effects, and placebo responses, these therapists had to be willing to learn and deliver the competing treatment and control procedures themselves – and be monitored in their performance. Five of the area's most highly regarded insight-oriented psychotherapists agreed to participate: Joe Becker, Alice Jonietz, Merle Ohlsen, Fred Proff, and Don Shannon. All were doctoral practitioners who had been previous supervisors of mine.

Commitments and funding. I obtained commitments from the numerous players, wrote the proposal, and had it approved by my doctoral committee. By concurrently submitting a proposal to the U. S. Office of Education, I received fast-track contract funds to purchase supplies and equipment, pay therapists, and support data analyses. Of course, notification of the award arrived only after the latest date that everyone had to commit to work on the project. Jo volunteered to handle the typing and supervise the many duplicating and scoring tasks.

As a sidelight on scientific progress in the clinical area, Erik and I had earlier approached the NIMH regarding possible grant support. We were told the proposed study could not be funded because symptom substitution was a highly probable outcome for two of the planned treatment conditions. By policy, the NIMH could not support treatments that would have negative outcomes on participants. My hypotheses obviously had support within the government agency that was responsible for looking after the mental health of the nation!

Design and Procedures

Some writers have mistakenly referred to this investigation as an "analogue study" of psychotherapy. That faulty inference apparently resulted from the fact that the clients were also students, concurrently enrolled in a course in public speaking, and because actual treatment contacts were time-limited to five sessions within a 6-week period.

As detailed elsewhere (Paul, 1966, 1967a, 1969e), I do not consider this study to be an analogue. Clients were "real clients" who requested treatment for personal difficulties following announcement of its availability. They sought treatment for serious "real-life problems," with no incentive provided beyond their own potential improvement in functioning. Therapists were "real therapists" with years of experience. The experienced therapists selected the number of sessions, based on their consensus of the usual number needed to treat the focal problem (given that identification and assessment of the problem occurred in advance). Treatment

General Design and Procedure

<table>
<tr><th>Group</th><th>Pretreatment Battery</th><th>Pretreatment Test Speech</th><th>Interview</th><th>Treatment</th><th>Posttreatment Test Speech</th><th>Follow-up Battery</th></tr>
<tr><td>D
(N = 15)</td><td rowspan="5">Anx. Diff.
PRCS
Extroversion
Emotionality
IPAT Anxiety
SR Inventory
Data Sheet</td><td rowspan="4">Anx. Diff.
PR
PSI
Checklist</td><td rowspan="4">Interview and Assignment to Treatment</td><td>Systematic De-Sensitization</td><td rowspan="4">Anx. Diff.
PR
PSI
Checklist</td><td rowspan="5">Anx. Diff.
PRCS
Extroversion
Emotionality
IPAT Anxiety
SR Inventory
Self-Ratings</td></tr>
<tr><td>I
(N = 15)</td><td>Insight Psychotherapy</td></tr>
<tr><td>AP
(N = 15)</td><td>Attention-Placebo</td></tr>
<tr><td>TC
(N = 29)</td><td>Classroom Only</td></tr>
<tr><td>CC
(N = 22)</td><td colspan="4">Classroom Only</td></tr>
</table>

Table 1. Design of the original study of insight vs. desensitization in psychotherapy (Reproduced from Paul, 1966).

sessions took place in the therapists' own clinical offices, in one of three "real clinical-service facilities," rather than in a laboratory setting. Finally, treatment procedures were applied as they would have been in ordinary practice, except for being monitored by audiotapes to ensure fidelity.

Treatment and control groups. The overall design and procedures for the focal study are summarized in Table 1. There were five groups in the study. Three were treatment groups – systematic desensitization (group D), insight-oriented psychotherapy (group I), and an attention-placebo control treatment (group AP). The same five therapists conducted all three of the individual treatments with one female and two male clients from each group. The attention-placebo condition involved therapists performing a believable set of actions and attending to clients. The clients, meanwhile, engaged in an irrelevant task that was presented as being helpful for anxiety reduction. The task also prevented therapists and clients from talking to each other for 45 minutes of each 50-minute session. This was an excellent control for the nonspecific effects of receiving treatment and attention from the same therapists. As shown later, it works!

The remaining two groups were control conditions. The treatment control group (group TC) was a wait-list control that received all assessments and classroom procedures, but no individual treatment. The no-contact control group (group CC) consisted of people who had requested treatment and met all other selection criteria, but received no personal contact. They merely continued in the speech course and completed the pretreatment and follow-up batteries with the entire class population. People in this group were unaware of their participation in a treatment study – providing a base for evaluation of possible improvement resulting from the additional attention, practice, and anticipation of treatment in group TC.

Pretreatment battery and subject selection. The pretreatment battery, noted in Table 1, was administered to the entire population at the beginning of the required speech course. This battery included self-report scales to assess anxiety levels in both the focal performance situation and in other theoretically relevant interpersonal-evaluative contexts. Nonfocal anxiety scales were included for later testing of hypotheses regarding generalization versus symptom substitution. Scales assessing general anxiety, extroversion, emotionality, and falsification were included for the latter purpose as well. These scales also served to describe the sample and to evaluate possible mediators of clients' response to treatment.

A cover letter in the pretreatment packet explained that treatment would be available free of charge to a few people. It said the psychology department was conducting a study of the way personality characteristics might interact with alternative treatments. What people benefit most from different approaches? Further, although treatment was to be paid by a federal grant, in return, anyone receiving services needed to commit 2-3 hours more for additional assessment. Demographic data were collected on a data sheet, which provided a place for people to request treatment and rate their degree of motivation.

A total of 380 people requested treatment following administration of the pretreatment battery. I selected the 96 who were the most debilitated by anxiety for participation in the study (68 males, 28 females). People in the resulting sample were "good bets" for psychotherapy, being young, intelligent, middle-class, highly motivated, and with strong to severe interpersonal-performance anxiety of 2-20 years standing. In most cases, anxiety was reported in nearly any social, evaluative, or interpersonal context – being most severe in the public speaking situation. Their scores on the focal anxiety scales were, in fact, higher than those of most people applying to community clinics with similar problems. The selected sample also scored significantly higher than the broad student population on both general anxiety and emotionality as well as scoring significantly lower on extroversion. The severity of the problem was further evident among those not selected for participation, although they had requested treatment. Even though the latter group scored lower on anxiety scales than those selected for participation, 32% dropped out without completing the speech course. None of the treated students dropped out.

Pretreatment test speech, treatment assignment, and interview. Of the 96 people in the selected sample, 74 underwent additional pretreatment assessment under stress conditions. This involved delivery of a test speech before an unfamiliar audience of 10-17 people. The audience included four trained observers (graduate students), introduced as "clinical psychologists and speech people who will be helping us to evaluate your reactions." During each presentation, the observers sat in the center front row, coding the presence or absence of 20 specific manifestations of anxiety on a timed-behavior checklist – every 30 seconds for 4 minutes (with reliabilities exceeding $r = .95$). Additional stress-condition measures were obtained just before each person presented his or her test speech. These included a self-report Anxiety Differential and two measures of physiological arousal – pulse rate and palmar sweat. At the end of the pretreatment test speech, each participant was scheduled for an interview with me.

The 74 "contact" people were then randomly assigned to one of the three treatment or control groups from stratified blocks based on pooled behavior checklist scores. Assignments were stratified within gender so that each therapist was randomly assigned one female and two male clients for each of the three treatment conditions. Each treatment group thus included 15 people while the no-treatment control group had 29 and the no-contact control group had 22 people. The five groups were equated on all relevant variables at the pretreatment assessment.

I met personally with each person who underwent pretreatment stress condition assessments to provide a common motivational induction and final screening. Each one assigned to a treatment group was given a standard rationale for the treatment and a description of the procedures. The intention had been to dismiss or reassign anyone whose expectations were opposed to the assigned treatment. This was necessary in only two instances. After checking schedules to assign the first session with a specific therapist, I then attempted to further induce common expectations by saying, "Oh, you'll be seeing Dr. X. (s)he is very good with problems of this sort.

(s)he's had a great deal of experience, and I think you'll find working with (her)him to be not only quite helpful, but interesting as well."

People assigned to group TC were told that time was not available for experienced therapists to see everyone that semester. Rather than ask anyone to work with a less competent therapist, names had been "picked from a hat" to determine who would have to wait until the following semester to receive treatment. I assured them that treatment would be provided for those who wanted it (and it was). It still would be necessary, however, for them to return for another evaluation speech in a few weeks, as our measures would be meaningless without them.

Treatment period. Treatments were conducted concurrently by the five therapists, rescheduling all missed appointments within a week. Written manuals were used prior to the treatment period to train therapists in their conduct of desensitization and attention-placebo treatments. Therapists described their own approach on a standardized instrument constructed for that purpose. I personally monitored audiotapes of every session and met weekly with each therapist to ensure fidelity and absence of cross-treatment contamination. Therapists provided self-ratings of their confidence in effecting change with each treatment approach. At the end of the treatment period therapists rated each of their client's improvement, prognosis, likability, and a variety of other features that might be of relevance.

People assigned to the no-treatment and no-contact control groups continued in the speech classes, without other contact during the treatment period.

Posttreatment test speech and follow-up battery. Within a week of treatment termination, clients in the three treatment groups and the wait-list controls (group TC) were brought back for posttreatment stress-condition assessments. All treated clients returned for this evaluation, but 7 of 29 in the wait-list condition were "no shows." These no shows were among the most anxious of that group at pretreatment. The same measures obtained before and during the pretreatment test speech were repeated for the posttreatment test speech. I also added blinding and other procedures to avoid carryover biases from the pretreatment test speech.

The follow-up battery was administered 6 weeks following termination of treatments. It was administered to the entire course population to protect the anonymity of the people within the five groups of the focal study. The follow-up battery consisted of the same self-report scales that had been administered in the pretreatment battery. It also included scales for each treated client to rate his or her therapist on likability and competence as well as self-ratings of improvement and satisfaction. A cover letter reemphasized the confidentiality of information and informed everyone of the opportunity to receive interpretation of his or her scores.

Results

Group and individual differences on all data were evaluated by analyses of variance, multiple comparisons of the difference between differences, regression analyses, and individually significant changes on each measure for each client. The results were surprisingly clear and consistent, with converging evidence from all information sources. The superiority I had hoped to demonstrate for insight-oriented psychotherapy was no where to be found. The attention-placebo treatment was, in fact, as effective as insight-oriented psychotherapy! Clients treated by systematic desensitization were, unmistakably, the most improved of all groups at treatment termination. In fact, systematic desensitization was remarkably effective on an absolute level. The 6-week follow-up demonstrated a similar pattern of focal treatment effects. For treated clients, only a few additional changes, beyond the focal effects, appeared at the 6-week follow-up. There was no evidence of symptom substitution. A few trends even suggested generalization of positive effects. The following highlights the major findings.

Stress condition results at treatment termination. Changes observed under stress conditions are the most stringent test of treatment effects. The percentages of significantly improved cases within each group under stress-condition assessments are presented in Figure 2. The dark bars at the top of each set in Figure 2 show that clients treated by systematic desensitization demonstrated significant improvement on all three classes of measurement – a much greater proportion of improved clients than either insight-oriented psychotherapy or attention-placebo treatments. In fact, 100% of clients treated by systematic desensitization showed improvement on both overt performance and self-report measures, with 87% also showing improvement on physiological measures.

The second and third bars of each set in Figure 2 reflect the percentages of improved cases treated, respectively, by insight-oriented psychotherapy and attention-placebo treatment. Both of these treatments produced greater rates of improvement than the no-treatment controls, but the insight and attention-placebo groups

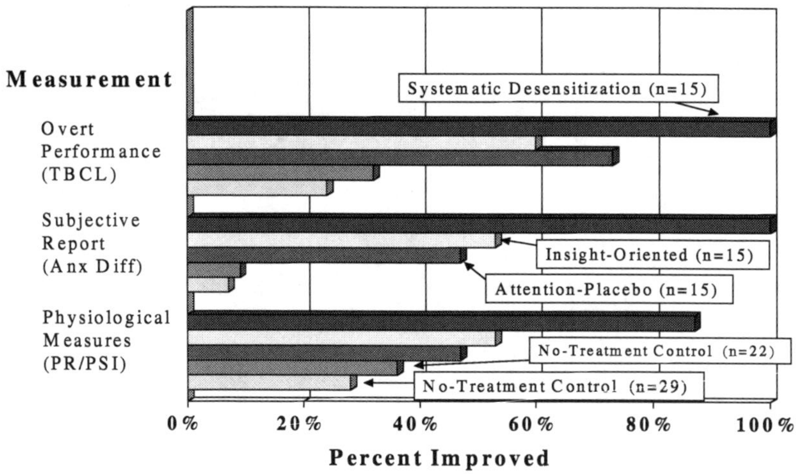

Figure 2. Percentage of cases significantly improved under stress conditions (Adapted from Paul, 1966).

did not differ in effectiveness from one another on a single measure! The bottom two bars of each set represent improvement rates for the no-treatment control group. The differing numbers reflect the "no shows" on the second assessment for those in the wait-list condition. Improvement rates that include the entire no-treatment control group, with no-shows treated as "no change," are in the lowest bars. The next to the lowest bar of each set shows improvement rates that include only those with complete data.

Six-week follow-up results. As noted earlier, the 6-week follow-up data generally showed a pattern among the four contact groups that was consistent with the stress-condition results at treatment termination. The no-treatment control group did show slight, but significant, gains compared to the no-contact control group – indicating that the additional attention, stress-condition assessments, and promise of treatment had produced some minimal benefits. However, the strength and clarity of results among the treatment groups left no doubt of the superiority of systematic desensitization over competing approaches, or of the essential equivalence of the insight and attention-placebo treatments.

No client or therapist characteristic interacted with response to treatment. Systematic desensitization was, without fail, more effective in the hands of all therapists, without moderating effects by any client attribute. Therapist and client ratings of improvement and prognosis in the focal problem area correlated with standardized improvement data from the self-report instruments and with improvements shown in the objective behavioral data. The *only*, even suggestive, superiority for the insight-oriented group came in a single rating by therapists – prognosis in areas other than the focal one – and this rating was unrelated to any other data. It was, however, consistent with the theory underlying the insight-oriented approach.

Two-year follow-up results (Paul, 1967a). The data just summarized are those that were included in my dissertation study (Paul, 1966). However, the 6-week follow-up in that study was too short to show the long-term effects predicted by psychodynamic theory. The early relapse and symptom substitution predicted for both systematic desensitization and attention-placebo clients, and the consolidation and spread of gains, for insight-oriented clients, all required the passage of time. Learning theory, in contrast, predicted no differential relapse in the focal area. Additional change in untreated areas was predicted by learning theory only to the extent of generalization of focal improvements, with naturally occurring reinforcement in the posttreatment environment.

A 2-year follow-up was undertaken to evaluate these contrasting predictions (Paul, 1967a). Other than archival records, all of this information was collected by mail as 64% of the total sample had moved from the area. Data collection included a third administration of the scales from the pretreatment and posttreatment batteries. The battery was supplemented by requests for information on the posttreatment frequency of stressful events, speech performances, and activities that might reflect predicted symptom-substitution effects (increased dependency, anxiety, or introversion). Information was also requested on receipt of either drug or psychological treatment during the follow-up period.

All but three of the earlier participants were located within 25-27 months following the end of the original treatment period. All treated clients returned requested data. Only 70% of controls returned data and 38% of those were excluded from analyses because they had been treated for the focal problem after the original study ended. The retained untreated controls were a positively biased subsample of the original control groups. Even so, the long-term follow-up results, again, demonstrated clear, convincing, and consistent findings in support of the learning theory interpretation. Not even suggestive support appeared for psychodynamic theory. Figure 3 presents the percentage of people in each group who showed continued improvement, generalized improvement, symptom substitution, or relapse on the 2-year follow-up.

Focal improvement among treated clients over the 2-year follow-up period was relatively reliable (***r***=.78) and predictable from improvements on stress condition assessments 2 years earlier (***r***=.61). The set of bars at the bottom of Figure 3 shows that systematic desensitization maintained its higher rate of significant improvement over the other two treatment groups. Insight and attention-placebo treatment continued to show no differences in improvement rates from one another. As noted at the top of Figure 3, there was no evidence of relapse for any treated client. No matter what treatment they had received, none showed an increase in self-reported anxiety in situations that involved public speaking. Of the positively biased group

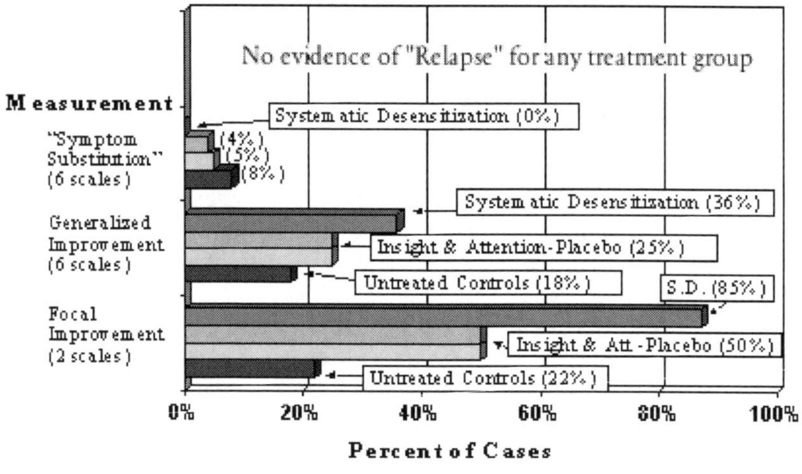

Figure 3. Relapse, symptom substitution, generalization of improvement, and continued focal improvement at the 2-year follow-up (Adapted from Paul, 1967a).

of untreated controls, 11% showed significant increases in focal anxiety that would qualify as relapse and 22% showed decreases that qualified as focal improvement.

The middle set of bars in Figure 3 shows evidence of generalized improvement, with the desensitization group showing more generalization of positive effects than other groups. The insight and attention-placebo groups failed to differ from each other, once again. As reflected in the top set of bars in Figure 3, changes that could provide evidence of possible symptom substitution occurred at exceptionally low rates. None of the groups, including controls, differed from chance-level changes and there were no differences among groups.

The results of the 2-year follow-up clearly substantiated the cause-effect relationships found earlier in my dissertation study. It also extended the evidence to show that the produced effects were lasting ones. Systematic desensitization not only worked but it worked best. No relapse. No symptom substitution. Insight-oriented psychotherapy produced no greater benefits than the nonspecific attention-placebo effects achieved by skilled therapists. Learning principles rather than psychodynamic theory accounted for the pattern of findings for all treatments.

Consequences of the Investigation

The impact of the focal study was substantial even before publication of the 1966 monograph. Emerging effects were apparent on the participating therapists and on me. I listened to audiotapes of every session to monitor the fidelity of treatment applications. Clients' in-session reports of progress in systematic desensitization were routinely positive and consistent with the underlying theory. Participating insight-oriented therapists began giving demonstrations of desensitization and using it in their own practices well before analyses of the objective data. Informal knowledge of the findings spread rapidly through local psychology, speech, and counseling departments as I analyzed the results. Word-of-mouth proliferation quickly extended beyond the university once committee members read the completed dissertation.

Adoption of a utility criterion to guide clinical work. The combination of my previously summarized personal experiences, accumulating evidence from the literature, and the findings of my own research finally forced me to discard the unsupported beliefs in the active unconscious and its clinical corollaries. I explicitly adopted a utility criterion for guidance in the clinical arena. That is, among sets of principles that can explain any given phenomenon, first use those that have firm evidential support. From among those sets of principles with empirical support, select the simplest set that can explain both the phenomenon and provide direction for how to change it. On that basis, I concluded that laboratory derived principles of learning and performance, including biological and social contexts, provide the best working hypotheses for understanding and ameliorating the great majority of clinical problems involving psychosocial functioning, be it motoric, emotional, or ideational.

This paradigm shift resulted in clinical practices that require more work on my part. I could occasionally see as many as 8-10 clients per day when I engaged in 50-minute insight-oriented psychotherapy sessions. After the shift, my limit for individual adult assessment and treatment became 4-5 hours per day – often using 2-hour sessions. Conducting functional analyses, designing and maintaining treatment programs, and engaging clients and their physical-social environments in the ongoing process of reeducation and change is simply harder work. The increased effort is justified by routine improvements in clients' functioning.

Additional consequences. The informal dissemination of information about the focal study by committee members and therapists led to my rapid entry to the talk circuit. Papers at regional conferences, invited addresses, and job-candidate colloquia all spread knowledge of the study and its findings before the monograph was published. This, in turn, resulted in networking with others who were engaged in what we now see as the behavioral revolution. For a period of 5 or 6 years, I participated several times each year in invited symposia with rosters that included some combination of the contributors to this volume and other notable players (e.g., Ted Ayllon, Nate Azrin, Izzy Goldiamond, Fred Kanfer, Peter Lang, Gerry Patterson, Bob Peterson, Len Ullmann, and Joe Wolpe). These symposia were so well attended that audiences often had standing room only. Job offers, invited chapters, and positions of influence on review panels and policy committees were early career consequences of the word-of-mouth dissemination.

The field was in ferment and clearly ready for change. Most people were interested in the clinical outcomes. Methodology became of interest as stakeholders in competing theoretical camps sought to embrace or dismiss the findings. The timeliness of work in this area is further reflected by the interest in the focal publication (Paul, 1966) and in the chapters in Cyril Franks' book that reviewed systematic desensitization studies (Paul, 1969d, 1969e) and methodological design and tactics (Paul, 1969a) – all of which became citation classics.

Intellectual Autobiography: Afterwards

My incorporation of the utility criterion resulted in consolidation and expansion of the new paradigm following completion of the focal study. The approach was strengthened during a postdoctoral year in California and through interactions with colleagues and further research at the University of Illinois, after I returned as faculty. These experiences also contributed to my later focus on psychoses, mental hospitals, and mental health systems in Illinois and Texas.

Consolidation and Expansion

Most professors at Illinois advised me to join the faculty of a major research university immediately upon graduation. However, a university appointment was not what I had in mind as a career goal. University faculty, I thought, had too much pressure to simply generate grants and publications. It seemed that accumulation of numbers often became the uppermost goal rather than using research to answer questions that really made a contribution. I still intended to make clinical practice my primary career focus. My interests had broadened to include supervision of clinical work and access to resources for researching questions that arose in clinical practice. I also wanted more direct experience with psychoses and hospitals before leaving the trainee role.

The willingness of my major professors to nominate me for faculty positions at top universities was very much appreciated. It was with some trepidation that I chose not to follow their advice. But, there were many reasons to pursue postdoctoral clinical training instead.

1964-65: VA postdoctoral training in Palo Alto/Menlo Park, CA. Our earlier experience in San Diego was so positive that Jo and I planned to return to California on completion of my doctorate. Selection of the VA Hospital in Palo Alto/Menlo Park for postdoctoral training was jointly determined by the desire to live there and by the remarkable intellectual activity in the area at that time. It was also close to Stanford University Press, where I had submitted the manuscript for the insight-versus-desensitization monograph. As noted earlier, Len Ullmann introduced me to Len Krasner, who helped arrange the postdoctoral position.

Still lacking finances, we replaced our old station wagon with a 48-passenger school bus to transport furniture and our other worldly goods. The bus became a moving van by removing all but four double front seats – one each for Jo and our three children. We licensed it as a camper. The bus trip involved many exciting events, but those are stories for another place. It was a bit embarrassing, after arriving in Palo Alto, when the bus was our "family car" for 6 weeks before we were able to replace it. Nevertheless, for the first time in our marriage, we lived in an ordinary single-family house and participated as regular community residents. The climate was great, the kids loved it, and we socialized a lot.

Professionally, the postdoctoral year in Palo Alto was even better than I anticipated. In addition to two formal 6-month rotations at the VA hospital, I also did some paid consulting and spent a few hours each week with private clients. As noted earlier, I was also active on the talk circuit during this period. VA trainees were treated to weekly seminars with Stanford University faculty, Mental Research Institute staff, and visiting professionals as well as some excellent VA staff. Influential instructors, beyond my direct supervisors, included Al Bandura, Walt Mischel, Ernest Hilgard, John Vitali, Don Jackson, Paul McReynolds, and Bob Weiss. Jerry Davison and I overlapped on the same ward for the last 6 weeks.

My first rotation was with chronically hospitalized folks on the Menlo Park campus. This placement provided direct experience in ward administration and staff training as well as expanding my intervention skills. My assignment, by prior arrangement, was in the experimental token-economy program run by Jack Atthowe and Len Krasner (Atthowe & Krasner, 1968). Bill Fairweather's social-milieu unit (Fairweather, 1964) was on the same campus. Visits there and to traditional programs allowed immediate contrasts of unit-wide organization and structures. The Atthowe/Krasner unit was the first full-fledged token economy for adults in the VA, after Ted Ayllon and Nate Azrin (1965) reported on their Illinois program at

Anna State Hospital. Consequently, a stream of behaviorally oriented psychologists and psychiatrists visited the ward. Those visits and the planning involved in daily operations provided many opportunities for discussing applications of learning theory – and reinforcement for my shift in orientation.

My second 6-month rotation was with acutely hospitalized folks on the Palo Alto campus. Unlike Menlo Park, explicit behavioral practices were rare there. Many psychologists were content to restrict their activities to testing. Chemotherapy predominated. Most professionals endorsed psychoanalytic or related psychodynamic orientations, providing the opportunity to argue and clarify differing positions. This helped consolidate my conversion.

For example, a series of psychological assessments were required on this rotation. The supervising psychologist insisted that I administer the Rorschach. Although I had been thoroughly trained in projective techniques, I found the literature failed to support their utility for most uses. I asked the supervisor to please specify the problems for which information was needed in a given case and let me select the best means for obtaining it. When I did not use any projectives, he asked where I would find the Rorschach more useful than other approaches? I suggested that it might provide information on subclinical cognitive slippage that had not otherwise impacted functioning, if anyone were really interested in that question outside of a research project. He assigned a clinical case with that very question the following week. I administered the Rorschach and wrote a short report for him. He stopped pressing for projectives once he knew that I could administer and interpret them. That was my last Rorschach – ever!

My primary assignment during the Palo Alto rotation was on a milieu unit that was one of four wards in a building run by the Stanford University Medical School. Clientele included high-frequency elopers, whom I often had to seek out in the San Francisco Bay area. Experimental studies with hallucinogens were conducted there. Jack Shelton, a Szaszian psychiatrist, ran the ward. He was an active practitioner of hallucinogens as well as an investigator of their use in treatment. To our surprise, Jack and I often gave identical advice to folks on the ward, although we arrived there from different conceptualizations. His non-disease, "myth of mental illness" approach (Szasz, 1961) was quite compatible with my own.

Weekly grand rounds with the combined staff of all four wards provided opportunities to contrast approaches. One of the other wards was organized as a therapeutic community. It was run by Rudy Moos, a psychologist who became well known for the study of ward atmosphere. A third-generation psychoanalyst, a psychiatrist, ran the other two wards. As the highest ranking VA professional in the building, the analyst felt obliged to give summaries at the end of case presentations. These often included self-styled insights, such as, "What we see here is a problem in impulse control deriving from unconscious anal conflict, for which massive doses of Thorazine are required to detoxify the id."

Such nonsensical discourse provided many occasions to consider contrasting conceptual principles. Open discussion of differing interpretations became even more active after Jerry Davison was assigned to our ward. Jack Shelton, Jerry, and I then regularly took seats in opposing corners of grand-rounds audiences to ask challenging questions when unsupported opinions were asserted as facts. It was great fun and further reinforced use of the utility criterion.

Another change in plans. Following postdoctoral training, the original plan had been to obtain a position in California that would allow time for private practice and perhaps a day per week for applied research. Once again, plans changed as a result of new experiences. The California climate was great. I enjoyed living on the edge of the "hip" culture, while maintaining more traditional values. However, Jo and I did not like the ideals that our children were developing. We decided that it would be better to raise the children in a community with more traditional mores than we observed in the bay area, especially with its high rate of broken homes.

I also found that I had come to equate time with money during the year of full-time applied work, to the extent that another client contact always won out over reading another journal article. In fact, I had fallen behind in the literature and I did not like that at all! I also came to a disturbing conclusion after presentations at several universities, public and private hospitals, and other mental health agencies. Namely, universities might be the only practical settings to allow all three of the major activities that I had come to value – clinical practice, training, and research. Although I was ambivalent about committing to a faculty position, a university that devoted equal resources and reinforcement to clinical training and applied research seemed to be worth a try. I received job offers from several top universities, but few of them placed the strong emphasis on clinical training that I wanted. An offer from Stanford University was tempting, but I declined it as they had terminated their clinical training program in psychology – and, paradoxically, the location had become undesirable as long as our children were young.

It was a surprise when Lloyd Humphreys inquired about my interest in returning to Illinois. He contacted me late in the year for recruiting. He was clearly ambivalent about violating the policy against hiring the department's own graduates. I was also ambivalent about returning. The department supported the three activities that I sought, but engaging in all of them would entail 75-80 hour workweeks. Did I want to continue working that hard? Not really! I was also a bit concerned about switching from student to faculty roles. However, discussions with the major players convinced me that this would not be a problem. The Illinois climate was lousy but the community was nearly ideal for child rearing and socializing in ways that we all enjoyed. Jo and the kids thought returning to Champaign-Urbana would be going home.

1965-1980: University of Illinois at Urbana-Champaign. I had planned to conduct long-term follow-ups of the subjects from my dissertation study. That would be easier from Illinois. We decided to return for a 2-year trial. That period of time should allow completion of the follow-up studies and a good test of job satisfaction as a faculty member. We remained at the University of Illinois at

Urbana-Champaign for 15 years. I continued a private practice with individual clients and became active in hospital consulting.

Teaching graduate courses in behavior disorders and interventions and supervising clinical practica involved immersion in the empirical and theoretical literature. The accumulating publications continued to undercut the basic assumptions of psychodynamic theory and to reinforce the utility of the alternate paradigm. The 1960's literature was rich in this regard. It included key articles (e.g., Baer, Wolf, & Risley, 1968; Eriksen & Pierce, 1968; Wilson, 1963) as well as books that became classics (e.g., Bandura, 1969; Bandura & Walters, 1963; Bijou & Baer, 1961; Franks, 1969; Kanfer & Phillips, 1970; Krasner & Ullmann, 1965; Patterson & Gullion, 1968; Ullmann & Krasner, 1965; Wolpe & Lazarus, 1966).

An exceptionally strong faculty in the Illinois department and affiliated institutes provided collegial support for the expanded application and evaluation of laboratory based principles. Wes Becker (who converted to a radical behaviorist position while I was in Palo Alto), Charles Eriksen, Hobart Mowrer, and Len Ullmann were all continuing members of the faculty whose work and personal relationships directly reinforced my change in orientation. Several additional behavioral clinicians joined the faculty as well, including Doug Bernstein, Sid Bijou, John Gottman, Fred Kanfer, Bob Peterson, Bob Nay, Bill Redd, Bob Sprague, and Warren Steinman.

Given the size of the Illinois faculty, those who identified with behavior therapy or behavior modification were still a minority. However, the thread that bound the entire faculty together was a commitment to interactional models of human functioning and the primacy of empirical evidence for guiding practices. Those values supported my expanding efforts.

In this context, my own studies of desensitization and related techniques continued to document the utility of a behavioral or social-learning approach. Besides the 2-year follow-up of subjects from the focal investigation (Paul, 1967a), these studies included evaluation of systematic desensitization in groups (Paul & Shannon, 1966) and long-term follow-up of those clients (Paul, 1968). A series of investigations on relaxation training and hypnosis further clarified the components of effective treatment procedures for anxiety related problems (Evans & Paul, 1970; Paul, 1969b, 1969c, 1969f; Paul & Trimble, 1970).

Many of these articles were reprinted over the years, long after my research interests had turned elsewhere. My last publications to specifically focus on systematic desensitization and related techniques appeared in the early 1970s. Coauthored with Doug Bernstein, these included a critique of analogue treatment studies (Bernstein & Paul, 1971) and a monograph on treatment of anxiety related problems (Paul & Bernstein, 1973). Both of these have been reprinted as well.

I continue to use these empirically based procedures in my own clinical work and to train practicum students in their application. At last count, I had personally used or supervised application of systematic desensitization and/or progressive relaxation training with more than 4000 clients. I try to keep up with the literature on treatment of sexual and other anxiety related problems. However, my interest waned for conducting further research on these topics, once I found the conceptualizations and technology to be routinely effective in clinical practice.

Psychoses, Mental Hospitals, and Mental Health Systems

When I joined the faculty at the University of Illinois, concurrent consulting work put emphasis on the absence of knowledge to support effective clinical practices in mental hospitals. My conversion was complete regarding the spuriousness of the basic assumptions underlying psychoanalytic practices. However, the utility criterion still called for empirical answers in those areas of practice where firm evidence was lacking. Traditional practices were clearly inadequate in the treatment of psychoses, especially for people who were chronically institutionalized. This attracted and maintained my interest. In fact, my work has primarily focused on institutionalized populations, observational assessment, and treatment of psychoses for more than 30 years.

1968-1984: Adolf Meyer Mental Health Center, Decatur, IL. For 5 years, I directed the Psychosocial Rehabilitation Unit at the Adolf Meyer Mental Health Center. The same staff on parallel residential treatment wards conducted Milieu Therapy and Social-Learning Programs. The unit was responsible for aftercare of discharged clientele as well. The research component was funded by a federal grant that I obtained to operationalize and evaluate the most promising approaches for treatment of people who were mental patients with the most severe disabilities. Comparison programs using traditional treatment approaches were located in a separate hospital.

After our treatment wards were terminated due to political changes in the state, I continued as director of the Clinical-Research Unit at the Meyer Center for another 11 years. This unit served as a base for continued follow-up of discharged clients as well as for grant-supported research and development of new observational assessment technologies. The latter work entailed statewide data collection and examination of mental health system operations.

The expansion to inpatient populations drew heavily on the work of colleagues who shared their ideas and innovations through personal interactions. Len Ullmann, Wes Becker, Don Peterson, Bob Peterson, Jerry Wiggins, Lloyd Humphreys, Sid Bijou, Lew Kurke, Bernie Wagner, Joe Williams, and John Nolte all contributed ideas to the development of inpatient assessment and treatment procedures. My coworkers and I sought guidance from Elaine Cumming and Alan Kraft on milieu practices. I had direct experience with the inpatient programs developed by Ted Ayllon and Nate Azrin, Jack Atthowe and Len Krasner, and Bill Fairweather. In the design of treatment programs, my coworkers and I incorporated procedural innovations from the work of all of these investigators as well as those developed by Ogden Lindsley, summarized in this volume. I am pleased to acknowledge other contributors to this volume – Don Baer, Monte Wolf, and Todd Risley – for providing the seminal technologies and templates with children that we adapted for use in developing effective treatment programs with adults.

I was the principle investigator and director of the clinical-research group that undertook the expanded work through the Meyer Center. That work, however, was a collaborative effort with a host of coworkers. Many were graduate students and interns who concurrently completed theses or dissertations as part of the ongoing operations. Senior clinical staff, who shared in the development and conduct of the treatment programs over the years, included: Titus McInnis, Beverly Holly, Dick Hagen, Ed Craighead, Kay Davidson, Jim Calhoun, Jim Curran, Al Litrownik, Dave Doty, Chris Power, Howard Himmelstein, Bill Kohen, Dale Theobald, Bob Paden, Carolyn Paden, Paula Griffith, Peggy Maynard, and Ralph Trimble.

Bob Lentz was a member of the clinical senior staff and supervisor of research personnel through completion of the residential treatment evaluations. Graduate research assistants, who contributed to the development of instruments and collection of assessment data, included: Dean Orris, Lester Tobias, George Montgomery, Roger Knudsen, Rich Edelson, Pat Vogel, Connie Duncan-Johnson, and Al Porterfield. Marco Mariotto, Joel Redfield, and Mark Licht were graduate research assistants who also took on the statistical analyses of the 6-year long comparative treatment evaluations (Paul & Lentz, 1977, 2001).

Mark Licht, Chris Power, Kathryn Engel, and Marco Mariotto continued as coworkers and collaborators through the Clinical-Research Unit and beyond. These former students and current colleagues were intimately involved with the practical development of the new observational assessment system. They were also responsible for the collection of data in the multi-institution samples to evaluate the feasibility and generalizability of the component instruments.

Many methodological and practical contributions emerged from the work at the Meyer Center. I found the laboratory-derived principles and theoretical formulations with greatest utility for anxiety-related problems were also the best for understanding and treating people's problems that were classified under the rubric of "schizophrenia" (Paul, 1974). My earlier formulation of the ultimate clinical question and necessary domains and classes of variables for research with outpatient treatments was extended to inpatient psychosocial and biomedical procedures and, ultimately, to the operation of treatment facilities and entire systems of service (Paul, 1986a, 1986b; Paul & Lentz, 1977, 2001).

Perhaps the most notable contribution from our Meyer Center work is a psychosocial treatment program that works for people who are the most severely disabled and chronically institutionalized of all mental patients (Paul, Stuve, & Menditto, 1997). This program – the Social-Learning Program – is the result of incorporating the principles and procedures from the work of previous researchers into a comprehensive, unit-wide treatment program. It is established as the treatment-of-choice on both absolute and comparative grounds, with superior cost-efficiency as well as effectiveness (Paul & Menditto, 1992). This program is ready for adoption in ongoing services as soon as the supporting assessment systems are available.

The basic developmental work on the observational assessment technology was also completed at the Meyer Center and other facilities in the state of Illinois. The quality of instruments had been demonstrated in earlier publications (e.g., ω^2s in the high .90s for reliabilities and prediction of discharge-readiness; *r*s in the .50s to .70s for prediction of postdischarge functioning in the community). However, analyses of the massive data set for evaluation of the instruments, prior to release for use elsewhere, was still in progress. Also, we needed to complete the materials for training others to implement an assessment and monitoring system that has been characterized as "revolutionary."

1980-present: University of Houston, Houston, TX. Jo and I moved to Texas in 1980. The University of Houston received funding to build a few prominent departments, and psychology was targeted as one of them. More than half of the faculty was newly recruited into a department that was to explicitly focus on solving applied problems. A Cullen Distinguished Chair and a group of stellar colleagues were part of the offer. Early on, the clinical program counted Dale Johnson, John Vincent, Roger Maley, Marco Mariotto, Lynn Rehm, and Len Ullmann among the faculty working on adult problems, with interests in the seriously mentally ill. The strongest incentive was the promise of establishing a combined service-research-training-demonstration center at Austin State Hospital in which to continue our work and disseminate findings (see Paul, 1990). Jo was willing to assume the secretarial duties of our clinical-research project. Houston had no snow. The kids were grown. It all looked very promising.

Unfortunately, the Austin center was trashed after 2 years of development. The Commissioner of the Texas Department of Mental Health and Mental Retardation (TDMHMR), with whom we had established agreements, fell into political disfavor. His replacement viewed "a proper DSM diagnosis and the right drug" as all that was needed for mental patients – certainly *not* a psychosocial unit run by people who were not even employees of his department. He terminated our agreements with Austin State Hospital and TDMHMR. He also refused to sign collaborative agreements with NIMH. That refusal killed grant support for our continuing operations in Illinois as well as planned expansions in Florida and Texas.

Following that disappointment, my co-authors and I committed our time to completing the assessment materials that would allow others to implement the Social-Learning Program. Marco Mariotto, Joel Redfield, Mark Licht, Chris Power, and I completed the theoretical analyses that underlies our science-based assessment approach (Paul, 1986b). We continued data analyses and development of the observational assessment technology with the assistance of our graduate students. The data set contains information on more than 1200 inpatients and 800 clinical staff in 35 different treatment units. It has served as a rich source of data for theses and dissertations.

Graduate seminars on our work have been preparing young psychologists to assist with dissemination, as the new technology becomes available. In addition to the developmental group noted below, several former students and current colleagues have remained affiliated with our clinical-research group. These include Bob Lentz, Chris Power, Kathryn Engel, Tony Menditto, Mark Schade, Gail Brothers Braun, Jan Cross, and Julian Salinas. With prepublication access to the assessment materials, Mark Licht, Mark Schade, and Tony Menditto have all spearheaded early implementations of the Social-Learning Program in different states. Under the direction of Tony Menditto, programs in Missouri are the most advanced at the time of this writing.

The new assessment technology was developed into the *Computerized TSBC/SRIC Planned-Access Observational Information System* (summarized in Mariotto, Paul, & Licht, 1995; Paul, 1987b). This assessment and monitoring system goes beyond support for the Social-Learning Program. It also stands, independently, as the best way to help residential treatment operations approach the status of an applied science. Three parts of a five-part series on the TSBC/SRIC System have been published (Paul, 1986b, 1987a, 1988). At the time of this writing, the developmental group led by Mark Licht is upgrading the TSBC/SRIC System computer programs. Coworkers in the group include Paul Stuve, James Coleman, Will Newbill, and Susan Hall. They are converting programs to a more powerful and user-friendly database system before we finish the final version of implementation materials (Paul, 2001a, 2001b). The TSBC/SRIC System has even more potential to improve ongoing practices than just having an effective treatment program for previously untreatable clientele. It will allow treatment facilities to offer ongoing services that are not only "new and improved" but "ever improving" (Paul, Stuve, & Cross, 1997).

Reflections and Recommendations

It has been quite a trip so far. What does it all mean? Can there be "take-home" messages that go beyond a list of platitudes and proverbs? The following includes a few things that struck me as I reflected on both the journey and the current state of the field. After reflections, I offer some recommendations derived from my in-route experiences. Others have said most of these things. I simply offer them as my own observations and beliefs, without attempting scholarly references to evidence, original sources, or to others who have expressed similar notions.

Reflections

I am struck by the degree to which my nonacademic life influenced my professional work. Family values, emotional experiences, and good and bad models of deportment all play the expected role. However, chance events and decisions based on irrelevant factors appear more influential than I imagined. Long-range planning is risky. Things change. It seems best to keep options open for as long as possible.

The role of political factors is noteworthy, especially for work involving residential units and mental health systems. Multiple stakeholders all want to protect their interests. Most political decisions are based on factors that should be peripheral. Gerry Klerman, former director of the Alcohol, Drug Abuse, and Mental Health Administration, suggested that clinical researchers need one trait if they hoped to bring about real change–tenacity in the face of adversity. I use the analogy of a broken-field runner in football to illustrate how therapists can direct a clinical session without being directive. Sometimes he zigs, sometimes he zags, sometimes he even runs in the opposite direction – but he is always focused on reaching the goal. The broken-field-runner also appears to be an apt analogy for our attempts to bring about change in the public mental health system.

The dissemination of behavioral interventions that could be imported to the lone clinician's office stands in sharp contrast to the political barriers just noted. These procedures were often adopted more rapidly than justified by the scientific evidence. In other cases, valid techniques were adapted and applied without the necessary training and rigor. It was a heady experience to be part of the early symposia, with packed rooms and active questioning. Unfortunately, the new techniques described by the careful research of those years were often adapted as a "bag of tricks." The necessary change in concepts and principles for understanding clinical problems – the real behavioral revolution – did not happen in those instances.

Things that still go "bump" in the night. Psychoanalytic theory no longer dominates psychiatry and psychology but it continues to flourish in the humanities and theatre arts. Psychoanalytically oriented treatment is clearly alive, if not well. Many still fail to attend to the empirical literature. This failure allows them to maintain a religious commitment to the active unconscious and its corollaries – and continue to argue articles of faith. They clearly have not shared the corrective emotional experiences of my history.

Unfortunately, the remedicalization of psychiatry seeks to supplant the disease analogies of psychodynamic thought with return to another religion – the presumption that all human problems result from defects that are based on real genetic or physical diseases. Criteria from the most recent round of voting are codified in the *Diagnostic and Statistical Manual* (DSM) and called a "nosology." Things people *do* are used to assign categories that refer to things they purportedly *have* – providing a pseudo-explanation, where naming activities supposedly accounts for their existence. Does the public notice this? Yes! Even in cartoons – Leroy Lockhorn says that Loretta cooks poorly because she "has" a "cooking disorder." Remedicalized professionals consider the disorders so named to be putative biological disease entities, for which drug treatment is assumed to be the proper intervention. "Biochemical imbalance" of the brain has become the panchreston, or explain-all-that-explains-nothing, of modern psychiatry.

Evidence-based practices. I endorse the past decade's initiatives to identify and promote empirically validated treatments as well as the fledgling work on empirically validated assessments. More generally, science-based practice and policy guidelines and evidence-based practices should be the best corrective to "things that still go 'bump' in the night."

My work has been identified among those that contributed to the development of these movements. I am pleased to offer Paul (1966) and Paul and Lentz (1977, 2001) and their follow-ups as practical models of the kind and scope of research that is needed to establish the comparative effectiveness of psychosocial and biomedical treatments. The manuals provide operational definitions of therapeutic procedures. They do so at a level of specification that allows training in the artful application of established principles and techniques, without being oversimplified "cookbooks." The assessment procedures provide converging evidence of reliably documented phenomena. They do so at a level of specificity that allows identification of aspects of functioning that are change-worthy as well as detection of the presence or absence of change.

As a note of caution, however, everyone should carefully examine the criteria used by professional groups to identify and sanction clinical procedures. Rather than undertaking a construct-validation approach, which fits the task, committees often develop rigid categorical checklists to ease their work. It is with some chagrin that neither of the award-winning monographs referenced above was included in the database of official psychiatric or psychological task forces that produced the first lists of effective treatments. Both groups defined the domain of evidence to include only articles in peer-reviewed journals. The psychology task force later included journal follow-ups and summaries of these studies as valid evidence. However, psychiatric groups continue to exclude these works, often on the basis that treatments were not specific to a single DSM diagnosis. Psychiatric guidelines are mostly for psychotropic drugs. It would be better if science-based rules of evidence played a greater role in these undertakings.

Recommendations

My major recommendation for all workers in the area is captured in the old adage, "Anything worth doing is worth doing well." Whether the activity involves learning new things, conducting research to solve problems, or engaging in clinical work to help others – do it right. Be responsible. Be thorough. Be rigorous. Do not take the easy way if a hard way is required.

Try to establish an environment that is rich in personal satisfactions and current reinforcers. External reinforcement, such as money, publications, promotions, or awards, is far too delayed to maintain good work let alone improve it. Avoidance schedules produce behavior but positive reinforcement feels better. Apply knowledge from life experiences to your discipline and vice versa. Learn what your reinforcers are and try to build new ones. Then use them to achieve balance. Take care of the important personal things – health, family, and friends – without which any degree of professional success will seem trivial.

Suggestions for students and young professionals. Beyond the recommendations just noted, my practical experiences provide some bases for suggestions to those who are just entering the field – students, young investigators, and young practitioners.

Take advantage of all possible educational experiences during your limited time in the trainee role. The best way to influence other professionals as well as clients is to understand their conceptual framework and the reinforcement system within which they operate. Do not let premature commitments to a career path or orientation limit your exposure to new ideas and practices. Always evaluate the evidence. Study, learn, and understand materials whether or not you find them intrinsically interesting or immediately applicable. They may become useful in ways you never imagined. They may even contribute to changes in direction of your own path.

Select problems for research about which you really care. Although passion has been described as the source of major achievements, luck also plays a role. You need not be passionate about the undertaking, but you should have a genuine interest in obtaining answers to the questions addressed by your research. This will help carry you through the inevitable hassles and pure drudgery that careful scientific work entails, especially for theses and dissertations. Of course, the problems should be ones that others care about as well. This is particularly true if you need outside funding to support your work. The greater the number of stakeholders concerned about the outcomes, the greater the degree of interest your research is likely to attract.

Make sure you have phenomena that can be reliably identified and measured. Do not become enamored with constructs that vanish under careful scrutiny. In most areas, a series of programmatic studies will probably make a greater contribution than isolated ones. However, investigations undertaken as part of degree requirements must be completed in a timely fashion. It is generally better to begin sequential investigations, where findings build on one another, than to try to answer all questions in a single study.

Suggestions for established investigators and practitioners. I do not presume to give advice to established investigators and practitioners unless they ask me. However, I encourage those who are well established in their discipline to consider some of the following suggestions that I give myself on occasion. Others will determine whether or not I follow my own advice.

Society should benefit from policies and practices that are informed by empirically based knowledge. Disseminate the products of your research. Just publishing findings is not enough. Collaborative negotiation is usually the best way to work with others. "Shape, don't rape," is a worthy proverb that I first heard from Len Ullmann. When rational discourse fails, however, senior people in a discipline can risk offending others in ways that junior people cannot. There is enough absurdity in the world that care must be taken to avoid simply becoming a chronic irritant. But do not just go-along-to-get-along when the issues are critical. Actively speak out on important things when you see "the emperor has no clothes." Provide leadership by example.

Surround yourself with energetic young people. They can help you from stagnating, personally and professionally. Be sure that those just entering the discipline become aware of common values and practices that underlie current procedures as well as those that are historically important – not just the new findings and technologies from recent publications. Do not rest on your laurels. Continue to evaluate the evidence. Continue to learn. Never fully retire.

Share what you know but recognize others for their knowledge and contributions. Try to be aware of when and where colleagues should take the major responsibility for continuing work that you may have started. The guru role, without the burden of day-to-day responsibility for activities, has many attractive features. In the words of my intellectual forefather, William James, "The great use of life is to spend it for something that will outlast it."

The "Ultimate" Answer

I originally formulated the "ultimate clinical question(s)" to summarize the domains and classes of variables needing description, measurement, or control – if firm evidence were to be obtained and accumulated across studies of psychotherapies and/or psychotropic drugs. The question, "What treatment, by whom, is most effective for this individual, with that specific problem, under which set of circumstances, and how does it come about?" could, of course, never be entirely answered. It was intended to guide investigators and practitioners. The extension of the question and organizational scheme of variables to inpatient and biomedical treatments as well as entire facilities and systems of service has also proven to be useful (see Hayes, 1991). Some instructors, I am told, even treat the ultimate question as a near mantra, requiring their students to memorize the words.

My final recommendation is this. Everyone should use the ultimate question for guidance, but add the "ultimate" answer as well. That should help to maintain focus on the interactional complexities of clinical phenomena. What is the ultimate answer? "It depends!"

References

Atthowe, J. M., & Krasner, L. (1968). Preliminary report on the application of contingent reinforcement procedures (token economy) on a "chronic" psychiatric ward. *Journal of Abnormal Psychology, 73*, 37-43.

Ayllon, T., & Azrin, N. H. (1965). The measurement and reinforcement of behavior of psychotics. *Journal of the Experimental Analysis of Behavior, 8*, 357-383.

Baer, D. M., Wolf, M. M., & Risley, T. R. (1968). Some current dimensions of applied behavior analysis. *Journal of Applied Behavior Analysis, 1*, 91-97.

Bandura, A. (1961). Psychotherapy as a learning process. *Psychological Bulletin, 58*, 143-159.

Bandura, A. (1969). *Principles of behavior modification.* New York: Holt.

Bandura, A., & Walters, R. H. (1963). *Social learning and personality development.* New York: Holt.

Bernstein, D. A., & Paul, G. L. (1971). Some comments on therapy analogue research with small animal "phobias." *Journal of Behavior Therapy and Experimental Psychiatry, 2*, 225-237.

Bijou, S. W., & Baer, D. (1961). *Child development* (Vol. 1). New York: Appleton-Century-Crofts.

Dollard, J., & Miller, N. E. (1950). *Personality and psychotherapy*. New York: McGraw-Hill.

Eriksen, C. W., & Pierce, J. (1968). Defense mechanisms. In E. F. Borgotta & W. N. Lambert (Eds.), *Handbook of personality theory* (pp.1007-1040). New York: Rand-McNally.

Evans, M. B., & Paul, G. L. (1970). Effects of hypnotically suggested analgesia on physiological and subjective responses to cold stress. *Journal of Consulting and Clinical Psychology, 35*, 362-372.

Eysenck, H. J. (1952). The effects of psychotherapy: An evaluation. *Journal of Consulting Psychology, 16*, 319-324.

Eysenck, H. J. (1961). The effects of psychotherapy. In H. J. Eysenck (Ed.), *Handbook of abnormal psychology* (pp. 697-725). New York: Basic Books.

Fairweather, G. W. (Ed.). (1964). *Social psychology in treating mental illness: An experimental approach*. New York: Wiley.

Franks, C. M. (Ed.). (1969). *Behavior therapy: Appraisal & status*. New York: McGraw-Hill.

Hayes, S. C. (1991). Pursuing the ultimate clinical question: An interview with Gordon L. Paul. *The Scientist-Practitioner, 1*(3), 6-16.

Kanfer, F. H., & Phillips, J. S. (1970). *Learning foundations of behavior therapy*. New York: Wiley.

Krasner, L., & Ullmann, L. P. (Eds.). (1965). *Research in behavior modification*. New York: Holt.

Marriotto, M. J., Paul, G. L., & Licht, M. H. (1995). Assessment in inpatient and residential settings. In J. N. Butcher (Ed.), *Clinical personality assessment: Practical approaches* (pp. 435-459). New York: Oxford University Press.

Nichols, T. (2001). The importance of case studies to methodology of science. In W. T. O'Donohue, D. Henderson, S. C. Hayes, J. Fisher, & L. J. Hayes (Eds.), *A history of the behavioral therapies: Founders' personal theories*. Reno, NV: Context Press.

Patterson, G. R., & Gullion, M. E. (1968). *Living with children*. Champaign, IL: Research Press.

Paul, G. L. (1963). Production of blisters by hypnotic suggestion: Another look: *Psychosomatic Medicine, 25*, 233-244.

Paul, G. L. (1966). *Insight versus desensitization in psychotherapy: An experiment in anxiety reduction*. Stanford, CA: Stanford University Press.

Paul, G. L. (1967a). Insight versus desensitization in psychotherapy two years after termination. *Journal of Consulting Psychology, 31*, 333-348.

Paul, G. L. (1967b). The strategy of outcome research in psychotherapy. *Journal of Consulting Psychology, 31*, 109-118.

Paul, G. L. (1968). Two-year follow-up of systematic desensitization in therapy groups. *Journal of Abnormal Psychology, 73*, 119-130.

Paul, G. L. (1969a). Behavior modification research: Design and tactics. In C. M. Franks (Ed.), *Behavior therapy: Appraisal and status* (pp. 29-62). New York: McGraw-Hill.

Paul, G. L. (1969b). Extroversion, emotionality, and physiological response to relaxation training and hypnotic suggestion. *International Journal of Clinical and Experimental Hypnosis, 17*, 89-98.

Paul, G. L. (1969c). Inhibition of physiological response to stressful imagery by relaxation training and hypnotically suggested relaxation. *Behavior Research and Therapy, 7*, 249-256.

Paul, G. L. (1969d). Outcome of systematic desensitization I: Background, procedures and uncontrolled reports of individual treatment. In C. M. Franks (Ed.), *Behavior therapy: Appraisal and status* (pp. 63-104). New York: McGraw-Hill.

Paul, G. L. (1969e). Outcome of systematic desensitization II: Controlled investigations of individual treatment, technique variations, and current status. In C. M. Franks (Ed.), *Behavior therapy: Appraisal and status* (pp. 105-159). New York: McGraw-Hill.

Paul, G. L. (1969f). Physiological effects of relaxation training and hypnotic suggestion. *Journal of Abnormal Psychology, 74*, 425-437.

Paul, G. L. (1974). Experimental-behavioral approaches to "schizophrenia." In R. Cancro, N. Fox, & L. Shapiro (Eds.), *Strategic intervention in schizophrenia: Current developments in treatment* (pp. 187-200). New York: Behavioral Publications.

Paul, G. L. (1986a). Can pregnancy be a placebo effect?: Terminology, designs, and conclusions in the study of psychosocial and pharmacological treatments of behavior disorders. *Journal of Behavior Therapy and Experimental Psychiatry, 17*, 524-544.

Paul, G. L. (Ed.). (1986b). *Principles and methods to support cost-effective quality operations: Assessment in residential treatment settings, Part I.* Champaign, IL: Research Press.

Paul, G. L. (Ed.). (1987a). *Observational assessment instrumentation for service and research – The Time-Sample Behavioral Checklist: Assessment in residential treatment settings, Part 2.* Champaign, IL: Research Press.

Paul, G. L. (1987b). Rational operations in residential treatment settings through ongoing assessment of client and staff functioning. In D. R. Peterson & D. B. Fishman (Eds.), *Assessment for decision* (pp. 145-203). New Brunswick, NJ: Rutgers University Press.

Paul, G. L. (Ed.). (1988). *Observational assessment instrumentation for service and research – The Staff-Resident Interaction Chronograph: Assessment in residential treatment settings, Part 3.* Champaign, IL: Research Press.

Paul, G. L. (1990). The role of the National Institute of Mental Health in attracting doctoral-level talent and improving training, research, and services: A proposal. In D. L. Johnson (Ed.), *Service needs of the seriously mentally ill: Training implications for psychologists* (pp. 45-50). Washington, DC: American Psychological Association Press.

Paul, G. L. (2000). Evidence-based practices in inpatient and residential facilities. *The Clinical Psychologist, 53,* 3-16.

Paul, G. L. (Ed.). (2001a). *Observational assessment instrumentation for service and research – The Computerized TSBC/SRIC Planned-Access Observational Information System: Assessment in residential treatment settings* [Part 4]. Manuscript in preparation, University of Houston.

Paul, G. L. (Ed.). (2000b). *Observational assessment instrumentation for service and research – The TSBC/SRIC System implementation package: Assessment in residential treatment settings, Part 5.* Manuscript in preparation, University of Houston.

Paul, G. L., & Bernstein, D. A. (1973). *Anxiety and clinical problems: Treatment by systematic desensitization and related techniques.* Morristown, NJ: General Learning Press.

Paul, G. L., & Eriksen, C. W. (1964). Effect of anxiety on "real-life" examinations. *Journal of Personality, 32,* 480-494.

Paul, G. L., Eriksen, C. W., & Humphreys, L. G. (1962). Use of temperature stress with cool air reinforcement for human operant conditioning. *Journal of Experimental Psychology, 64,* 329-335.

Paul, G. L., & Lentz, R. J. (1977). *Psychosocial treatment of chronic mental patients: Milieu versus social-learning programs.* Cambridge: Harvard University Press.

Paul, G. L., & Lentz, R. J. (2001). *Psychosocial treatment of chronic mental patients; Milieu versus social-learning programs* [2nd ed.]. Manuscript in preparation, University of Houston.

Paul, G. L., & Menditto, A. A. (1992). Effectiveness of inpatient treatment programs for mentally ill adults in public psychiatric facilities. *Applied and Preventive Psychology: Current Scientific Perspectives, 1,* 41-63.

Paul, G. L., & Shannon, D.T. (1966). Treatment of anxiety through systematic desensitization in therapy groups. *Journal of Abnormal Psychology, 71,* 123-135.

Paul, G. L., Stuve, P., & Cross, J. V. (1997). Real-world inpatient programs: Shedding some light – A critique. *Applied and Preventive Psychology: Current Scientific Perspectives, 6,* 193-204.

Paul, G. L., Stuve, P., & Menditto, A. A. (1997). Social-learning program (with token economy) for adult psychiatric inpatients. *The Clinical Psychologist,* 50, 14-17.

Paul, G. L., & Trimble, R. W. (1970). Recorded versus "live" relaxation training and hypnotic suggestion: Comparative effectiveness for reducing physiological arousal and inhibiting stress response. *Behavior Therapy, 1,* 285-302.

Reichenbach, H. (1938). *Experience and prediction.* Chicago: University of Chicago Press.
Szasz, T. S. (1961). *The myth of mental illness.* New York: Hoeber-Harper.
Ullmann, L. P., & Krasner, L. (Eds.). (1965). *Case studies in behavior modification.* New York: Holt.
Wilson, R. S. (1963). On behavior pathology. *Psychological Bulletin, 60,* 130-146.
Wolpe, J. (1958). *Psychotherapy by reciprocal inhibition.* Stanford, CA: Stanford University Press.
Wolpe, J., & Lazarus, A. A. (1966). *Behavior therapy techniques.* New York: Pergamon.

Footnote

[1] Preparing the prelude to my intellectual autobiography involved revisiting aspects of my youth that are laden with emotions. Some involve people and experiences that I simply had not recently thought about – at least, not regarding their impact on my own development. Others involved painful experiences that I had diligently worked to suppress. The redintegration of strong emotional reactions, both positive and negative, that I experienced in considering these aspects of my history – even while writing this chapter – suggests that I have, indeed, selected relevant material for inclusion.

Chapter 18

Values and Constructionism in Clinical Assessment: Some Historical and Personal Perspectives on Behavior Therapy[1]

Gerald C. Davison
University of Southern California

It's been said that key decisions in life are determined or at least strongly influenced by unforeseen chance events. A social gathering we decide only at the last minute to attend turns out to be the place we meet our future spouse. A careless moment while driving leads to a terrible accident that affects our health and our family's well-being for the rest of our lives. Though the idea that chance events play a major role in shaping our existence may not fully satisfy our existential needs, I've been struck many times by how germane this perspective is in reflecting upon the careers of many of my friends and colleagues. It certainly applies to mine.

The task set for participants in the Reno Conference on the History of Behavior Therapy was to present what we see as the formative influences in our professional lives, discuss a publication that we believe has had some importance in behavior therapy, and reflect on the nature of that influence on the field. This paper is an effort to fulfill this unusual and intriguing assignment.

My High School and College Years

I spent grades 7 through 12 at Boston Latin School, at the time not a particularly reinforcing or supportive secondary school and known for a number of notable graduates like several signers of the Declaration of Independence, among them Samuel Adams and John Hancock. Another signer was Benjamin Franklin, who enrolled in the school in 1714 and was doing very well when his father withdrew him after just one year. It seemed that Josiah Franklin did not consider his son pious enough for the ministry, which was the profession that most of the boys were oriented towards after they graduated and went on to Harvard. Other well-known graduates were Cotton Mather, George Santyana, Ralph Waldo Emerson, Arthur Fiedler, and Leonard Bernstein. Not too much pressure on contemporary students! For generations this school has been the way out of several of the Boston ghettoes for the children of parents and grandparents who immigrated from Europe and who saw a rigorous education as the most reliable way for the kids to make it into the mainstream of American society.

Nearly all of my 240 classmates of the class of 1957 went to college, and about a fifth of these entered Harvard as I did. Like many other Jewish boys, I was supposed to become either a physician or a lawyer. I spent the first year studying German, Russian, political science, biology, western civilization, and other general education topics that were supposed to enable me to declare a major (or "concentration," the term favored by Harvardians). By the beginning of my sophomore year, however, I had managed only to reject political science as a major and to locate myself in the German department, where I found myself intrigued more by the characters in the novels I was reading than by the language or whatever else it was that a literature major was supposed to find interesting.

Then something unexpected happened during the first day of classes of my sophomore year. Having read during the previous summer Freud's Clark University lectures and being both drawn to and annoyed by Freud's ingenious speculations about people's putative unconscious motivations, I found myself deciding at the last minute to drop into a class that was sandwiched between my 9:00 and 11:00 AM lectures. It was called Social Relations 10, the first of two semesters of a massive introductory course in a department that had been created after the second world war as a combination of anthropology, sociology, and psychology. There was also a department called Psychology, where Skinner was situated, but there was little more than animosity and mutual suspicion between the pigeon and rat-runners of Psychology and those more interested in complex human interactions in Social Relations.

So, with a long-standing curiosity about why people – especially myself – behaved as they did, and with the summer's reading of Freud still knocking around in my head, I veered off my intended path and entered Emerson Hall to listen to the first lecture of the introductory Soc. Rel. course. And my life changed.

The lecture was by Robert White, a courtly New Englander and, in what would be an irony for me fifteen years later, author of what was at the time one of the leading abnormal psychology textbooks. What White did in this opening lecture was place psychology in context, as an approach to understanding the human condition that straddled biology, sociology, anthropology, political science and other social sciences, and even philosophy and theology. While my reaction may have fallen short of being an epiphany, I nonetheless made the decision to alter my fall schedule so that I could enroll in the course – while continuing as a German major for the nonce.

Throughout the two semesters that year, I had as lecturers in addition to White the following senior professors: Clyde Kluckhohn, Talcott Parsons, and Jerome Bruner. Not too shabby for a poor Jewish kid from Dorchester. We read widely in the several domains of what was called Social Relations, but there was one set of readings and experiences that were pivotal for me. In discussion section, we were examining a clinical case history of Benjamin Feingold, a young man with lots of insecurities and anxieties. One day the topic of discussion was a dream he had of sitting at the wheel of a car and then seeing to his right his brother-in-law coming to a stop next to him so close to his car that the two cars scraped together. What did the dream mean, the teaching fellow asked us. A lively conversation ensued during which everyone in the section except myself saw very clearly that the dream was a disguised expression of Benjamin's homosexuality: the two cars scraping together obviously signified a wish on his part to rub up against the body of his brother-in-law. The Radcliffe students in the class – "Cliffies," we called them with a mixture of envy and resentment since most of them were smarter and more verbal than the Harvard students – were especially vocal in this rendition of the dream.

Now it turns out – as I have learned at the several reunions I've attended over the past thirty years – that most of us were somewhat intimidated by our peers, all of whom appeared brighter and better read than we. I was certainly no exception. I recall looking around the room and deciding that even if I were not downright stupid, I was certainly poorly suited to any specialization of psychology that had to do with trying to understand and help people in emotional distress. No matter. There were other areas of psychology that intrigued me, and I spent the next three years working with two faculty, Richard Alpert (aka Baba Ram Dass) and Jerome Bruner on topics relating to motivation and cognition. I ended up doing an honors thesis with Bruner on perceptual problem-solving under conditions of degraded but improving stimulus input. This early interest in cognition diminished drastically at Stanford, as seen below, but returned soon thereafter with my involvement in cognitive behavior therapy. Towards the end of my senior year – after a dalliance with applying to law schools – I found myself with an acceptance to Stanford, to study cognitive dissonance with Leon Festinger.

But the uncertainty earlier in my senior year – whether to go to law school or to graduate school in psychology – had led me to seek ways to postpone a firm decision. I applied for several foreign study fellowships and was awarded a Fulbright Scholarship to study for a year in Germany following graduation in June 1961.

My Graduate School Years

The year abroad was, well, broadening. I immersed myself in the culture, language, and wine of the southwestern part of Germany, took courses at the University of Freiburg in dream analysis, handwriting analysis, the Colored Pyramids Test, and psychoanalysis, and sang in Freiburg's Russian Chorus. By the time June came around, I was ready to trek out to Stanford and begin a new life.

Eager to become a Festinger-type social psychologist at Stanford beginning in Fall 1962, I was dismayed to learn that he had switched into eye movement research, both forcing and freeing me to explore a bit that first year. Having an NSF fellowship, I was able to move pretty much as I wanted and decided to do some research in something I had never had contact with or even given any thought to, physiological psychology. This found me learning about brain stimulation of the rat brain from J.A. Deutsch, who had recently published an unusual book on what he called "a structural theory of behavior." Deutsch had studied at Oxford, where much of the teaching is done via individual tutorials, so we had innumerable seemingly discursive conversations in his lab, with me watching him run rats while he peppered me with questions on what I had been reading. I found it very intellectually stimulating but somehow constraining, because as complex and challenging as rat's appetitive behavior was as understood by Deutsch's ingenious theorizing, I continued to feel unfulfilled.

And now another unexpected event. Because my mother was worried that I would not eat well in California, she'd prevailed on me to join a meal plan for at least my first quarter at Stanford. This found me eating dinner each evening in the graduate dining hall with other first year students in psychology. Some of these were clinical students (Stanford had an APA-approved clinical program at the time), and they often talked about a professor named Bandura and something called "behavior therapy." The basic notion was that all the stuff I'd been learning as an experimental psychologist had relevance for understanding and treating abnormal behavior. This was a new notion for me. None of my professors at Harvard had ever mentioned this viewpoint – and recall that Wolpe's classic book had been published in 1958, while I was a sophomore. Recall also that Skinner was at Harvard and had published a couple of papers with Ogden Lindsley on operant conditioning of regressed schizophrenics. But these new-fangled notions had not found their way into the ego-analytic, psychodynamic stronghold of Emerson Hall.

These dinner conversations bounced around in my mind during the fall and winter quarters of my first year, and then another unexpected thing happened. Visiting that year from the University of Illinois was a young associate professor named Perry London, whose courses I had of course been avoiding because they had to do with clinical. Somehow we found ourselves playing tennis, and during a break, he asked me what I wanted to do when I grew up. When I confessed that I had little idea except that I thought I'd like to be an academic like him, he took me back to his office and showed me a few vitas of colleagues of his. He asked me whether anything struck me about the publications. They were all very different from each other, and each vita was, within itself, very heterogeneous. Precisely, he said, but one thing they had in common was that all the people were clinical psychologists. Clinical psychology, he said with obvious relish, is a bastard discipline. And that's what makes it exciting and promising. That conversation with London was pivotal.

Soon I found myself in Bandura's office, doing a song and dance about why he should let me switch into clinical. I interpreted his mm-hmms and nods as signs that I should continue my persuasion attempts, but after a while he interrupted me and said "OK." "OK, what?" I asked. "OK, you can switch into clinical," he said with some bemusement. And that was it. Stanford was a remarkably flexible place, and I am forever grateful for that. For I knew then and there that I would not have found myself now in a clinical program had I gone to either of the other two places that had been options for me, Berkeley and Michigan. I had finally found a true intellectual and professional home in a department whose earlier appeal had had nothing to do with clinical psychology. Indeed, I hadn't known what area of psychology I would specialize in, only that it would not be clinical.

Dumb luck continued. I took Bandura's course that spring, worked with some autistic children at a nearby daycare center, read virtually everything that had ever been published in behavior therapy, and then found myself in my second year taking an assessment course with Walter Mischel and a behavior therapy course with a visitor from South Africa named Arnold Lazarus.

This triumvirate – unbeknownst to them, I think – presented me with a marvelous apprenticeship in theory, research, and practice in what we then called social learning approaches to psychotherapy, or sometimes just behavior therapy. Lazarus began to see private patients at a greatly reduced fee and permitted a few of the clinical students to sit in with him. I must have spent at least 10 hours a week during my second year, from September 1963 to June 1964, watching Lazarus work with patients. Somewhere along the line the conceptual introduction I had received from Bandura and Mischel came to life in my sessions with Lazarus, such that behavior therapy had a completely different meaning for me at the end of that incredible year than it had had in the beginning.[2]

Lazarus returned to South Africa in the summer of 1964 and I globbed onto a dissertation project on systematic desensitization (which I would have been very reluctant to undertake had I not learned the procedure and related things from Lazarus) that went well and enabled me to complete my degree by July of the following year. In those days one could do an internship postdoctorally, and that is what happened. I spent a good internship year at the Veterans Administration (VA) Hospital in Palo Alto.

One last tidbit from my formative Stanford years is in the form of another chance event. I began my internship in July 1965 and was assigned to a ward on which Gordon Paul had been working as an intern the previous several months. It turned out that he was not leaving till August, so we had one month's overlap. During that time I did pretty much what I'd done with Lazarus – I followed him around and sat in on practically every meeting and session he had. (My advice to graduate students has for some years been: Find someone good and follow that person around.) I hate to think what my internship year would have been like had it not been for Paul's calm and skillful introduction into the sometimes surreal world of the VA mental hospital.

My Stony Brook Years

After completing my internship in August 1966, I migrated to SUNY-Stony Brook to join a dedicated, sometimes hypomanic group of behavior therapy enthusiasts in an avowedly behavioral Ph.D. program set up by Len Krasner (director of clinical training) and Harry Kalish (department chair). I arrived there along with the first cohort of graduate students as well as the first group of postdoctoral fellows in what was the very first postdoctoral training program in behavior therapy.

It was a heady time. Here was a program that, well before the empirically supported treatments movement, elected to focus on assessment and intervention that enjoyed some measure of empirical support, eschewing unvalidated approaches and procedures without a concern that our students would be unable later on to obtain clinical internships. True, we were narrow, but the Krasner-Kalish vision was to specialize in something that we all believed had more promise than the traditional clinical fare.

I worked most closely with three colleagues during my Stony Brook years, and these collaborations enriched my professional life immeasurably. First there was my attribution research in the late 1960s with Stu Valins, a Schachter-trained social psychologist. Together we published the first experiment showing that attribution of behavior changes to oneself rather than to a drug leads to greater maintenance of therapeutic change (Davison & Valins, 1969). Second was getting together with John Neale to write our abnormal psychology textbook, the first edition being published in 1974. It was an instant success, and we recently completed our 8th edition (Davison & Neale, 2001). And finally there was *Clinical Behavior Therapy* with Marv Goldfried, published in 1976 and reissued in 1994 in an expanded form (Goldfried & Davison, 1976, 1994). This book helped bring research and theoretical abstractions to life, contributed to the cognitive trend in behavior therapy, and made a case for trying to integrate ideas and procedures from the non-behavioral psychotherapies. I was very fortunate to have had such talented colleagues as these as well as other Stony Brook faculty.

During the 1970s a number of Stony Brook faculty were doing sex research. I was spending a lot of time with two colleagues in particular, Jim Geer in Psychology and John Gagnon in Sociology. We planned and we plotted, and at one point Gagnon and I co-taught a graduate seminar in human sexuality that attracted a lot of interesting and occasionally unconventional students and colleagues.

Around 1971, I began doing a good deal of reading in what was then known as the radical gay literature, books like *Lesbian/Woman* by Martin and Lyon (1972) and *Homosexual Behavior Among Males* by Churchill (1967). Between 1971 and 1973 I taught two advanced graduate seminars on homosexuality, which were well attended by students in Stony Brook's clinical program, postdoctoral fellows in the behavior therapy program I was directing, and a few selected undergraduates and graduate students from other departments. It was my impression that some of the students had a very personal interest in the subject matter, but most of the seminar members were involved in the subject more from an intellectual than from a personal or political point of view. A couple of colleagues mentioned to me a few years afterwards that they wondered if these might have been the first courses taught in a psychology department with the focus primarily on homosexuality.

Much of what we read and discussed in seminar was new to us, and some of it was disturbing. The disturbing part came from the anger expressed in many of the books and articles towards scientists who were investigating the causes of homosexuality and towards practitioners who were engaged in sexual reorientation programs. It took me a while to understand the source of that anger.

Why focus on the etiology of homosexuality, this literature asked, rather than on the etiology of heterosexuality? The reason, it was asserted, was that the latter was viewed as the universal norm and that the only thing worth looking into were aberrations from that norm, i.e., homosexuality. A not-always-articulated agenda was at work, therefore: By focusing on the causes of homosexuality more than on the causes of heterosexuality, the message was being conveyed that the former was intrinsically abnormal and needed special scrutiny. Psychoanalytic theorizing of course viewed homosexuality as deviant, and while the rhetoric of behavior therapy disclaimed intrinsic abnormality in favor of a socially relative view – it depends on the culture one is in – the reality was that some of the earliest work in behavior therapy entailed efforts to eliminate homosexuality in favor of heterosexuality.

Of more interest to me, though, was the brief against sexual reorientation treatment. Simply stated, why spend so much time and effort developing, evaluating, and providing change-of-orientation therapies when they are aimed at a "problem" that is socially defined?

This was a toughie for me. I had already written on sexual reorientation in a paper with my student Terry Wilson (Wilson & Davison, 1974) and had even made a training film with Bob Liebert, *Behavior Therapy for Homosexuality* (Davison & Liebert, 1971) that demonstrated the "orgasmic reorientation" technique I had published on several years earlier (Davison, 1968). The basic theme of the article with Wilson was that there were more sophisticated ways to analyze and change homosexuality than were prevalent in the behavior therapy literature, and we offered an analysis that we believed would eventuate in more effective and more humane – little or no aversion therapy – ways to alter sexual orientation from the homosexual to the heterosexual. In fact, it was the material in this paper that formed the basis for the workshop I gave at the AABT convention in October 1972, a pivotal event for the contribution that I've selected to focus on as important in my professional development and of some significance as well for the field.

The 1972 AABT Convention

Chance rears its head once again, but in this case the foundations had already been laid.

One of the people attending my 1972 AABT workshop on better ways to change homosexuals into heterosexuals was Charles Silverstein, a recent Ph.D. from the Rutgers clinical program. I recall Chuck sitting in the meeting room with an interested and fairly friendly expression on his face, occasionally asking questions about why I was involved in this sort of scholarship and application. My answer, which was the standard response of behavior therapists at the time, was that I would never impose such conversion treatment on an unwilling homosexual patient, but that I saw it as appropriate and, indeed, inherent to my professional role to make such reorientation interventions available to gay and lesbian patients who asked for sexual reorientation. He never seemed quite satisfied with my answer but he didn't push the issue. Not during the workshop.

During a break, he came up to me and asked if he could circulate some flyers for a symposium he had organized for the last day of the convention. He showed me the flyer, and it looked like one of those radical political diatribes that were prevalent in the early 1970s on a variety of social issues. I thought to myself that I would certainly not attend the symposium but felt it would be imprudent and uncollegial not to permit him to distribute it to the members of my workshop (assuming that I actually had a choice in the matter, since he could easily have handed them to people as they left the workshop).

Now here's where chance enters the picture again. I had intended to leave the New York Hilton at a time on Sunday that would enable me to catch a late-morning train from Penn Station out to Port Jefferson, a town I lived in just east of Stony Brook. But I fell into unplanned conversations with some friends as I was trying to leave the hotel and then realized that I would never make my intended train. I found myself with a couple of extra hours, and then Silverstein's symposium came to mind. With no one in particular to talk to and deciding it would be more interesting to spend the extra time at the convention as it was ending rather than cooling my heels elsewhere, I found the room where the radicals were to hold forth.

It was a boisterous affair. Silverstein enraged me. He accused people like me of strengthening the unjustifiable bias against and discrimination towards homosexuals by virtue of even making conversion programs available. Others spoke in a similar vein, but what I remember most was that Silverstein was not radical enough for some members of the audience (some of whom may not have been actual convention registrants – but that's how it was in those days). So this man, whose views I reacted to with a mixture of outrage, curiosity, and a nescent respect, was accused in angry tones of selling out to the oppressing establishment, to the behavior therapy fascists, by the very fact of his participating in the convention.

I returned to Stony Brook and over the next several weeks began discussing these events and my reactions to them with several friends and colleagues, and with my homosexuality seminar. I wish I could remember how my ideas evolved after that, but it could not have been more than a few weeks before I concluded that Silverstein and the radical therapists were right.

Being President of AABT in 1973-1974

During my presidential year, I initiated a motion in the AABT Board of Directors, which passed the following resolution at its meeting of May 11-12, 1974. It was supported by an overwhelming vote of the membership later that spring:

> The AABT believes that homosexuality is not in itself a sign of behavioral pathology. The Association urges all mental health professionals to take the lead in removing the stigma of mental illness that has long been attributed to these patterns of emotion and behavior. While we recognize that this long-standing prejudice will not be easily changed, there is no justification for a delay in formally according these people the basic civil and human rights that other citizens enjoy.

But this position statement, as forward-looking as it was, went only just so far. The implications (as I saw them) had yet to be drawn out. This would be the theme of my 1974 presidential address, which I entitled "Homosexuality: The Ethical Challenge."

The Context of My AABT Address

The AABT convention in Chicago in November 1974 was a tense affair. Behavior therapy had been lambasted in the media the preceding year by several groups – by the ACLU and by Senator Sam Ervin's committee that was looking into behavior modification for denying people their civil liberties (especially prisoners in the federal penitentiary in Springfield, Missouri)[3]. Also critical of behavior therapy was an unruly and violence-threatening group of self-appointed guardians of The American Dream who saw fit to engage in such activities as circulating the home addresses of fascists like myself, Israel Goldiamond, and other putative enemies of the people. Since Goldiamond was a featured presenter at the 1974 convention, we had to arrange for plainclothes as well as uniformed police to ensure the orderliness and safety of the proceedings.

It was in this context that I presented the arguments summarized below. For reasons that I believe will be evident, I was fairly nervous. But with the support of a number of friends who sat down front in the large ballroom and gave me encouraging nonverbals – even though most of them disagreed with the substance of my remarks – I got through the address.

Homosexuality: The Ethical Challenge

Below is a brief rendition of my AABT address (Davison, 1974/1976), expanded in recent years to encompass more general issues of the constructive nature of clinical assessment (Davison, 1991).

We Only Want to Help

API (Apocryphal Press International). The governor recently signed into law a bill prohibiting discrimination in housing and job opportunities on the basis of membership in a Protestant Church. This new law is the result of efforts by militant Protestants, who have lobbied extensively during the past ten years for relief from institutionalized discrimination. In an unusual statement accompanying the signing of the bill, the governor expressed the hope that this legislation would contribute to greater social acceptance of Protestantism as a legitimate, albeit unconventional, religion.

At the same time, the governor authorized funding in the amount of twenty million dollars for the upcoming fiscal year to be used to set up within existing mental health centers special units devoted to research into the causes of people's adoption of Protestantism as their religion and into the most humane and effective procedures for helping Protestants convert to Catholicism or Judaism. The governor was quick to point out, however, that these efforts, and the therapy services that will derive from and accompany them, are not be imposed on Protestants, rather are only to be made available to those who express the voluntary wish to change. "We are not in the business of forcing anything on these people. We only want to help," he said.

The Myth of Therapeutic Neutrality

Therapists never make ethically or politically neutral decisions. "Any type of psychiatric [psychological] intervention, even when treating a voluntary patient, will have an impact upon the distribution of power within the various social systems in which the patient moves. The radical therapists are absolutely right when they insist that psychiatric neutrality is a myth" (Halleck, 1971).

This is the thesis of Seymour Halleck's noted – and too little read – book, *The Politics of Therapy*, and it plays a major role in my argument about sexual conversion therapy. Most of the time the very naturalness of and familiarity with our therapeutic practices blind us to the nonempirical biases that affect how we construe the patient's problems and the goals we regard as acceptable to work towards. Better to be aware of and own up to our biases than to pretend that we have none.

Differences Do Not Imply Pathogens

Sometimes those who have argued in favor of sexual conversion therapies for gays and lesbians seek to justify their position by asserting that homosexuality is pathological and that, as doctors of the mind, it is our duty and right to set things straight (pun intended). One form that the argument takes is that homosexuals differ from heterosexuals in how they were raised, and that this difference indicates something pathogenic. The classic study in this vein is by Bieber, Dain, Dince, Drellich, Grand, Gunlach, Kremer, Rifkin, Wilbur, & Bieber (1962), a survey so flawed both conceptually and methodologically that it is hard to believe that it has been taken seriously by anyone. The logic of the findings takes the following form: the parents of male homosexuals more often reflect a pattern of a "close-binding intimate mother" and a cold and detached father. Ergo, homosexuality is a mental illness.

A moment's reflection reveals the absurdity of the argument. Simply put, what is wrong with such child-rearing unless one has decided before the fact that homosexuality is an illness? Post hoc ergo propter hoc. Weak reasoning indeed.

No Cure Without a Disease

Clinicians devote effort to developing and analyzing therapeutic procedures only if they are concerned about a problem. Until the 1980s behavior therapists spent a good deal of time and effort reducing homosexual attraction and increasing heterosexual attraction in homosexuals (and for the most part, the target population was men only). Again, until recently little if any time – and none at all when I first made my remarks – was spent by mainstream therapists encouraging health professionals to change their biases against homosexuality and foster gay-affirmative attitudes and behavior in patients who happened to be homosexual. The question for me was and still is the following: How can therapists honestly speak of nonprejudice when they participate in or tacitly support therapy regimens that by their very existence and regardless of their effectiveness condone the societal prejudice and perhaps also impede social change? As Begelman pointed out many years ago (1975), sexual reorientation therapies

> ...*by their very existence constitute a significant causal element in reinforcing the social doctrine that homosexuality is bad.* Indeed, the point of the activist protest is that behavior therapists [and other therapists] contribute significantly to preventing the exercise of any *real* option in decision making about sexual

> identity by further strengthening the prejudice that homosexuality is a "problem behavior" since treatment may be offered for it. . .homosexuals tend to seek treatment *for being homosexuals*. . .contrary to the disclaimer that behavioral therapy is "not a system of ethics" (Bandura, 1969, p. 87), the very act of providing therapeutic services for homosexual "problems" indicates otherwise (p. 180, emphasis in original).

I would add that the availability of a technique encourages its use. For example, Wolpe's (1958) systematic desensitization ushered in a period in which behavior therapists looked vigorously for antecedent cues that could be arranged on an anxiety hierarchy and be paired in imagery with deep muscle relaxation. Thus, a problem like social isolation might be viewed at least in part as a consequence of unnecessary anxiety that could be translated into an anxiety hierarchy and then desensitized. The therapist's assessment and problem-solving efforts are shaped by the availability of therapeutic techniques that are believed to be effective. This is not a bad thing! But it does skew what the therapist sees and finds out about a patient, a topic we turn to next.

Clinical Problems as Clinicians' Constructions

As I have argued elsewhere (e.g., Davison & Neale, 2001; Davison & Lazarus, 1995; Goldfried & Davison, 1994), clients seldom come to mental health clinicians with problems as clearly delineated and independently verifiable as what patients often bring to a physician. A client usually goes to a psychologist or psychiatrist in the way described by Halleck (1971). That is, the person is unhappy; life is going badly; nothing is meaningful; sadness and despair are out of proportion to life circumstances; the mind wanders and unwanted thoughts intrude, etc. The clinician *transforms* these often vague and complex complaints into a diagnosis or functional analysis, a set of ideas of what is wrong, what the controlling variables are, and what might be done to alleviate the suffering and maladaptation. My argument, then, is that psychological problems are for the most part *constructions* of the clinician. Clients comes to us in pain, and they leave with a more clearly defined problem or set of problems that we *assign* to them.

In the case of homosexuality, I argue that when a person with such attractions/behavior goes to a therapist, whatever psychological woes they have are generally construed as caused entirely or primarily by their sexual orientation. This happens because (a) their sexual orientation is usually the most salient part of their personhood, to the clinician and usually to the clients themselves because of the negative salience homosexuality has been accorded by society; and (b) it is regarded as abnormal, regardless of the liberal stance the clinician may take overtly. Even with the changes in the DSM over the past 25 years, but especially when I first articulated this position in 1974, the clinician's perceptions and problem-solving are skewed in a direction that implicates homosexuality – no matter what the actual presenting problems are (cf. Davison & Friedman, 1981) – and, most importantly, imply the desirability of a change in sexual orientation.

None of this is to gainsay that being homosexual in our society is difficult psychologically and that it can occasion people considerable distress – particularly a generation ago but even now, given the disproportionate exposure to hate crimes and simple everyday prejudice that homosexuals are subject to (discussed in next section). The moral point I tried to make in 1974 and, despite incredulousness on the part of some of my friends and colleagues I still hold to, is that mental health professionals have a responsibility not to be co-opted by the societal pressures that, sometimes subtly, channel our clinical problem-solving and decision-making into narrowly defined domains that result in a maintenance of a status quo that, in official pronouncements, we say we do not support.

Discrimination, Hate Crimes, and the "Voluntary" Desire to Change Sexual Orientation

I'd like to expand in this section on a theme that was not fully developed in my original presentation and that may provide the context not only for my holding to my position against sexual conversion therapies but also for the importance I attach to applying the analysis to other psychological issues that come to the attention of health professionals.

Although most states have dropped their sodomy laws, which used to be enforced selectively against homosexual acts, some legal pressure against homosexuality remains. A 1986 U.S. Supreme Court decision (*Bowers v. Hardwick*, 106 S.Ct. 284 [1986]), still valid, refused to find constitutional protection of the right to privacy for consensual adult homosexual activity and thereby upheld a Georgia law that prohibits oral – genital and anal – genital acts, even in private and between consenting adults. (Such laws can be applied to heterosexual sex as well, but straight people don't have to worry about that as much as do gays and lesbians.)

But legal pressures are not the whole story. Research supports the view that gays and lesbians are discriminated against in all kinds of ways and that this discrimination takes a particularly heavy toll on their emotional well-being. So-called "hate crimes" highlight this problem. A hate crime (sometimes referred to as a bias crime) is an assault that is based primarily or solely on a person's (perceived) membership in a group against which the perpetrator is prejudiced. The ultimate modern-day hate crime was, of course, the Holocaust in Germany and other parts of Europe prior to and during World War II. The Nazis sought out for imprisonment and execution millions of Jews and hundreds of thousands of gypsies, Communists, and homosexuals. The more recent "ethnic cleansing" in Bosnia and Kosovo and in many other parts of the world shows us that humankind has not learned much from the Holocaust experience. But hate crimes as well as hurtful discrimination are carried out every day in less organized and less dramatic fashion.

Recent research shows that as many as 92 percent of gays and lesbians have been subjected to verbal abuse and threats – often from members of their own family – and that as many as 24 percent have been physically attacked because of their sexual orientation (Herek, 1989; Herek, Gillis, Kogan, & Glunt, 1996). A quarter of gay youth are ejected from their homes when they come out to their families, and as many as half of the homeless young people in New York City are gay. The lifetime risk of suicide and suicidal behaviors is much higher among homosexual men than among heterosexuals (Herrell, Goldberg, True, Ramakrishnan, Lyons, Eisen, & Tsuang, 1999).

As compared to non-hate crimes, bias crimes and verbal assaults may create more psychological distress, perhaps because they are an attack not just against the person as a physical being but against the person's very identity (Garnets Herek, & Levy, 1990). Furthermore, such crimes may impart to the victim a pervasive sense of danger and even loathing of an aspect of the self that might otherwise be a source of pleasure and pride.

In addition to violence from strangers and acquaintances, lesbians and gay men experience "invisibility, isolation, lack of information, lack of role models, negative attitudes from others, lack of family and social support, uninformed or biased helping professionals, religious prohibitions, workplace discriminations, lack of legal supports, and internalized homophobia" (Fassinger & Richie, 1997, p. 90). Fassinger (1991) concluded that, while growing up, most gays and lesbians acquire the same negative attitudes towards gays as heterosexuals do, and this internalized homophobia makes it all the more difficult for them to confront their sexual orientation and to consider it in a positive light.

Anti-gay attitudes are strong, sometimes virulent, with many people believing that homosexuals are sick and their behavior disgusting (Herek, 1994). These negative attitudes can take the form of open heterosexism – as when people directly insult a gay person with epithets like *faggot* or *dyke* – or a more subtle, indirect kind of anti-homosexual stance – as when people tell jokes that deride homosexuality without knowing (or caring) if a gay person is present. This prejudice creates what has been termed "minority stress", a source of pressure and tension that is a special burden of those in despised or feared minorities (Meyer, 1995) and no doubt is the major factor in gay and lesbian people suffering particularly high levels of depression (Herek et al., 1996).

In light of all this, is it surprising that gays may seek out sexual reorientation treatment? Being subjected to verbal and physical assault for being gay is not likely to enhance one's sense of comfort with and acceptance of one's sexual orientation. Little wonder, then, that questions have been raised about how voluntary is the desire of some gays to change their sexual orientation.

A Proposal Regarding Sexual Reorientation Therapy

These several considerations led me to make a proposal that surprised no one more than myself, an idea that was present for several years in some of the gay activist literature (see especially Silverstein, 1977): *Therapists should stop engaging in change-of-orientation programs, whether the client makes the request or someone else does.* The social pressures, discrimination, and in some cases violent hatred directed toward people with homosexual inclinations make it highly doubtful that client-requests for conversion therapy approach what we regard as voluntary. In a sense, by attending to the reasons for a "voluntary" request for change, we are, I believe, doing nothing less than remaining true to our deterministic stance. And without entering the free will-determinism morass, we can, I believe, consider more carefully than we have the societal pressures that would seem to underlie "voluntary" requests for conversion therapy.

Long ago, Perry London (1969) warned of an unappreciated danger in behavior control technology, namely clinicians' increasing ability to engineer what we have tended to regard as free will on the part of our patients. In his view, therapists are capable of making patients want what is available and what they believe their patients *should* want. Moreover, even if therapists assert that they do not work against the will of their patients, this does not free them from the responsibility of examining those factors that determine what is considered free expression of intent and desire on the part of our patients. Indeed, I would argue that the therapist sets the goals in therapy more than does the patient.

Halleck put the matter thus:

> At first glance, a model of psychiatric [or psychological] practice based on the contention that people should just be helped to learn to do the things they want to do seems uncomplicated and desirable. But it is an unobtainable model. Unlike a technician, a psychiatrist [or psychologist] cannot avoid communicating and at times imposing his own values upon his patients. The patient usually has considerable difficulty in finding the way in which he would wish to change his behavior, but as he talks to the psychiatrist [or psychologist], his wants and needs become clearer. In the very process of defining his needs in the presence of a figure who is viewed as wise and authoritarian, the patient is profoundly influenced. He ends up wanting some of the things the psychiatrist [or psychologist] thinks he should want (1971, p. 19).

Not Can but Ought

As mentioned below in my discussion of a critique by Sturgis and Adams (1978), there is an important and oft-overlooked distinction between being able to achieve a goal and whether it is proper to try to do so. Empirical evidence as to whether we *can* change sexual orientation is not relevant to whether we *ought to* – except that we ought not to engage in a given change effort when there is no evidence that we can actually do so. This may well be the case with conversion therapies. The ethical argument against an ineffective treatment is that patients are bound to be disappointed and likely to feel even worse and "sicker" if they have made an effort to alter something that cannot be changed. The patient has not only failed to achieve a goal that has been set forth by the therapist as important but is likely to come away from the unsuccessful therapy continuing to believe that their behavior is bad and that they are really hopeless and unworthy.

But the two domains – empirical and ethical – are best kept separate.

Psychotherapy, Politics, and Morality

And this takes us to the final aspect of my argument. I hadn't considered myself a community psychologist until the formulation of my brief against conversion therapy, but I think the characterization is apt. In Rappaport's (1977) terms, I am working at an institutional level, which is the domain of community psychology. In contrast, most therapists operate at the individual level. An institutional analysis of human problems examines those values and ideologies that guide the decision-making of a society. Individual therapy work, in contrast, assumes that society is benign and that psychological suffering can best be alleviated by helping the patient adjust to prevailing values and conditions. My underlying assumption is that issues surrounding therapy for homosexuality should be addressed at an institutional level, and that greater societal acceptance of homosexuality as a normal variation of human sexuality rather than as a problem that needs to be fixed will, in fact, redound to the benefit of the individual by reducing the discrimination and oppression described earlier that, I firmly believe, accounts for the distress that can be associated with homosexuality and ultimately the desire of some homosexual individuals to seek sexual reorientation.

Do therapists have some kind of abstract responsibility to satisfy a patient's expressed desires and wishes, as asserted by some (e.g., Sturgis & Adams, 1978)? No. Therapists constrain themselves in many ways when patients ask for assistance, and under some circumstances, therapists are even legally required to break the confidentiality that is inherent in the relationship. In any event, requests alone have never been a sufficient justification for providing a particular service to a patient.

Finally, am I arguing against trying to help homosexuals in therapy? Not at all. It is one thing to argue that therapists should not try to alter patients' sexual orientation; it is quite another to suggest that therapists should not work therapeutically with people who are gay or lesbian. (This seems straightforward enough, but over the years some critics have alleged that I have urged people not to treat homosexuals at all.) Indeed, the implication of my thesis is that therapists consider seriously the problems in living experienced by people who happen to prefer members of their own sex as sexual partners. For example, while a gay person may be depressed because his sexual orientation is mocked or attacked and he feels insecure about standing up for himself, gay people also get depressed because their professional aspirations are thwarted by circumstances having nothing to do with their sexual orientation. And it would be nice if alcohol abusers who happen to be homosexual could be helped to reduce their excessive drinking without having their sexual orientation questioned. Freed of the inclination of trying to alter a homosexual's sexual preferences, therapists will find many other ways that they might help that individual lead a more fulfilling life.

Aftermath of The Paper

To return to the circumstances of my AABT presidential address in 1974, the immediate aftermath was pretty emotional. The audience had been very attentive, with the silence deepening when I articulated the main point that we should not be engaging in sexual conversion therapy even when the patient asked for it. (Friends commented afterwards that one gets that kind of silence when everyone in a room full of 1,000 people stops breathing at the same time.) There was a reception of sorts right after the talk, and I recall some colleagues seeking me out to shake my hand and others keeping their distance, with looks on their faces too complex to interpret. But the most memorable reaction came from a young woman who approached with glistening eyes and told me that she could not believe what she'd just heard and that she just wanted to thank me. I've been told that other people who have been personally affected by conversion efforts and their promulgation reacted similarly, albeit privately. I have found these reactions very gratifying, especially as the years have gone by and I have seen the argument become, if not universally accepted, at least more mainstream and one that can no longer be ignored.

It may or may not have been assumed by some that I was gay. Besides some occasional heterosexist kidding from a colleague or friend, I'm not aware of this consequence of which I'd been forewarned (not that it mattered to me one way or the other). And of course this admonition assumes that only a gay person would hold the point of view against sexual conversion therapies that I'd articulated – a position that I've always seen as a strategy, perhaps unconsciously employed, to denigrate the message by denigrating the messenger.

More important is what happened a month later when I submitted for publication a manuscript based on my AABT address. For reasons that I hope are obvious, I selected the *American Psychologist.* Only a week or two after sending it in, I received a letter from the editor handling the manuscript (an APA staff person of no scholarly credentials that I was aware of) that he had decided not to send it out for review because it was not "of general enough interest" to warrant consideration for a journal sent to all APA members as part of their dues. Think about this. I was not surprised that he was offended by the content of the paper – and, yes, I am presuming that this was the reason he rejected it without obtaining input from appropriate referees – but I was taken aback at the peremptory judgment that a paper examining the ethical bases of psychotherapy as applied to the case of sexual conversion treatment was not of "general enough interest" to an organization like APA.

Well, no one likes rejection letters, but I did my best to let go of my pique and decided to submit the same manuscript to the *Journal of Consulting and Clinical Psychology*, edited at the time by Brendan Maher. Again I got a very speedy response in a thin envelope, and I feared for the worst as I opened it. But Maher's decision could not have been more different or gratifying. He told me that he wanted to publish it without having it vetted by outside reviewers, provided that I would agree to his inviting several accompanying critiques. I could not have been more pleased. At his request, I made two suggestions: Irving Bieber, who I was confident would excoriate my paper (which he did); and Seymour Halleck, whom I had relied on extensively in formulating my argument on the politics of therapy and whose opinion of my effort I was certain the readership would be interested in. The commentaries followed my paper, which was published as the lead article (Davison, 1976). Interestingly, Halleck's comments did not, as I read them, fully embrace the conclusion I had come to, but his commentary was, I think, the most supportive of my effort.

A year after its publication, Maher sent me a manuscript to review for JCCP. It was a critique of my article by Ellen Sturgis and Henry Adams (Sturgis was Adams' graduate student at the University of Georgia). I found the manuscript to be an interesting and thoughtful paper on how better to change people's homosexual orientations. The only problem was that I found it irrelevant to my earlier article, for the question to me was not *whether* we can change sexual orientation but whether therapists *should* help people do so. Clearly my belief was and is that we should not. So I told Maher that I would not be an appropriate reviewer because I would have to reject the manuscript out of hand as not relevant. His response was that he wanted to publish the paper provided I write a rebuttal (instead of the review he had asked me to write). This seemed a very sensible editorial decision, and I agreed to do so. Basically "Not Can But Ought: The Treatment of Homosexuality" (Davison, 1978) responded to Sturgis and Adams (1978) in the aforementioned fashion, that is, that their paper was irrelevant to my argument. I don't believe my rebuttal was convincing to the authors, but I found it interesting some years later to be told by Sturgis that she had changed her views on the matter and now agreed with my position. Adams, on the other hand, continued to believe that therapists have an obligation to change people's sexual orientations if they seek such treatment. Interestingly, he and his students conducted some very interesting and ingenious research on homophobia, a focus that I was delighted to see for his considerable research skills.[4]

Importance of My AABT Presidential Address

It is both a treat and an embarrassment to be asked to comment on the importance of one's work. The only thing one can really do is suspend modesty and try to comment on it as if it were the work of someone else. I will try to do that.

Empirical versus Ethical Questions

I think my paper, and the rebuttal to the Sturgis-Adams critique, have contributed to a clearer understanding of the difference between what we as psychotherapists *can* or think we can do and what we *ought* to be doing. It is surprising to me how difficult it is for some folks to see this essential and simple difference. In my teaching I sometimes use an intentionally bizarre example to make the point. I tell students that I have a one-session cure for any mental/emotional/behavioral problem. In fact, it works in much less than one session. Indeed, it works in much less than one minute. It is a bullet in the head of the patient. With death comes an end to all the person's psychological suffering and/or maladaptive behavior. No more panic attacks, no more depression, no more disordered thinking, no more shy withdrawal, no more non-assertiveness, no more autistic aloneness, no more psychopathic finagling, no more aggression. All gone in an instant.

So, what's the problem?

The concepts of values and biases are not as anathema in professional circles now as I found them to be when I was in graduate school in the mid-1960s. This is a good thing, and perhaps my paper has contributed to the clarification of the issue, whether or not people agree with the particulars of my argument.

The Therapist as Secular Priest

Related to this point are Perry London's writings on moral issues in psychotherapy (e.g., London, 1964). This influence from my graduate school days did not show up fully until I became obsessed with the sexual conversion issue. As indicated earlier, his concept of therapist as secular priest defines our role as inherently moral, whether we like it or not. Especially behavior therapists unabashedly try to shape the patient in ways that they believe will benefit the patient and not infringe on the rights and sensibilities of others. But we also are good at engineering what the patient ends up wanting, as Halleck said so eloquently in his 1971 book. I believe that my article has helped sensitize people to the issue, regardless of how they think about it. As a teacher it is enough for me to know that I may have helped frame the debate and made it legitimate, if not actually necessary, to consider the influence that therapists have on their patients, even when therapists think of themselves as hands-off when it comes to therapeutic goals. I just don't believe that patients don't get shaped in this way. At the very least, I think it is better to assume this shaping rather than, as we have been doing, assume its absence.

Liberalization on the part of the APA and APA re Homosexuality

It's possible that my 1974 address and the publications based on it played some role in discussions that led stagewise to the dropping of homosexuality entirely from the DSM as well as to the recent position of APA against sexual conversion therapies. I am not in a position to know this, but friends and colleagues have suggested this to be the case. Certainly my own "conversion" in 1973-1974 took place at a time that changes in organizational viewpoints were occurring. I cannot help but be pleased if the position I took was at all instrumental.

Fewer Requests for Sexual Reorientation and Fewer Articles in the Professional Literature

Over the past 25 years there seems to have been a sharp decline in people seeking conversion therapy and there certainly has been a decline in articles published on the subject in the professional mental health literature (Campos & Hathaway, 1993). With respect to the latter, one can inspect the tables of contents of journals such as *Behaviour Research and Therapy*, *Journal of Abnormal Psychology*, and *Journal of Consulting and Clinical Psychology*, as well as the titles of psychotherapy books, and readily verify the decline. This does not mean that some therapy efforts do not continue to involve attempts at sexual reorientation – nearly all that happens in therapy settings remains hidden from view, with practically none of it seeing the light of publication. But I suspect the incidence is down, consistent with the decrease in our journals and professional books.

Psychosocial Interventions as Part of Social Institutions

As I argued in my original paper, an institutional perspective is important in understanding the conduct of psychotherapy. As private and walled-off-from-the-world as outpatient and some inpatient mental health intervention is, therapists and patients do not work together in a social vacuum. As Halleck argued in 1971, the decisions made in the consulting room reflect and have effects on the politics and social fabric of the place and time in which therapy is conducted. Therapists' behavior is constrained by multiple factors – from theoretical orientation, to personal taste, to religious values, to legal requirements and strictures, and most recently to reporting requirements and treatment decisions from insurance companies. Patients' behavior is also influenced by multiple factors, and the emphasis in my writings on homosexuality is on the manner in which societal prejudices and biases shape the very way people come to understand what is wrong and what is right about themselves, what they might wish to change and what they might prefer to leave alone. I continue to focus on the specific issue of homosexuality because so many people have been and continue to be hurt by prejudice and discrimination. But as I hope is clear, the issues are much more general, going to the heart of how researchers and clinicians set their professional agendas, which in turn affect what they learn and the decisions they make. I believe and hope that the position I took in 1974 has contributed to the debate.

References

Bandura, A. (1969). *Principles of behavior modification*. New York: Holt, Rinehart, & Winston.

Begelman, D. A. (1975). Ethical and legal issues of behavior modification. In M. Hersen, R., Eisler, & P. M. Miller (Eds.), *Progress in behavior modification* (pp. 159-189). New York: Academic Press.

Bieber, I., Dain, H. J., Dince, P. R., Drellich, M. G., Grand, H. G., Gundlach, R. H., Kremer, M. W., Rifkin, A. H., Wilbur, C. B., & Bieber, T. B. (1962). *Homosexuality: A psychoanalytic study*. New York: Basic Books.

Campos, P. E., & Hathaway, B. E. (1993). Behavioral research on gay issues: 20 years after Davison's ethical challenge. *The Behavior Therapist, 16*, 193-197.

Churchill, W. (1967). *Homosexual behavior among males: A cross-cultural and cross-species investigation*. New York: Hawthorn Books.

Davison, G. C. (1968). Elimination of a sadistic fantasy by a client-controlled counterconditioning technique. *Journal of Abnormal Psychology*, *73*, 84-90

Davison, G. C. (1974, November). *Homosexuality: The ethical challenge*. Presidential address to the annual convention of the Association for Advancement of Behavior Therapy, Chicago.

Davison, G. C. (1976). Homosexuality: The ethical challenge. *Journal of Consulting and Clinical Psychology*, *44*, 157-162.

Davison, G. C. (1978). Not can but ought: The treatment of homosexuality. *Journal of Consulting and Clinical Psychology*, *46*, 170-172.

Davison, G. C. (1991). Constructionism and morality in therapy for homosexuality. In J. C. Gonsiorek & J. Weinrich (Eds.), *Homosexuality: Research findings for public policy* (pp. 137-148). Beverly Hills, CA: Sage.
Davison, G. C., & Friedman, S. (1981). Sexual orientation stereotypy in the distortion of clinical judgment. *Journal of Homosexuality, 6*, 37-44.
Davison, G. C., & Lazarus, A. A. (1995). The dialectics of science and practice. In S. C. Hayes, V. M. Follette, T. Risley, R. D. Dawes, & K. Grady (Eds.), *Scientific standards of psychological practice: Issues and recommendations* (pp. 95-120). Reno, NV: Context Press.
Davison, G. C., & Liebert, R. M. (1971). *Behavior therapy for homosexuality* [16 mm. film]. Psychological Cinema Register, Pennsylvania State University.
Davison, G. C., & Neale, J. M. (2001). *Abnormal psychology* (8th ed.). New York: Wiley.
Fassinger, R. E. (1991). Counseling lesbian women and gay men. *The Counseling Psychologist, 19*, 157-176.
Fassinger, R. E., & Richie, B. S. (1997). Sex matters: Gender and sexual orientation in training for multicultural competency. In D. B. Pope-Davis & H. L. K. Coleman (Eds.), *Multicultural counseling competencies: Assessment, education and training, and supervision* (pp. 83-110). Thousand Oaks, CA: Sage Publications.
Garnets, L., Herek, G. M., & Levy, B. (1990). Violence and victimization of lesbians and gay men: Mental health consequences. *Journal of Interpersonal Violence, 5*, 366-383.
Goldfried, M. R., & Davison, G. C. (1976). *Clinical behavior therapy*. New York: Holt, Rinehart, & Winston.
Goldfried, M. R., & Davison, G. C. (1994). *Clinical behavior therapy*. [Exp. ed.]. New York: Wiley-Interscience.
Halleck, S. L. (1971). *The politics of therapy*. New York: Science House.
Herek, G. M. (1989). Hate crimes against lesbians and gay men: Issues for research and policy. *American Psychologist, 44*, 948-955.
Herek, G. M. (1994). Assessing heterosexuals' attitudes towards lesbians and gay men: A review of the empirical research with the ATLG scale. In B. Greene & G. M. Herek (Eds.), *Contemporary perspectives on lesbian and gay issues in psychology* (pp. 206-228). Newbury Park, CA: Sage.
Herek, G. M., Gillis, R., Kogan, J. C., & Glunt, E. K. (1996). Hate crime victimization among lesbian, gay, and bisexual adults. *Journal of Interpersonal Violence, 12*, 195-215.
Herrell, R., Goldberg, J., True, W. R., Ramakrishnan, V., Lyons, M., Eisen, S., & Tsuang, M. T. (1999). Sexual orientation and suicidality: A co-twin control study in adult men. *Archives of General Psychiatry, 56*, 867-874.
London, P. (1964). *The modes and morals of psychotherapy*. New York: Holt, Rinehart & Winston.
London, P. (1969). *Behavior control*. New York: Harper & Row.

Martin, D., & Lyons, P. (1972). *Lesbian/woman*. San Francisco: Glide Publications.
Meyer, I. (1995). Minority stress and mental health in gay men. *Journal of Health Sciences and Social Behavior, 36*, 38-56.
Rappaport, J. (1977). *Community psychology: Values, research, and action*. New York: Holt, Rinehart, & Winston.
Silverstein, C. (1972). *Behavior modification and the gay community*. Paper presented at the annual convention of the Association for Advancement of Behavior Therapy, New York City.
Silverstein, C. (1977). Homosexuality and the ethics of behavioral intervention: Paper 2. *Journal of Homosexuality, 2*, 205-211.
Sturgis, E. T., & Adams, H. E. (1978). The right to treatment: Issues in the treatment of homosexuality. *Journal of Consulting and Clinical Psychology, 46*, 165-169.
Wilson, G. T., & Davison, G. C. (1974). Behavior therapy and homosexuality: A critical perspective. *Behavior Therapy, 5*, 16-28.
Wolpe, J. (1958). *Psychotherapy by reciprocal inhibition*. Stanford: Stanford University Press.

Footnotes

[1] For helpful comments on an early draft of this paper, I thank Asher Davison. This article is dedicated to the memory of one of my mentors and a best friend, Perry London.

[2] This brings to mind something that Jerome Bruner said in a lecture in his cognitive psychology course back in 1959. He was discussing concept formation and how, once we have attained a concept of something, it is hard to recall what life was like before that understanding. I think his example was that we look at a chair, consider what it is, and try to remember what it looked like before we knew it was a chair. In an analogous fashion, I came away from my yearlong clinical apprenticeship with Lazarus with a new understanding of behavior therapy, different from what I had had before seeing him in action with patients.

[3] In those days behavior modification encompassed – in the view of many laypersons like Senator Ervin's committee – psychosurgery and electroconvulsive shock therapy. The reason was that these and other techniques modified behavior. This was the kind of misconception we were dealing with at the time.

[4] Sadly, Hank Adams died a few months before the present paper went to press.